INDIGENOUS PEOPLES AND HUMAN RIGHTS

Indigenous Peoples and Human Rights explores how general human rights standards have enabled, empowered and constrained indigenous peoples in claiming and defending their essential economic, social, cultural, civil and political interests. The book examines the jurisprudence of United Nations treaty committees and regional human rights bodies (in Africa, the Americas and Europe) that have interpreted and applied human rights standards to the special circumstances and experiences of indigenous peoples. It focuses particularly on how human rights laws since the 1960s have been drawn upon by indigenous activists and victims to protect their interests in ancestral lands, natural resources, culture and language. It further explores the right to indigenous self-determination; civil and political rights; economic, social and cultural rights (including labour rights); family and children's rights; violence and discrimination against indigenous peoples; and access to justice and remedies for violations. The book also discusses international and regional efforts to define who is 'indigenous' and who is a 'minority', and the legal relationship between indigenous individuals and their communities. The jurisprudence considered in this book significantly shaped the UN Declaration on the Rights of Indigenous Peoples 2007, which particularises and adapts general human rights standards for indigenous peoples. The book concludes by exploring future normative and implementation challenges in the light of the standard setting and consolidation, and political momentum, surrounding the UN Declaration and associated UN human rights mechanisms.

Indigenous Peoples and Human Rights

International and Regional Jurisprudence

Ben Saul

• HART •
PUBLISHING
OXFORD AND PORTLAND, OREGON
2016

Hart Publishing
An imprint of Bloomsbury Publishing plc

Hart Publishing Ltd
16C Worcester Place
Oxford
OX1 2JW
UK

Bloomsbury Publishing Plc
50 Bedford Square
London
WC1B 3DP
UK

www.hartpub.co.uk
www.bloomsbury.com

Published in North America (US and Canada) by
Hart Publishing
c/o International Specialized Book Services
920 NE 58th Avenue, Suite 300
Portland, OR 97213-3786
USA

www.isbs.com

First published 2016

British Library Cataloguing-in-Publication Data

A catalogue record for this book is available from the British Library.

ISBN: PB: 978-1-90136-240-4
ePDF: 978-1-78225-227-6
ePub: 978-1-78225-228-3

Library of Congress Cataloging-in-Publication Data
Names: Saul, Ben, author.

Title: Indigenous peoples and human rights : international and regional jurisprudence / Ben Saul.

Description: Portland, Oregon : Hart Publishing, 2016. | Includes bibliographical references and index.

Identifiers: LCCN 2016001022 (print) | LCCN 2016001592 (ebook) | ISBN 9781901362404 (pbk. : alk. paper) | ISBN 9781782252283 (Epub)

Subjects: LCSH: Indigenous peoples—Legal status, laws, etc. | Human rights.

Classification: LCC K3247 .S28 2016 (print) | LCC K3247 (ebook) | DDC 342.08/72—dc23

LC record available at http://lccn.loc.gov/2016001022

Typeset by Compuscript Ltd, Shannon
Printed and bound in Great Britain by
CPI Group (UK) Ltd, Croydon CR0 4YY

Acknowledgements

I thank my research assistants for their work on this book: Naomi Hart, Giselle Kenny, Katherine Bones, Kathleen Heath, Ella Alexander, Harrison Grace, Alexander Horne, Alice Gardoll, Lucinda Bradshaw, Ellen Moore, Natalie Mendes, Katya Pesce and Lucy Cameron. I am also grateful for discussions with Thalia Anthony and Larissa Behrendt about indigenous legal issues, and for the support of the Sydney Centre for International Law at Sydney Law School at the University of Sydney.

Contents

Abbreviations

ACHPR	African Commission on Human and Peoples' Rights
ACHR	American Convention on Human Rights
ACtHPR	African Court on Human and Peoples' Rights
AIPP	Asia Indigenous Peoples' Pact
ASEAN	Association of Southeast Asian Nations
AU	African Union
CAT	UN Committee Against Torture
CEACR	ILO Committee of Experts on the Application of Conventions and Recommendations
CEDAW	Convention on the Elimination of All Forms of Discrimination Against Women
CEDAW Committee	UN Committee on the Elimination of Discrimination Against Women
CERD	UN Committee on the Elimination of Racial Discrimination
CESCR	UN Committee on Economic, Social and Cultural Rights
COHRE	Centre on Housing Rights and Evictions
CRC	UN Committee on the Rights of the Child
CROC	Convention on the Rights of the Child
CRPD	Convention on the Rights of Persons with Disabilities
CRPD Committee	UN Committee on the Rights of Persons with Disabilities
ECHR	European Convention on Human Rights
ECommHR	European Commission on Human Rights
ECOSOC	Economic and Social Council
ECSR	European Committee on Social Rights
ECtHR	European Court of Human Rights
EMRIP	Expert Mechanism on the Rights of Indigenous Peoples
ESC	European Social Charter 1961
ETS	European Treaty Series

EU	European Union
FAO	Food and Agriculture Organization
HRC	UN Human Rights Committee
IACHR	Inter-American Commission on Human Rights
IACtHR	Inter-American Court of Human Rights
ICCPR	International Covenant on Civil and Political Rights
ICERD	International Convention on the Elimination of All Forms of Racial Discrimination
ICESCR	International Covenant on Economic, Social and Cultural Rights
ICJ	International Court of Justice
ICMW	International Convention on the Protection of the Rights of All Migrant Workers and Members of Their Families
IFC	International Finance Corporation
IGC	Intergovernmental Committee on Intellectual Property and Genetic Resources, Traditional Knowledge and Folklore (WIPO)
ILO	International Labour Organization
ILO CEACR	ILO Committee of Experts on the Application of Conventions and Recommendations
IUCN	International Union for Conservation of Nature and Natural Resources
IWGIA	International Working Group for Indigenous Affairs
NGO	Non-governmental organisation
OAS	Organization of American States
OAU	Organization of African Unity
OHCHR	UN Office of the High Commissioner for Human Rights
PFII	Permanent Forum on Indigenous Issues
PM	Precautionary Measures (of the IACHR)
RAIPON	Association of Small Peoples of the Soviet North
SERAC	Social and Economic Rights Action Center
UDHR	Universal Declaration of Human Rights
UN	United Nations

UNDP	UN Development Programme
UNDRIP	UN Declaration on the Rights of Indigenous Peoples
UNESCO	UN Educational, Scientific and Cultural Organization
UNGA	UN General Assembly
UNGAOR	UN General Assembly Official Records
UNHCR	UN High Commissioner for Refugees
UNICEF	UN Children's Fund
UNTS	United Nations Treaty Series
WGIP	Working Group on Indigenous Populations
WHO	World Health Organization
WIPO	World Intellectual Property Organization
WTO	World Trade Organization
YATAMA	The Organization of the People of Mother Earth

Table of Cases

1. Views of United Nations Treaty Bodies

1.1. Committee against Torture

1.2. Committee on the Elimination of Discrimination against Women

1.3. Committee on the Elimination of Racial Discrimination

1.4. Human Rights Committee

2. Decisions of Regional Bodies

2.1. African Commission on Human and Peoples' Rights

2.2. Inter-American Court of Human Rights

2.3. Inter-American Commission on Human Rights

Reports on the Merits

Friendly Settlements

Special Reports

Precautionary Measures

2.4. European Court of Human Rights

2.5. European Commission on Human Rights

2.6. European Committee on Social Rights

2.7. Advisory Committee on the Framework Convention on the Protection of National Minorities

3. Other International Cases

4. Domestic Cases

Table of Instruments

1. International Instruments

Treaties

General Comments/General Recommendations

Guidelines and Other 'Soft' Law

Draft Instruments

2. Regional Instruments

Treaties

Other Regional Legal Materials

3. Bilateral Treaties

4. Domestic Legislation

Introduction

Indigenous Peoples and Human Rights: Institutions and Influences

FOR A LONG time indigenous peoples were scarcely mentioned in international human rights law. They appear neither in the Universal Declaration of Human Rights of 1948 nor in most of the major human rights conventions, including those on racial discrimination (1965), civil and political rights (1966), economic, social and cultural rights (1966), women's rights (1979), torture (1986), migrant workers (1990), or enforced disappearances (2007).[1] There is a only a fleeting reference to discrimination on the basis of indigenous origin in the UN Convention on the Rights of Persons with Disabilities 2006, and then only in the Preamble. Only the Convention on the Rights of the Child 1989 directly addresses indigenous peoples, in three contexts: media communication in indigenous languages; education in a pluralistic society; and the right to enjoy indigenous culture, religion and language.[2] As yet there is still no specialised treaty on indigenous rights, such as exists for some other vulnerable groups.

Despite the near absence of binding standards explicitly recognising indigenous rights, international and regional human rights systems have creatively adapted general human rights standards to protect a range of critical indigenous interests. This book focuses on the jurisprudence developed by United Nations human rights treaty bodies and regional human rights bodies in interpreting and adapting general human rights standards to the specific circumstances and experiences of indigenous peoples. Most of this work began in the 1980s and has accelerated since the 1990s.

[1] International Covenant on Civil and Political Rights (ICCPR) (adopted 16 December 1966, entered into force 23 March 1976, 999 UNTS 171); International Covenant on Economic, Social and Cultural Rights (ICESCR) (adopted 16 December 1966, entered into force 3 January 1976, 993 UNTS 3); Convention on the Elimination of All Forms of Discrimination Against Women (CEDAW) (adopted 18 December 1979, entered into force 3 September 1981, 1249 UNTS 13); Convention Against Torture and Other Cruel, Inhuman or Degrading Treatment or Punishment (adopted 10 December 1984, entered into force 26 June 1987, 1465 UNTS 85); International Convention on the Protection of the Rights of All Migrant Workers and Members of Their Families (adopted 18 December 1990, entered into force 1 July 2003, 2220 UNTS 3); International Convention for the Protection of All Persons from Enforced Disappearance (adopted 20 December 2006, entered into force 23 December 2010, 2716 UNTS 3).

[2] Convention on the Rights of the Child (adopted 20 November 1989, entered into force 2 September 1990, 1577 UNTS 3). Article 17(d) requires states to encourage the mass media to have regard to the linguistic needs of indigenous children. Article 29(1)(d) requires states to ensure that education prepares children for responsible life in a free society, 'in the spirit of … friendship amongst all peoples, ethnic, national and religious groups and persons of indigenous origin'. Article 30 guarantees that indigenous children 'shall not be denied the right, in community with other members of his or her group, to enjoy his or her own culture, to profess and practise his or her own religion, or to use his or her own language'.

The committees' jurisprudence has also helped to lay the intellectual groundwork for further standard-setting initiatives by other UN human rights bodies, while later interacting with the standards issued by those bodies.

UN TREATY COMMITTEE JURISPRUDENCE

Within the UN system, the focus is on the Human Rights Committee (HRC) (concerning civil and political rights) in chapter 2, and, in chapter 3, on the Committee on Economic, Social and Cultural Rights (CESCR), Committee on the Elimination of Racial Discrimination (CERD), Committee on the Elimination of Discrimination Against Women (CEDAW Committee), Committee on the Rights of the Child (CRC) and Committee Against Torture (CAT).

The term 'jurisprudence' is deployed liberally in relation to the outputs of these bodies. The committees are not courts. Their 'general comments' providing guidance on particular rights, 'concluding observations' on states' periodic reports, and 'views' in individual cases (where states accept the complaints procedures) are recommendatory and not strictly binding at law. Their pronouncements are, however, highly authoritative interpretations of states' convention obligations, both at a standard setting level and in the resolution of particular factual and legal disputes in individual cases. As the HRC has stated in relation to its role in individual cases (and which applies equally to the other committees):

> While the function of the Human Rights Committee in considering individual communications is not, as such, that of a judicial body, the views issued by the Committee under the Optional Protocol exhibit some important characteristics of a judicial decision. They are arrived at in a judicial spirit, including the impartiality and independence of Committee members, the considered interpretation of the language of the Covenant, and the determinative character of the decisions. ...
>
> The views of the Committee under the Optional Protocol represent an authoritative determination by the organ established under the Covenant itself charged with the interpretation of that instrument. These views derive their character, and the importance which attaches to them, from the integral role of the Committee under both the Covenant and the Optional Protocol.[3]

Chapters 2 and 3 show that, in the absence of indigenous-specific standards in most human rights treaties, indigenous peoples have sought to apply general human rights standards in ways that are particular to their distinctive circumstances. Chapter 2 suggests the HRC's focus has been on adapting the right of minorities to take part in cultural life (ICCPR, Article 27) to indigenous circumstances, particularly to protect interests in land and resources. To a lesser extent the HRC has also tailored the right of self-determination and other civil and political rights to address the specificities of indigenous experiences. Chapter 3 reviews the practice of the remaining UN treaty committees. It shows that all have been concerned with cross-cutting

[3] HRC, *General Comment No 33: The Obligations of States Parties under the Optional Protocol to the International Covenant on Civil and Political Rights* (5 November 2008), [11] and [13].

issues of discrimination, violence and a lack of access to justice affecting indigenous peoples. Most committees have been concerned to varying degrees about violations of economic and social rights, and particularly in relation to indigenous lands and resources. The CESCR has mostly focused on self-determination and cultural rights. The CERD and CEDAW have been especially interested in indigenous political participation, while the CRC has been most concerned with family rights and child rights in the family.

REGIONAL JURISPRUDENCE

At the regional level, the book's emphasis, in chapters 4 and 5, is on developments in the Inter-American and African human rights systems, where indigenous issues have been most prominently raised. Chapter 4 shows how these regions have developed a distinctive rights jurisprudence to protect distinctive indigenous interests in land, natural resources and culture, most commonly by expansively interpreting ordinary property rights. Chapter 5 then considers how the regional systems have creatively dealt with cultural, socio-economic and physical integrity rights in relation to indigenous peoples.

The lynchpin of the Inter-American system, a creation of the 35 members of the Organization of American States (OAS), is the binding American Convention on Human Rights 1969, and, to a lesser extent, the American Declaration on the Rights and Duties of Man 1948, which is formally non-binding but reflective of regional customary law. States' human rights performance is supervised through recommendations of the Inter-American Commission on Human Rights and binding decisions of the Inter-American Court of Human Rights. In the African system, the foundational instrument is the African Charter on Human and Peoples' Rights 1981, now part of the African Union (comprising 54 member states). States are monitored through recommendations of the African Commission on Human and Peoples' Rights (ACHPR) and binding decisions of the African Court of Human and Peoples' Rights (ACtHPR). The book touches to a lesser extent on European systems,[4] in which indigenous issues have been comparatively scarce. It does not, however, consider certain other sub-regional procedures which have occasionally protected indigenous rights.[5]

[4] Including under the: European Convention for the Protection of Human Rights and Fundamental Freedoms (ECHR) (adopted 4 November 1950, entered into force 3 September 1953, 213 UNTS 2) (supervised by the European Court of Human Rights and the former European Commission on Human Rights until its abolition in 1998); Council of Europe Framework Convention on the Protection of National Minorities (adopted 1 February 1995, entered into force 1 February 1998, ETS No 157) (supervised by an Advisory Committee); and European Social Charter (adopted 18 October 1961, entered into force 26 February 1961, 529 UNTS 89) (supervised by the European Committee on Social Rights). The book does not consider the Charter of Fundamental Rights of the European Union (adopted 7 December 2000, entered into force 1 December 2009, OJ C364/01) or its enforcement by the European Court of Justice.

[5] Such as the Caribbean Court of Justice decision of 30 October 2015 ordering Belize to protect the customary and constitutional land tenure rights of Maya Toledo people and fund consultations for land demarcation: *Maya Leaders' Alliance and others v Attorney General of Belize* [2015] CCJ 15 (Appellate Jurisdiction).

Again, 'jurisprudence' is mentioned advisedly. Some regional bodies, such as the Inter-American and African courts, indeed issue binding judgments in particular cases, which have precedent-like effects, albeit confined to the respective regional system. At the same time, however, such decisions often have a wider, external influence on other regional systems and international law bodies grappling with indigenous issues. Horizontal judicial dialogue on indigenous rights, and legal borrowing and adaptation, is common. The opinions of the Inter-American and African human rights commissions, on the other hand, are only recommendatory not binding within their respective spheres. Nonetheless, they too have been influential in shaping regional and international norms on indigenous rights.

BACKGROUND INFLUENCES ON INTERNATIONAL AND REGIONAL JURISPRUDENCE

The articulation of indigenous rights by the UN treaty committees and regional bodies has not taken place in a vacuum. The respective international and regional treaty regimes are not self-contained, but have been permeated by an array of antecedent and concurrent background influences. While this book is limited to jurisprudence of the UN treaty committees and regional bodies, it must be emphasised that the contemporary international story of indigenous rights begins long before the post-Second World War UN and regional treaties.

International Labour Organization

The contribution of the International Labour Organization (ILO), established in 1919 under the League of Nations, and later absorbed as a specialised agency of the UN from 1945, has been seminal. Prompted by concerns about forced labour and exploitation, seven conventions dealing with the labour rights of indigenous peoples were adopted by states through the ILO between 1936 and 1989.[6] While all remain in force, the first six are now closed for ratification ('shelved') and only the last, ILO Convention No 169 concerning Indigenous and Tribal Peoples 1989, is regarded

[6] ILO Convention No 50 concerning the Recruiting of Indigenous Workers (adopted 20 June 1936, entered into force 8 September 1939, 40 UNTS 110); ILO Convention No 64 concerning Contracts of Employment (Indigenous Workers) (adopted 27 June 1939, entered into force 8 July 1948, 40 UNTS 282); ILO Convention No 65 concerning Penal Sanctions (Indigenous Workers) (adopted 27 June 1939, entered into force 8 July 1948, 40 UNTS 312); ILO Convention No 86 concerning the Contracts of Employment (Indigenous Workers) (adopted 11 July 1947, entered into force 13 February 1953, 161 UNTS 114); ILO Convention No 104 concerning the Abolition of Penal Sanctions (Indigenous Workers) (adopted 21 June 1955, entered into force 7 June 1958, 305 UNTS 267); ILO Convention No 107 concerning the Protection and Integration of Indigenous and Other Tribal and Semi-Tribal Populations in Independent Countries (adopted 26 June 1957, entered into force 2 June 1959, 328 UNTS 247); ILO Convention No 169 concerning Indigenous and Tribal Peoples in Independent Countries (adopted 27 June 1989, entered into force 5 September 1991, 1650 UNTS 383). See also ILO, *Eliminating Discrimination against Indigenous and Tribal Peoples in Employment and Occupation: A Guide to ILO Convention No. 111* (ILO, Geneva, 2007).

as a contemporary standard (an 'up-to-date' convention). The ILO's definition of 'indigenous', stemming from these treaties, is discussed in chapter 1.

The earlier conventions are now regarded as paternalistic and/or assimilationist, even if, in their time, they were progressive in many respects. Convention No 107 of 1957, for instance, recognised indigenous land rights in Article 11. The current standard, Convention No 169, recognises an extensive array of indigenous rights to land, territory, natural resources and a healthy environment; protection from displacement; cultural, language, religious and education rights; recognition of customary laws and indigenous peoples' cultural, social and political institutions; participation and consultation in decision-making affecting them; control over development; and equality and non-discrimination.

The implementation of state obligations is supervised by a number of ILO mechanisms, themselves generative of a jurisprudence that is roughly comparable to that issued by the UN treaty bodies, namely through state reporting and individual complaints.[7] First, states must periodically report on their ratification and implementation of ILO conventions,[8] and in response the ILO's Committee of Experts on the Application of Conventions and Recommendations engages states through 'direct requests' for information and 'observations' on their compliance. States are encouraged, but not required, to consult with their indigenous peoples in relation to their implementation of Convention No 169 and their reporting to the ILO, but in practice this is rare (with Norway being the exception). Individual complaints have only been received from nine countries since 1989, and all but one came from Latin America.[9]

Secondly, while indigenous peoples cannot complain directly to the ILO,[10] workers' and employers' organisations can make representations' (on their behalf) about non-compliance with ILO conventions.[11] Representations are considered by a tripartite committee (of employer, worker and state representatives). The state is given an opportunity to respond before the committee reports its conclusions and recommendations to the ILO's Governing Body for adoption. The Committee of Experts may also be tasked to follow-up on the state's implementation of the recommendations.

Monitoring under the ILO system is more specific but less dense than that under the UN and regional procedures. It is more specific because ILO Convention No 169 is exclusively devoted to indigenous (and tribal) rights, whereas the UN and regional conventions articulate more general norms. But it is less dense because there are only

[7] See, eg, ILO, *Indigenous and Tribal Peoples' Rights in Practice: A Guide to ILO Convention No. 169* (ILO, Geneva, 2009) (compiling the comments of the ILO supervisory bodies); ILO, *Monitoring Indigenous and Tribal Peoples' Rights through ILO Conventions: A Compilation of ILO Supervisory Bodies' Comments 2009–2010* (ILO, Geneva, 2010); Fergus MacKay, *A Guide to Indigenous Peoples' Rights in the International Labour Organization* (Forest Peoples Programme, Moreton-in-Marsh, 2003); Tanja Joona, 'International Norms and Domestic Practices in Regard to ILO Convention No. 169, with Special Reference to Articles 1 and 13–19' (2010) 12 *International Community Law Review* 213. See also James Anaya, *Indigenous Peoples in International Law* (Oxford University Press, 2004), 228–30.

[8] ILO Constitution, Art 22.

[9] Argentina, Bolivia, Brazil, Colombia, Denmark, Guatemala, Ecuador, Mexico and Peru: ILO, *Indigenous and Tribal Peoples' Rights in Practice* (n 7) 182.

[10] Indigenous peoples can informally send information to the ILO, which may be included in country files.

[11] ILO Constitution, Art 24. States can also complain about other states' compliance under Art 26.

20 states party to ILO Convention No 169, whereas the regional conventions have roughly at least double that number,[12] while most states are parties to the key UN treaties. Admittedly the raw figures understate the normative effects of ILO mechanisms, since they also engage ILO member states on ILO instruments that states have not ratified, including Convention No 169.

Further, ILO Convention No 169 has been frequently considered outside of the ILO system, by international, regional and national courts, and has been particularly influential in Latin American courts,[13] the region where it has the highest number of ratifications. While the ILO treaties are confined to labour issues, they have influenced the evolution of wider human rights standards on indigenous peoples, including by shaping ideas about who is 'indigenous' (discussed in chapter 1) and catalysing the work of other UN bodies. ILO Convention No 169 is often mentioned by the UN committees and regional bodies when dealing with indigenous issues.

It must be noted, however, that ILO Convention No 169 is more restrictive in certain respects than contemporary international and regional standards on indigenous rights.[14] To mention just a few examples, it recognises aspects of internal autonomy but not a right of self-determination. It requires consultations on development projects to aim to secure indigenous consent but it does not require actual consent even where a project would jeopardize subsistence rights and cultural survival, and states retain ultimate decision-making authority. It protects indigenous rights in traditional land where it is currently used or occupied but not where indigenous peoples have been historically dispossessed from their lands. In recognises indigenous rights in land but not necessarily a right to full ownership. Its procedures for considering land claims are also not sufficiently protective or robust.

Other UN Mechanisms

Beyond the ILO, much of the standard setting on indigenous rights has been through the non-binding but normatively influential 'soft law'[15] developed by various political UN bodies. These have foremost emanated from the various special procedures and mechanisms devoted to indigenous issues in the UN system since the 1970s. Particularly important was a ground-breaking study undertaken by a UN Special Rapporteur, Martínez Cobo, from 1972–86, within the UN Sub-Commission on Prevention of Discrimination and Protection of Minorities (under the then UN Commission on Human Rights). The Martínez Cobo study laid much of the conceptual groundwork for contemporary thinking about who are indigenous peoples (the subject of chapter 1 of this book), what are their legal rights, and areas for the progressive development

[12] Thirty-five states in the Inter-American and 53 in the African systems, respectively.

[13] See ILO, *Application of Convention No. 169 by Domestic and International Courts in Latin America: A Casebook* (ILO, Geneva, 2009).

[14] Mackay, *A Guide to Indigenous Peoples' Rights* (n 7) 16–19.

[15] Such as resolutions, reports, guidelines, and other texts with normative intentions or implications. Despite not being formally binding, soft law is often invoked by governments, courts, UN bodies, international organisations (such as the World Bank), NGOs and corporations when dealing with indigenous issues. Over time, soft law standards can crystallise into customary international law, given sufficiently widespread and representative state practice accompanied by the requisite legal intention (*opinio juris*).

of the law. While not binding, it has heavily influenced subsequent standard setting through the (non-binding) resolutions of the UN Commission on Human Rights and the work of other UN and regional human rights bodies.

Working Group on Indigenous Populations (WGIP) 1982–2007 and the UN Declaration on the Rights of Indigenous Peoples 2007

Next came the landmark establishment in 1982 of the Working Group on Indigenous Populations (WGIP), as a subsidiary organ of the Sub-Commission.[16] The Working Group met annually in Geneva until 2007 and had a mandate to review human rights developments and promote the evolution of international standards on indigenous rights. The Working Group consisted of independent experts and state members from the Sub-Commission representing all geopolitical regions. It was also open to indigenous peoples (with funding from the UN Voluntary Fund, established in 1985), non-governmental organisations (NGOs), states and UN agencies, and over time indigenous representatives became very active, even dominant, in its proceedings.[17]

Between 1985 and 1993, the WGIP prepared a draft declaration on the rights of indigenous peoples, which was eventually adopted by a resolution of the UN General Assembly in 2007,[18] after a long deliberative process involving states and indigenous peoples.[19] The instrument adopted, the UN Declaration on the Rights of Indigenous Peoples of 2007 (UNDRIP), covers a spectrum of rights, including on self-determination;[20] culture, identity, religion, language and history; non-discrimination; life, liberty and security; education, employment and health; participation in decision-making and sustainable development, including through free, prior and informed consent; and land, resources and the environment.

The UNDRIP is increasingly viewed, and utilised, as a cornerstone of contemporary international legal standards on indigenous rights. While it does not have the status of a binding treaty, there has been, and remains, considerable debate about the extent of its normative implications.[21] In the General Assembly in 2007, it was

[16] Pursuant to UN Economic and Social Council Resolution 1982/34, 'Study of the problem of discrimination against indigenous populations', 28th Plenary Session (7 May 1982).

[17] Anaya, *Indigenous Peoples in International Law* (n 7) 221.

[18] UN General Assembly Resolution 61/295, 'Declaration on the Rights of Indigenous Peoples' (13 September 2007) (144 states in favour, 4 against (Australia, Canada, New Zealand, United States), 11 abstaining). The WGIP's draft declaration was approved by the UN Sub-Commission in 1993, carried forward from 1995 by the UN Commission on Human Rights, and approved by the new UN Human Rights Council in Resolution 2006/2 (29 June 2006) (30 states in favour, 2 against, 12 abstentions, and 3 absentees).

[19] Benedict Kingsbury, 'Indigenous Peoples' in *Max Planck Encyclopedia of Public International Law*, online subscription database, [11]–[13].

[20] See Karen Engle, 'On Fragile Architecture: The UN Declaration on the Rights of Indigenous Peoples in the Context of Human Rights' (2011) 22 *European Journal of International Law* 141.

[21] See generally Stephen Allen and Alexandra Xanthaki (eds), *Reflections on the UN Declaration on the Rights of Indigenous Peoples* (Hart Publishing, 2011); James Anaya and Siegfried Wiessner, 'The UN Declaration on the Rights of Indigenous Peoples: Towards Re-empowerment', *Jurist*, 3 October 2007.

adopted by 144 votes in favour to four against, with 11 abstentions;[22] more states have since expressed their support,[23] including some which originally voted against it. The UN's Permanent Forum on Indigenous Issues (PFII), discussed below, has argued that the UNDRIP 'forms a part of universal human rights law' that was 'almost universally agreed upon' through an extensive deliberative process, and is 'part of a practice that has advanced a growing "rapprochement" between declarations and treaties'.[24] It has further suggested that the UNDRIP has a 'growing legal status' and that its 'entirety' may have already 'acquired the status of being part of binding international law', or at least some of its provisions have.[25] Certain scholars also support the view that all or most of the UNDRIP reflects customary law.[26]

Others are more sceptical, emphasising that some states view the UNDRIP as an aspirational political programme rather than as reflecting legal obligations.[27] The fact that only 20 states are parties to the only binding treaty on indigenous rights, ILO Convention No 169, is a stark reminder that many—if not most—states remain reluctant to assume binding legal obligations that are specific to indigenous peoples, notwithstanding that an overwhelming majority of states support the UNDRIP, and that almost 100 states have indigenous populations.

Insofar as the UNDRIP particularises general human rights law for indigenous peoples and circumstances,[28] it can hardly be opposed by states as reflecting binding international standards. Indeed, much of its content, and thus its normative force, stems from the particularised application, over recent decades, of general human rights law to indigenous peoples by the UN treaty committees, regional bodies and national legal practice, as discussed in this book. This was deliberate; the drafters of the UNDRIP paid careful attention to existing state practice in order to come up with a text that would maximise state support. However, the devil is in the detail of particular provisions, especially in how far the UNDRIP pushes the boundaries of the existing law in genuinely new directions, or recognises unique indigenous rights which cannot be readily extrapolated from general norms applicable to everyone. Certain issues, such as the scope of self-determination; the extent of consultation and consent; and the retrospective reach of indigenous rights in lands from which they have been historically dispossessed,[29] among others, remain contested.

[22] The four states against were Australia, Canada, New Zealand and the United States; the 11 abstentions were Azerbaijan, Bangladesh, Bhutan, Burundi, Colombia, Georgia, Kenya, Nigeria, Russian Federation, Samoa and Ukraine.

[23] See, eg, OHCHR, *Outcome Document of the Durban Review Conference* (24 April 2009), [73] (the Outcome Document was adopted by consensus of 182 states).

[24] PFII, *Report on the Eighth Session to ECOSOC*, E/C.19/2009/L.3 (2009), Annex: General Comment No 1 (2009) on Article 42 of the UNDRIP, [7], [9], [10].

[25] Ibid [12].

[26] Anaya and Wiessner, 'The UN Declaration on the Rights of Indigenous Peoples' (n 21).

[27] Stephen Allen, 'The UN Declaration on the Rights of Indigenous Peoples and the Limits of the International Legal Project' in Allen and Xanthaki (eds) (n 21), 226, 228–29, 254.

[28] Ibid 231.

[29] Article 28(1) of the UNDRIP recognises a right of restitution where 'lands, territories and resources which they have traditionally owned or otherwise occupied or used … have been confiscated, taken, occupied, used or damaged without their free, prior and informed consent'. See Allen, 'The UN Declaration on the Rights of Indigenous Peoples' (n 27) 240.

Overall, the UNDRIP variously consolidates existing norms, clarifies certain rules, and progressively develops others. It is gradually filtering into the practice of the UN treaty committees, regional bodies and states, and its up-take and acceptance in this manner will be the ultimate litmus test of its normativity. In 2014, the General Assembly's World Conference on Indigenous Peoples encouraged the UN treaty committees to consider the UNDRIP in their work, and urged states to report to the committees (and the Human Rights Council's Universal Periodic Review) on measures taken to advance its objectives.[30]

While the WGIP has made a vital contribution to standard setting, a limitation of its mandate was its limited ability to formally monitor the situation of indigenous peoples on the ground. Certainly it informally received and reviewed information from governments and indigenous groups, NGOs and international organisations,[31] and in some cases acted as a de facto monitoring procedure and even issued public statements of concern about situations in particular countries.[32] However, it had no formal mandate to demand state reports, receive and resolve individual complaints, function as an early warning mechanism, or react to crises.[33] Once it had concluded the drafting of the UNDRIP, doubts about its effectiveness and future led to its replacement in 2007.

Expert Mechanism on the Rights of Indigenous Peoples (EMRIP) 2007–present

The WGIP was replaced in 2007 by an Expert Mechanism on the Rights of Indigenous Peoples (EMRIP), created as a subsidiary body of the Human Rights Council[34] comprised of five independent experts.[35] The EMRIP provides thematic advice (through studies and research) to the Council and can suggest proposals for its adoption. Its annual session is attended by states, indigenous peoples, NGOs, academics and interested UN bodies. Thus far its advices have addressed issues concerning education; participation in decision-making; languages and cultures; extractive industries; access to justice; restorative justice and indigenous legal systems; and disaster risk reduction.[36]

The EMRIP has also encouraged better state implementation of the UNDRIP. In 2014 it observed that few states have adopted comprehensive plans or strategies

[30] UN General Assembly Resolution 69/2, 'Outcome Document of the World Conference on Indigenous Peoples' (22 September 2014), [29].

[31] Anaya, *Indigenous Peoples in International Law* (n 7) 221.

[32] Ibid 222.

[33] Gaetano Pentassuglia, 'Evolving Protection of Minority Groups; Global Challenges and the Role of International Jurisprudence' (2009) 11 *International Community Law Review* 185, 191; Anaya, *Indigenous Peoples in International Law* (n 7) 222.

[34] By UN Human Rights Council Resolution 6/36 (11 December 2007).

[35] Having regard to indigenous origin, gender balance and geographic representation.

[36] Respectively, Advice Nos: 1 (2009) on the Rights of Indigenous Peoples to Education; 2 (2011) on Indigenous Peoples and the Right to Participate in Decision-making; 3 (2012) on Indigenous Peoples' Languages and Cultures; 4 (2012) on Indigenous Peoples and the Right to Participate in Decision-making, with A Focus on Extractive Industries; 5 (2013) on Access to Justice in the Promotion and Protection of the Rights of Indigenous People; 6 (2014) on Restorative Justice, Indigenous Juridical Systems and Access to Justice for Indigenous Women, Children and Youth, and Persons with Disabilities; and 7 (2014) on Promotion and Protection of the Rights of Indigenous Peoples in Disaster Risk Reduction Initiatives.

to implement it, or provided information to the EMRIP on the effectiveness of measures taken.[37] Some states have objected to ambiguities in the UNDRIP (such as who is indigenous) or perceive positive measures for indigenous peoples as unequal treatment.[38] At the World Conference on Indigenous Peoples in 2014, the UN General Assembly asked the Human Rights Council to consider improving the EMRIP so that it can more effectively promote respect for the UNDRIP.[39] It was specifically envisaged that the EMRIP could better assist states to monitor, evaluate and improve their implementation of the UNDRIP. The development of an Optional Protocol to the UNDRIP has been separately suggested to enable individual complaints and strengthen supervision and monitoring. That suggestion has, however, been controversial.[40]

UN Permanent Forum on Indigenous Issues (PFII) 2000–present

A fourth UN standard setting process is the UN Permanent Forum on Indigenous Issues (PFII),[41] established by ECOSOC in 2000 and meeting for the first time in 2002, following initial discussions at the Vienna Conference on Human Rights in 1993. The PFII is comprised of 16 independent experts serving in their personal capacity: eight nominated by governments, and eight by indigenous organisations in the various regions. The PFII advises ECOSOC on indigenous issues in six areas: economic and social development; culture; the environment; education; health; and human rights.[42] It provides expert advice and recommendations to the Human Rights Council and other UN bodies and programmes; raises awareness of indigenous issues, and coordination and integration, in the UN system; and prepares and disseminates information. Its initial focus was on review and coordination of UN bodies and programmes.[43]

The PFII also has a 'soft mandate' under Article 42 of the UNDRIP to 'promote respect for and full application of' the UNDRIP and to 'follow up … [its] effectiveness'. It has issued its own 'General Comment' (deliberately borrowing from the practice of the UN treaty bodies) and asserted an implied power to engage in dialogue with states about their compliance.[44] It has even conducted in-country investigations of alleged violations (as on forced labour and servitude amongst the Guaraní people in Bolivia and Paraguay).[45]

[37] EMRIP, *Report to the Human Rights Council*, A/HRC/27/67 (25 July 2014), 22.

[38] Ibid.

[39] UN General Assembly Resolution 69/2, *Outcome Document of the World Conference on Indigenous Peoples* (n 30), [28].

[40] See Permanent Forum on Indigenous Issues, *Expert Group Meeting on the Theme 'Dialogue on an Optional Protocol to the United Nations Declaration on the Rights of Indigenous Peoples'*, Note by the Secretariat, UN Doc E/C.19/2015/8 (17 February 2015).

[41] There is a 2015 proposal to change the name to the 'Permanent Forum on the Rights of Indigenous Peoples'.

[42] It also works on the cross-cutting topics of gender and women; children and youth; the Millennium Development Goals and the post-2015 Agenda; and data and indicators.

[43] Anaya, *Indigenous Peoples in International Law* (n 7) 220.

[44] PFII, *Report on the Eighth Session to ECOSOC*, E/C.19/2009/L.3 (2009), Annex: General Comment No 1 (2009) on Article 42 of the UNDRIP, [20]–[22]; see Kingsbury, 'Indigenous Peoples' (n 19), [16].

[45] Ibid.

The PFII contributes to soft law formation through elaborating on thematic issues and fleshing out the application of existing standards to particular factual situations. Thus far the PFII has issued reports on a wide variety of topics, many of which address legal and human rights issues. Some have considered normative and institutional questions, such as human rights mechanisms;[46] an Optional Protocol to the UNDRIP;[47] truth commissions;[48] the UNDRIP and national constitutions;[49] criminal defence rights;[50] the impact of the doctrine of discovery;[51] decolonisation in the Pacific;[52] and participation in Arctic governance and resource development.[53]

Many reports address land, resource and environment issues. These have included best practices in resolving land disputes and claims;[54] land tenure and management[55] (including the impact of oil palm and other commercial tree plantations, and monocropping);[56] fishing rights;[57] extractive industries;[58] corporations;[59] World Bank policies;[60] the rights of Mother Earth;[61] protecting traditional knowledge, genetic resources and folklore;[62] development;[63] and indicators of well-being, poverty and sustainability.[64] Climate change[65] and disaster risk reduction[66] have also received attention.

Some reports focus on sub-groups such as women (concerning violence[67] and political participation);[68] young people (concerning participation in decision-making,[69] boarding schools,[70] and the inclusion of indigenous knowledge in education;[71]

[46] E/C.19/2008/2 (19 December 2007).
[47] E/C.19/2014/7 (4 March 2014).
[48] E/C.19/2013/13 (14 February 2013).
[49] E/C.19/2013/18 (20 February 2013).
[50] E/C.19/2011/4 (8 February 2011).
[51] E/C.19/2014/3 (20 February 2014); E/C.19/2010/13 (4 February 2010).
[52] E/C.19/2013/12 (20 February 2013).
[53] E/C.19/2012/10 (3 March 2012).
[54] E/C.19/2014/4 (27 February 2014).
[55] E/C.19/2010/CRP. 7 (21 April 2009).
[56] E/C.19/2007/CRP.6 (7 May 2007).
[57] E/C.19/2010/2 (8 January 2010) (Australia and Norway).
[58] E/C.19/2013/11 (14 February 2013) (in Mexico); E/C.19/2013/16 (20 February 2013) (consolidated report); E/C.19/2013/20 (5 March 2013) (in Australia).
[59] E/C.19/2012/3 (24 April 2012); E/C.19/2011/12 (10 March 2011); E/C.19/2010 CRP.1 (19 January 2010).
[60] E/C.19/2013/15 (20 February 2013).
[61] E/C.19/2010/4 (15 January 2010).
[62] E/C.19/2014/2 (19 February 2014) (in Africa); E/C.19/2007/10 (20 March 2007) (traditional knowledge).
[63] E/C.19/2010/CRP. 4 (25 March 2010).
[64] E/C.19/2008/9 (20 February 2008).
[65] E/C.19/2013/7 (12 February 2013) (rights and safeguards in emissions reduction projects involving deforestation and forest degradation); E/C.19/2012/4 (23 February 2012) (impact on reindeer herding); E/C.19/2010/7 (2 February 2010) (consistency of policies and projects with the UNDRIP); E/C.19/2010/15 (12 February 2010) (impacts of adaptation and mitigation measures on reindeer herding); E/C.19/2010/18 (4 March 2010) (implications of Copenhagen meeting for indigenous local adaptation and mitigation measures); E/C.19/2008/10 (20 March 2008) (impact of mitigation measures).
[66] E/C.19/2013/14 (20 February 2013).
[67] E/C.19/2013/9 (12 February 2013).
[68] E/C.19/2013/10 (19 February 2013).
[69] E/C.19/2013/8 (12 February 2013).
[70] E/C.19/2010/11 (1 February 2010).
[71] E/C.19/2013/17 (20 February 2013).

and their living conditions in Mesoamerica[72]); and indigenous people with disabilities.[73] Geographical case studies have also featured, such as the implementation of the Chittagong Hill Tracts Accord 1997 in Bangladesh;[74] and participation in democracy and elections in Latin America.[75]

The Permanent Forum is still a relatively new body. Criticism of its work thus far has centred on its capacity to influence other states or other UN bodies,[76] as well as whether it has marginalised or co-opted alternative indigenous voices and 'deradicalised' resistance.[77] There is also discussion about its representativeness,[78] since half of its members are nominated by states rather than indigenous peoples, although indigenous peoples may attend its meetings. Concerns have also been expressed about resource and expertise limitations.[79]

UN Special Rapporteur on the Situation of Human Rights and Fundamental Freedoms of Indigenous Peoples 2001–present

A final UN standard setting process is the UN Special Rapporteur on the Situation of Human Rights and Fundamental Freedoms of Indigenous Peoples, established by the Commission on Human Rights in 2001[80] and subsequently maintained by the Human Rights Council. The Special Rapporteur is an independent expert mandated to promote good laws and practices on the implementation of international standards; report on indigenous rights in particular countries; address specific violations of indigenous rights; conduct thematic studies; and cooperate with other UN bodies.

Specialised Branches of International Law

Beyond these UN mechanisms dedicated to indigenous issues, three other areas of international law, also of concern to specialised UN bodies, have influenced the appreciation of indigenous issues by the UN treaty committees and regional human rights bodies. These include aspects of international environmental law; cultural heritage and cultural property law; and international law concerning finance and development.[81]

[72] E/C.19/2014/5 (27 February 2014).

[73] E/C.19/2013/6 (5 February 2013).

[74] E/C.19/2011/6 (18 February 2011).

[75] E/C.19/2014/6 (26 February 2014).

[76] Mary Lawlor, 'Indigenous Internationalism: Native Rights and the UN' (2003) 1 *Comparative American Studies: A Journal* 351.

[77] Isabelle Schulte-Tenckhoff and Adil Hasan Khan, 'The Permanent Quest for a Mandate: Assessing the UN Permanent Forum on Indigenous Issues' (2011) 20 *Griffith Law Review* 673.

[78] Irene Watson, 'De-colonisation and Aboriginal Peoples: Past and Future Strategies, Sharon Venne Interviewed by Irene Watson' (2007) 26 *Australian Feminist Law Journal* 111, 112.

[79] Anaya, *Indigenous Peoples in International Law* (n 7) 220.

[80] UN Human Rights Council Resolution 15/14, 'Human Rights and Indigenous Peoples: Mandate of the Special Rapporteur on the Rights of Indigenous Peoples' (6 October 2010).

[81] Indigenous peoples have shaped many other areas of international law not considered here, including on sovereignty, acquisition of title to territory (by conquest, discovery and occupation of *terra nullius*, treaty and the like), statehood, legal personality, law of treaties, law of the sea, international criminal law

International Environmental Law

Environmental regulation is one of the few areas of international law to establish binding treaty standards protecting indigenous interests and has informed human rights interpretation. First, indigenous sealing, whaling and polar bear hunting are permitted in certain circumstances under the relevant conventions,[82] exceptions which admit the cultural and economic importance of those traditional activities. Secondly, local communities (implicitly including indigenous peoples) must be consulted, and 'local and traditional knowledge' protected, under the UN Convention to Combat Desertification 1994.[83] Thirdly, and most significantly, the Convention on Biological Diversity 1992 recognises the role of indigenous communities in conserving and sustainably using biological diversity, by requiring states to:

> respect, preserve and maintain knowledge, innovations and practices of Indigenous and local communities embodying traditional lifestyles relevant for the conservation and sustainable use of biological diversity and promote their wider application with approval and involvement of the holders of such knowledge, innovations and practices and encourage the equitable sharing of the benefits arising from the utilisation of such knowledge, innovations and practices.[84]

The subsequent Nagoya Protocol to the Convention on Biological Diversity 2010 further regulates genetic resources and the fair and equitable sharing of benefits from their utilisation.[85] Article 12 addresses indigenous traditional knowledge (including customary laws, community protocols and procedures) associated with genetic resources. States must secure indigenous communities' prior informed consent, and fair and equitable benefit-sharing, in the light of community laws and procedures and customary use and exchange.

(particularly 'cultural' genocide, slavery, forced labour, apartheid, and crimes against humanity), diplomatic protection, and procedural doctrines (such as estoppel, acquiescence, good faith, abuse of rights and laches): see, eg, Benedict Kingsbury, '"Indigenous Peoples" in International Law: A Constructivist Approach to the Asian Controversy' (1998) 92 *American Journal of International Law* 414, 436–37; Ben Saul, 'Indigenous Peoples, Laws and Customs in the Teaching of Public and Private International Law' (2012) 4 *Ngiya: Talk the Law* 63. With the adoption of the UN Charter 1945, indigenous peoples have shaped decolonisation, self-determination, and the doctrines of inter-temporal law (whereby an act is judged by the law in force at the time) (see *Island of Palmas* (*Netherlands v United States*) (1928) 2 RIAA 829) and the stability of territorial boundaries (*uti possidetis*) (see Anaya, *Indigenous Peoples in International Law* (n 7) 107–8).

82 Respectively: Convention on the Conservation of North Pacific Fur Seals, Art VII (adopted 7 May 1976, entered into force 12 October 1976, 314 UNTS 105); International Convention for the Regulation of Whaling (adopted 2 December 1946, entered into force 10 November 1948, 161 UNTS 72), as amended by the International Whaling Commission Amendments to the Schedule, 24 October 1997, [13(b)(2)]; International Agreement for the Conservation of Polar Bears, Art 3(d) (adopted 15 November 1973, entered into force 26 May 1976).

83 Convention to Combat Desertification, Art 16(g) (adopted 17 June 1994, entered into force 26 December 1996, 1954 UNTS 3).

84 Convention on Biological Diversity, Art 8(j) (adopted 5 June 1992, entered into force 29 December 1993, 1760 UNTS 79).

85 Nagoya Protocol on Genetic Resources and the Fair and Equitable Sharing of Benefits arising from their Utilization to the Convention on Biological Diversity (adopted 29 October 2010, entered into force 12 October 2014).

At the level of soft law, the Rio UN Conference on Environment and Development of 1992 also acknowledges certain indigenous interests. States committed to a non-binding action plan on sustainable development, Agenda 21, Chapter 26 of which is dedicated to 'Recognising and Strengthening the Role of Indigenous Peoples and their Communities'. Its objectives include establishing processes to empower indigenous peoples, and strengthening their participation in resource management, sustainable development and conservation. Further, the UN Forest Principles of 1992 encourage national forest policies to recognise and protect indigenous peoples' rights, including economic rights in forest exploitation.[86] Other actors have also developed their own policy guidance, including the International Union for Conservation of Nature and Natural Resources.[87]

International Cultural Heritage and Cultural Property Law

Given the centrality of cultural distinctiveness to the conceptualisation of peoples as indigenous (as discussed in chapter 1), international law has afforded some express protection to indigenous cultural heritage and property.[88] Cultural heritage and property overlap with, but are legally distinct from, the human right to take part in cultural life (ICESCR, Article 15) and the cultural rights of minorities (ICCPR, Article 27). International cultural heritage and cultural property law have influenced the interpretation of those cultural rights.

Indigenous peoples are modestly mentioned in two recent treaties adopted under the auspices of the UN Educational, Scientific and Cultural Organization (UNESCO). First, the Preamble to the Convention for the Safeguarding of the Intangible Cultural Heritage 2003 recognises that 'communities, in particular indigenous communities, groups and, in some cases, individuals, play an important role in the production, safeguarding, maintenance and re-creation of the intangible cultural heritage, thus helping to enrich cultural diversity and human creativity'. Intangible cultural heritage is defined as 'the practices, representations, expressions, knowledge, skills—as well as the instruments, objects, artefacts and cultural spaces associated therewith—that communities, groups and, in some cases, individuals recognize as part of their

[86] UN General Assembly, 'Non-Legally Binding Authoritative Statement of Principles for a Global Consensus on the Management, Conservation and Sustainable Development of All Forests' in *Report of the UN Conference on Environment and Development*, UN Doc A/CONF 151/26 (14 August 1992), vol III, Art 5(a).

[87] Javier Beltran, *Indigenous and Traditional Peoples and Protected Areas: Principles, Guidelines and Case Studies*, World Commission on Protected Areas, Best Practice Protected Areas Guideline Series No 4 (International Union for Conservation of Nature and Natural Resources (IUCN), Cardiff University, and World Wildlife Fund, 2000).

[88] See generally Alexandra Xanthaki, 'Indigenous Cultural Rights in International Law' (2000) *European Journal of Law Reform* 343; Anaya, *Indigenous Peoples in International Law* (n 7), 131–41; Tony Simpson, 'Claims of Indigenous Peoples to Cultural Property in Canada, Australia, and New Zealand' (1995) 18 *Hastings International and Comparative Law Review* 195; Robert Paterson, 'Claiming Possession of the Material Cultural Property of Indigenous Peoples' (2001) 16 *Connecticut Journal of International Law* 283; Maureen Tehan, 'To Be or Not to Be (Property): Anglo-Australian Law and the Search for Protection of Indigenous Cultural Heritage' (1996) 15 *University of Tasmania Law Review* 273.

cultural heritage'.[89] The Convention's operative provisions, however, apply to indigenous communities in the same way as to other groups.

Secondly, an operative provision of the Convention on the Protection and Promotion of the Diversity of Cultural Expressions 2005 calls for equal respect for all cultures, including 'indigenous peoples'.[90] It also calls on the parties to pay 'due attention to the special circumstances and needs of various social groups, including ... indigenous peoples'.[91] Again, indigenous peoples are entitled to the same protections as other groups. The Preamble emphasises the importance of traditional knowledge, particularly indigenous knowledge, as a source of intangible and material wealth and in contributing to sustainable development.

Indigenous peoples are not mentioned in other important UNESCO instruments that may affect them, including standards on underwater cultural heritage, world cultural and natural heritage, illicit dealings in cultural property, the protection of cultural property in conflict, and copyright and intellectual property.[92] While indigenous peoples may be able to benefit from the norms in some of these conventions, the lack of specific attention to indigenous issues has sometimes been controversial. For example, indigenous peoples have criticised the failure of the World Heritage Committee, under the UNESCO Convention Concerning the Protection of the World Cultural and Natural Heritage 1972, to enable indigenous participation and consultation in the nomination, declaration and management of World Heritage sites. In some cases, World Heritage listing can negatively impact on indigenous land, resource and cultural rights.[93] Proposals to formalise indigenous involvement in these processes have thus far been unsuccessful.[94]

Some soft law standards issued by UNESCO have mentioned indigenous peoples. For example, its Universal Declaration on Cultural Diversity 2002 guarantees the cultural diversity of indigenous peoples,[95] while in 1982 UNESCO and the World Intellectual Property Organization (WIPO) adopted model provisions on the protection of folklore.[96]

[89] Convention for the Safeguarding of the Intangible Cultural Heritage, Art 2(1) (adopted 17 October 2003, entered into force 20 April 2006, 2368 UNTS 1).

[90] Convention on the Protection and Promotion of the Diversity of Cultural Expressions, Art 2(3) (adopted 20 October 2005, entered into force 18 March 2007, 2440 UNTS 311).

[91] Ibid Art 7(1)(a).

[92] Respectively: UNESCO Convention for the Protection of the Underwater Cultural Heritage (adopted 2 November 2001, entered into force 2 January 2009, 2562 UNTS 3); Convention for the Protection of the World Cultural and Natural Heritage (adopted 16 November 1972, entered into force 17 December 1975, 1037 UNTS 151); Convention on the Means of Prohibiting and Preventing the Illicit Import, Export and Transfer of Ownership of Cultural Property (adopted 14 November 1970, entered into force 24 April 1972, 823 UNTS 231); Convention on the Protection of Cultural Property in the Event of Armed Conflict with Regulations for the Execution of the Convention (adopted 14 May 1954, entered into force 7 August 1956, 249 UNTS 215); and Universal Copyright Convention (adopted 6 September 1952, entered into force 16 September 1955, 216 UNTS 132) as revised (24 July 1971, entered into force 10 July 1974, 943 UNTS 178).

[93] IWGIA, *The Indigenous World 2013* (IWGIA, Copenhagen, 2013), 476–83.

[94] See Lynn Meskell, 'UNESCO and the Fate of the World Heritage Indigenous Peoples Council of Experts (WHIPCOE)' (2013) 20 *International Journal of Cultural Property* 155.

[95] UNESCO, Universal Declaration on Cultural Diversity, Art 4 (adopted 2 November 2001).

[96] UNESCO and WIPO, Model Provisions for National Laws on the Protection of Expressions of Folklore against Illicit Exploitation and Other Prejudicial Actions (1985).

It should also be noted that the extent of protection for indigenous culture has been controversial in some areas of international law. For example, during the drafting of the Convention on the Prevention and Punishment of the Crime of Genocide 1948,[97] a proposal to specifically prohibit 'cultural genocide'[98] was rejected. In part this was because of objections by states that had problematic relations with their indigenous peoples.[99] The last remaining vestige of a concept of cultural genocide in the Convention concerns the forced transfer of children from one group to another, where intended to destroy (in whole or in part) the first national, ethnical, racial or religious group (Article II(e)). That practice has been claimed to constitute genocide, for example, in past Australian indigenous policies.[100] More broadly, a number of national courts have convicted persons of genocide for the attempted physical extermination of indigenous peoples,[101] while there has been national political acknowledgement of genocide against indigenous peoples in a number of other cases.[102]

International Intellectual Property Law

There has also been much debate about the adequacy of the related field of international intellectual property law in protecting indigenous interests in their natural resources (such as wildlife and plant products), genetic material, and traditional knowledge.[103] The WIPO's Intergovernmental Committee on Intellectual Property

[97] Convention on the Prevention and Punishment of the Crime of Genocide (adopted 9 December 1948, entered into force on 12 January 1951, 78 UNTS 277).

[98] ECOSOC, Ad Hoc Committee on Genocide, *Report of the Committee and Draft Convention Drawn up by the Committee*, UN Doc E/794 (24 May 1948), 17–19 (Draft Article III: 'any deliberate act committed with the intent to destroy the language, religion or cultural of a national, racial or religious group on grounds of national or racial origin or religious belief').

[99] William Schabas, *Genocide in International Law* (Cambridge University Press, Cambridge, 2000), 184 (such as Sweden, Brazil, New Zealand, Canada and South Africa).

[100] Human Rights and Equal Opportunity Commission, *National Inquiry into the Separation of Aboriginal and Tomes Strait Islander Children from their Families, Bringing Them Home* (April 1997); cf *Nulyarimma v Thompson* [1997] Federal Court of Australia 1192 (the international crime of genocide cannot be prosecuted in Australia in the absence of domestic legislative incorporation); *Kruger v Commonwealth (Stolen Generations Case)* (1997) 190 Commonwealth Law Reports 1 (the High Court of Australia found that even if genocide were a crime, the removal of Aboriginal children from the parents, in their own best interests by welfare authorities, would not constitute genocide). See Ben Saul, 'The International Crime of Genocide in Australian Law' (2000) 22 *Sydney Law Review* 527. Genocide was legislatively criminalised in Australia in 2002.

[101] Such as convictions in Brazil's courts for private attacks by Brazilian nationals on the Yanomami in Venezuela (see *Yanomami Indigenous People of Xaximu v Venezuela (Friendly Settlement)*, IACHR, Report No 32/12, Petition 11.706, 20 March 2012); the conviction of the former President of Equatorial Guinea for targeting the Bubi indigenous minority and the deaths of 80,000 people (of a population of 300,000) (see Alejandro Artucio, *The Trial of Macias in Equatorial Guinea: The Story of A Dictatorship* (International Commission of Jurists and the International University Exchange Fund, 1979)).

[102] Such as Germany's 2004 apology for imperial Germany's killing of 100,000 Herero indigenous people in south-west Africa, between 1904 and 1908; and the Report of Guatemala's Historical Clarification Commission (Comisión para el Esclarecimiento Histórico), *Memory of Silence* (25 February 1999), finding that the armed forces committed genocide against the Mayans between 1980–83, and a Presidential apology in 2009 for genocide against the Mayan people.

[103] Silke von Lewinski (ed), *Indigenous Heritage and Intellectual Property: Genetic Resources, Traditional Knowledge and Folklore* (2nd edn, Kluwer Law International, 2008); Chidi Oguamanam, *International Law and Indigenous Knowledge: Intellectual Property Rights, Plant Biodiversity and Traditional Medicine* (University of Toronto Press, 2006); Tony Simpson, *Indigenous Heritage and Self-Determination: The Cultural and Intellectual Property Rights of Indigenous Peoples* (International Work Group for

and Genetic Resources, Traditional Knowledge and Folklore (IGC), established in 2000, has been attempting to develop binding instruments on genetic resources, traditional knowledge and traditional cultural expressions. The instruments would apply to indigenous peoples but also certain other groups. The first set of Draft Articles would prevent misappropriation of *genetic resources* and associated traditional knowledge through the intellectual property system, including by preventing patenting. Traditional knowledge is defined as that held by indigenous peoples, and which is traditionally generated, dynamic and evolving, and inter-generationally transmitted.[104]

A second set of Draft Articles would enable indigenous peoples to prevent misappropriation, misuse or unauthorised use of their *traditional knowledge*; control how such knowledge is used in non-traditional ways; share equitably in the benefits from its use with prior informed consent; and encourage its creation and innovation.[105] Traditional knowledge refers to know-how, skills, innovations, practices, teachings and learnings of indigenous peoples, and may be associated with agriculture, the environment, healthcare and medicine, biodiversity, traditional lifestyles, natural or genetic resources, and architecture and construction. It would be protected where it is linked to indigenous cultural and social identity and cultural heritage and is inter-generationally transmitted, and regardless whether it is in codified, oral or other form, or is dynamic and evolving.[106] One proposal suggests traditional knowledge must have persisted for at least 50 years to gain protection.

A third set of Draft Articles would enable indigenous peoples to prevent the misappropriation and misuse of their *[traditional] cultural expressions*; control non-traditional uses; prevent the unauthorised or inappropriate grant or exercise of intellectual property rights over them, while enabling fair use; provide legal certainty; promote equitable sharing of benefits from their use with prior informed consent; and encourage their creation and innovation.[107] Traditional cultural expressions are defined to include any forms of artistic and literary, creative and other spiritual expression, tangible or intangible, or a combination thereof, such as actions, materials, music and sound, verbal and written, and regardless of form.[108] Again,

Indigenous Affairs, 2007); Sarah Harding, 'Defining Traditional Knowledge: Lessons from Cultural Property' (2004) 11 *Cardozo Journal of International and Comparative Law* 511; David Jordan, 'Square Pegs and Round Holes: Domestic Intellectual Property Law and Native American Economic and Cultural Policy: Can it Fit?' (2001) 25 *American Indian Law Review* 93; Terri Janke, 'Respecting Indigenous Cultural and Intellectual Property Rights' (1999) 22 *UNSW Law Journal* 631; Robert Paterson and Dennis Karjala, 'Looking beyond Intellectual Property in Resolving Protection of the Intangible Cultural Heritage of Indigenous Peoples' (2004) 11 *Cardozo Journal of International and Comparative Law* 633; Tamara Kagan, 'Recovering Aboriginal Cultural Property at Common Law: A Contextual Approach' (2005) 63 *University of Toronto Faculty Law Review* 1; Angela Riley, 'Straight Stealing: Towards an Indigenous System of Cultural Property Protection' (2005) 80 *Washington Law Review* 69.

104 WIPO IGC, *Consolidated Document Relating to Intellectual Property and Genetic Resources*, Rev. 2, 26th Session, WIPO/GRTKF/IC/26/4 (3–7 February 2014), Annex, List of Terms (the definition is subject to debate).

105 WIPO IGC, 'The Protection of Traditional Knowledge: Draft Articles, Rev. 2', WIPO/GRTKF/IC/27/4 (28 March 2014), Policy Objectives.

106 Ibid Art 1 (the elements of definition remain subject to debate).

107 WIPO IGC, 'The Protection of Traditional Cultural Expressions, Rev. 2', WIPO/GRTKF/IC/25/7 (19 July 2013), Objectives.

108 Ibid, List of Terms (the elements of definition remain subject to debate).

such expression must be associated with the cultural and social identity and cultural heritage of indigenous peoples, be inter-generationally transmitted, persist for a minimum period, and may be dynamic and evolving.[109]

Development Finance and Investment

A final domain of international law which has (grudgingly) acknowledged indigenous rights is development finance and investment, which has also influenced human rights interpretation in those contexts. Most prominently, in multilateral development financing, the World Bank has adopted a detailed operational safeguard policy which requires borrowers in its projects to engage in a process of free, prior and informed consultation and to secure broad community support.[110] Measures must be adopted to avoid adverse effects on indigenous peoples or to minimise, mitigate or compensate for such effects. The Bank's policy has influenced other development banks, financial institutions and corporations, and had trickle-down effects into the national laws of state beneficiaries of the Bank's finance.

The International Finance Corporation (IFC) has adopted Performance Standard 7 on Indigenous Peoples[111] to guide businesses involved in projects which have social and environmental impacts. It addresses the avoidance of adverse impacts; the participation and consent of indigenous peoples in development; a higher obligation of free, prior and informed consent where a project impacts on indigenous lands and resources, would involve relocation, or affect critical cultural property; and the mitigation of impacts and benefit sharing.

Other financial institutions have adopted the Equator Principles to assess and manage environmental and social risks in projects.[112] Principle 5 recognises the vulnerability of indigenous peoples and requires a process of informed consultation and participation. Following the IFC, it further requires free, prior and informed consent for projects which have particular adverse impacts. Independent environmental and social assessment is also required for projects affecting indigenous peoples and their cultural systems and values. More broadly, the commentary to the UN Guiding Principles on Business and Human Rights of 2011 encourages corporations to take into account indigenous peoples' rights, although the Guiding Principles themselves do not explicitly draw attention to indigenous peoples.

Besides banks, financial institutions and corporations, other development actors have developed policies addressing indigenous peoples. The UN Development Group, a consortium of 27 UN actors, adopted Guidelines on Indigenous Peoples' Issues in 2008, which advise on international human rights standards and practical programme design. Some field agencies have developed their own guidance, including the UN Development Programme (UNDP), UN Children's Fund (UNICEF), and

[109] Ibid Art 1.
[110] World Bank Operational Policy 4.10: Indigenous Peoples (July 2005).
[111] International Finance Corporation, Performance Standard 7 (1 January 2012).
[112] Equator Principles (June 2013).

Food and Agriculture Organization (FAO), among others.[113] UNESCO launched a process to adopt guidelines on indigenous peoples in 2011.[114]

Finally, some multilateral and bilateral free trade agreements contain safeguard provisions that allow states to adopt special measures for indigenous peoples without infringing equal treatment protection for foreign investors.[115] There are, however, serious concerns about the adverse impacts of free trade and investment treaties on indigenous economic self-determination, control of lands and resources, environmental health and cultural rights.

Grey Law: 'Treaties' with Indigenous Peoples

As suggested above, the application of human rights law to indigenous peoples is affected by a penumbra of other international norms and soft standards that influence interpretation. One further source of external normative influence is relevant: 'treaties' with indigenous peoples, which often preserve certain indigenous rights in land, resources and self-governance (albeit usually not within a modern human rights framework). Historically many agreements were concluded between indigenous peoples and colonial 'white settler' societies such as the United States, Canada and New Zealand, many of which remain in effect. More than 370 treaties were agreed between the United States and native American (or 'American Indian') nations under the treaty-making powers of the US Constitution.[116]

At the time, the states entering into such treaties seemed to recognise a distinctive international legal personality of indigenous peoples, since the treaties often purported to transfer 'sovereignty' (as it was then understood in western international law); they were not typically understood as mere contracts for the sale of land. The status of such treaties in international law has, however, been controversial. In the legal systems of the states concerned, over time many treaties have been 'reduced to domestic law' by court decisions or legislation,[117] precisely so as to avoid international legal complications or challenges to the manner of acquiring sovereignty. On the international plane, indigenous peoples have often not subsequently been recognised as bearing a legal personality equivalent or opposable to states, or the capacity to make international claims and seek remedies for breaches of the treaties.

[113] See UNDP, *UNDP and Indigenous Peoples: A Practice Note on Engagement* (2001); UNICEF, *Indigenous and Minority Children* (3 September 2013), available at www.unicef.org/policyanalysis/rights/index_60331.html; FAO, *FAO Policy on Indigenous and Tribal Peoples* (2010).

[114] UNESCO, 'Indigenous Peoples: Knowledge Systems, Knowledge Diversity, Knowledge Societies: Towards a UNESCO Policy on Engaging with Indigenous Peoples', available at www.unesco.org/new/en/indigenous-peoples/related-info/unesco-policy-on-indigenous-peoples/launch-event-policy-on-indigenous-people/.

[115] Kingsbury, 'Indigenous Peoples' (n 19) [26] (citing the North American Free Trade Agreement 1992, Canada-Chile Free Trade Agreement 1996, New Zealand-Singapore Closer Economic Partnership Agreement 2000, Australia-US Free Trade Agreement 2004, and Singapore-Australia Free Trade Agreement 2003).

[116] Gudmundur Alfredsson, 'Indigenous Peoples, Treaties with', in *Max Planck Encyclopedia of Public International Law*, online entry (last updated March 2011).

[117] Ibid.

So far, international courts and tribunals have not provided much comfort to indigenous peoples. In a well-known case involving the international law on territorial disputes, the *Island of Palmas* case (1928), the Permanent Court of Arbitration refused to recognise treaties between indigenous peoples and the Dutch East India Company[118] (the latter being a corporation representing a state). A similar denial of legal personality occurred in the *Cayuga Indian Claims Arbitration* (1926) between the United Kingdom and the United States.[119] In the *Western Sahara Advisory Opinion* (1975), however, the International Court of Justice appeared to implicitly acknowledge that the socially and politically organised nomadic peoples there had a recognisable legal personality. The Court observed that agreements between colonial powers and such peoples conferred 'derivative roots of title, and not original titles obtained by occupation of terrae nullius'.[120]

The modern international law of treaties does not exclude the possibility of international agreements involving subjects of international law other than states.[121] A UN study concluded in 1999 that treaties with indigenous peoples are agreements under international law and remain in effect.[122] Article 37 of the UNDRIP 2007 recognises the legal force of such treaties:

1. Indigenous peoples have the right to the recognition, observance and enforcement of treaties, agreements and other constructive arrangements concluded with States or their successors and to have States honour and respect such treaties, agreements and other constructive arrangements.
2. Nothing in this Declaration may be interpreted as diminishing or eliminating the rights of indigenous peoples contained in treaties, agreements and other constructive arrangements.

On the one hand, the enforcement of such treaties can provide important strategic points of leverage by which indigenous peoples can seek to vindicate their interests. Treaties often protect indigenous interests in land, resources, culture and self-governance, matters which have rough correlates in modern human rights standards. At the same time, the validity of such treaties is often questionable because of their manner of adoption, as where tainted by fraud, error or coercion, or undermined by material breaches by states.[123] While the political settlement agreed in a treaty can sometimes deliver indigenous peoples more than the more limited guarantees of modern human rights law, the content of treaties can equally fall short of guaranteeing

[118] Claire Charters, 'Indigenous Peoples and International Law and Policy' in Benjamin Richardson, Shin Imai and Kent McNeill (eds), *Indigenous Peoples and the Law: Comparative and Critical Perspectives* (Hart Publishing, 2009), 162; see *Island of Palmas* (*United States v Netherlands*) (1928) 2 RIAA 829.

[119] Ibid; see *Cayuga Indians (Great Britain) v United States* (1926) 6 RIAA 173.

[120] *Western Sahara (Advisory Opinion)* [1975] ICJ Rep 12, 39.

[121] Vienna Convention on the Law of Treaties, Art 3 (adopted 23 May 1969, entered into force 27 January 1980, 1155 UNTS 331).

[122] UN Special Rapporteur Miguel Alfonso Martínez, *Study on Treaties, Agreements and Other Constructive Arrangements between States and Indigenous Populations: Final Report*, UN Doc E/CN.4/Sub.2/1999/20 (22 June 1999).

[123] Alfredsson, 'Indigenous Peoples, Treaties with' (n 116).

contemporary protections. Much depends on the bargaining power of the parties at the time, and indigenous peoples were rarely in a position of equality with adversary states.

In practice, treaties perhaps operate as *sui generis* instruments: neither the same as treaties between states, nor purely domestic law, but grey law somewhere in between. They often confer an entrenched or privileged legal status in domestic law, albeit subject to the state's purportedly superior sovereignty. They can lie dormant for long periods, before reviving with the right confluence of political and legal factors, as with the resurrection of New Zealand's Treaty of Waitangi 1840 from the 1970s onwards.

Importantly, treaties are not just historical artefacts but continue to be created; the Draft Nordic Saami Convention is a case in point, under negotiation between Sweden, Norway, Finland and their Saami peoples since 2011. There was also a recent, inconclusive debate about the need for a treaty in Australia, where no treaties were concluded with indigenous peoples during the British colonial conquest from 1788. The prospect of future treaties with indigenous peoples also offers an opportunity to entrench human rights standards in specific, binding contracts with the state (as long as international standards are not bargained away).

This book is mindful of these many external influences on the application and development of human rights standards relating to indigenous peoples. Before turning to the practice of the UN treaty committees and regional human rights bodies in chapters 2 to 5, one critical threshold issue first needs to be considered: who qualifies as an 'indigenous' people and which individuals are entitled to be recognised as members of those indigenous communities.

Chapter 1 accordingly considers various international and regional efforts to identify the indigenous peoples entitled to the rights and protections that have been incrementally recognised and tailored to their needs. In a world of startlingly diverse indigenous communities, and of governments with divergent political interests and ideologies, the question of who is indigenous has been notoriously difficult and controversial to resolve. As will be seen, however, although no definitive answer has been possible, the absence of a conclusive definition has not precluded the international community from forging a workable, functional understanding of who is 'indigenous'—and thus of who benefits from that status.

1

Identifying 'Indigenous' Peoples in International Law

AT FIRST SIGHT it may seem obvious who is 'indigenous'. In many countries, there are communities or groups that are well recognised by wider society as 'indigenous', whether Australian 'aborigines', American 'Indians', or the Inuit in the Arctic. Sometimes recognition stems from old treaties adopted during colonisation, as between what is now Canada and its Aboriginal peoples or 'First Nations', the United States with native American tribes, and New Zealand with the Maori. Some countries even constitutionally recognise indigenous peoples[1] and many more countries legislatively acknowledge them in some way.

From time to time there are certainly controversies (technical or political) over whether a particular group is 'indigenous' or a certain person is a member of a group. Some countries do not recognise any legal category of 'indigenous' at all, even where groups claim to be indigenous and are recognised as such internationally. Much of the time, however, there is a wide consensus in a given society. Who counts as indigenous in a particular country is shaped by a range of historical, cultural, political and social factors and the combination of factors can vary from place to place.

Taken literally, the term 'indigenous' refers to the descendants of the first or original inhabitants of a place, in contrast to later arrivals from elsewhere with different cultures. As shown below, however, this definition is deceptively simple and fails to capture the experience of other kinds of indigenous peoples, particularly in Africa and Asia.

Despite the apparent ease of identifying indigenous peoples in many countries, translating such intuitions into legal concepts of who is indigenous has proved surprisingly difficult. Law is in the business of conferring rights and obligations on people and other actors like governments, corporations and organisations. In order to decide who gets what, and who must do or refrain from doing certain things, the law typically needs to define the legal entities or individuals to whom the law applies and seeks to regulate. This 'gatekeeper' role is true of many kinds of law, whether customary, religious, national, regional or international. Identifying as indigenous can also be particularly important in helping indigenous peoples to assert their identity,

[1] Argentinian Constitution, art 75(17); Bolivian Constitution (2009), art 30; Constitution of Malaysia, arts 160(2) ('Aborigines') and 161(a)(6) ('natives'); Interim Constitution of Nepal (2007), arts 13 and 21; Russian Federation Constitution (1993), art 69; Cameroon Constitution (1996), Preamble.

dignity, sense of community and political claims in the face of historical injustice and contemporary marginalisation.

It can therefore matter a great deal who is recognised by the law as 'indigenous'. Legal definitions determine who is entitled to rights in critical resources such land and water, to vote in elections for representative institutions, to exercise cultural practices and control over traditional knowledge, and so on. Definitions can equally identify obligations on governments to provide social services, or on mining, agricultural or fishing companies to negotiate with indigenous groups to access their resources. Internationally, law can determine who has access to 'an international platform from which to analyse their situation, voice their concerns and seek recognition and protection of their rights' as indigenous peoples.[2]

The problem of legal definition is perhaps most difficult in international law, where any common concept of 'indigenous' peoples must accommodate the vast diversity of groups worldwide. It is roughly estimated that there are 370 million indigenous peoples in 90 countries, speaking 4,000 languages,[3] and comprising around 5,000 distinct groups.[4]

The universal labelling of such groups as 'indigenous' is comparatively recent, with the term only becoming widespread in the late twentieth century. In part this was because of efforts by international organisations. For example, Article 22 of the League of Nations Covenant of 1919 refers to state obligations to (paternalistically) safeguard the interests of the 'indigenous population' in the limited context of mandate territories; International Labour Organization (ILO) treaties in the 1930s addressed the labour rights of 'indigenous' workers;[5] and some regional organisations mentioned 'indigenous' inhabitants in the 1930s.[6] The term 'indigenous' was occasionally used in even earlier legal settings, as at a conference of the European 'Great Powers' on Africa in 1885, which committed to the 'protection of indigenous populations' in Africa[7] (meaning those other than the colonists).

After the Second World War, the United Nations Charter of 1945 committed the international community to decolonisation[8] and the self-determination of 'peoples'. It did not, however, mention 'indigenous' communities or identify them as peoples entitled to assert the right of self-determination. At that time the right of self-determination was understood to exclusively apply to the whole population

[2] ACHPR and International Working Group for Indigenous Affairs, *Report of the ACHPR's Working Group of Experts on Indigenous Populations/Communities*, adopted by the ACHPR at its 28th ordinary session (2005), 90.

[3] UN Department of Economic and Social Affairs, *State of the World's Indigenous Peoples* (UN, 2009), 1.

[4] Ibid 84.

[5] See, eg, ILO Convention No 50 concerning the Recruiting of Indigenous Workers (1936); ILO Convention No 65 concerning Penal Sanctions (Indigenous Workers) (1939); and ILO Recommendation concerning Labour Inspectorates (Indigenous Workers) (1939).

[6] See, eg, Eighth International Conference of American States, Resolution XI (21 December 1938) ('the indigenous inhabitants, as descendants of the first inhabitants of the lands which today form America').

[7] UN Commission on Human Rights, Working Group on Indigenous Populations, *Standard-Setting Activities: Evolution of Standards Concerning the Rights of Indigenous Peoples: Working Paper by the Chairperson-Rapporteur, Mrs Erica-Irene Daes, on the Concept of 'Indigenous People'*, UN Doc E/CN.4/Sub.2/AC.4/1996/2 (10 June 1996), [11], citing the Berlin Africa Conference 1885, Final Act, Art 6.

[8] Ibid [17]–[20] (discussing non-self-governing territories and 'peoples' entitled to self-determination).

of a colonial territory. Since then, the ILO,[9] various UN bodies and increased international advocacy by indigenous groups since the 1960s,[10] have helped to popularise 'indigenous' as a legal concept.

Before the rise of the term 'indigenous', what are now known generically as indigenous peoples were referred to (including in national and international law) by a variety of disparate and localised terms, many of which persist in various forms. Today some are regarded as pejorative and no longer used, such as the word 'Eskimo' (now known as Inuit) and, in many places, 'natives'. Some terms were originally used by colonial powers to describe their encounters with the inhabitants of foreign lands, but have since been reclaimed and are now used by some indigenous peoples today. This is true, for instance, of some of the very earliest international law debates about the rights of 'Indians', as during the Spanish conquest of the New World (the Americas) in the fifteenth and sixteenth centuries.[11]

Sometimes the terminology is contested inter-generationally within indigenous groups themselves, as in North America where some prefer the term 'native American' while others still use the earlier term 'American Indian', or in Australia where 'aboriginal',[12] 'indigenous' and 'First Peoples' are all in circulation. Even the term 'indigenous' can be problematic, as where it is used in a derogatory sense by some governments or chauvinistically by one ethnic group claiming rights over another.[13]

Nowadays, most indigenous groups retain their own distinctive group names, while appropriating the universal 'indigenous' label when engaging strategically with laws, institutions and social movements. As Kingsbury notes, '[t]he choice and evolution of an overarching self-conception to unify the international political movement of indigenous peoples has necessarily involved abstracting from a highly diverse range of self-understandings and political discourses among different groups'.[14] This strategic positioning is well explained by Asian indigenous networks as follows:

> We are using the term Indigenous Peoples with a meaning that is different from that given in many dictionaries, or how it is understood by many governments. Over the past decades, the concept of Indigenous Peoples has evolved beyond the original meaning found in dictionaries, and it is now well established in international law. That is why we are writing it with capital initial letters.

[9] See Andrew Erueti, 'The International Labour Organisation and the Internationalisation of the Concept of Indigenous Peoples' in Stephen Allen and Alexandra Xanthaki (eds), *Reflections on the UN Declaration on the Rights of Indigenous Peoples* (Hart Publishing, 2011), 93.

[10] Benedict Kingsbury, '"Indigenous Peoples" in International Law: A Constructivist Approach to the Asian Controversy' (1998) 92 *American Journal of International Law* 414, 421; James Anaya, *Indigenous Peoples in International Law* (2nd edn, Oxford University Press, 2004), 56–58.

[11] Anaya, *Indigenous Peoples in International Law* (n 10) 16–19.

[12] (Australian) Aboriginal and Torres Straight Islander Commission, *A Definition of 'Indigenous Peoples'?, Information Received from Indigenous Peoples' Organizations*, UN Commission on Human Rights (Working Group on Indigenous Populations), UN Doc E/CN.4/Sub.2/AC.4/1996/2/Add.1 (10 June 1996), [7].

[13] *Report of the ACHPR's Working Group on Indigenous Populations* (n 2) 86, 102.

[14] Kingsbury, '"Indigenous Peoples" in International Law' (n 10) 414, 421–22.

> It is a foreign term for most of us, and it is often difficult to translate into our own languages. Some governments in Southeast Asia use names to refer to us collectively—like 'ethnic minorities', 'hill tribes', 'native people'. There are also the names given by outsiders, some of which are not appreciated by many of us, since they often imply notions of cultural inferiority, being 'primitive' or 'backward'. Examples are *chuncheat* (meaning 'ethnicity', or literally 'national people' in Cambodia) or *sakai* (literally meaning 'slave') used in Thailand for some hunter-gatherer groups. We ourselves though prefer to use the names which our ancestors have given us.[15]

Linguistically, the term 'indigenous' entered the English language (which has dominated the global legal debates and social movements) around the seventeenth century, from Latin origins (*indigenus*) meaning 'born in a country, native'.[16] This original meaning points to a key characteristic of many indigenous peoples: that they preceded or took priority in time over other inhabitants of a place, particularly colonial conquistadors, settlers and migrants. Often there is a further sense that indigenous peoples were also the 'first' or 'original' inhabitants, as in the word 'aborigine' ('from the beginning').[17] In some cases, however, priority in time between different groups cannot be easily established.[18] In other cases, an indigenous group today may have displaced earlier groups that no longer exist.[19] 'First occupancy', or alternatively priority in time, alone are also not compelling moral bases for providing differential rights to such groups,[20] as opposed to the marginalisation caused by later arrivals or more dominant groups.

There is a wide variety of definitions of 'indigenous' in national laws. Despite various efforts, the international community, however, has never agreed on a comprehensive legal definition of 'indigenous'. There is no widely accepted treaty and the International Court of Justice has not considered the question.[21] In part this is because it is technically difficult to agree on a definition which is neither under- nor over-inclusive, that is, too narrow so it excludes some groups that ought to be recognised, or too wide that it may be open to abuse or fail to provide meaningful differentiation.

It is also because there are political sensitivities amongst certain governments about recognising indigenous peoples. For example, quite a few Asian, African and Pacific governments have objected that indigenous peoples do not exist in their countries because all of their inhabitants can be said to be native or autochthonous there. In Asia these include, for instance, major countries in the region such as China,

[15] Asia Indigenous Peoples' Pact (AIPP), the International Working Group for Indigenous Affairs (IWGIA) and Asian Forum for Human Rights and Development, *ASEAN's Indigenous Peoples* (2010), 2.

[16] Oxford English Dictionary, www.oed.com/.

[17] Other examples include the Bengali word 'adivasi' ('original inhabitant') and the Malay expression 'orang asli' ('original peoples' or 'first peoples'): Patrick Thornberry, *Indigenous Peoples and Human Rights* (Manchester University Press, 2002), 39.

[18] Ibid 38.

[19] See the Kennewick example in North America given by Thornberry, *Indigenous Peoples and Human Rights* (n 17) 35–37.

[20] See, eg, Jeremy Waldron, 'Indigeneity: First Peoples and Last Occupancy' (2003) 1 *New Zealand Journal of Public and International Law* 55, 78–79.

[21] *Western Sahara (Advisory Opinion)* [1975] ICJ Rep 12, concerned nomadic but socially and politically organised 'tribes' or 'peoples' at the time of Spanish colonisation in the nineteenth century, who later became entitled to exercise the right of self-determination during decolonisation. The case did not turn on the Saharawis' status as 'indigenous': [75]–[83].

India, Indonesia, Thailand, Myanmar and Bangladesh. In African countries, there is 'very little' formal legal recognition of (the many)[22] indigenous peoples, with rare (and modest) exceptions in Cameroon, Republic of Congo and South Africa.[23] Some countries recognise only ethnic 'groups' or 'minorities', or otherwise utilise their own unique terminology, such as 'local populations'[24] or 'scheduled tribes' (in India) or 'tribal areas' (in Pakistan).[25]

The difficulties inherent in precisely defining 'indigenous' at the international level have not, however, been fatal to agreeing international legal standards on indigenous peoples. As the United Nations notes, 'the prevailing view today is that no formal universal definition is necessary for the recognition and protection of their rights'.[26] This was the consensus view reached by indigenous observers,[27] and many states, during extensive debates in the UN Working Group on Indigenous Populations in the 1990s.

Rather, a flexible and open-ended approach has been purposefully adopted by the UN and actors like the World Bank.[28] Normative agreement and practical cooperation on indigenous issues have been possible notwithstanding the absence of a firm legal definition. This is not unusual in international law: other concepts have also not been defined, from 'minorities' to 'terrorism', yet cooperation is still possible. This flexible approach to defining indigenous has been labelled 'constructivist', one which:

> takes the international concept of 'indigenous peoples' not as one sharply defined by universally applicable criteria, but as embodying a continuous process in which claims and practices in numerous specific cases are abstracted in the wider institutions of international society, then made specific again at the moment of application in the political, legal and social processes of particular cases and societies.[29]

The most recent and authoritative statement on indigenous legal issues by the international community, the UN Declaration on the Rights of Indigenous Peoples (UNDRIP), adopted by the UN General Assembly in 2007, does not attempt to define 'indigenous peoples'. Instead, Article 33 refers to the rights of indigenous peoples to decide their own identities and procedures of belonging. Self-identification is regarded as important because otherwise governments ruled by dominant majority populations could simply choose not to recognise a group as indigenous and hence deny its legal existence and rights. The drafters rejected proposals, including from

[22] *Report of the ACHPR's Working Group on Indigenous Populations* (n 2) 15–19.

[23] ILO and ACHPR, *Overview Report on the Constitutional and Legislative Protection of the Rights of Indigenous Peoples in 24 African Countries* (2009), 17, 20.

[24] Republic of Congo Forest Code, Law No. 004/74, cited in ibid 21.

[25] Indian Constitution 1949, art 342; Pakistan Constitution 1973, art 246.

[26] UN Development Group Guidelines on Indigenous Peoples' Issues, 8–9, available at www2.ohchr.org/english/issues/indigenous/docs/guidelines.pdf (February 2008).

[27] Working Group on Indigenous Populations, *Report of the Working Group on Indigenous Populations on its Fourteenth Session to the Commission on Human Rights Sub-Commission on Prevention of Discrimination and Protection of Minorities*, UN Doc E/CN.4/Sub.2/1996/21 (July–August 1996).

[28] World Bank Operational Policy 4.10: Indigenous Peoples (July 2005), [3].

[29] Kingsbury, '"Indigenous Peoples" in International Law' (n 10) 414, 415.

the United States, to include a list of non-exhaustive factors that may be taken into account when a state decides whether to recognise an indigenous group.[30]

By contrast, the international law approach enables indigenous peoples to assert their existence and claim their rights from governments and assert them against other actors. Of course, in practice some governments still refuse to recognise indigenous peoples under domestic law, but international law still provides opportunities to pressurise governments, at the national and international levels, so that they realign their domestic law with international obligations. It also recognised that self-identification alone is not sufficient to identify indigenous peoples; otherwise, anyone could claim such status and its attendant rights, including in ways which conflicted with the rights of genuine indigenous peoples. Other factors are therefore necessary to help make out the meaning of who is 'indigenous'.

INTERNATIONAL LABOUR ORGANIZATION APPROACHES

While the UNDRIP does not otherwise define the concept, over time the international community has developed well accepted working guidelines on the meaning of 'indigenous'. One of the most important early efforts was in ILO Convention No 107 of 1957 concerning the Protection and Integration of Indigenous and Other Tribal and Semi-Tribal Populations in Independent Countries. The ILO is the oldest specialised United Nations agency and has a mandate to advance workers' rights. Convention No 107 was prompted by the ILO's concern about forced labour by indigenous peoples,[31] particularly farmers and forest peoples in Latin America and hill peoples in South and Southeast Asia.[32] At its height, Convention No 107 achieved 27 ratifications and it remains in force for 18 countries.[33]

The Convention describes as 'indigenous' certain 'tribal' populations that descended from those who inhabited a country, or part of it, 'at the time of conquest or colonisation', and who 'irrespective of their legal status, live more in conformity with the social, economic and cultural institutions of that time than with the institutions of the nation to which they belong'.[34]

[30] Commission on Human Rights, *Report of the Working Group Established in Accordance with Commission Resolution 1995/32 of 3 March 1995 on its Eleventh Session*, E/CN.4/2006/79 (22 March 2006), Annex I: Revised Chairman's Summary and Proposals, 28–29 (including: whether the group self-identifies as indigenous; whether the group is comprised of descendants of persons who inhabited a geographic area prior to the sovereignty of the state; whether the group historically had been sovereign; whether the group maintains a distinct community and aspects of governmental structure; whether the group has a cultural affinity with a particular area of land or territories; whether the group has distinct objective characteristics such as language, religion, culture; and whether the group has been historically regarded and treated as indigenous by the State).

[31] UN Department of Economic and Social Affairs, *State of the World's Indigenous Peoples* (UN, 2009), 2.

[32] Andrew Erueti, 'The International Labour Organisation and the Internationalisation of the Concept of Indigenous Peoples' in Stephen Allen and Alexandra Xanthaki (eds), *Reflections on the UN Declaration on the Rights of Indigenous Peoples* (Hart Publishing, 2011), 94–95.

[33] ILO Normlex, Ratifications of C107, available at www.ilo.org/dyn/normlex/en.

[34] ILO Convention No 107 concerning the Protection and Integration of Indigenous and Other Tribal and Semi-Tribal Populations in Independent Countries, Art 1(1)(b) (adopted 26 June 1957, entered into force 2 June 1959, 328 UNTS 247).

Tribal populations in turn are defined as those 'whose social and economic conditions are at a less advanced stage than … other sections of the national community' and who maintain their own customs or traditions or are regulated by special laws.[35] As such, the Convention regards all indigenous groups as tribal but only some tribal groups as indigenous.[36] The distinction is immaterial in the sense that both groups are entitled to the same rights and protections.[37]

Semi-tribal populations are also covered, being those 'who, although they are in the process of losing their tribal characteristics, are not yet integrated into the national community'.[38] The latter could include marginalised people who are neither part of continuing indigenous communities nor accepted as part of the national society, including urban fringe dwellers.[39]

While Convention No 107 was well intentioned, it was a creature of its time and was later criticised by indigenous peoples for promoting assimilation,[40] that is, integration into the mainstream national community, and being paternalistic. As its title suggests, the Convention encourages 'integration' of indigenous peoples into mainstream society, and defines indigenous peoples in part by them being 'less advanced' and assumes they must be somehow 'developed' or modernised. The very use of the term 'tribal' carries implications of primitiveness or backwardness.[41] It is also unduly restrictive, by only recognising indigenous peoples if they are able to maintain their own customs and tradition. In reality this may not be possible since colonisation almost always disrupted (and even destroyed) indigenous customs and traditions. In addition, all cultures change over time and continuity of pre-colonial customs and traditions is an unreasonable expectation.

The ILO eventually responded by adopting Convention No 169 of 1989 concerning Indigenous and Tribal Peoples in Independent Countries, a process which involved consultation with indigenous groups.[42] Unlike the early ILO treaty, Convention No 169 does not define indigenous peoples as a sub-set of tribal peoples but separates them out as a distinct category. Article 1(1)(b) thus refers to:

> peoples in independent countries who are regarded as indigenous on account of their descent from the populations which inhabited the country, or a geographical region to which the country belongs, at the time of conquest or colonization or the establishment of present state boundaries and who irrespective of their legal status, retain some or all of their own social, economic, cultural and political institutions.

A connection to pre-colonial populations remains a central criterion, although this is now framed in ancestral, racial or biological terms of 'descent' (which has a problematic history given the legacy of eugenics in the subjugation of indigenous

[35] Ibid art 1(1)(a).
[36] Thornberry, *Indigenous Peoples and Human Rights* (n 17) 43.
[37] Daes, *Working Paper on the Concept of 'Indigenous People'* (n 7) [22].
[38] ILO Convention No 107, art 1(2).
[39] Thornberry, *Indigenous Peoples and Human Rights* (n 17) 43.
[40] United Nations Department of Economic and Social Affairs, *State of the World's Indigenous Peoples* (UN, 2009), 2.
[41] Thornberry, *Indigenous Peoples and Human Rights* (n 17) 39.
[42] Anaya, *Indigenous Peoples in International Law* (n 10) 58–59.

peoples). Domestic legal status also remains irrelevant. But the Convention also accommodates situations where colonisation did not occur, as in parts of Asia and Africa, by referring to peoples that inhabited an area prior to the establishment of present state boundaries. The Convention also only expects that indigenous peoples retain 'some' of their own social, economic, cultural and political institutions, thereby allowing for the disruptive impacts of colonialism. Unlike in the previous convention, indigenous people also need not be regulated by special domestic laws to be recognised, signifying a shift away from state-based identification of indigenous peoples.

The distinction between indigenous and tribal populations is sharpened further by recognition of indigenous 'institutions' in contrast to tribal 'customs or traditions', implying semi-autonomous structures of social life. Tribal peoples are defined as those 'in independent countries whose social, cultural and economic conditions distinguish them from other sections of the national community and whose status is regulated wholly or partially by their own customs or traditions or by special laws or regulations' (Article 1(2)(a)). Both indigenous and tribal peoples remain, however, sub-state actors that subsist within existing 'independent countries', and recognition does not imply, for instance, an international legal right of secession from such states. Both also enjoy the same legal rights under the Convention,[43] and UN practice often refers synonymously to tribal and indigenous groups.[44]

Most importantly, Article 1(2) of Convention No 169 newly emphasises that '[s]elf-identification as indigenous or tribal shall be regarded as a fundamental criterion for determining the groups to which' the Convention applies. This represents a fundamental shift away from external, objective tests for indigeneity towards a more subjective approach grounded in lived experience. Self-identification enables indigenous peoples to assert their own identity, rather than having it imposed upon them by state authorities, as occurred during colonial periods when indigenous peoples were often classified according to scales of colour blood or civilisation, including by racial or anthropological archetypes and the pseudo-science of eugenics. Self-identification can also aid in distinguishing indigenous peoples from ethnic or other minorities, where the latter otherwise exhibit similar defining characteristics.[45] There has, however, been debate about the extent to which self-identification is an individual or collective process,[46] or involves elements of both, an issue discussed further below.

It has been suggested that the definition in Convention No 169 'may well reflect customary international law'.[47] It is certainly true that this Convention's definition has influentially shaped international debates and state practice about indigenous issues, well beyond its formal applicability to those countries that have ratified it. It has, for instance, helped to frame debates about indigeneity within various United Nations and ILO mechanisms.

43 Daes, *Working Paper on the Concept of 'Indigenous People'* (n 7) [31].

44 UN Secretariat of the Permanent Forum on Indigenous Issues, *The Concept of Indigenous Peoples*, UN Doc PFII/2004/WS.1/3 (19–21 January 2004), 3.

45 Thornberry, *Indigenous Peoples and Human Rights* (n 17) 46.

46 Ibid.

47 Benedict Kingsbury, 'Indigenous Peoples' in *Max Planck Encyclopedia of Public International Law*, online entry, last updated November 2006.

However, only about 11 per cent of all countries are parties to the Convention. Of the 22 countries that are parties, most (15) come from one region, Latin America. Only one country from Africa is a party (Central African Republic); one from Asia (Nepal); one from the Pacific (Fiji); and four from Europe (Spain, Norway, Denmark and the Netherlands). Most countries with indigenous populations are not parties, including, for instance, Russia, China and India, and the so-called 'white settler' societies of Canada, Australia, New Zealand and the United States. Asian and African states in particular have baulked at becoming parties to Convention No 169, whereas some had signed the less protective Convention No 107, which is still in force for 18 states.[48]

The Convention is also confined to addressing certain labour-related issues and does not purport to cover the field of indigenous issues. Article 1(3) of the Convention expressly disclaims that 'the use of the term *peoples* in this Convention shall not be construed as having any implications as regards the rights which may attach to the term under international law'. In light of all of this, it is hard to escape the conclusion that the Convention's definition of 'indigenous' does not reflect customary international law, but is rather one important source, among others, which has influenced the development of international law. The Convention's definition also does not address all pertinent indicia of the indigenous experience and is thus too limiting to serve as a guide for all relevant applications of international law.

UNITED NATIONS APPROACHES

Various processes within the United Nations system have further elucidated the meaning of 'indigenous'. A ground-breaking *Study on the Problem of Discrimination against Indigenous Populations* was undertaken by a Special Rapporteur of the UN Sub-Commission on Prevention of Discrimination and Protection of Minorities, José Martínez Cobo, between 1972 and 1986.[49] Martínez Cobo described indigenous characteristics as follows:

> Indigenous communities, peoples and nations are those which, having a historical continuity with pre-invasion and pre-colonial societies that developed on their territories, consider themselves distinct from other sectors of the societies now prevailing in those territories, or parts of them. They form at present non-dominant sectors of society and are determined to preserve, develop and transmit to future generations their ancestral territories, and their ethnic identity, as the basis of their continued existence as peoples, in accordance with their own cultural patterns, social institutions and legal systems.[50]

[48] Notably including Angola, Bangladesh, India, Egypt, Ghana, Iraq, Malawi, Pakistan, Syria and Tunisia.

[49] UN Commission on Human Rights, *Study of the Problem of Discrimination against Indigenous Populations, Final Report of the Special Rapporteur, Mr José Martínez Cobo* (1981–83), available at http://undesadspd.org/IndigenousPeoples/LibraryDocuments/Mart%C3%ADnezCoboStudy.aspx.

[50] UN Commission on Human Rights, Sub-Commission on Prevention of Discrimination and Protection of Minorities, *Study of the Problem of Discrimination against Indigenous Populations: Final Report of the Special Rapporteur Martínez Cobo*, UN Doc E/CN.4/Sub.2/1983/21/Add.8 (30 September 1983), [379]–[382].

The Martínez Cobo definition has been endorsed by indigenous groups at the UN,[51] and is largely reflected in the guidelines of other actors such as the World Bank.[52] The definition shares many elements of ILO Convention No 169, emphasising historical continuity, self-identification as socially distinct groups, and distinctive ethnic identity, culture and institutions. It is further recognised that indigenous peoples may possess their own 'legal systems' (such as customary or traditional laws) and implicitly that such legal pluralism can co-exist within countries without undermining state sovereignty.

'Peoples'

Likewise, in referring to indigenous 'nations' alongside 'peoples' and 'communities', the definition suggests indigenous solidarity as a nation within a state is feasible. The shift in terminology is significant and not merely semantic. The Martínez Cobo definition refers interchangeably to 'communities, peoples and nations', whereas in some earlier ILO and UN practice, the term 'peoples' was avoided and 'populations' was used instead.[53] Some states were historically hesitant to recognise indigenous groups as 'peoples', since that word has a specific connotation in the international law of self-determination,[54] namely the right to freely determine one's own political and economic future, including through statehood. 'Peoples' is now commonly used,[55] including in the UN Declaration on the Rights of Indigenous Peoples.

This does not mean, however, that indigenous peoples in independent countries enjoy the right of self-determination to the same extent as a 'people' comprising the whole population of a country. Specifically, there is no right of statehood or secession, but rather rights to limited autonomy and control over resources with the parameters of existing states. Even so, during the drafting of the UN Declaration on

[51] Working Group on Indigenous Populations, *Report of the Working Group on Indigenous Populations on its Fourteenth Session to the Commission on Human Rights Sub-Commission on Prevention of Discrimination and Protection of Minorities*, UN Doc E/CN.4/Sub.2/1996/21 (July–August 1996).

[52] World Bank Operational Policy 4.10: Indigenous Peoples (July 2005), [4], provides that: 'For purposes of this policy, the term "Indigenous Peoples" is used in a generic sense to refer to a distinct, vulnerable, social and cultural group possessing the following characteristics in varying degrees: (a) self-identification as members of a distinct indigenous cultural group and recognition of this identity by others; (b) collective attachment to geographically distinct habitats or ancestral territories in the project area and to the natural resources in these habitats and territories; (c) customary cultural, economic, social, or political institutions that are separate from those of the dominant society and culture; and (d) an indigenous language, often different from the official language of the country or region'.

[53] For instance, in ILO Convention No 107; the UN Working Group on Indigenous Populations (1982–2007); UN General Assembly: *UN Voluntary Fund for Indigenous Populations*, Resolution 40/131 (13 December 1985).

[54] Thornberry, *Indigenous Peoples and Human Rights* (n 17) 40–41.

[55] See, eg, ILO Convention No 169 concerning Indigenous and Tribal Peoples in Independent Countries (adopted 27 June 1989, entered into force 5 September 1991, 1650 UNTS 383); Special Rapporteur on the Situation of Human Rights and Fundamental Freedoms of Indigenous Peoples (2001–); Expert Mechanism on the Rights of Indigenous Peoples (2007–); see also International Year of the World's Indigenous People (1993); International Decades of the World's Indigenous People (1995–2004) and (2005–2014).

Indigenous Peoples in 2007, the African Group of states objected that reference to 'peoples' would imply a right of secession.[56]

Non-dominance

An important additional attribute identified by Martínez Cobo is that indigenous peoples are 'non-dominant sectors of society'. Non-dominance has two potential meanings. One is that indigenous peoples are less numerous than a majority of the population in a country, in other words, that they are in the minority. This does not, however, imply arbitrary numerical limits on the size of a group population in order to qualify it as indigenous. For instance, under Russian law, only groups of less than 50,000 people are recognised as indigenous,[57] with 46 such groups (mostly in the north) officially recognised. Larger peoples are thus excluded, such as the Komi-Izhma/Izvatas, Sakha/Yakuts, Tuvans, Buryat, Nogay, Khakass, Karelians and Chechens.[58] In the international law sense, such groups are still non-dominant vis-à-vis the Russian population as a whole. This is also true of situations, as in Danish Greenland, where an indigenous people comprises a majority of part of the state's territory, but are still in the minority in relation to the whole population of the state.

Another meaning of non-dominance refers to the relative lack of power of indigenous groups in relation to others in society. In this sense, being indigenous correlates with an experience of subjugation, marginalisation, dispossession, exclusion or discrimination.[59] This criterion is particularly important in capturing the experience of groups in places which did not undergo 'saltwater' colonialism, as in parts of Africa and Asia, but where traditional tribal or rural groups have been marginalised by dominant (equally 'native') populations.[60] Of course, disadvantage alone is insufficient to differentiate indigenous peoples from other vulnerable groups, from slum dwellers to lower caste Hindus in India.

A paradox in the strict application of this criterion is that the attainment of equal rights could render a people no longer indigenous (as no longer being disadvantaged). However, UN practice suggests that the historical experience of marginalisation is

[56] African Group of Experts, *Response Note to the Draft Aide Memoire of the African Group on the UN Declaration on the Rights of Indigenous Peoples* (21 March 2007), 4.

[57] Russian Federal Law #82-FZ (30 April 1999): Guarantees of the Rights of Small Indigenous Peoples of the Russian Federation; Russian Federal Law #104-FZ (20 July 2000): General Principles of Organisation of Communities of Small Indigenous Peoples in the North, Siberia and the Far East of the Russian Federation. See generally Alexandra Xanthaki, 'Indigenous Rights in the Russian Federation' (2004) 26 *Human Rights Quarterly* 74; Alexandra Tomaselli and Anna Koch, 'Implementation of Indigenous Rights in Russia' (2014) 5(4) *International Indigenous Policy Journal*, article no 3; Vladimir Kryazhov, 'Development of Russian Legislation on Northern Indigenous Peoples' (2013) 4(2) *Arctic Review on Law and Politics* 140; Johannes Rohr, *Indigenous Peoples in the Russian Federation* (International Working Group for Indigenous Affairs, 2014).

[58] See, eg, Indra Overland, 'Indigenous Rights in the Russian North' in Elana Wilson Rowe (ed), *Russia and the North* (University of Ottawa Press, 2009), 168.

[59] Daes, Working Paper on the Concept of 'Indigenous People' (n 7) [69].

[60] United Nations Department of Economic and Social Affairs, *State of the World's Indigenous Peoples* (UN, 2009), 6.

also critical, not whether it always persists[61] (if it does, it affects the measures that may be necessary to improve the situation rather than the existence of the group as such).

Historical Continuity

Significantly, the Martínez Cobo definition further outlines non-mandatory indicia of 'historical continuity' with pre-colonial societies, as follows:

> This historical continuity may consist of the continuation, for an extended period reaching into the present, of one or more of the following factors:
>
> (a) Occupation of ancestral lands, or at least part of them;
> (b) Common ancestry with the original occupants of these lands;
> (c) Culture in general, or in specific manifestations (such as religion, living under a tribal system, membership of an indigenous community, dress, means of livelihood, life-style etc);
> (d) Language (whether used as the only language, as mother-tongue, as the habitual means of communication at home or in the family, or as the main, preferred, habitual, general or normal language);
> (e) Residence in certain parts of the country, or in certain regions of the world;
> (f) Other relevant factors.

The definition thus moves away from the strict requirement of 'descent' in ILO Convention No 169, and the attendant risks of biological essentialism or determinism, and instead adopts a more flexible approach, albeit still insisting on some kind of historical continuity. The factors are not mandatory, cumulative or exhaustive, but are indications of indigeneity that may be present in various combinations in different cases. The definition thus accounts for the diversity of indigenous experiences without excluding the most vulnerable groups. Strict priority in time, or pre-colonial heritage, are not essential criteria.

For example, many indigenous peoples were dispossessed of their traditional lands during conquest and colonisation and so no longer occupy them.[62] Some indigenous people face difficulties in tracing their ancestry because of, for instance, forced child removals, adoptions, family disintegration, miscegenation or historical stigmas associated with identifying as indigenous. Cultural continuity can be problematic due to the dislocation or separation of communities, urbanisation, the decline or extinction of languages, cultural disintegration in the face of social problems, or the normal processes of dynamic cultural change. Expectations that indigenous peoples must continue to pursue a static 'traditional life-style' (as under Russian law)[63] are unreasonable. There is also a risk that emphasis on cultural distinctiveness may artificially

[61] Ibid.

[62] The World Bank also recognises that a group that has lost its collective attachment to ancestral lands will still be regarded as indigenous even if it has been forcibly displaced by development activity: World Bank Operational Policy 4.10: Indigenous Peoples (July 2005), [4].

[63] Russian Federal Law #82-FZ (30 April 1999).

ossify indigenous cultures as 'authentic' museum relics, when all cultures are subject to change—and more so in times of colonialism and modernity.

Contemporary identity politics are complex. Indigenous peoples often have their feet in the door of more than one culture, just as many people today possess multiple identities (say as a British, Muslim woman of Asian background; or based on disability or sexuality). This complexity must be accommodated by contemporary approaches to indigeneity.

Consider, for example, some real hard cases at the margins from Australia. What if a celebrated novelist is raised believing he is aboriginal and experiences life (including racism) as an indigenous person, only to discover late in life that his father was African American?[64] Or what if a person was raised thinking she is a white child, only to learn as an adult that she is of indigenous descent, and wishes to reconnect with that heritage and identify as indigenous—and goes on to become a celebrated indigenous painter?[65]

To pose some hypotheticals, what about a person who has no indigenous 'blood' or life experience, but wishes to 'become' indigenous, just as one might convert to another faith, or marry into an ethnic minority, or become naturalised as a citizen of another nation? What if an indigenous person migrates to another country (voluntarily or where forced) and is 'faced with the dilemma of no longer having the opportunity of identifying as indigenous'?[66] The answer to some of these dilemmas is partly provided by the emphasis in the Martínez Cobo definition on the twin processes of self-identification and community acceptance.

A flexible approach to definition means that the precise combination of factors constituting an indigenous people will vary by context. A concrete example is the Draft Nordic Saami Convention, negotiated by three states (Finland, Norway and Sweden) in consultation with Saami representatives. Draft Article 4 defines who is Saami by reference to a combination of language, livelihood/culture, descent and national legal recognition:

> The Convention applies to persons residing in Finland, Norway or Sweden that identify themselves as Saami and who
>
> 1. have Saami as their domestic language or have at least one parent or grandparent who has or has had Saami as his or her domestic language, or
> 2. have a right to pursue Saami reindeer husbandry in Norway or Sweden, or
> 3. fulfil the requirements to be eligible to vote in elections to the Saami parliament in Finland, Norway or Sweden, or
> 4. are children of a person referred to in 1, 2 or 3.

Comparable requirements are found in national laws establishing Saami Parliaments in each of the Nordic states.[67]

[64] Mudrooroo (Colin Thomas Johnson).

[65] Sally Morgan.

[66] International Expert Workshop on Data Collection and Disaggregation for Indigenous Peoples was convened from 19–21 January 2004, in New York.

[67] Act on the Sámi Parliament (974/1995) (Finland), s 3; Sami Parliament Act 1992 (Sweden), s 2.

Self-Identification and Community Acceptance

In addition to the objective indicia of indigeneity, as quoted above the Martínez Cobo definition acknowledges that indigenous peoples subjectively constitute themselves when they 'consider themselves distinct' from other parts of society. The definition goes further to describe a subjective bilateral process of individual self-identification as indigenous and acceptance by the indigenous community:

> On an individual basis, an indigenous person is one who belongs to these indigenous populations through self-identification as indigenous (group consciousness) and is recognised and accepted by these populations as one of its members (acceptance by the group).
>
> This preserves for these communities the sovereign right and power to decide who belongs to them, without external interference.[68]

As noted earlier, self-identification enables indigenous peoples to fashion their own identity on their own terms. Often this is accomplished by reference to indigenous customary law rules, regardless whether custom is formally recognised by a state's law. Community acceptance can also tip the balance in an individual's favour where other indicia of indigeneity are uncertain, as where evidence of descent is weak.[69]

This process of self-identification and acceptance sometimes gives rise to tensions between individuals and communities. Certainly, some indigenous groups have a stronger collective orientation than, for instance, more individualistic 'western' cultures (although there are obvious dangers in generalising or essentialising whole societies). While modes of authority and decision-making may be culturally specific to an indigenous community, like any human group, indigenous communities are also marked by power dynamics, hierarchies, political and identity struggles, and questions concerning representativeness, participation, fairness, gender equality and human rights. Those who are legally defined as indigenous may not necessarily be accepted as such by 'tribal constitutions' or practices[70] (and vice versa).

For example, in *Lovelace v Canada* (1981) before the UN Human Rights Committee,[71] a woman born and registered as a Maliseet Indian lost her legal rights and status as an Indian after marrying a non-Indian man. As a result, she could not live on an Indian reserve or receive the education, housing and social assistance benefits to which Indians were entitled. Indian men who married non-Indian women did not lose Indian status, so she claimed sex discrimination and a violation of minority cultural rights (under Article 27) of the ICCPR.

While she lost her rights under Canadian legislation, Canada defended the law in part by arguing that traditional Indian family relationships were patrilineal; that reserve land was more threatened by non-Indian men than non-Indian women (so the law protected Indian communities); and that the law could only be changed in

[68] UN Commission on Human Rights, *Final Report of the Special Rapporteur Martínez Cobo* (n 50) [379]–[382].

[69] See, eg, *Attorney-General (Commonwealth) v State of Queensland* (1990) 94 ALR 515, 517–18.

[70] See Kirsty Gover, *Tribal Constitutionalism: States, Tribes and the Governance of Membership* (Oxford University Press, 2010).

[71] *Lovelace v Canada*, HRC Communication No 24/1977 (30 July 1981).

consultation with Indians, who were divided on equal rights.[72] In addition, after her marriage ended and she sought to reside on the reserve, the Band Council refused to provide her with a house because she was not registered.

The Human Rights Committee avoided the issue of sex discrimination and instead found that Lovelace was a member of a minority whose rights had been infringed:

> Persons who are born and brought up on reserves who have kept ties with their community and wish to maintain these ties must normally be considered as belonging to that minority within the meaning of the Covenant. Since Sandra Lovelace is ethnically a Maliseet Indian and has only been absent from her home reserve for a few years during the existence of her marriage, she is ... entitled to be regarded as 'belonging' to this minority and to claim the benefits of article 27 of the Covenant ...
>
> ... the right of Sandra Lovelace to access to her native culture and language 'in community with the other members' of her group, has in fact been, and continues to be interfered with, because there is no place outside the Tobique Reserve where such a community exists.[73]

The Committee then determined that the restrictions on her right to live on the reserve did not have a reasonable and objective justification and were not consistent with Article 27:

> The case of Sandra Lovelace should be considered in the light of the fact that her marriage to a non-Indian has broken up. It is natural that in such a situation she wishes to return to the environment in which she was born, particularly as after the dissolution of her marriage her main cultural attachment again was to the Maliseet band. Whatever may be the merits of the Indian Act in other respects, it does not seem to the Committee that to deny Sandra Lovelace the right to reside on the reserve is reasonable, or necessary to preserve the identity of the tribe. The Committee therefore concludes that to prevent her recognition as belonging to the band is an unjustifiable denial of her rights under article 27 of the Covenant, read in the context of the other provisions referred to.[74]

The Committee did not frame the case by reference to indigenous peoples or rights, and did not squarely confront the definition of an 'Indian' or the human rights limits on the criteria or procedure for deciding who is Indian. The case also targeted a legislative definition of Indian, said to reflect Indian preferences, rather than the actual practices or decisions of the Indian community. Nonetheless, the case illustrates how UN treaty bodies are prepared to assess legal standards for indigenous group membership for consistency with human rights, and to assert individual interests against purported group preferences encoded in state law, at least in a case where a person's core cultural identity has been disenfranchised. As former UN Special Rapporteur Daes notes, the Committee 'implicitly decided that she remained a part of the Maliseet Indian band from which she came'.[75] The Band itself was not directly consulted.

The authority to decide who is indigenous is complex and varies by context. It involves individuals and indigenous groups, but also states (and their legal institutions) and other actors. At the United Nations, for example, operational agencies

[72] Ibid [4].
[73] Ibid [14]–[15].
[74] Ibid [17].
[75] Daes, *Working Paper on the Concept of 'Indigenous People'* (n 7) [36].

such as the UN Development Programme must determine who is indigenous for the purposes of its development programming; UNESCO is concerned to protect indigenous culture;[76] while policy fora (such as ECOSOC, human rights bodies or indigenous mechanisms) have accreditation procedures for recognising the participation of groups.

Likewise, the World Bank and regional development banks have 'safeguard policies' on human rights, and multinational corporations may have corporate social responsibility policies, which necessitate the identification of indigenous groups affected by development projects or corporate activities. The World Bank's screening process for recognising affected indigenous peoples involves what it calls a 'technical judgment of qualified social scientists' with local expertise and consultation with indigenous peoples and the project borrower.[77] In addition, as noted earlier, the ILO has a long history of engaging with governments to protect indigenous peoples falling within the scope of the ILO instruments.

Former UN Special Rapporteur Erica-Irene Daes emphasised the need for a fair procedure 'so there is room for the reasonable evolution and regional specificity in the concept of "indigenous" in practice'.[78] The global community of indigenous peoples also has an interest in regulating claimants to indigenous status,[79] as evidenced by controversies in the 1990s over the attendance of white South African Boers and white Nambinian Basters at UN indigenous meetings.[80] As Thornberry notes, '[n]either governments nor indigenous peoples favour the exponential growth of indigenism as a vehicle to carry all kinds of claims by sundry collectives',[81] particularly when rights and state assistance and funding are at stake.

Relationship to Minorities

Throughout international efforts to conceptualise indigeneity, there has been considerable analytical overlap with the concept of minorities (which can also encompass 'tribal' groups, in the language of the ILO, that are not also indigenous; though many minorities are not 'tribal'). In part this stems from the identical rights accorded to tribal and indigenous groups under ILO Convention No 169. National courts have also sometimes elided the legal categories of minorities and indigenous groups.[82] Some indigenous groups have also strategically used international law on minority rights to advance their interests,[83] not least because key UN human rights treaties refer to minorities[84] but not indigenous peoples. In many ways the indigenous

[76] UNESCO, Universal Declaration on Cultural Diversity (2 November 2001), art 4.
[77] World Bank, Operational Policy 4.10: Indigenous Peoples (July 2005), [4], [8].
[78] Daes, *Working Paper on the Concept of 'Indigenous People'* (n 7) [74].
[79] See also ibid [68].
[80] Thornberry, *Indigenous Peoples and Human Rights* (n 17) 33.
[81] Ibid 57.
[82] *Lemeiguran and others v Attorney-General and others* (2006) AHRLR 281 (KeHC 2006), [102].
[83] See chapter 2.
[84] Such as art 27 of the International Covenant on Civil and Political Rights (adopted 16 December 1966, entered into force 23 March 1976, 999 UNTS 171) (concerning minority rights) and the Convention on the Elimination of Racial Discrimination (adopted 7 March 1966, entered into force 4 January 1969, 660 UNTS 195) (mentioning racial and ethnic groups throughout).

rights movement grew out of and sought to expand the narrower aperture of rights for minorities. Many indigenous peoples now insist on their distinctiveness from minorities and emphasise that the respective rights and identity issues are different.[85]

Like the term 'indigenous', the concept of minorities has a long pedigree in international law. Minorities were addressed by refugee and peace treaties and international institutions since the time of the League of Nations after the First World War, which dealt principally with sub-national minorities in European states. Article 27 of the ICCPR now guarantees persons belonging to 'ethnic, religious or linguistic minorities' within existing states, 'in community with other members of their group ... [to] enjoy their own culture, to profess and practise their own religion, or to use their own language'. A UN Declaration of 1992 additionally recognises 'national' minorities,[86] as does a European instrument (exclusively).[87]

Like the term 'indigenous', 'minority' has not been defined in international law and has its own conceptual difficulties.[88] In the *Greco-Bulgarian Communities Advisory Opinion* (1930), the Permanent Court of International Justice described the analogous category of 'community' as:

> a group of persons living in a given country or locality having a race, religion, language and traditions of their own, and united by this identity ... in a sentiment of solidarity, with a view to preserving their traditions, maintaining their form of worship, securing their instruction and upbringing of their children in accordance with the spirit and tradition of their race and mutually assisting one another.[89]

Similarly, an influential UN Special Rapporteur in 1992 understood minorities as:

> A group numerically inferior to the rest of the population of a State, in a non-dominant position, whose members—being nationals of the State—possess ethnic, religious or linguistic characteristics differing from those of the rest of the population and show ... a sense of solidarity, directed towards preserving their culture, traditions, religion or language.[90]

As discussed earlier, many of these traits are shared by indigenous peoples,[91] as is the contemporary acceptance of self-identification also as a means of identifying minorities.[92] As will be seen in later chapters, there is also considerable cross-over between the international legal rights of indigenous peoples and minorities, including as regards: non-discrimination; cultural, religious and linguistic rights; participation

[85] Asia Indigenous Peoples' Pact (AIPP), the International Working Group for Indigenous Affairs (IWGIA) and Asian Forum for Human Rights and Development, *ASEAN's Indigenous Peoples* (2010), 3 ('Though both ethnic minorities and we, Indigenous Peoples, face the same experience of discrimination and marginalization, we are very different in terms of our rights and our identity').

[86] UN General Assembly Resolution 47/135, Declaration on the Rights of Persons Belonging to National or Ethnic, Religious and Linguistic Minorities (18 December 1992).

[87] Council of Europe Framework Convention on the Protection of National Minorities (adopted 1 February 1995, entered into force 1 February 1998, ETS No 157).

[88] See, eg, Thornberry, *Indigenous Peoples and Human Rights* (n 17) 52–53.

[89] *Greco-Bulgarian Communities Advisory Opinion*, PJIJ Series B, No 17 (31 July 1930), 22.

[90] UN Commission on Human Rights, Special Rapporteur Francesco Capotorti of the Sub-Commission on Prevention of Discrimination and Protection of Minorities, *Study on the Rights of Persons Belonging to Ethnic, Religious and Linguistic Minorities*, UN Doc E/CN.4/Sub.2/384/Rev.1, (1979) [568].

[91] Thornberry, *Indigenous Peoples and Human Rights* (n 17) 52.

[92] OHCHR, 'Minorities under International Law', available at www.ohchr.org/EN/Issues/Minorities/Pages/internationallaw.aspx.

in social, economic and political life; the right to participate effectively in decisions; the right to establish and maintain associations; protection and positive measures of assistance by the state; measures in education to encourage knowledge of history, traditions, language and culture; and the right to participate in economic progress and development.

The distinction does, however, matter fundamentally in certain other respects. Indigenous rights are far more extensive in certain areas of 'survival' rights, such as land rights, control over resources, political institutions, and (indigenous) self-determination. The main points of definitional distinction between indigenous peoples and minorities concerns the former's attachment to ancestral lands as well as their priority in time before the rest of the population.[93] However, some minorities exhibit these qualities too[94] (consider, for instance, the Kurds in parts of Turkey and neighbouring states), rendering any distinction difficult to maintain in cases not involving 'saltwater' colonialism. It may then depend on the group's self-characterisation as one or the other, at the risk of opportunistically pursuing whichever legal category affords the greatest benefit (or least disadvantage) under prevailing circumstances.

It is also commonly suggested that minority rights are individual whereas indigenous rights are collective.[95] Such a dichotomy is, however, too simple. Individual minority rights are necessarily defined in relation to the collective; a person cannot speak a language to him or herself alone. Conversely, indigenous rights frequently possess individual dimensions, as is apparent from the very process of individual self-identification as indigenous. The matter is perhaps one of degree but not of kind. In general, the overlap and slippage between the categories of indigenous peoples and minorities may lead, particularly since the adoption of the UN Declaration on the Rights of Indigenous Peoples in 2007, to less divergence between the categories over time.[96]

Relationship to 'Peoples'

A further complication is the persisting analytical confusion about the legal term 'peoples' and its application to, or differentiation from, indigenous groups and minority communities. As mentioned earlier, the classical right of 'external' self-determination under the UN Charter and human rights treaties was reserved to the 'people' of a whole colonised territory, not particular sub-national groups within it.[97] There has since been lively debate about whether self-determination extends, or should extend, internally or remedially to sub-national groups within existing independent states, whether minorities or indigenous groups.

[93] Daes, *Working Paper on the Concept of 'Indigenous People'* (n 7) [60].

[94] cf ibid [60] (these two factors have 'never been associated with the concept of "minorities"').

[95] *Report of the ACHPR's Working Group on Indigenous Populations* (n 2) 96.

[96] Will Kymlicka, 'Beyond the Indigenous/Minority Dichotomy?' in Stephen Allen and Alexandra Xanthaki (eds), *Reflections on the UN Declaration on the Rights of Indigenous Peoples* (Hart Publishing, 2011), 183, 188.

[97] James Crawford, *Brownlie's Principles of Public International Law* (8th edn, Oxford University Press, 2012), 141.

A closely related debate is whether indigenous groups are 'peoples' even if they are not entitled, for instance, to the maximal rights of self-determination in the form of secession from a state. As noted earlier, such debates were reflected in the terminology used to describe particular UN and ILO instruments and processes. Efforts to reclaim the word 'peoples' represent a strategic attempt by indigenous groups themselves to increase their visibility, recognition and rights on the international plane, even if indigenous 'peoples' are not legally identical to the 'peoples' of colonial territories or the populations of independent states. Most states now squarely accept that indigenous groups are 'peoples', as evidenced by the title of the UN Declaration on the Rights of Indigenous Peoples.

The terminology nonetheless still throws up legal questions in particular contexts. For example, at the regional level, under the African Charter on Human and Peoples' Rights of 1981, indigenous groups are not mentioned but Article 20 recognises the right of self-determination of all peoples; Article 21 entitles peoples to freely dispose of their natural resources; and Article 22 accords a right of peoples to development.[98] In the case of *Katangese Peoples' Congress v Zaire* (2000), the African Commission on Human and Peoples' Rights noted that there may be 'controversy as to the definition of peoples' but implied that it might include an ethnic minority within a state.[99]

In the later case of *Mgwanga Gunme v Cameroon* (2009), the African Commission noted that the meaning of 'peoples' rights' was not defined by the drafters of the African Charter, has not been defined in international law, and has long been controversial.[100] It nonetheless found that 'there is recognition that certain objective features attributable to a collective of individuals, may warrant them to be considered as "people"'.[101] These guiding characteristics include 'a common historical tradition, a racial or ethnic identity, cultural homogeneity, linguistic unity, religious and ideological affinities, territorial connection, and a common economic life', and self-consciousness (or self-identification) as a people.[102] It noted further that under the African Charter 'the notion of "people" is closely related to collective rights, which 'can be exercised by a people, bound together by their historical, traditional, racial, ethnic, cultural, linguistic, religious, ideological, geographical, economic identities and affinities, or other bonds'.[103] On the facts the Commission accepted that 'the people of Southern Cameroon can legitimately claim to be a "people"',[104] including because 'they manifest numerous characteristics and affinities, which include a

[98] African Charter on Human and Peoples' Rights (adopted 27 June 1981, entered into force 21 October 1986, 1520 UNTS 217).

[99] *Katangese Peoples' Congress v Zaire*, ACHPR Communication No 75/1992, 2000 AHRLR 72, [4]: 'The issue in the case is not self-determination for all Zaireoise as a people but specifically for the Katangese. Whether the Katangese consist of one or more ethnic groups is, for this purpose immaterial and no evidence has been adduced to that effect'.

[100] *Kevin Mgwanga Gunme and others v Cameroon*, ACHPR Communication No 266/2003 (27 May 2009), [169].

[101] Ibid [169]–[170].

[102] Ibid [169]–[170].

[103] Ibid [174].

[104] Ibid [178].

common history, linguistic tradition, territorial connection and political outlook', and 'identify themselves as a people with a separate and distinct identity'.[105]

Similarly, in *COHRE v Sudan* (2009), the Commission found that the three major Black African tribes of the Darfur region of Sudan (the Zaghawa, the Fur and the Marsalit) constituted a 'people' entitled not to be dominated by other races in Sudan, such as the Arab Sudanese.[106] It noted that the jurisprudence may be 'very fluid', but held that 'peoples' are not only defined by external aggression, oppression or colonisation, but also by internal abuse of minorities or even majorities.[107] Factors relevant to identifying peoples included self-identification and external identification, language, religion, culture, territory, history, ethno-anthropological factors and race.[108] The Commission regretted that African states tend to deny the existence of peoples because of the racial legacy of colonialism, but argued that 'racial and ethnic diversity on the continent contributes to the rich cultural diversity which is a cause for celebration'.[109]

What is significant about African regional practice is that the term 'peoples' is primarily legally operative, rather than concepts of indigenous groups or minorities, and that the term peoples can undoubtedly cover those groups in certain circumstances. In other words, indigenous peoples can be a sub-set of the wider legal category of 'peoples'. As the next section shows, over time the African human rights system has also come to attach particular legal significance to the idea of being 'indigenous', and sought to loosely define the concept.

REGIONAL APPROACHES

Africa

In Africa, recognition of indigenous peoples has been strongly contested by many African governments. The central objection is that all Africans are said to be indigenous to Africa, so it makes no sense to differentiate between different groups in a country. Any such attempt is also thought to be socially divisive, particularly in countries already riven by ethnic tensions. For many African countries that were historically affected by colonialism, indigenous peoples are principally seen as those subjugated by European colonialism, not by the practices of independent African countries. Many such arguments were made during the drafting of the UNDRIP, when the African Group of states insisted that a definition of indigenous peoples was necessary to avoid implementation problems and inter-ethnic tensions.[110]

105 Ibid [179].

106 *Sudan Human Rights Organisation and Centre on Housing Rights and Evictions (COHRE) v Sudan*, ACHPR Communication No 279/2003-296/2005 (May 2009), [217]–[223].

107 Ibid [220], [222].

108 Ibid [220].

109 Ibid [221].

110 African Group of Experts, *Response Note to the Draft Aide Memoire of the African Group on the UN Declaration on the Rights of Indigenous Peoples* (21 March 2007), 1.

It is true that 'all Africans are indigenous to Africa in the sense that they were there before European colonialists arrived and that they have been subject to subordination during colonialism'.[111] In the African context it is therefore not helpful to define indigenous peoples as coming first or as the descendants of pre-colonial 'native' populations, in contrast to people who came from elsewhere.[112] Other characteristics assume greater importance.

In an Advisory Opinion on UNDRIP in 2007, the African Commission found that 'a definition is not necessary or useful as there is no universally agreed definition of the term and no single definition can capture the characteristics of indigenous populations'.[113] Instead the Commission found it 'more relevant and constructive to try to bring out the main characteristics allowing the identification of the indigenous populations and communities in Africa'.[114] As an earlier study by the African Commission warned, the danger of a strict definition is that governments may use it as an excuse not to recognise certain groups.[115] The Advisory Opinion thus adopted the same flexible approach as at the international level:

(a) Self-identification [as indigenous and distinctly different from other groups];
(b) A special attachment to and use of their traditional land whereby their ancestral land and territory have a fundamental importance for their collective physical and cultural survival as peoples;
(c) A state of subjugation, marginalisation, dispossession, exclusion, or discrimination because these peoples have different cultures, ways of life or mode of production than the national hegemonic and dominant model.[116]

The Advisory Opinion was influenced by a similar definition in the report of the African Commission's Working Group of Experts on Indigenous Populations/Communities in 2005.[117]

The Commission's Advisory Opinion notes that in Africa 'the term indigenous populations does not mean "first inhabitants"' and that this 'distinguishes Africa from other continents where native communities have been almost annihilated by non-native populations'.[118] As such, 'any African can legitimately consider him/herself as indigene to the Continent'.[119] Such approach is designed to avoid

[111] *Report of the ACHPR's Working Group on Indigenous Populations* (n 2) 88; see also ibid 2; Daes, *Working Paper on the Concept of 'Indigenous People'* (n 7) [64].

[112] *Report of the ACHPR's Working Group on Indigenous Populations* (n 2) 92.

[113] ACHPR, *Advisory Opinion on the United Nations Declaration on the Rights of Indigenous Peoples*, 41st Session (16–30 May 2007), [10]; see also *Report of the ACHPR's Working Group on Indigenous Populations* (n 2) 87.

[114] ACHPR, *Advisory Opinion* (n 113) [10]; see also *Report of the ACHPR's Working Group on Indigenous Populations* (n 2) 87.

[115] *Report of the ACHPR's Working Group on Indigenous Populations* (n 2) 87.

[116] ACHPR, *Advisory Opinion* (n 113) [12].

[117] *Report of the ACHPR's Working Group on Indigenous Populations* (n 2) 87. See also ACHPR, *Principles and Guidelines on the Implementation of Economic, Social and Cultural Rights in the African Charter on Human and Peoples' Rights* (November 2010), 8.

[118] ACHPR, *Advisory Opinion* (n 113) [13].

[119] Ibid [13].

questioning the identity of other groups.[120] Instead, the African Commission's Expert Working Group emphasised that:

> When some particular marginalized groups use the term *indigenous* to describe their situation, they use the modern analytical form of the concept (which does not merely focus on aboriginality) in an attempt to draw attention to and alleviate the particular form of discrimination they suffer from ... and by which they can seek protection in international human rights law and moral standards.[121]

As noted earlier, this produces the paradox that ending discrimination could conceptually terminate indigenous status in Africa. The question may also be asked why the focus is not simply on targeting structural inequality and discrimination, including its collective dimensions, instead of constructing a problematic separate group status.

These problems are, however, largely more conceptual than real. In practice, despite governmental protests, the identification of indigenous groups in Africa is often straightforward. As one group of African international lawyers argues, indigenous communities are usually 'clearly identified and identifiable by the rest of their fellow citizens and governments'.[122] The experts give many examples.[123] Often they are hunter-gatherers or nomadic pastoralists in remote areas whose land uses and ways of life have been marginalised by settled agriculture, modern economic development, majority cultural domination (including in education and language), or forced relocation due to national parks.[124] The survival of their way of life and culture depends on access to traditional lands and natural resources.[125] They are often excluded from political and development processes.[126] The High Court of Kenya, for instance, has differentiated indigenous minorities in Kenya from other Kenyan tribes by emphasising that the former have 'a strong attachment to their culture as opposed to the homogenous ones who have adapted to change with very little attachment to the old ways'.[127]

The definitional approach in the African Commission's Advisory Opinion, and of the African Expert Working Group, has been applied by the African Commission in individual cases. In *Endorois Welfare Council v Kenya* (2010), the African Commission accepted that the Endorois people of Kenya were 'indigenous' in a case involving a 'people's' right to freely dispose of natural resources under Article 21 of the

[120] *Report of the ACHPR's Working Group on Indigenous Populations* (n 2) 88.

[121] Ibid; see also African Group of Experts, *Response Note to the Draft Aide Memoire of the African Group on the UN Declaration on the Rights of Indigenous Peoples* (21 March 2007).

[122] Ibid.

[123] Ibid: 'the "Pygmies" of the African tropical forests, the San or "Bushmen" of southern Africa, the Hadzabe, Akie, Ogiek, Yaaku, Sengwer and other hunter-gatherer groups in East Africa, various pastoralist groups in eastern, western and northern Africa such as the Maasai, Samburu, Turkana, Barabaig, Mbororo, Toubou, Tuareg etc'.

[124] *Report of the ACHPR's Working Group on Indigenous Populations* (n 2) 92; African Group of Experts, *Response Note to the Draft Aide Memoire of the African Group on the UN Declaration on the Rights of Indigenous Peoples* (21 March 2007), 1–2.

[125] *Report of the ACHPR's Working Group on Indigenous Populations* (n 2) 89.

[126] Ibid.

[127] *Lemeiguran and others v Attorney-General and others* (2006) AHRLR 281 (KeHC 2006), [102].

African Charter.[128] The Endorois had been denied access to their ancestral lands and resources by the declaration of a wildlife sanctuary around Lake Bogoria in Kenya in 1973.

The Commission first noted that the notions of 'peoples' and 'indigenous peoples' are both contested and there is 'no universal and unambiguous definition of the concept' capable of capturing the global diversity of either.[129] It noted the similarity between marginalised and vulnerable groups in Africa and marginalised indigenous groups.[130] It rejected a formalistic approach to the definition of indigenous in light of the Charter's human rights objectives. It approved the finding of the Inter-American Court of Human Rights that groups beyond a narrow 'aboriginal' or pre-colonial understanding can be indigenous.[131]

The Commission proceeded to identify indigenous peoples as a sub-set of 'peoples' as mentioned in the African Charter. The Commission first endorsed the approach of the African Commission's Expert Working Group, which is 'not intended to create a special class of citizens, but rather to address historical and present-day injustices and inequalities'.[132] It summarised the Working Group's four criteria for identifying indigenous peoples as: 'the occupation and use of a specific territory; the voluntary perpetuation of cultural distinctiveness; self-identification as a distinct collectivity, as well as recognition by other groups; an experience of subjugation, marginalisation, dispossession, exclusion or discrimination'.[133] In addition, it noted that the Working Group had suggested hunter-gatherers and pastoralists were typically indigenous in Africa, because 'the survival of their particular way of life depends on access and rights to their traditional land and the natural resources thereon'.[134]

The Commission further endorsed the definition of indigenous proffered by the UN Working Group on Indigenous Populations, read in the light of the African Commission's Expert Working Group.[135] It also stated that although many African countries are not parties to ILO Convention No 169, its definition shares the 'common thread' of all the various attempts to describe indigenous characteristics, namely 'that indigenous peoples have an unambiguous relationship to a distinct territory' and that there are 'linkages between people, their land, and culture'.[136] The Commission further emphasised the need for collective self-identification or the consciousness of a people that they are an indigenous people.[137] This view in turn was based on the 'emerging consensus' on the objective features that a collective

[128] *Centre for Minority Rights Development (Kenya) and Minority Rights Group International on behalf of Endorois Welfare Council v Kenya*, ACHPR Communication No 276/2003, 2009 AHRLR 75 (4 February 2010).

[129] Ibid [147].

[130] Ibid [148].

[131] Ibid [159], citing *Moiwana v Suriname (Preliminary Objections, Merits and Reparations)* (2005) IACtHR (Ser C) No 145 (15 June 2005) and *Saramaka v Suriname (Preliminary Objections, Merits, Reparations and Costs)* (2007) IACtHR (Ser C) No 172 (28 November 2007).

[132] Ibid [149].

[133] Ibid [150].

[134] Ibid [150].

[135] Ibid [152]–[153].

[136] Ibid [154].

[137] Ibid [151].

of individuals should manifest to be considered as a 'peoples', namely 'a common historical tradition, racial or ethnic identity, cultural homogeneity, linguistic unity, religious and ideological affinities, territorial connection, and a common economic life or other bonds, identities and affinities they collectively enjoy or suffer collectively from the deprivation of such rights'.[138]

On the facts, the African Commission found that the Endorois were an indigenous people. They were a pastoralist community who had lived for centuries in their traditional territory around Lake Bogoria.[139] Their culture, religion, traditional way of life and identity were found to be intimately intertwined with their ancestral lands,[140] and distinct from surrounding groups. The Endorois also identified themselves as a distinct people,[141] sharing a common history, culture and religion[142] which depended on access to their ancestral lands.[143]

The Kenyan government had argued that the integration of the Endorois into modern society had dissipated their cultural distinctiveness from other tribal groups.[144] It suggested that different individuals in the Endorois community adhered to different degrees to traditional laws, customs and economic life, and some members did not identify with the group.[145] The Commission drew on the *Saramaka* case of the Inter-American Court of Human Rights to reject these arguments. It found that lack of identification with the group by some members, or their living outside traditional territory, did not diminish the group's overall distinctiveness and communal interests.[146] Moreover, the Commission deferred to the group's own rules as to whether particular individuals were entitled to the group's collective rights:

> [the] question of whether certain members of the community may assert certain communal rights on behalf of the group is a question that must be resolved by the Endorois themselves in accordance with their own traditional customs and norms and not by the State. The Endorois cannot be denied a right to juridical personality just because there is a lack of individual identification with the traditions and laws of the Endorois by some members of the community.[147]

The Americas

The judicial dialogue between the African and the American jurisprudence indicates that these regions share a flexible approach to characterising indigenous peoples. As under the African Charter, the American Convention on Human Rights does not mention indigenous peoples. In 1989, the General Assembly of the Organization of

138 Ibid [151].
139 Ibid [154].
140 Ibid [156].
141 Ibid [157] [162].
142 Ibid [162].
143 Ibid [156].
144 Ibid [161].
145 Ibid.
146 Ibid [161]–[162].
147 Ibid [162].

American States asked the Inter-American Commission on Human Rights to draft a legal instrument on the rights of 'indigenous populations'.

The Commission delivered its final Proposed American Declaration on the Rights of Indigenous Peoples to the OAS Assembly in 1997.[148] Draft Article 1(1) provided that the Declaration 'applies to indigenous peoples as well as peoples whose social, cultural and economic conditions distinguish them from other sections of the national community, and whose status is regulated wholly or partially by their own customs or traditions or by special laws or regulations'. Article 1(2) additionally regarded '[s]elf-identification as indigenous' as a 'fundamental criterion'. As is apparent, the definition was influenced in part by ILO Convention No 169, which various American states had ratified, covering both pre-colonial and tribal groups as indigenous.

The OAS Assembly then asked the OAS Permanent Council to further develop the draft and in 1999 established a Working Group of the Council to continue the process. As of 2016, the drafting continues, reflecting the significant disagreements amongst participants (state and indigenous peoples' representatives) over the content of the Declaration, notwithstanding the successful adoption of the UN Declaration in 2007. In 2006, however, consensus was reached on the guiding definition of 'indigenous',[149] although Canada and the United States signalled formal reservations about the whole process.[150] The agreed Article I(1) applies the Declaration to 'the indigenous peoples of the Americas', and Article I(2) emphasises self-identification, reflecting the contemporary UN, ILO and African approaches:

> Self-identification as indigenous peoples will be a fundamental criteria for determining to whom this Declaration applies. The states shall respect the right to such self-identification as indigenous, individually or collectively, in keeping with the practices and institutions of each indigenous people.[151]

The agreed definition in Article I thus moved away from the more prescriptive 1997 draft, which had also emphasised group distinctiveness. By 2009 the Draft Declaration also recognised multi-ethnicity in stating that '[i]ndigenous persons and communities have the right to belong to one or more indigenous peoples, in accordance with the identity, traditions, customs, and systems of belonging of each people', without discrimination (Article VIII).[152] This approach is at odds with some national laws in the Americas, as under the Bolivian Constitution, where indigenous peoples must predate 'the Spanish colonial invasion', or the Paraguayan Constitution which

[148] Approved by the IACHR, 1333rd session, 95th Regular Session (26 February 1997).

[149] Seventh Meeting of Negotiations in the Quest for Points of Consensus, agreed by consensus (25 March 2006).

[150] Luis Rodriguez-Pinero, 'The Inter-American System and the UN Declaration on the Rights of Indigenous Peoples: Mutual Reinforcement' in Stephen Allen and Alexandra Xanthaki (eds), *Reflections on the UN Declaration on the Rights of Indigenous Peoples* (Hart Publishing, 2011), 457, 475.

[151] Working Group to Prepare the Draft American Declaration on the Rights of Indigenous Peoples (of the Permanent Council of the Organization of American States, Committee on Juridical and Political Affairs), *Record of the Current Status of the Draft American Declaration on the Rights of Indigenous Peoples*, UN Doc OAS Doc GT/DADIN/doc.334/08 rev. 7 (2 May 2012).

[152] Twelfth Meeting of Negotiations in the Quest for Points of Consensus, approved 30 November 2009.

recognises cultural groups prior to the establishment of the state.[153] Many issues other than the definition remain to be settled in the Draft Declaration.

In the absence of an explicit regional standard defining indigenous peoples, the Inter-American human rights system has incrementally addressed the meaning of 'indigenous'. In particular, as in Africa, the right to property (under Article 21 of the American Convention on Human Rights) has been interpreted by the Inter-American Court and Commission to also protect collective or communal property. This includes indigenous rights in property.[154]

In the early case of *Mayagna (Sumo) Awas Tingni Community v Nicaragua* (2001), the Inter-American Court recognised the Awas Tingni Community as an indigenous community of the Atlantic Coast of Nicaragua.[155] The Awas Tingi alleged that Nicaragua had not demarcated their communal lands or protected their legal interests in such lands and their resources, and had granted a logging concession on their lands without their consent.

The Court did not, however, advance a general definition of 'indigenous' peoples, largely because there was no factual dispute over the group's characterisation as indigenous. The Nicaraguan Constitution and other national laws already recognised indigenous property rights, and the Awas Tingni Community had been accorded domestic legal recognition. The Court also had the benefit of expert evidence from anthropologists, academics and government authorities that the Community was regarded as indigenous. Most subsequent cases decided by the Inter-American Court have likewise involved no dispute over whether a claimant group is indigenous for the same reason that the group was already recognised as indigenous under national law.[156]

The dispute in the *Awas Tingni Community* case centred instead on whether the Awas Tigni had maintained links to their ancestral lands and whether their claimed lands were ancestral at all. Nicaragua argued that the Community had been affected by separation and demographic shifts; they occupied non-ancestral lands or lacked evidence of links to ancestral lands; other indigenous groups already had title to, or better claims to, some of the areas; and that its claims were excessive relative to the size of the group and its subsistence needs.[157]

Consequently, while the parties agreed that the petitioners were 'indigenous', and the Court found it unnecessary to resort to a general definition of 'indigenous',

[153] Bolivian Constitution 2009, art 30(I): 'A nation and rural native indigenous people consists of every human collective that shares a cultural identity, language, historic tradition, institutions, territory and world view, whose existence predates the Spanish colonial invasion'; Paraguay Constitution 1992, art 68.

[154] *Awas Tingni Community v Nicaragua (Merits, Reparations and Costs)* (2001) IACtHR (Ser C) No 79 (31 August 2001), [148].

[155] Ibid [103].

[156] See, eg, *Yakye Axa Indigenous Community v Paraguay (Merits, Reparations and Costs)* (2005) IACtHR (Ser C) No 125 (17 June 2005), [140]; *Sawhoyamaxa Indigenous Community v Paraguay (Merits, Reparations and Costs)* (2006) IACtHR (Ser C) No 146 (29 March 2006), [124]; *Xákmok Kásek Indigenous Community v Paraguay (Merits, Reparations and Costs)* (2010) IACtHR (Ser C) No 214 (24 August 2010), [88]–[89]; *Kichwa Indigenous People of Sarayaku v Ecuador (Merits and Reparations)* (2012) IACtHR (Ser C) No 245 (27 June 2012), [124].

[157] *Awas Tingni Community v Nicaragua* (n 154) [141].

in reality the disagreement about links to ancestral lands was partly a proxy for a debate about definition. That is, does being indigenous require a connection to ancestral lands in cases where colonisation and subsequent development have precisely alienated people from their lands? On the evidence the Court found it unnecessary to address this legal question because it accepted that the 'the members of the Awas Tingni Community have a communal property right to the lands they currently inhabit, without detriment to the rights of other indigenous communities'.[158] The Community's links to land had not been severed, and its distinctive identity fractured, to the degree contended by Nicaragua. Because the land in question had not been fully titled, the Court left open the extent to which the Community's claims might be limited by reference to stronger claims by other indigenous groups over the same territory, and instead required Nicaragua to complete the land titling process.

The Court also indicated some characteristics of indigenous peoples' relationship with land which implicitly help to define such groups, and which it found to be satisfied by the Awas Tingni. Thus, the Court found that indigenous peoples have a strong communitarian tradition of communal or collective property ownership; and that their ties to land 'must be recognized and understood as the fundamental basis of their cultures, their spiritual life, their integrity, and their economic survival', as well as inter-generational identity.[159] A lingering question remains, however, on the facts of other cases, whether a total alienation of links to traditional lands (as in the case of urbanised groups) would deny such peoples an indigenous status.

In *Xákmok Kásek Indigenous Community v Paraguay* (2010), the state objected to the admissibility of a complaint on the basis that there were contradictions in the name and ethnic roots of the indigenous complainants concerned, such that they did not meet the requirements of indigenous peoples under international law.[160] The Inter-American Court rejected that argument. It emphasised that it is the right of an indigenous community, not the Court or the state, to determine its name and ethnic identity.[161] The community in question identified itself as indigenous, and this was objectively based on their immemorial ancestral ties to particular territories and their social and linguistic commonalities.[162] This was the case despite colonisation displacing their communities, leading to mixing and intermarriage, and reconstituting their society and language from a larger and diverse community; differences in names corresponded to these historical circumstances.

The *Awas Tingni Community* case concerned a classical pre-colonial indigenous people. What it means to be indigenous was more controversial in the later case of *Moiwana Village v Suriname* (2005). There the Inter-American Court of Human Rights recognised a group of 'Maroons' as indigenous in interpreting the communal aspect of the right to property under Article 21.[163] Maroons are not the pre-colonial inhabitants of Suriname but are descendants of African slaves from Dutch plantations in the seventeenth century. The case concerned Suriname's failure to investigate

[158] Ibid [153].
[159] Ibid [149].
[160] *Xákmok Kásek Indigenous Community v Paraguay* (n 156) [33].
[161] Ibid [37].
[162] Ibid [39]–[42].
[163] *Moiwana v Suriname* (2005) IACtHR (Ser C) No 145 (15 June 2005).

a massacre and forced eviction of Maroon villagers, preventing them from returning to their lands.

The Inter-American Court found that while the Moiwana villagers were not indigenous (in the sense of being pre-colonially native or aboriginal) to the region, the village was settled by N'djuka clans in the nineteenth century and since then 'the community members lived in the area in strict adherence to N'djuka custom'.[164] Further, the Court stated that:

> the Moiwana community members, a N'djuka tribal people, possess an 'all-encompassing relationship' to their traditional lands, and their concept of ownership regarding that territory is not centered on the individual, but rather on the community as a whole. Thus, this Court's holding with regard to indigenous communities and their communal rights to property under Article 21 of the Convention must also apply to the tribal Moiwana community members.[165]

The Court was influenced by expert evidence that the N'djuka are 'inextricably tied' to their ancestral lands and sacred sites, denial of access to which 'deprived them of a fundamental aspect of their identity and sense of well being', including their culture and religion.[166]

The subsequent case of *Saramaka People v Suriname* (2007) also dealt with Maroons in a matter concerning the right to (communal) property under Article 21 of the American Convention.[167] Suriname also questioned whether the Saramaka could be juridically recognised as a people because some of their members had voluntarily embraced modern society, diluting the group's distinctiveness.[168] The Inter-American Court rejected this argument, finding that:

> the fact that some individual members of the Saramaka people may live outside of the traditional Saramaka territory and in a way that may differ from other Saramakas who live within the traditional territory and in accordance with Saramaka customs does not affect the distinctiveness of this tribal group nor its communal use and enjoyment of their property.[169]

The question of who represents the people in making such claims was to be determined by the Saramaka people in accordance with their traditions and customs.[170]

As to the identity of the Saramaka more broadly, the Court found that the Saramaka people are not strictly indigenous (that is, pre-colonial), but 'tribal'. The Court noted that their 'social structure is different from other sectors of society inasmuch as the Saramaka people are organized in matrilineal clans (*lõs*), and they regulate themselves, at least partially, by their own customs and traditions'.[171] The Court characterised them as 'tribal' because they 'maintain a strong

164 Ibid [132].
165 Ibid [133].
166 Ibid [132].
167 *Saramaka v Suriname* (n 131).
168 Ibid [162].
169 Ibid [164].
170 Ibid [164].
171 Ibid [181].

spiritual relationship with the ancestral territory they have traditionally used and occupied'.[172] In this regard the Court stated further:

> Land is more than merely a source of subsistence for them; it is also a necessary source for the continuation of the life and cultural identity of the Saramaka people. The lands and resources of the Saramaka people are part of their social, ancestral, and spiritual essence. In this territory, the Saramaka people hunt, fish, and farm, and they gather water, plants for medicinal purposes, oils, minerals, and wood. Their sacred sites are scattered throughout the territory, while at the same time the territory itself has a sacred value to them. In particular, the identity of the members of the Saramaka people with the land is inextricably linked to their historical fight for freedom from slavery, called the sacred 'first time'.[173]

The Court emphasised that 'their economy can also be characterized as tribal', with food, implements and building materials coming from the land.[174] Thus, the Court concluded that the Saramaka:

> make up a tribal community whose social, cultural and economic characteristics are different from other sections of the national community, particularly because of their special relationship with their ancestral territories, and because they regulate themselves, at least partially, by their own norms, customs, and/or traditions.[175]

Although the Court drew a distinction between indigenous and tribal peoples, its analysis indicates that both categories share similar characteristics, but for the precolonial descent of the former. As in the earlier *Moiwana Village* case, the Court in Saramaka also rendered the distinction one without difference, since it concluded that:

> the Court's jurisprudence regarding indigenous peoples' right to property is also applicable to tribal peoples because both share distinct social, cultural, and economic characteristics, including a special relationship with their ancestral territories, that require special measures under international human rights law in order to guarantee their physical and cultural survival.[176]

As may be apparent, in a number of cases the Inter-American Court has been influenced by ILO Convention No 169, ratified by many American states, when dealing with communal (tribal or indigenous) property rights under Article 21 of the American Convention.[177] Thus far the Court has not, however, explicitly endorsed its definitions of 'tribal' or 'indigenous' as operative ones in the Inter-American system, instead preferring a more open-ended approach.

Asia

Around two-thirds of the world's indigenous peoples are estimated to live in Asia,[178] yet legal recognition of indigenous peoples and their rights is perhaps weakest there

[172] Ibid [82].
[173] Ibid [82].
[174] Ibid [83].
[175] Ibid [84].
[176] Ibid [86].
[177] *Yakye Axa v Paraguay* (n 156) [131].
[178] Asia Indigenous Peoples' Pact (AIPP), the International Working Group for Indigenous Affairs (IWGIA) and Asian Forum for Human Rights and Development, *ASEAN's Indigenous Peoples* (2010), 5.

of all regions, along with the Middle East. As in Africa, many Asian governments, including countries with large populations such as China, India, Bangladesh, Pakistan, Indonesia and Vietnam, do not recognise indigenous peoples.

State views in the region about the meaning of 'indigenous' have been strongly shaped by the legacy of colonialism, as in Africa. Some governments understand the term as describing the whole non-European populations of colonial territories during the decolonisation period.[179] The Indonesian Constitution of 1949, for example, defines Indonesian citizens as 'indigenous Indonesian peoples' (Article 26), meaning all Indonesians. Asian states' understanding of 'indigenous' is also shaped by the residue of colonial administrative practices in their classification of non-majority ethnic groups,[180] which shaped subsequent social relations.

There have also been practical objections that because of 'centuries of migration, absorption and differentiation, it is impossible to say who came first'.[181] Further, it is sometimes thought that the recognition of special rights for some groups might fuel chauvinistic claims and produce inter-ethnic tensions,[182] especially given the real experience of communal violence (in India, Pakistan and Bangladesh) and ethnic conflict (in Myanmar, Indonesia and the Philippines). Some Asian states also emphasise community solidarity over ethnic differences, although quite a few states recognise ethnic groups by other names, such as minorities (as in China and Vietnam) or 'tribes' (in India and Pakistan). In some cases, neglect or hostility fuel non-recognition, as with the Bedouin in parts of the Middle East or 'Marsh Arabs' earlier in Iraq.

At the regional level, unlike in Africa and the Americas, the roughly 50 countries of Asia (from west to east) have not established a binding regional human rights system. The closest is within the eight country grouping of the Association of Southeast Asian Nations (ASEAN), which created an Inter-Governmental Commission on Human Rights in 2009 and adopted an ASEAN Human Rights Declaration in 2012. The ASEAN Declaration does not, however, mention indigenous peoples or even minorities, although it mentions 'marginalised groups' (Article 4) and 'racial and religious groups' (Article 31(3)). It has been much criticised by indigenous groups in the ASEAN region.[183] Indigenous peoples' representative organisations, such as the Indigenous Peoples' Task Force and Asia Indigenous Peoples Pact, do, however, attempt to engage with the ASEAN institutions.

The increased global consciousness of indigenous peoples and rights, and the growth of indigenous networks in Asia itself, has nonetheless gradually expanded recognition of indigenous peoples over time. There is now some official recognition of indigenous peoples in countries such as the Philippines, Japan, Nepal, Malaysia and Taiwan.[184] Such recognition is often partial, as in Japan where the Ainu,

[179] Kingsbury, '"Indigenous Peoples" in International Law' (n 10) 414, 426.

[180] Ibid 427.

[181] Ibid 435.

[182] Ibid.

[183] See Yogeswaran Subramaniam, 'The ASEAN Human Rights Declaration and Indigenous Rights' (2013) 8(4) *Indigenous Law Bulletin* 3.

[184] Indigenous Peoples Rights Act 1997 (Congress of the Philippines); Resolution to Acknowledge the Ainu are an Indigenous People, 6 June 2008 (Japanese Diet); Land Law 2001, Part 2 (National Assembly of Cambodia); Indigenous Peoples Basic Law 2005 (Taiwan); National Foundation for Development

previously classified as an 'ethnic minority',[185] were eventually recognised in 2008 (following Japan's support for the UN Declaration in 2007) but other groups still are not (such as the Ryukyuan of Okinawa).[186] National and transnational networks of indigenous peoples continue to pressure Asian governments to recognise them, utilising the national, regional, ILO and UN processes discussed in this book.

CONCLUSION

The contemporary international legal concept of 'indigenous' people is not limited to its literal or textual meaning, namely the original inhabitants of a place. Like many legal concepts, it derives meaning from the social and political movements that have popularised it, the institutional and legal processes within which is it claimed, and from the policy purposes it is mobilised to secure. The latter include protecting (as well as constituting) the human rights of a distinctive kind of marginalised group, as well as facilitating their identity, dignity and recognition. All the while the umbrella concept of 'indigenous' allows for the global diversity of indigenous peoples, without subsuming the particularity of local contexts.

The main characteristics or indicia of indigenous peoples can be briefly summarised.[187] First, they have an historical continuity with respect to particular territories. Such continuity may be indicated by factors such as occupation of or other connection to ancestral or other identifiable lands, ancestry and culture (including religion, language, laws and institutions). Historical continuity need not, however, involve a strict priority in time over other groups, descent from pre-colonial populations, the exclusion of the indigeneity of other groups, the maintenance of 'traditional' or rural lifestyles or continuous, exclusive possession of ancestral lands.

Secondly, the group must consider itself a distinct group, identify as indigenous, and be determined to preserve and transmit its identity, culture, lands, laws and institutions, as relevant. Thirdly, the group's members must individually identify as indigenous and be recognised by the group as such. Recognition by national laws is unnecessary. Fourthly and finally, the group must be non-dominant in the sense of experiencing subjugation, marginalisation, dispossession, exclusion or discrimination (whether or not this persists).[188]

of Indigenous Nationalities Act 2002 (Nepal) and Interim Constitution of Nepal 2007, arts 13 and 21; Constitution of Malaysia, arts 160(2) ('Aborigines') and 161(a)(6) ('natives') and Aboriginal Peoples Act 1954 (Malaysia).

[185] *Kayano and others v Hokkaido Expropriation Committee (Nibutani Dam Decision)*, Judgment of the Sapporo District Court (Civil Division No 3), 27 March 1997, (1999) 38 *International Legal Materials* 397.

[186] David McGrogan, 'A Shift in Japan's Stance on Indigenous Rights, and Its Implication' (2010) 17 *International Journal on Minority and Group Rights* 355.

[187] Based on an assimilation of the definitions of Martínez-Cobo and Daes: UN Commission on Human Rights, *Final Report of the Special Rapporteur Martínez Cobo*, (n 50), [379]–[382]; Daes, *Working Paper on the Concept of 'Indigenous People'* (n 7).

[188] Daes, *Working Paper on the Concept of 'Indigenous People'* (n 7).

The identification and recognition of who is indigenous occurs in different contexts and at different levels. These processes involve individuals, communities, the wider population, transnational NGO networks, state authorities, the ILO and UN bodies, and economic actors such as the World Bank and corporations. Flexible rather than prescriptive criteria have proven best suited to the task. The criteria alone do not provide automatic answers, and in the end tight conceptual lines between indigenous peoples and other legal categories (such as minorities) may sometimes be hard to draw. As Kingsbury notes, it is also necessary to rely 'on the dynamic processes of negotiation, politics, legal analysis, institutional decision-making and social interaction to work out the application of these criteria to the innumerable nuances of specific cases'.[189]

As mentioned at the outset, often who is indigenous is not controversial, although difficult struggles for visibility and recognition continue in many countries. Disputes arise even more frequently over the legal rights to which indigenous peoples are entitled after they have been recognised, as well as in efforts to secure their implementation. The rest of this book charts indigenous struggles to secure rights through cases and situations brought before international and regional human rights bodies—from self-determination to land rights, and from civil and political rights to social, economic and cultural rights.

[189] Kingsbury, '"Indigenous Peoples" in International Law' (n 10) 414, 457.

2

The United Nations Human Rights Committee and Indigenous Peoples

AS MENTIONED IN the introductory chapter, most international and regional human rights treaties do not specifically mention indigenous peoples. In the absence of indigenous-specific standards, indigenous peoples have often resorted to general human rights law to protect their interests. The UN human rights treaty bodies have been especially significant, as this chapter and the next explain. The UN treaty bodies are committees of independent experts elected by states parties to each of the major international human rights treaties. While there is some variation in their mandates, the committees typically perform three core functions. First, they set normative standards and provide prospective guidance by issuing 'General Comments' interpreting and elaborating on particular treaty rights. Secondly, they monitor states' implementation of treaty obligations, through a dialogic process of periodic state reporting to the committees and responses from the committees in the form of 'Concluding Observations'. Thirdly, they make quasi-judicial decisions ('Views') on complaints brought by individuals ('communications'), where states have opted to allow them to be made.

This chapter focuses on the UN treaty body that has addressed indigenous issues most often and more thoroughly than the others to date: the UN Human Rights Committee (HRC), charged with monitoring states' implementation of the International Covenant on Civil and Political Rights (ICCPR) 1966.[1] While it is mandated to deal principally with individual civil and political rights (and has applied these to indigenous peoples in various ways), it has also considered the application of a number of ICCPR rights that have a collective orientation. In particular, in monitoring states' reports it has affirmed the application of the right of self-determination under Article 1 of the ICCPR to indigenous peoples, albeit in a qualified form. It has, however, refused to entertain individual complaints about self-determination for jurisdictional (admissibility) reasons.

Most commonly, indigenous issues have raised concerns (in state reporting and individual complaints) in relation the right of 'minorities' to enjoy their own culture under Article 27 of the ICCPR. Many such cases have turned on the significance of indigenous economic and cultural attachments to traditional lands and natural

[1] For early monitoring of indigenous issues by the HRC, see also James Anaya, *Indigenous Peoples in International Law* (2nd edn, Oxford University Press, 2004), 228–30 and 253–58.

resources.[2] Minority rights have provided an aperture through which indigenous peoples have been able to make human rights claims in the absence of indigenous-specific standards. As noted in chapter 1, there is considerable overlap between the concepts of minorities and indigenous peoples. However, forcibly 'fitting' indigenous interests into the framework of minority rights has proven too restrictive to vindicate the full suite of rights to which indigenous peoples are now entitled. The development of the UN Declaration on the Rights of Indigenous Peoples was partly driven by the indigenous experience of the UN treaty bodies, both in terms of consolidating the gains from them and seeking to progressively overcome the limitations of those procedures.

RIGHT TO SELF-DETERMINATION (ICCPR, ARTICLE 1)

State Reporting

In monitoring states through the state reporting and Concluding Observations process, since the late 1990s the HRC has recognised that the right of self-determination (in its economic, cultural and political aspects) applies to indigenous peoples, albeit not as extensively as it applies to the whole populations of colonial territories or independent countries. In general international law, self-determination refers to the right of a people to freely determine their political status and freely pursue their economic, social and cultural development.[3] In the case of populations of colonial or occupied territories, this encompasses the right to choose to become, or resume being, an independent state. Thus far the HRC has recognised a qualified right of self-determination for indigenous peoples, which entitles them to a high degree of internal autonomy in arranging their own communities and controlling their resources but stopping short of a right of secession or independent statehood.

Most commonly the HRC has emphasised self-determination in the context of indigenous land rights, whether in white settler societies, the Nordic/Arctic countries, and Latin America. Thus it found that Canada's 'practice of extinguishing inherent aboriginal rights is incompatible with article 1 and should be abandoned'.[4] It also linked the economic and political dimensions of self-determination by finding that 'without a greater share of land and resources institutions of aboriginal self-government [in Canada] will fail'.[5] Likewise the HRC was concerned that Australia had not sufficiently protected indigenous self-determination and asked it to 'take the necessary steps in order to secure for the indigenous inhabitants a stronger role in decision-making over their traditional lands and natural resources (art. 1, para. 2)'.[6]

[2] The HRC's consideration of membership and exclusion from membership of indigenous groups was considered in chapter 1 on the definition of indigenous peoples, particularly the decision in *Lovelace v Canada*, HRC Communication No 24/1977 (30 July 1981).

[3] ICCPR 1966 and ICESCR 1966, common art 1.

[4] HRC, *Concluding Observations: Canada*, UN Doc A/54/40 (1999), vol I, [230].

[5] Ibid [230].

[6] HRC, *Concluding Observations: Australia*, UN Doc A/55/40 (2000), vol I, [506]–[507].

In Scandinavia, the HRC raised indigenous self-determination in criticising Finland for failing to settle Sami land rights and the impact of competing (public and private) land users on the Sami's traditional means of subsistence, namely reindeer breeding, 'thus endangering their traditional culture and way of life, and hence their identity'.[7] Sweden was criticised under Article 1 for unduly limiting the role of the Sami Parliament in making decisions about Sami traditional lands and economic activities, and for the impact of various development projects (such as hydroelectricity, mining and forestry and land privatisation) on their environment and means of subsistence.[8] In the Americas, the HRC has invoked Article 1 in urging Mexico to ensure the effective consultation of indigenous peoples in decision-making in all areas that impact on their rights,[9] and to increase indigenous participation in state institutions.[10] It asked Chile to ensure that all negotiations respect indigenous land rights.[11]

The HRC's treatment of self-determination has, however, been somewhat inconsistent. In quite a few situations, the HRC has applied only the framework of minority cultural rights (for example, to 'Highlanders' in Thailand, or Maroon and Amerindian communities in Suriname),[12] even where such groups have indigenous-like attachments to land or are elsewhere recognised as indigenous peoples entitled to self-determination. It is not always clear why the HRC refers to some groups as 'minorities' and others as 'indigenous', since it seldom elaborates on the characteristics of either group in reviewing state reports under Article 1 (or Article 27).

Individual Communications

While the HRC has occasionally commented on the right of self-determination of indigenous peoples in its Concluding Observations on state reports, it has been reluctant to address the issue when raised in individual communications under the First Optional Protocol to the ICCPR. The case of *Ominayak (Lubicon Lake Band) v Canada* (1990)[13] was brought by Chief Ominayak, the leader and representative of a Cree Indian band living in Alberta, Canada. Ominayak claimed that the Canadian government had permitted the provincial Alberta government to expropriate Lubicon territory for the benefit of corporate interests, such as oil and gas leases, contrary to a federal law and an 1899 treaty that recognised the band's right to continue its traditional way of life.[14] Ominayak argued that this violated the band's right to freely determine its political status and to pursue its economic, social and cultural development (under Article 1(1) of the ICCPR); and to freely dispose of its natural

[7] HRC, *Concluding Observations: Finland*, UN Doc A/60/40 (2004), vol I, [81(17)].
[8] HRC, *Concluding Observations: Sweden*, UN Doc A/57/40 (2002), vol I, [79(15)].
[9] HRC, *Concluding Observations: Mexico*, UN Doc CCPR/C/MEX/CO/5 (2010), [22].
[10] HRC, *Concluding Observations: Mexico*, UN Doc A/54/40 (1999), vol I, [331].
[11] HRC, *Concluding Observations: Chile*, UN Doc CCPR/C/CHL/CO/5 (2007), [19].
[12] HRC, *Concluding Observations: Thailand*, UN Doc A/60/40 (2005), vol I, [95(24)]; HRC, *Concluding Observations: Suriname*, UN Doc A/59/40 (2004), vol I, [69(21)].
[13] *Chief Bernard Ominayak and Lubicon Lake Band v Canada*, HRC Communication No 167/1984 (26 March 1990).
[14] Ibid [2.3].

wealth and resources (under Article 1(2)). As a result, it was arguably deprived of its means of subsistence under Article 1, including because of environmental and economic harms.

The HRC ruled that the claims under Article 1 were inadmissible because individuals (such as Chief Ominayak) cannot claim under the Protocol to be a victim, since self-determination was regarded as a collective right 'which deals with rights conferred upon peoples, as such'.[15] The HRC further decided that it could not consider whether the Lubicon Lake Band constituted a 'people' under Article 1, since the Protocol provides a procedure under which only 'individuals can claim that their individual rights have been violated' (specifically, in Articles 6–27 of the ICCPR).[16] The HRC added that '[t]here is, however, no objection to a group of individuals, who claim to be similarly affected, collectively to submit a communication about alleged breaches of their rights',[17] as long it concerns any of Articles 6–27. The HRC duly considered the complainant's separate claim under Article 27, discussed in the next section.

In another case decided in the same year, *EP v Colombia* (1990), the HRC reiterated its finding that under the Protocol only individuals can claim that their individual rights (under Articles 6–27 of the ICCPR) have been violated.[18] It further emphasised that 'no individual, or group of individuals, can in the abstract, by way of *actio popularis*, challenge a law or practice deemed to be contrary to the Covenant'.[19] Rather, '[a]n individual, or a group of individuals, can only claim to be a victim … if he or she, or they, are actually affected'.[20]

While the complaints had also claimed violations of ICCPR rights beyond Article 1 (such as Articles 25, 26 and 27), the HRC held these were inadmissible because domestic remedies had not been exhausted.[21] The complaint was brought by English-speaking 'indigenous' islanders on an archipelago over which Colombia had established sovereignty by force in the early nineteenth century.[22] Colombia had dispossessed many islanders from their land, including by a policy to 'Colombianise' the islands through transmigration and exclusive, discriminatory use of the Spanish language.[23] Such policies had caused overpopulation, environmental harms (such as water scarcity and pollution), destruction of traditional livelihoods (such as farming and fishing) and discrimination in employment, services and public office.[24]

Likewise in *RL and others v Canada* (1991), the HRC held that an Article 1 self-determination claim was inadmissible because the HRC may not consider communications from individuals claiming violations of individual rights.[25] In this case,

[15] Ibid [13.3].
[16] Ibid [32.1].
[17] Ibid [27.6], [32.1]; see also *AD (The Mikmaq Tribal Society) v Canada*, HRC Communication No 78/1980 (29 July 1984), [8.2].
[18] *EP v Colombia*, HRC Communication No 318/1988 (25 July 1990), [8.2].
[19] Ibid.
[20] Ibid [8.2].
[21] Ibid [8.3].
[22] Ibid [1], [2.1].
[23] Ibid [2.2], [2.5].
[24] Ibid [2.3]–[2.4], [2.6]–[2.7].
[25] *RL and others v Canada*, HRC Communication No 358/1989 (5 November 1991), [6.2].

the Whispering Pines Indian Band of the Shuswap Nation in British Columbia claimed that a 1985 federal law, which amended the rules on membership of Indian bands, infringed their right, as a distinct people, to determine the form and membership of their own economic, social and political institutions under Article 1(1) of the ICCPR.[26] In particular, the law admitted new members whom the community could not house or support, and deprived current members' children and grandchildren of membership and the right to live on the reserve.[27] The law was adopted in response to the HRC's recommendation in *Lovelace v Canada* (1981) (discussed in chapter 1) to remove sex discrimination in Indian membership rules, but it also deprived certain others of their pre-existing Indian status on the basis of a racial quota. The other grounds of challenge to the law (Articles 17, 22, 23, 26 and 27) were inadmissible for failure to exhaust domestic remedies.

In a case almost a decade later, the HRC showed a greater willingness to take into account self-determination in individual communications under the Protocol. In *Diergaardt (Late Captain of the Rehoboth Baster Community) v Namibia* (2000), the complainant submitted that Namibia had violated the right to (internal) self-determination of the Baster community by preventing it from pursuing its economic, social and cultural development, or freely disposing of its wealth and resources.[28] The Rehoboth Basters are descendants of indigenous Khoi and (Dutch) Afrikaans settlers who migrated to Namibia in 1872 and enjoyed considerable political, economic and cultural autonomy under German colonial and South African mandate rule, until Namibia attained independence in 1990.[29] Thereafter, their communal land was expropriated under the new Constitution, allegedly affecting their means of subsistence (cattle raising and the sharing of communal lands during droughts).

The HRC found that the Article 1 claim was inadmissible for the reasons given in its earlier cases, but conceded that 'the provisions of article 1 may be relevant in the interpretation of other rights protected by the Covenant, in particular articles 25, 26 and 27'.[30] On the merits, however, the HRC did not explicitly deploy Article 1 in the interpretation and application of those ICCPR rights that were found to be admissible,[31] discussed in the next section.

The broader question remains whether the HRC is correct to dismiss Article 1 claims outright under the Protocol. Article 1 of the Protocol provides that complaints may be made in respect of a violation of 'any' ICCPR right.[32] Article 1 complaints are thus not expressly excluded, nor are claims restricted to those made in respect of Articles 6–27 of the ICCPR, as the HRC has held. The HRC's restrictive

[26] Ibid [3.8].

[27] Ibid [3.1].

[28] *JGA Diergaardt (Late Captain of the Rehoboth Baster Community) and Others v Namibia*, HRC Communication No 760/1997 (25 July 2000), [3.2].

[29] Ibid [2.1]–[2.6].

[30] Ibid [10.3] and Individual Opinion of Martin Scheinin (concurring). See also *Gillot v France*, HRC Communication No 932/2000 (15 July 2002), [13.4]; *Mahuika and others v New Zealand*, HRC Communication No 547/1993 (27 October 2000), [9.2].

[31] International Covenant on Civil and Political Rights (ICCPR), Arts 14, 17, 25(a), (c), 26 and 27 (adopted 16 December 1966, entered into force 23 March 1976, 999 UNTS 171).

[32] Optional Protocol to the International Covenant on Civil and Political Rights (adopted 16 December 1966, entered into force 23 March 1976, 999 UNTS 171).

approach rests upon an artificially strict conceptualisation of self-determination rights as exclusively 'collective' and thus as inappropriate for individual vindication, as well as on an overly restrictive approach to standing.

In an appropriate case, where the author of a communication is recognised as the legitimate representative of a 'people', it is hard to see why a blanket inadmissibility rule should be upheld. For instance, in *Ominayak v Canada*, Chief Ominayak was the unanimously elected leader of the Lubicon Lake Band and had lodged the communication on its behalf.[33] Collective rights can only be enjoyed by the individuals who comprise a group. General international law on self-determination already contains certain principles to identify a people's legitimate representatives, such as through recognition by the relevant regional organisation or through other UN bodies or procedures. The HRC is part of that UN system. In the same vein, the HRC has already recognised that individual minority rights under Article 27 have collective dimensions; so too with self-determination, it is a question of degree not kind.

It would remain necessary for a person to prove that s/he was individually affected by the violation of the group's rights, but that too is conceivable in the right case. Under the Optional Protocol to the ICESCR (unlike under the Optional Protocol to the ICCPR) there is express provision for communications to be submitted on behalf of groups,[34] lending further support to the view that collective claims to self-determination ought to be recognised. (The right of self-determination is common to Article 1 of the ICESCR and ICCPR.)

RIGHT TO TAKE PART IN CULTURAL LIFE (ICCPR, ARTICLE 27)

The HRC's General Comments have infrequently mentioned indigenous peoples in interpreting most civil and political rights. The HRC's most explicit statement concerns the right of 'ethnic, religious or linguistic minorities', in Article 27 of the ICCPR, 'to enjoy their own culture, to profess and practise their own religion, or to use their own language'. In General Comment No 23, the HRC recognised 'indigenous communities' as capable of constituting minorities protected by Article 27.[35] It further observed that the rights of individuals under Article 27, including to enjoy a particular culture, 'may consist in a way of life which is closely associated with territory and use of its resources', which 'may particularly be true of members of indigenous communities constituting a minority'.[36] It elaborated further on aspects of indigenous cultural rights coming within Article 27:

> culture manifests itself in many forms, including a particular way of life associated with the use of land resources, especially in the case of indigenous peoples. That right may include such traditional activities as fishing or hunting and the right to live in reserves protected by

[33] Ibid [7].

[34] *Optional Protocol to the International Covenant on Economic, Social and Cultural Rights* (adopted 10 December 2008, entered into force 5 May 2013), Art 2.

[35] HRC, *General Comment No 23: The Rights of Minorities (Article 27)*, UN Doc CCPR/C/21/Rev.1/Add.5 (8 April 1994), [3.2], [7].

[36] Ibid [3.2].

law. The enjoyment of those rights may require positive legal measures of protection and measures to ensure the effective participation of members of minority communities in decisions which affect them.[37]

State Reporting

Recognition as Indigenous

In monitoring states through the state reporting and Concluding Observations process, the HRC has regarded state non-recognition of groups as indigenous as jeopardising the right to take part in cultural life under Article 27. It was thus concerned that the Danish Supreme Court did not recognise the Thule Tribe of Greenland, an Inuit people, as a separate group capable of vindicating its traditional rights, despite the tribe's own perception to the contrary.[38] It accordingly emphasised that states should pay special attention to self-identification as indigenous.[39] The HRC was likewise concerned that Japan had not recognised the Ainu (an indigenous people from Hokkaido and Honshi islands) and the Ryukyu/Okinawa islanders as indigenous peoples.[40] The HRC was further concerned about a Slovenian law that differentiated between '"autochthonous" (indigenous)' and "non-autochthonous" (new)' Roma communities.[41] Elsewhere it urged the United States to provide for full judicial review of determinations of federal recognition of Indian tribes.[42] The HRC was also concerned about the inter-generational denial of Indian status to the descendants of women who had lost Indian status by marriage.[43]

Land and Resources

The key focus of the HRC under Article 27 has been indigenous attachment to land as an expression of their minority cultural rights. The HRC has been concerned where states fail to recognise indigenous land or property rights,[44] or accord them appropriate weight in evaluating competing land uses.[45] Where land titling or demarcation processes are underway, the HRC has highlighted delays and unresolved or incomplete distributions;[46] procedural obstacles to vindicating land rights (such as

[37] Ibid [7].

[38] HRC, Concluding Observations: Denmark (2008), UN Doc CCPR/C/DNK/CO/5, [13].

[39] Ibid [13].

[40] HRC, *Concluding Observations: Japan*, UN Doc CCPR/C/JPN/CO/5 (2008), [32].

[41] HRC, *Concluding Observations: Slovenia*, UN Doc A/60/40 (2005), vol I, [93(16)].

[42] HRC, *Concluding Observations: United States of America*, UN Doc A/50/40 (1995), [302].

[43] HRC, *Concluding Observations: Canada*, UN Doc CCPR/C/79/Add.105 (1999), [19] (concerning legal amendments responding to the HRC's Views in *Lovelace v Canada*, HRC Communication No 24/1977 (30 July 1981)).

[44] HRC, *Concluding Observations: Japan*, UN Doc A/54/40 (1999), vol I, [156] (concerning the Ainu); HRC, *Concluding Observations: Colombia*, UN Doc A/59/40 (2004), vol I, [67(20)].

[45] HRC, *Concluding Observations: Australia*, UN Doc A/55/40 (2000), vol I, [510].

[46] HRC, *Concluding Observations: Brazil*, UN Doc A/51/40 (1996), vol I, [320]; HRC, *Concluding Observations: Australia*, UN Doc A/55/40 (2000), vol I, [508]; HRC, *Concluding Observations: Paraguay*, UN Doc CCPR/C/PRY/CO/2 (2006), [23]; HRC, *Concluding Observations: Guyana*, UN Doc A/55/40 (2000), vol I, [379]; HRC, *Concluding Observations: Nicaragua*, UN Doc CCPR/C/NIC/CO/3 (2008), [21] (delays despite a decision of the Inter-American Court of Human Rights six years previously, in the *Awas Tingni* case (*Awas Tingi v Nicaragua* [2001] IACtHR (Ser C) No 79)).

high costs, complexity and strict evidentiary rules;[47] and unsatisfactory legal aid or inadequate means to enforce rights[48]); and inequitable land distributions.[49]

Where indigenous land rights are recognised, the HRC has been concerned where rights can be extinguished by a political body without due process and compensation,[50] or sold to private companies without consultation;[51] where there are unacceptable restrictions on such rights;[52] or where the amount of land is insufficient on which to pursue traditional economic activities.[53] The HRC has also highlighted where indigenous land rights are unacceptably impinged upon by competing public and private land uses[54] (including, for example, a law permitting anyone to fish and hunt on public lands;[55] pastoral leases;[56] agrarian reform;[57] or lawsuits by private landowners prohibiting traditional land uses such as reindeer herding[58]), thus impairing traditional livelihoods.

A prevalent concern of the HRC has been where indigenous land has been adversely affected by public or private development projects, whether legally or illegally. The impacts of natural resource exploitation on indigenous culture, land, environment and identity has been a particular focus, including logging and/or mining;[59] oil exploitation;[60] outside settlers;[61] hydroelectricity;[62] game reserves;[63] road building;[64] or military bases.[65] Often such activities have been accompanied by violence against indigenous peoples, and/or forced evictions, displacement, dispossession or relocation.[66] The HRC has accordingly called on states to investigate and punish those responsible.[67]

47 HRC, *Concluding Observations: Australia*, UN Doc CCPR/C/AUS/CO/5 (2009), [16].

48 HRC, *Concluding Observations: Norway*, UN Doc A/55/40 (2000), vol I, [81].

49 HRC, *Concluding Observations: Mexico*, UN Doc (A/49/40) (1994), vol I, [177], [182].

50 HRC, *Concluding Observations: United States of America*, UN Doc A/50/40 (1995), [290]; HRC, *Concluding Observations: United States of America*, UN Doc CCPR/C/USA/CO/3 (2006), [37] (where Native American rights on reservations or accruing from long use and possession can be extinguished by Congress).

51 HRC, *Concluding Observations: Paraguay*, UN Doc CCPR/C/PRY/CO/3 (2008), [27].

52 HRC, *Concluding Observations: United States of America*, UN Doc CCPR/C/USA/CO/3 (2006), [37] (as resulting from the concept of permanent trusteeship over the Indian and Alaska native tribes and their land and their exercise through Individual Indian Money (IIM) accounts).

53 HRC, *Concluding Observations: Guyana*, UN Doc A/55/40 (2000), vol I, [379].

54 HRC, *Concluding Observations: Norway*, UN Doc A/55/40 (2000), vol I, [81].

55 HRC, *Concluding Observations: Sweden*, UN Doc A/51/40 (1996), vol I, [90].

56 HRC, *Concluding Observations: Australia*, UN Doc A/55/40 (2000), vol I, [508].

57 HRC, *Concluding Observations: Mexico*, UN Doc A/49/40 (1994), vol I, [177], [182].

58 HRC, *Concluding Observations: Norway*, UN Doc A/55/40 (2000), vol I, [81].

59 HRC, *Concluding Observations: Guyana*, UN Doc A/55/40 (2000), vol I, [379]; HRC, *Concluding Observations: Suriname*, UN Doc A/59/40 (2004), vol I, [69(21)].

60 HRC, *Concluding Observations: Ecuador*, UN Doc A/53/40 (1998), vol I, [292].

61 HRC, *Concluding Observations: Nicaragua*, UN Doc CCPR/C/NIC/CO/3 (2008), [21].

62 HRC, *Concluding Observations: Chile*, UN Doc A/54/40 (1999), vol I, [218].

63 HRC, *Concluding Observations: Tanzania*, UN Doc CCPR/C/TZA/CO/4 (2009), [26].

64 HRC, *Concluding Observations: Bolivia*, UN Doc CCPR/C/BOL/CO/3 (2013), [25].

65 HRC, *Concluding Observations: Denmark*, UN Doc A/52/40 (1998), vol I, [69]; HRC, *Concluding Observations: Denmark*, UN Doc A/56/40 (2001), vol I, [73(11)].

66 HRC, *Concluding Observations: Argentina*, UN Doc CCPR/C/ARG/CO/4 (2010), [25]; HRC, *Concluding Observations: Kenya*, UN Doc CCPR/C/KEN/CO/3 (2012), [24] (where the state had not implemented the orders of the ACHPR in *Centre for Minority Rights Development (Kenya) and Minority Rights Group International on behalf of Endorois Welfare Council v Kenya* 267/2003, ACHPR (4 February 2010)).

67 HRC, *Concluding Observations: Argentina*, UN Doc CCPR/C/ARG/CO/4 (2010), [25].

Where indigenous lands are potentially affected by development projects or competing land uses, the HRC has repeatedly insisted that indigenous peoples have a right to be consulted on and participate in decisions that affect their rights (whether concerning land and natural resources, or other policy areas).[68] While the precise language and formulation used by the HRC has varied, the standard is drawn from ILO Convention No 169 and the HRC has recognised that it comprises a number of inter-related elements. It is a right not only to be informed and consulted, but also for the 'free, prior and informed consent'[69] of indigenous peoples to be obtained before decisions or measures are taken that 'substantially compromise or interfere with their culturally significant economic activities'.[70] On this basis, the HRC criticised Peruvian and Bolivian laws which provided for consultation but not free, prior or informed consent.[71] The HRC has held the standard of consent to be high, expressing concern, for example, where a road-building project did not have the support of 'all' affected communities.[72] It has also called on indigenous representative institutions to be mandated to be involved in decisions about land and resources.[73] In terms of remedies, the HRC has indicated that '[r]elocation and compensation may not be appropriate in order to comply with article 27' where the sustainability of indigenous culture and way of life is at stake.[74]

The principles of consultation and participation are not limited to decisions or measures affecting land and natural resources, but extend to other policy areas.[75] Thus, at the political level, for instance, the HRC was concerned that indigenous peoples were not sufficiently consulted on Mexican constitutional reforms that affected their rights,[76] or on an Australian proposal to replace a national representative indigenous body.[77] Further, indigenous peoples were not adequately consulted

68 See, eg, HRC, *Concluding Observations: Chile*, UN Doc A/54/40 (1999), vol I, [218]; HRC, *Concluding Observations: Panama*, UN Doc CCPR/C/PAN/CO/3 (2008), [21]; HRC, *Concluding Observations: Togo*, UN Doc CCPR/C/TGO/CO/4 (2011), [21]; HRC, *Concluding Observations: Guatemala*, UN Doc CCPR/C/GTM/CO/3 (2012), [27]; HRC, *Concluding Observations: Suriname*, UN Doc A/59/40 (2004), vol I, [69(21)]; HRC, *Concluding Observations: Colombia*, UN Doc A/59/40 (2004), vol I, [67(20)]; HRC, *Concluding Observations: Paraguay*, UN Doc CCPR/C/PRY/CO/3 (2008), [27]; HRC, *Concluding Observations: Australia*, UN Doc CCPR/C/AUS/CO/5 (2009), [13]; HRC, *Concluding Observations: Bolivia*, UN Doc CCPR/C/BOL/CO/3 (2013), [25].

69 HRC, *Concluding Observations: Panama*, UN Doc CCPR/C/PAN/CO/3 (2008), [21]; HRC, *Concluding Observations: Togo*, UN Doc CCPR/C/TGO/CO/4 (2011), [21]; HRC, *Concluding Observations: Guatemala*, UN Doc CCPR/C/GTM/CO/3 (2012), [27]; HRC, *Concluding Observations: Bolivia*, UN Doc CCPR/C/BOL/CO/3 (2013), [25].

70 HRC, *Concluding Observations: Peru*, UN Doc CCPR/C/PER/CO/5 (2013), [24].

71 Ibid [24]; HRC, *Concluding Observations: Bolivia*, UN Doc CCPR/C/BOL/CO/3 (2013), [25].

72 Ibid [25].

73 HRC, *Concluding Observations: Sweden*, UN Doc A/57/40 (2002), vol I, [79(15)] (concerning the Sami Parliament).

74 HRC, *Concluding Observations: Chile*, UN Doc A/54/40 (1999), vol I, [218].

75 HRC, *Concluding Observations: Mexico*, UN Doc A/49/40 (1994), vol I, [182]; HRC, *Concluding Observations: Guyana*, UN Doc A/55/40 (2000), vol I, [380]; HRC, *Concluding Observations: Suriname*, UN A/59/40 (2004), vol I, [69(21)].

76 HRC, *Concluding Observations: Mexico*, UN Doc CCPR/C/MEX/CO/5 (2010), [22].

77 HRC, *Concluding Observations: Australia*, UN Doc CCPR/C/AUS/CO/5 (2009), [13].

on measures taken by Australia in response to indigenous child abuse which involved the suspension of racial discrimination laws.[78]

Language and Other Cultural Rights

The HRC has highlighted other dimensions of indigenous minority cultural rights under Article 27. Language has been a particular focus. The HRC has called on states to take measures to guarantee, protect and promote indigenous languages and stem their decline.[79] States have been urged to provide adequate opportunities for indigenous children to receive instruction and education in their own language about their culture and history in the school curriculum.[80] States have also been asked to distribute summaries of the HRC's reports in indigenous languages.[81]

Other aspects of cultural rights raised under Article 27 include: respect for cultural traditions, including agricultural activities;[82] protection of customary rights;[83] ensuring indigenous peoples can effectively take part in elections with due regard for their traditions, conventions and customs;[84] and the need for indigenous representation in parliament, high public offices, the liberal professions and the senior civil service.[85]

Individual Communications

The HRC has also addressed various aspects of cultural rights in individual communications. Out of 12 communications brought by indigenous peoples alleging violations of Article 27 and decided by the HRC between 1981 and 2015, the HRC found breaches in three cases.[86] The first, *Lovelace v Canada* (1981), discussed in chapter 1, concerned the denial of membership of an indigenous community and consequent denial of the right to live on a reserve. The second, *Ominyak v Canada* (1990), involved an indigenous group whose traditional way of life had been adversely affected by the expropriation of land for corporate oil and gas development.[87] The third, *Poma Poma v Peru* (2006), involved the destruction of traditional subsistence grazing activities by a state's diversion of groundwater. Of the many

[78] Ibid [14].
[79] HRC, *Concluding Observations: Venezuela*, UN Doc A/48/40 (1993), part I, [310]; HRC, *Concluding Observations: Canada*, UN Doc CCPR/C/CAN/CO5 (2006), [10]; HRC, *Concluding Observations: Costa Rica*, UN Doc CCPR/C/CRI/CO/5 (2007), [5].
[80] HRC, *Concluding Observations: Japan*, UN Doc CCPR/C/JPN/CO/5 (2008), [32].
[81] HRC, *Concluding Observations: Panama*, UN Doc CCPR/C/PAN/CO/3 (2008), [22].
[82] HRC, *Concluding Observations: Cambodia*, UN Doc A/54/40 (1999), vol I, [311].
[83] HRC, *Concluding Observations: Sweden*, UN Doc A/51/40 (1996), vol I, [98].
[84] HRC, *Concluding Observations: Nicaragua*, UN Doc CCPR/C/NIC/CO/3 (2008), [20].
[85] HRC, *Concluding Observations: New Zealand*, UN Doc A/50/40 (1995), [182].
[86] *Lovelace v Canada*, HRC Communication No 24/1977 (30 July 1981); *Chief Bernard Ominayak and Lubicon Lake Band v Canada*, HRC Communication No 167/1984 (26 March 1990); *Poma Poma v Peru*, HRC Communication No 1457/2006 (27 March 2009).
[87] *Chief Bernard Ominayak and Lubicon Lake Band v Canada*, HRC Communication No 167/1984 (26 March 1990) (although the HRC found that the case was already being appropriately remedied by the state at the time of the HRC's decision).

unsuccessful cases, most have involved challenges to public or private interference with Sami reindeer herding in Scandinavia, in relation to which the HRC has taken a very cautious approach. All 12 cases are considered below. It is noteworthy that virtually all of the cases have been brought against developed western states (Finland, Norway, Sweden, Canada and New Zealand), plus Peru and Namibia. This distortion may be explained by a number of factors, including patterns of ratification of the Optional Protocol to the ICCPR, the inaccessibility of justice in developing states, official discouragement of the concept of 'indigenous' peoples in some developing states (particularly in Asia and Africa) and an alternative recourse to regional human rights mechanisms (particularly in Latin America, and increasingly in Africa, as discussed in chapters 4 and 5).

Conflict Between Individual and Community Cultural Rights

In *Lovelace v Canada* (1981),[88] the complainant was born and registered as a 'Maliseet Indian', which gave her rights under national law, including the right to live on an Indian reserve. Following her marriage to a non-Indian, she lost these rights and was not entitled to return to the reserve, even when her marriage broke up. The complainant claimed that this constituted a violation of her right, under Article 27, to enjoy her own culture. The measures she complained of were designed, in part, to preserve the identity of the Indian tribe, and thus to ensure their collective right to enjoy their culture. The HRC nonetheless indicated that measures affecting the right of an individual to enjoy their own culture 'must have both a reasonable and objective justification and be consistent with the other provisions of the Covenant'.[89] On the facts, the HRC found that it was not reasonable or necessary to preserve the identity of the tribe to deny her the right to reside on the reserve.[90] The HRC thus contemplated, in principle, that individual interests could be subordinated to collective interests, but that there was no justification for the collective to prevail in the present case.

The similar case of *Kitok v Sweden* (1988)[91] concerned a law which denied an ethnic Sami formal membership of the Sami community and the consequent right to carry out reindeer husbandry. The law restricted the right of reindeer husbandry to Sami who undertook it as their 'permanent occupation' and had not 'gone over to any other main economic activity'.[92] The complainant, an ethnic Sami, had left full-time reindeer farming for financial reasons. Sweden argued that the law was justified for economic and ecological reasons, to ensure the future of reindeer breeding for those for whom it is their primary source of income, and to preserve the well-being of the Sami community.[93] The HRC accepted that the method selected by Sweden to secure these objectives—limiting the right to engage in reindeer breeding to members of the Sami villages—was reasonable and consistent with Article 27.

[88] *Lovelace v Canada*, HRC Communication No 24/1977 (30 July 1981).
[89] Ibid [16].
[90] Ibid [17].
[91] *Ivan Kitok v Sweden*, HRC Communication No 197/1985 (27 July 1988).
[92] See ibid [9.6].
[93] Ibid [9.5].

The HRC nonetheless expressed 'grave doubts' about the compatibility of certain aspects of the Swedish law with Article 27, since ignoring objective ethnic criteria for membership may be disproportionate to the legitimate end sought by the law.[94] This was particularly so because Mr Kitok had always retained links with the Sami community, by always living on Sami lands and seeking to return to full-time reindeer farming as soon as it became financially possible. Nonetheless, the HRC observed that the case involved an apparent conflict between the protection of the rights of the minority as a whole and a single member of it.[95]

In resolving the conflict, the HRC followed its principle in *Lovelace* that 'a restriction upon the right of an individual member of a minority must be shown to have a reasonable and objective justification and to be necessary for the continued viability and welfare of the minority as a whole'.[96] The HRC concluded that there was no violation in this case because Mr Kitok was permitted by the Sami board, albeit not equally to others, to graze and farm his reindeer, and to hunt and fish free of charge on the community's pasture.[97] He was thus not prevented from enjoying his own culture.[98]

Conflict between the cultural rights of minority groups as a whole and their members, and between individuals and the state, also arose in *Mahuika v New Zealand* (1993).[99] The case was brought by Maori individuals who claimed that their traditional rights to fish were affected by legislation based on an agreement between the New Zealand government and Maori representatives. Although the majority of Maori tribes supported the agreement, those bringing this case did not. The HRC acknowledged that 'economic activities may come within the ambit of Article 27, if they are an essential element of the culture of a community'.[100] On the facts it recognised that 'the use and control of fisheries is an essential element of [Maori] culture',[101] including not only as a traditional means of livelihood but as adapted to a modern way of life and modern technology (such as through commercial fishing).[102]

Restriction of access to fish stocks could, in an appropriate case, be contrary to Article 27. The HRC found that such rights may not be interfered with unless the indigenous people had the 'opportunity to participate in the decision-making process' and as long as 'they will continue to benefit from their traditional economy'.[103] The HRC found New Zealand had undertaken a complicated process of consultation and had secured substantial Maori support for a nation-wide settlement and the regulation of fishing activities.[104] The HRC held that where the right of individuals to enjoy their own culture conflicts with parallel rights of other members

[94] Ibid [9.6]–[9.7].
[95] Ibid [9.8].
[96] Ibid.
[97] Ibid.
[98] Ibid [4.2].
[99] *Mahuika and others v New Zealand*, HRC Communication No 547/1993 (27 October 1993).
[100] Ibid [9.3].
[101] Ibid.
[102] Ibid [9.4].
[103] Ibid [9.5].
[104] Ibid [9.6].

of the minority group, or the minority as a whole, the HRC will focus on whether the limitation is in the interests of all members of the minority and whether it is reasonably and objectively justified.[105] On the facts, the HRC found that there had been no violation of Article 27. It was significant that the settlement accorded the Maori greater access to and control over commercial fisheries, paid special attention to the cultural and religious significance of fishing, and preserved customary (non-commercial) food gathering rights.[106]

Non-Indigenous Interference in Indigenous Lands and Resources

The remaining HRC decisions have involved claims that the public or private, non-indigenous exploitation of indigenous lands and natural resources infringes minority cultural rights under Article 27. Those arguments have so far only succeeded in *Ominayak (Lubicon Lake Band) v Canada* (1990), and even then the HRC accepted that remedies already proposed by the state party were adequate. As noted earlier, the case concerned Canada's failure to protect the Lubicon Lake Band from corporate oil and gas developments on their land. While the HRC dismissed the Article 1 self-determination claim, it proactively suggested that the case might raise issues of minority cultural rights under Article 27 (which had not been argued by Ominayak) and it was thus admissible on that basis.[107]

On the merits the HRC observed that Article 27 includes 'the right of persons, in community with others, to engage in economic and social activities which are part of the culture of the community to which they belong'.[108] It then found on the facts, without elaborating, that '[h]istorical inequities, to which the State party refers, and certain more recent developments threaten the way of life and culture of the Lubicon Lake Band and constitute a violation of article 27 so long as they continue'.[109] In so doing, the HRC again acknowledged the collective dimensions of the individual right to culture, as well as the impacts on members of the band who were not strictly the 'victims' of the complaint.

While finding violations of Article 27, the HRC nonetheless accepted that remedies already proposed by Canada were appropriate.[110] Canada had committed to implementing an agreement with Alberta to set aside 95 square miles of land for a reserve, and negotiated with the band on the modalities to transfer the land, including issues of band membership, the size of the reserve, community construction and the delivery of services and programmes.[111] In addition, while the band had withdrawn from the negotiations over a dispute about cash compensation, Canada had made a standing offer of CAN$45 million in benefits and programmes, which was equivalent to CAN$500,000 for each family of five in a band of 500 members.[112]

105 Ibid [9.6].
106 Ibid [9.7]–[9.8].
107 Ibid [13.4].
108 Ibid [32.2].
109 Ibid [33].
110 Ibid.
111 Ibid [29.7]–[29.8].
112 Ibid [29.8], [29.10].

The offer was without prejudice to ongoing litigation by the band seeking CAN$167 million in compensation for economic and other losses.[113]

In *Ilmari Länsman and Others v Finland* (1994) ('*Länsman I*'),[114] the HRC considered whether stone quarrying on lands traditionally used by indigenous Sami people for reindeer husbandry (organised through the Muotkatunturi Herdsmen's Committee), and related transport through reindeer fences, would violate Article 27. The HRC noted that 'reindeer husbandry is an essential element of [Sami] culture', including in its modern, technologically-assisted form.[115] It noted further that 'mountain Riutusvaara [where the quarrying was to be carried out] continues to have a spiritual significance relevant to their culture', and that there were also concerns about the quality of slaughtered reindeer being affected by the environmental disturbance.[116] The HRC acknowledged the state's interest in economic development and indicated that development which denies the right to culture is incompatible with Article 27, while that which has only a limited impact on a minority's way of life may be consistent with it.[117] The state must, however, ensure the effective participation of minority communities in decisions which affect them.[118]

On the facts, the HRC found that the complainants and other indigenous representatives were consulted, and their interests considered, during the process for issuing the quarrying permit.[119] Further, the conditions of the permit were designed to minimise the impact on reindeer herding and the environment, including by quarrying outside the period used for reindeer pasturing.[120] Necessary changes in herding methods could also be accommodated by the local forestry authorities and the company.[121] The HRC concluded that reindeer herding had not appeared to have been adversely affected by the scale of the quarrying undertaken or approved (a maximum of 5,000 cubic metres of stone).[122] As such, there was no denial of the right to enjoy their culture under Article 27. The HRC noted, however, that if mining were to be approved on a larger scale and significantly expanded by the authorised companies, there might then arise a violation.[123]

Two years later the HRC decided a second case involving Sami reindeer herders from the same community. The case of *Jouni Länsman and Others v Finland* (1996) ('*Länsman II*')[124] concerned a plan by the Finnish forestry board to approve logging and road construction in 3,000 hectares of winter herding lands used by the Muotkatunturi Herdsmen's Committee, an area over which ownership was unsettled.

[113] Ibid [29.10].
[114] *Ilmari Länsman and 47 Other Members of the Muotkatunturi Herdsmen's Committee and Members of the Angeli Local Community*, HRC Communication No 511/1992 (8 November 1994).
[115] Ibid [9.2]–[9.3].
[116] Ibid [9.3].
[117] Ibid [9.4].
[118] Ibid [9.5].
[119] Ibid [9.6].
[120] Ibid.
[121] Ibid [9.7].
[122] Ibid [9.6].
[123] Ibid [9.8].
[124] *Jouni E. Länsman, Jouni A. Länsman, Eino Länsman and Marko Torikka (All Members of the Muotkatunturi Herdsmen's Committee) v Finland*, HRC Communication No 671/1995 (30 October 1996).

The complainants argued that the lichen covering the ground and trees in this area of old untouched forests was essential food for their reindeer, and that the quiet and undisturbed area was also where reindeer gave birth.[125] They also emphasised that a decline in the economic viability of reindeer herding, in part because of development activities such as quarrying, should be taken into account.[126]

The HRC found that the Herdsmen's Committee had been consulted in the planning process and had not reacted negatively.[127] The authorities were found to have duly weighed the complainants' interests and the general economic interests in determining forest management measures, with regard to logging methods, choice of areas and road construction.[128] The domestic courts had also determined that there would be no denial of Article 27 rights. The HRC concluded that there was no denial of Article 27 or error by the domestic courts. The scale of logging approved, although imposing additional work and expenses on the herders, did not appear to threaten the survival of reindeer husbandry, and its low economic profitability was considered to be a result of other, external economic factors.[129]

The HRC acknowledged, however, that if logging were subsequently approved on a larger scale, or the effects of the logging already approved were more serious than foreseen, then it would need to be reconsidered whether there was a violation of Article 27.[130] In particular, the HRC noted, in light of the quarrying challenged in *Länsman I*, that different development activities, while not a violation of Article 27 by themselves, 'taken together, may erode the rights of Sami people to enjoy their own culture'.[131] It was precisely these cumulative effects that became the subject of a third challenge by Finnish Sami reindeer herders decided by the HRC almost a decade later.

In *Jouni Länsman and Others v Finland* (2005) ('*Länsman III*'),[132] the areas approved for logging that were considered in *Länsman II* had been logged, further areas of the Herdsmen's Committee had been logged, and another, unexpected, unplanned logging operation was imminent.[133] The complainants argued that since the 1980s, 1,600 hectares of one of their grazing areas had been logged, accounting for 40 per cent of lichen there.[134] Logging was said to destroy the lichen for hundreds of years, and waste in logged areas prevented grazing and compacted the snow, which impeded reindeer digging for food.[135] Reindeer also avoided areas being logged, instead straying onto other pastures and incurring additional labour for the herders. Finland argued that the declining economic profitability of reindeer herding was in part due to over-population, not logging.[136]

125 Ibid [2.4].
126 Ibid [2.5]–[2.6].
127 Ibid [10.5].
128 Ibid.
129 Ibid [10.6].
130 Ibid [10.7].
131 Ibid.
132 *Jouni E. Länsman, Eino Länsman, and the Muotkatunturi Herdsmen's Committee v Finland*, HRC Communication No 1023/2001 (17 March 2005).
133 Ibid [2.3]–[2.4].
134 Ibid [3.1].
135 Ibid [3.2].
136 Ibid [10.3].

The HRC considered the overall effects of development over a period of time and in more than one area on the complainants' right to enjoy their own culture, to determine whether it had been merely limited (not violating Article 27) or denied (thus violating the right).[137] It accordingly considered the effects of past, present and future logging on the complainants' ability to enjoy their culture, through reindeer herding, in community with other members of their group.[138] The HRC acknowledged that logging potentially impacted on reindeer husbandry based on natural pastures, but also identified other factors affecting its economic profitability.[139] It noted further that the overall number of reindeer remained high despite these difficulties. As such, the HRC concluded that the effects of logging 'have not been shown to be serious enough as to amount to a denial of the authors' right to enjoy their own culture in community with other members of their group under article 27'.[140]

The case of *Äärelä and Näkkäläjärvi v Finland* (2001)[141] concerned the effects of logging on land used by Sami members of the Sallivaara Reindeer Herding Co-operative. The Co-operative was entitled to use 286,000 hectares of state-owned land for reindeer husbandry, and argued that plans to log 92 hectares would violate their cultural rights. It was undisputed that the complainants were members of a minority culture and that reindeer husbandry was an essential element of their culture.[142] The issue was whether the logging was so substantial that it denied their right to enjoy their culture. A Finnish lower court had found that the area was essential to the Sami's cultural rights, whereas an appellate court, reviewing conflicting expert evidence, found that Article 27 rights would not be infringed.

The HRC observed that the complainants and other stakeholders were consulted during the planning of the logging and that alterations were duly made.[143] The HRC also recounted the appellate court's reasoning that the particular area was of secondary importance relative to the Collective's lands overall (since it was not the main winter pasture and had not been used as a back-up area in recent years), and that logging there would contribute to the long-term sustainability of reindeer husbandry by allowing the regeneration of ground lichen.[144] The appellate court had also found that the small area to be logged would not involve road works and would have minimal effects on tree lichen.[145] The HRC concluded that it did not have sufficient information to draw independent conclusions on the factual importance of the area to husbandry and its sustainability, and thus on the Article 27 consequences. It accordingly could not conclude that the logging would amount to a failure by Finland to protect the right to enjoy Sami culture.

The situation of Sami reindeer herders was also addressed by the HRC in a case concerning Norway. The complaint in *Jonassen v Norway* (2002), supported by

137 Ibid [10.1]–[10.2].
138 Ibid [10.2].
139 Ibid [10.3].
140 Ibid [10.3].
141 *Äärelä and Näkkäläjärvi v Finland*, HRC Communication No 779/1997 (24 October 2001).
142 Ibid [7.5].
143 Ibid [7.6].
144 Ibid [7.6], [2.4].
145 Ibid [2.4].

Norway's Sami Assembly, the Board of Reindeer Husbandry and the Sami Reindeer Herders Association, was found to be inadmissible for failure to exhaust domestic remedies.[146] The complainants argued that a Norwegian law on reindeer husbandry denied them their traditional rights to graze reindeer in certain areas.[147] They claimed that this infringed their right to enjoy their culture (including its economic or material aspects), as interpreted in the light of Article 1 of the ICCPR (by which peoples are entitled to freely dispose of their natural wealth and resources, and not be deprived of their means of subsistence).[148]

The complainants sought to differentiate their situation from that of the Finnish Sami in *Länsman I and Länsman II*, arguing that their cultural rights were denied by the cumulative exclusion from multiple herding areas, not merely disturbed by isolated acts, and because of the related discriminatory impacts of Norway's justice system.[149] As a result, there was a risk of their entire reindeer husbandry closing down in certain areas because of the expenses involved in adapting to the grazing area exclusions (such as new fences or more labour costs).[150] They further argued that, unlike in *Länsman II*, the Norwegian courts had not specifically considered their cultural rights under Article 27. Instead, the courts had relied upon old judicial precedents from a time when the Sami were discriminated against, subject to forced integration, and reindeer breeding was regarded as a burden on Norwegian farmers.[151]

The complainants also argued that the Norwegian law recognising grazing rights on the basis of immemorial usage violated Article 27 because it did not take into account Sami culture and perceptions of law, or the specific features of reindeer herding (such as sporadic grazing over extensive areas). Rather, the law treated the acquisition of reindeer herding rights in the same way as other property law matters and in the light of the characteristics of ordinary livestock.[152] To legally show that they had used the area for over 100 years was claimed to be impractical, including because of their sporadic lifestyle, the use of materials for their huts and fences that decomposed, and their lack of a written culture.[153]

In yet another Sami case, *Paadar and Alatorvinen Families v Finland* (2014),[154] the complainants were full-time reindeer herders, all of whose animals were slaughtered as a result of decisions by their reindeer herding cooperative. While the cooperative aimed to sustainably manage the reindeer population, the complainants were part of the smaller of two herding villages comprising it and hence in the minority in decision-making. Reindeer herd sizes were calculated based on detailed formulas. The cooperative was a public law entity created by legislation. The complainants

[146] *Jonassen v Norway*, HRC Communication No 942/2000 (25 October 2002), [8.10].
[147] Ibid [2.4]–[2.17].
[148] Ibid [3.3].
[149] Ibid [3.4].
[150] Ibid [3.5].
[151] Ibid [3.6]–[3.7].
[152] Ibid [3.8]–[3.10].
[153] Ibid [3.9], [3.11].
[154] *Paadar and Alatorvinen Families v Finland*, HRC Communication No 2102/2011 (26 March 2012).

were the only families still making a living from herding, and then only by utilising natural pastures. They argued that the forced slaughtering of their reindeer violated their right under Article 27 of the ICCPR to enjoy their indigenous culture in community with other Sami, since it would deprive them of their way of life and livelihood.[155] They also alleged that it contravened Article 26 by discriminating against them on account of their Sami way of herding, ethnicity and opposition to logging on Sami lands. They further claimed that their language (only spoken by 300 people) would disappear with their livelihood. Finally, they argued that they did not receive a fair hearing in the Finnish courts, contrary to Article 14 of the ICCPR.

The HRC accepted that reindeer husbandry is an essential element of Sami culture and an economic activity protected under Article 27.[156] It noted that the case concerned alleged different treatment between Sami members of the cooperative rather than between Sami and non-Sami herders.[157] The HRC was unable to find a violation of either Article 26 or 27 because of limited evidence about the number of calf losses sustained by the complainants, and the number of forced reductions to their herd and the herds of others in the cooperative in previous years.[158] It recalled, however, that cumulative measures may violate Article 27 even if individual acts do not.[159] The HRC also dismissed the Article 14 claim because there was no evidence that the Finnish courts acted arbitrarily or that the proceedings were flawed or denied justice.[160]

Four HRC members dissented, finding that the slaughter of all of the complainants' reindeer constituted a 'particularly grave interference' with their Article 27 rights.[161] It would deprive them of their livelihood, which was essential to enjoy their traditional culture. The dissenting members accepted that it was legitimate to impose reindeer quotas for economic and ecological reasons, to preserve Sami minority culture. However, Finland had not shown that slaughtering all of the complainants' animals was necessary for the continued viability and welfare of the minority as a whole, or that alternative measures could not have achieved the same objectives.

In another natural resources case, *Howard v Canada* (2005),[162] the complainant had taken fish from a river just outside his nation's reserve and was convicted and fined for unlicensed fishing out of season. The issue was whether Ontario's fishing regulations thereby deprived him, as a member of the Hiawatha community of the Mississauga First Nation, of his ability to exercise, individually and in community with other members, his aboriginal fishing rights, contrary to Article 27 of the ICCPR. Fishing was said to be essential to his cultural, spiritual and social survival and the inter-generational transmission of his culture.[163] He also argued that

155 Ibid [3.2].
156 Ibid [7.5].
157 Ibid [7.4].
158 Ibid [7.7].
159 Ibid [7.7].
160 Ibid [7.2].
161 Ibid, Individual Opinion of Committee Members Kälin, Rodriguez Rescia, Seibert-Fohr and Shany.
162 *Howard v Canada*, HRC Communication No 879/1998 (26 July 2005).
163 Ibid [3.1].

Article 27 must be interpreted in the light of Article 1 given his people's domestic legal status as a First Nation.[164]

It was undisputed that he was a member of a minority group (a legally recognised Aboriginal people of Canada) and that fishing was an integral part of his right to enjoy his own culture under Article 27.[165] Canada argued, however, that under a 1923 treaty, his nation had surrendered its fishing rights in the relevant area and that any continuing rights were lawfully extinguished by the clear and plain intention of the Crown.[166] Canada also noted that he was entitled to fish in other areas open for fishing, when areas adjacent to the reserves were closed, as long as he obtained a licence.[167] The complainant objected that there were insufficient fish in adjacent waters, and waters farther afield were not his nation's traditional grounds, such that these formal rights were not culturally or practically meaningful.

The HRC found that it was unable to determine whether the 1923 treaty extinguished the complainant's aboriginal right to fish outside his nation's reserves or adjacent waters.[168] It accepted the right of a state to regulate the cultural activities of minorities, as long as it does not amount to a de facto denial of the right.[169] For this reason, it rejected the argument that requiring a fishing licence violated Article 27. The HRC further accepted that he could fish, by treaty rights, on adjacent waters, or with a licence elsewhere, but the question was whether these possibilities were sufficient to allow him to enjoy his culture.[170]

On this critical point, the HRC noted that the evidence conflicted on the availability of fish in and adjacent to the reserves, and on the extent of his nation's traditional fishing grounds.[171] The HRC noted that the evaluation of facts and evidence is primarily a matter for the domestic courts and that, in this case, these matters had not been brought before the Canadian courts, impeding the HRC's task.[172] As a result, while the HRC understood the complainant's concerns about the small size of the reserves and the limits on fishing elsewhere, it found itself unable to draw independent conclusions on the facts so as to find a violation of Article 27.[173]

In *Poma Poma v Peru* (2006),[174] a family of alpaca and llama farmers in the Andean mountains complained that the state's diversion of groundwater from their land (in the 1950s and 1990s) had dried out the wetlands and destroyed the pastures on which their subsistence activities depended. Thousands of livestock died and poverty resulted. Environmental impact assessments had not been properly carried out. The complainants alleged that the impacts violated their right to self-determination under Article 1(2) of the ICCPR, because it deprived them of their means of survival

164 Ibid [3.5].
165 Ibid [12.4].
166 Ibid [2.1]–[2.8].
167 Ibid [12.6].
168 Ibid [12.3].
169 Ibid [12.7].
170 Ibid [12.8].
171 Ibid [12.9].
172 Ibid [12.10].
173 Ibid [12.11].
174 *Poma Poma v Peru*, HRC Communication No 1457/2006 (27 March 2009).

and livelihood.[175] They also argued that it infringed their right to private and family life under Article 17 of the ICCPR, since it concerned their customs, social relations, language and methods of grazing and caring for animals and way of life for thousands of years.[176] Further, they alleged that their right to equality before the courts under Article 14(1) was violated, because their attempts to seek domestic remedies had not succeeded due to discriminatory treatment of them as indigenous people.[177] Finally, they claimed they were denied an effective remedy, contrary to Article 2 of the ICCPR, because domestic proceedings had failed to bring them justice.

The HRC dismissed the Article 1 claim because individual complaints cannot be made about self-determination.[178] It also held inadmissible the Article 14 claim, because the complainants had not substantiated that they were discriminated against as indigenous.[179] The HRC accepted that Article 2 was violated because domestic remedies were ineffective.[180] Concerning Article 17, the HRC decided that the facts raised issues more related to Article 27 and considered the complaint on that basis.[181]

As regards Article 27, the HRC recalled General Comment No 23,[182] then reiterated that it protects 'the right of persons, in community with others, to engage in economic and social activities which are part of the culture of the community to which they belong'.[183] It noted that it was undisputed that the complainants were part of an 'ethnic minority' and that 'raising llamas is an essential element of the culture of the Aymara community, since it is a form of subsistence and an ancestral tradition handed down from parent to child'.[184] The HRC also recalled that states may legitimately take steps to promote economic development, and that the state's leeway extends to limiting but not denying the rights in Article 27.[185]

On the facts, the HRC emphasised that the diversion of water had led to thousands of livestock dying, which ruined the complainants' way of life and economy, forcing their members to abandon their land and traditional activities.[186] Further, the complainants and the community had not been consulted by the state, independent studies of the impacts had not been carried out, and measures had not been taken to mitigate the adverse effects.[187] The HRC reiterated that 'participation in the decision-making process must be effective, which requires not mere consultation but the free, prior and informed consent of the members of the community'.[188] The HRC concluded that the state had 'substantively compromised the way of life and

[175] Ibid [3.2].
[176] Ibid [3.3].
[177] Ibid [3.4].
[178] Ibid [6.3].
[179] Ibid [6.4].
[180] Ibid [7.8].
[181] Ibid [6.3].
[182] Ibid [7.2].
[183] Ibid [7.3].
[184] Ibid [7.3].
[185] Ibid [7.4].
[186] Ibid [7.5].
[187] Ibid [7.7].
[188] Ibid [7.6].

culture' of the complainants, violating Article 27. The HRC found it unnecessary to determine if Article 17 had also been violated.[189]

In a final case concerning Article 27, *Diergaardt v Namibia* (2000), the HRC did not accept that the Basters' economic activity of cattle raising was sufficiently related to their culture so as to engage the protection of Article 27 at all. The HRC acknowledged that the right of members of a minority to enjoy their culture includes protection of a particular way of life associated with the use of land resources through economic activities, such as hunting and fishing, especially for indigenous peoples.[190] On the facts, however, the HRC found that '[a]lthough the link of the Rehoboth community to the lands in question dates back some 125 years, it is not the result of a relationship that would have given rise to a distinctive culture'.[191] Further, while its historical forms of self-government were distinctive, they were not based on cattle raising. As such, Article 27 had not been violated.[192] The separate claims in this case under Articles 14 (the right to a fair hearing) and 17 (the right to privacy) are considered in the next section.

OTHER CIVIL AND POLITICAL RIGHTS

Non-discrimination

Beyond Article 27, in monitoring states the HRC has drawn attention to the special needs of indigenous peoples in relation to other civil and political rights. The HRC has expressed frequent concern about discrimination against and inequality experienced by indigenous peoples (under Articles 3 and 26 of the ICCPR), whether in state laws or practices, or at the hands of the general population.[193] The HRC has called for the legal prohibition and criminalisation of discrimination and xenophobia against indigenous peoples.[194] It has called on states to take measures to ensure that discrimination is investigated and that victims receive reparation.[195] It has criticised discriminatory special laws for indigenous peoples which are exempt from the state's human rights laws.[196] The HRC has encouraged states to adopt positive measures to promote equal opportunities and non-discriminatory access to all services by indigenous people.[197] It has accepted positive discrimination, for instance to permit 'limitations on the freedom [of non-indigenous people] to settle in areas inhabited by indigenous or minority communities'.[198]

[189] Ibid [7.9].
[190] Ibid [10.6].
[191] Ibid.
[192] Nor was there any separate issue arising under Art 17 of the ICCPR.
[193] HRC, *Concluding Observations: Panama*, UN Doc CCPR/C/PAN/CO/3 (2008), [21].
[194] HRC, *Concluding Observations: Guatemala*, UN Doc CCPR/C/GTM/CO/3 (2012), [10].
[195] HRC, *Concluding Observations: Peru*, UN Doc CCPR/C/PER/CO/5 (2013), [7].
[196] HRC, *Concluding Observations: Canada*, UN Doc CCPR/CAN/CO/5 (2006), [6] (where the Canadian Human Rights Act cannot affect any provision of the Indian Act).
[197] HRC, *Concluding Observations: Paraguay*, UN Doc CCPR/C/PRY/CO/3 (2008), [9].
[198] HRC, *General Comment No 27: Freedom of Movement (Article 12)*, UN Doc CCPR/C/21/Rev.1/Add.9 (2 November 1999), [16].

The HRC dealt with an individual complaint alleging discrimination in *LNP v Argentina* (2011).[199] In that case, a 15-year-old girl belonging to the Qom indigenous group living in the Chaco Province of Argentina was sexually assaulted by three Creole (non-indigenous) youths. She argued that she was discriminated against because of her gender and ethnicity during the ensuing police and medical investigations (Article 26 of the ICCPR); that this treatment was cruel, inhuman or degrading (Article 7); that her rights as a child (Article 24) and to privacy, honour and reputation (Article 17) were violated; and that she was denied equal access to the courts (Article 14(1)) and an effective remedy (Article 2(3)).

The HRC found that Argentina had discriminated against her on the basis of gender and ethnicity, contrary to Article 26.[200] It was uncontested that the police kept her waiting for several hours, 'in tears and with traces of blood on her dress, and that they did not take down any complaint'.[201] At the medical centre, she was subjected to unnecessary painful and irrelevant tests, including a test for her virginity. In court, the girl's supposed 'long-standing defloration' was invoked to supposedly prove that there was no lack of consent to sex. All of the witnesses were asked whether she was a prostitute. This and her sexual life were relied upon by a domestic court. Together the relevant authorities had discriminatorily cast doubt on the morality of the victim.

Such treatment also constituted a failure by the state to protect her as a child under Article 24.[202] Further, her physical and mental suffering before state authorities, including her re-victimisation, in light of her status as a minor, violated Article 7.[203] Irrelevant inquiries by a social worker, medical staff and the court about her sexual life and morality additionally constituted arbitrary interference with her privacy and an unlawful attack on her honour and reputation under Article 17.[204] Her equal access to the courts was denied, contrary to Article 14(1), because she was not informed of her right to sue; she was unable to participate in court proceedings; she was not notified of the acquittal of her attackers; and the trial of her attackers was wholly in Spanish, which she and other witnesses had difficulty communicating in.[205] Finally, she was denied an effective remedy because domestic law prevented her from challenging the above-mentioned judicial acts.[206]

Excessive Use of Force and Arbitrary Law Enforcement

In other areas when monitoring states, the HRC has often been concerned about the excessive use of force against indigenous peoples by law enforcement officials[207]

199 *LNP v Argentina*, HRC Communication No 1610/2007 (18 July 2011).
200 Ibid [13.3].
201 Ibid.
202 Ibid [13.4].
203 Ibid [13.6].
204 Ibid [13.7].
205 Ibid [13.5].
206 Ibid [13.8].
207 HRC, *Concluding Observations: Australia*, UN Doc CCPR/C/AUS/CO/5 (2009), [21]

or security forces,[208] including during demonstrations,[209] in areas of counter-insurgency,[210] by lethal attacks on human rights defenders,[211] or by methods such as electro-muscular disruption devices (EMDs) or 'TASERs'.[212] It has called on states to promptly, effectively and impartially investigate and punish violations.[213] It has further encouraged states to strengthen human rights training of law enforcement officials (including by compliance with the UN Basic Principles on the Use of Force and Firearms by Law Enforcement Officials).[214]

The related problems of arbitrary or mass arrests, and preventive administrative detention, of indigenous peoples, without adequate evidence, has also attracted the HRC's attention.[215] So too have legal systems which produce the over-incarceration of indigenous peoples, or allow for mandatory imprisonment for minor offences, leading to disproportionate punishments.[216] The lack of adequate access to justice generally (under Article 14 of the ICCPR) by indigenous peoples has also been emphasised,[217] including where it results from geographical isolation, language barriers and lack of interpreters, or the insensitivity of legal officials.[218] Indigenous justice systems too have come under scrutiny, with the HRC concerned about their compatibility with the ICCPR,[219] including in respect of the ICCPR's prohibition on corporal punishment.[220]

In the individual complaint of *Jose Vicente et al (Arhuacos Community) v Colombia* (1997),[221] the HRC considered allegations by indigenous victims of violations of the right to life (Article 6 of the ICCPR), freedom from torture (Article 7), and freedom from arbitrary detention (Article 9). The case was brought by two members of the indigenous Arhuaco community in Colombia who were detained and tortured, and relatives of three indigenous leaders who were abducted and killed, all by state officials, on suspicion of their involvement with the guerilla group Ejército de Liberación Nacional (ELN). Although the interpretation of the rights in question did not turn on the indigenous identity of the victims,[222] to a significant extent they were indirectly targeted because of their perceived involvement in organised indigenous

208 HRC, *Concluding Observations: Bolivia*, UN Doc A/52/40 (1997), vol I, [215].
209 HRC, *Concluding Observations: Bolivia*, UN Doc CCPR/C/BOL/CO/3 (2013), [15].
210 HRC, *Concluding Observations: Philippines*, UN Doc CCPR/CO/79/PHL (2003), [15].
211 HRC, *Concluding Observations: Paraguay*, UN Doc CCPR/C/PRY/CO/3 (2008), [15].
212 HRC, *Concluding Observations: Australia*, UN Doc CCPR/C/AUS/CO/5 (2009), [21].
213 HRC, *Concluding Observations: Philippines*, UN Doc CCPR/CO/79/PHL (2003), [8]; HRC, *Concluding Observations: Colombia*, UN Doc CCPR/C/COL/6 (2010), [20]; HRC, *Concluding Observations: Bolivia*, UN Doc CCPR/C/BOL/CO/3 (2013), [15].
214 HRC, *Concluding Observations: Bolivia*, UN Doc CCPR/C/BOL/CO/3 (2013), [15].
215 HRC, *Concluding Observations: Colombia*, UN Doc CCPR/C/COL/6 (2010), [20].
216 HRC, *Concluding Observations: Australia*, UN Doc A/55/40 (2000), vol I, [522].
217 HRC, *Concluding Observations: Australia*, UN Doc CCPR/C/AUS/CO/5 (2009), [25].
218 HRC, *Concluding Observations: Guatemala*, UN Doc CCPR/C/GTM/CO/3 (2012), [26].
219 HRC, *Concluding Observations: Bolivia*, UN Doc CCPR/C/BOL/CO/3 (2013), [22].
220 Ibid [16].
221 *Jose Vicente and Others (Arhuacos Community) v Colombia*, HRC Communication No 612/1995 (29 July 1997), [8.3]–]8.5], [9].
222 This was also the case in *Brough v Australia*, HRC Communication No 1184/2003 (17 March 2006), where an indigenous prisoner alleged violations of Arts 7 (freedom from ill-treatment) and 10 (humane conditions of detention) but his indigenous status was not determinative of or directly relevant to the rights at issue.

resistance. While certain domestic investigations and disciplinary and administrative proceedings had taken place, the HRC found that they were not sufficient to provide effective remedies under Article 2 of the ICCPR, particularly for serious violations such as of the right to life.[223]

Specifically, the HRC noted that Colombian authorities had already found state agents responsible for the disappearance and deaths of the three indigenous leaders and concluded that Colombia had violated their right to life under Article 6.[224] Further, they had been tortured prior to being shot, such that the HRC also found violations of Article 7 (the prohibition on torture or cruel, inhuman or degrading treatment).[225] Domestic investigations also established that the three had been arbitrarily arrested and detained without a warrant or charges being laid, contrary to the freedom from arbitrary detention under Article 9.[226] Domestic inquiries established that the two others had been blind-folded and dunked in a canal by soldiers, also amounting to torture contrary to Article 7.[227] They too were arbitrarily detained contrary to Article 9, but since no charges were brought, there was no violation of the right to a fair trial under Article 14, despite their interrogation by the military without due process or a lawyer.[228] As regards remedies, the HRC found that the state had a duty to thoroughly investigate rights violations and to criminally prosecute and punish those responsible, particularly when the perpetrators had been identified.[229] The state was also required to compensate the victims and the relatives for loss and injury; expedite existing criminal proceedings; and ensure that similar events did not occur in future.[230]

Right to a Fair Hearing (ICCPR, Article 14)

Quite a few individual complaints decided by the HRC have involved alleged denials of the right of indigenous persons to equal access to the courts, or a fair hearing, under Article 14 of the ICCPR. In *Hopu v France* (1997),[231] the complainants claimed that their right to a fair hearing under Article 14(1) of the ICCPR was violated because they were denied access to an independent and impartial tribunal in the determination of land disputes.[232] They argued that the only tribunals competent to adjudicate such matters were indigenous ones, which were not available to them. The HRC noted that they could have brought their case before a French tribunal but chose not to do so.[233] Further, a tribunal had already determined the dispute over the land as long ago as 1961. That decision was not appealed by the

223 *Jose Vicente and others* (n 221) [8.2].
224 Ibid [8.3].
225 Ibid [8.4].
226 Ibid [8.6].
227 Ibid [8.5].
228 Ibid [8.7].
229 Ibid [8.8].
230 Ibid [10].
231 *Hopu and Bessert v France*, HRC Communication No 549/1993 (29 July 1997), [10.2]–[10.3].
232 Ibid [10.2].
233 Ibid.

previous owners and no other step was taken by the complainants to challenge the land's ownership or use, except by peaceful occupation. As such, the HRC found no violation of Article 14(1).

In *Diergaardt v Namibia* (2000), the HRC held that the complainants were also unable to show how being forced to use English (which was not their mother tongue and in which they were not fluent) during court proceedings adversely affected their right to a fair hearing under Article 14(1) of the ICCPR.[234] On the other hand, the HRC held that a Namibian government instruction to public servants not to respond to the complainant's communications in the Afrikaans language, 'even when they are perfectly capable of doing so', possibly targeted them and violated Article 26 of the ICCPR (equality before the law and equal protection of law). Six members of the HRC dissented on this point,[235] mainly on the basis that Afrikaans was not treated differently from other tribal languages in a state in which there was only one official language (English).

In *Mahuika and Others v New Zealand* (2000),[236] the complainants' court challenges were discontinued following a national negotiated settlement of Maori fishing rights, and a bar on court challenges in the new law implementing the settlement. They argued that this violated their right to access the courts for the determination of rights and obligations in a suit at law under Article 14(1) of the ICCPR. The HRC noted that ordinarily it would be objectionable if a court discontinued pending cases or a statute barred future challenges.[237] However, the HRC concluded that, in the circumstances, the discontinuance and the bar occurred in the framework of a national negotiated settlement of pending court claims that had been adjourned pending the settlement, and which the settlement aimed to resolve.[238] As such, there was no violation of Article 14(1). It was also noted that other aspects of fisheries rights could still be litigated, such as commercial quota allocations and customary rights.

In *Äärelä and Näkkäläjärui v Finland* (2001),[239] which concerned the effects of logging on Sami reindeer herding, the complainants argued that the award of substantial costs against them in unsuccessful domestic litigation to vindicate their cultural rights violated their right to equal access to the courts under Article 14(1) of the ICCPR. While the HRC found no violation of their cultural rights under Article 27, it nonetheless held that 'a rigid duty under law to award costs to a winning party may have a deterrent effect on the ability of persons who allege their rights under the Covenant have been violated to pursue a remedy before the courts'.[240] On the facts the HRC found that awarding costs without a discretion to consider the impact on the complainants or the effect on access to the courts by them or similarly situated

234 *Diergaardt and Others v Namibia*, HRC Communication No 760/1997 (25 July 2000), [10.9].

235 Ibid, Separate Opinions of Abdalfattah Amor, Nisuke Ando, PN Bhagwati, Lord Colville, Maxwell Yalden and Rajsoomer Lallah.

236 *Mahuika and others v New Zealand*, HRC Communication No 547/1993 (27 October 2000), [11].

237 Ibid [9.10]–[9.11].

238 Ibid.

239 *Äärelä and Näkkäläjärui v Finland*, HRC Communication No 779/1997 (24 October 2001).

240 Ibid [7.2].

complainants violated Article 14(1) in conjunction with Article 2 (the right to an effective remedy).[241] It also noted that intervening amendments to Finland's judicial procedure law had given the courts such a discretion. The HRC recommended that the costs already paid be restituted to the complainants, and that no further recovery of costs against them be pursued.[242]

The complainant also argued that the domestic court's procedure was unfair because it required an oral hearing and denied an on-site inspection.[243] The HRC stated a general principle that domestic courts are entitled to determine their own procedures and that a complainant must demonstrate unfairness in the particular case.[244] On the facts, the HRC found that the oral hearing was considered necessary to determine the reliability and weight to be accorded to oral testimony and that this was not manifestly arbitrary or a denial of justice.[245] Further, the refusal of an on-site inspection (and reliance on a lower court's earlier inspection) did not inject unfairness into the hearing or demonstrably alter the outcome. Hence the HRC found no violation of Article 14(1) on these counts.

A final claim was that the complainants were denied a fair trial because they were denied an opportunity to comment on a brief submitted by the forestry authority after the expiry of filing time limits.[246] On this point the HRC noted that 'it is a fundamental duty of the courts to ensure equality between the parties, including the ability to contest all the argument and evidence adduced by the other party'.[247] The domestic court had found it 'manifestly unnecessary' to invite the complainants to respond, while having 'special reason' to take account of the submission by one party before deciding in its favour. The HRC concluded that the court's failure to provide a 'full opportunity to each party to challenge the submissions of the other' violated Article 14(1). As a result, the HRC further found that Finland was obliged to reconsider the complainants' claims.[248]

Right to Take Part in Public Affairs (ICCPR, Article 25)

Two individual complaints decided by the HRC have dealt with alleged violations of the right to take part in public affairs under Article 25 of the ICCPR. In *Marshall (Mikmaq Tribal Society) v Canada* (1991),[249] representatives of the Mikmaq tribal society in Nova Scotia claimed that Canada's refusal to invite them to constitutional conferences, the purpose of which was to identify and define aboriginal and treaty rights, violated their right to take part in public affairs, directly or through freely chosen representatives, under Article 25(a) of the ICCPR. Around 600 other aboriginal groups were represented in the consultations through four national associations.

241 Ibid.
242 Ibid [8.2].
243 Ibid [7.3].
244 Ibid.
245 Ibid.
246 Ibid [7.4].
247 Ibid.
248 Ibid [8.2].
249 *AD (Mikmaq Tribal Society) v Canada*, HRC Communication No 78/1980 (29 July 1984).

The HRC first found that the constitutional conferences involving aboriginal representatives constituted 'the conduct of public affairs' within the meaning of Article 25(a), even though constitutional conferences normally only involved elected government officials.[250] The HRC noted, however, that Article 25(a) does not entitle every citizen to take part directly or freely choose their representatives, but rather permits the legal and constitutional system of a state to provide for the modalities of participation.[251] The conduct of public affairs is ordinarily the task of elected representatives and appointed public officials, and variably affects the whole population, parts of it or specific social groups.[252]

The HRC acknowledged that prior consultations (such as public hearings with interested groups) are often provided for by law or policy, but found that Article 25(a) 'cannot be understood as meaning that any directly affected group, large or small, has the unconditional right to choose the modalities of participation in the conduct of public affairs'.[253] The HRC concluded that Canada's failure to invite Mikmaq representatives did not infringe Article 25(a), and that participation and representation at the conferences had not been unreasonably restricted.[254]

In *Diergaardt v Namibia* (2000), the HRC found that the termination of self-government, and the diminished political influence of the Basters as a result of becoming a minority in the newly independent Namibia, did not violate the individual right to take part in the conduct of public affairs directly or through freely chosen representatives (under Article 25(a) of the ICCPR), or the right of equal access to public service (Article 25(c)).[255] One HRC member, while agreeing with the decision, believed that the HRC unduly emphasised the individual nature of rights of political participation under Article 25.[256] He believed that members of minorities and indigenous peoples may additionally require forms of local, regional or cultural autonomy. In this respect he reiterated the HRC majority's observation that the right of self-determination under Article 1 affects the interpretation of Article 25.

Women's, Children's and Family Rights

In monitoring states, the situation of indigenous women has been of special interest to the HRC. It has criticised discrimination and inequality,[257] including in relation to participation in political life,[258] matrimonial real property on reserve lands,[259] and in the harsh working conditions, low pay and excessive hours experienced by

250 Ibid [5.3].
251 Ibid [5.4].
252 Ibid [5.5].
253 Ibid.
254 Ibid [6].
255 Ibid [10.8].
256 *Diergaardt and Others v Namibia*, HRC Communication No 760/1997 (25 July 2000), Individual Opinion of Martin Scheinin (concurring), [15]–[26].
257 HRC, *Concluding Observations: Guatemala*, UN Doc CCPR/C/GTM/CO/3 (2012), [8].
258 HRC, *Concluding Observations: Bolivia*, UN Doc CCPR/C/BOL/CO/3 (2013), [8].
259 HRC, *Concluding Observations: Canada*, UN Doc CCPR/CAN/CO/5 (2006), [22].

indigenous domestic workers.[260] States have been encouraged to develop policies which include 'a specific perspective in favour of' indigenous women, along with special programmes for them.[261] The HRC has also addressed violence against indigenous women, including higher rates of domestic violence[262] and forced sterilisation.[263]

Likewise the HRC has regularly expressed concern at the situation of indigenous children. It has criticised the lack of registration at birth,[264] as well as procedural barriers to later registration.[265] It has also been alarmed by child labour,[266] and the continuing, unremedied effects of a state policy for the removal of indigenous children from their parents (known as the 'Stolen Generations' in Australia).[267] In relation to the latter, the HRC welcomed a parliamentary apology to the victims but regretted that the state refused to grant reparation, including compensation.[268]

Family rights were the subject of a complaint in *Hopu and Bessert v France* (1997).[269] Article 23 of the ICCPR requires the protection of the family as the fundamental unit of society. In this case, some Polynesian Tahitians claimed that their family rights would be violated by the building of a hotel on their ancestral burial grounds, which represented an important place in their history, culture, family life and identity.[270] For a similar reason they also alleged a violation of the right to privacy in Article 17 of the ICCPR, which protects individuals against arbitrary or unlawful interference in their privacy, family, home or correspondence. France countered that the complainants could not prove a kinship link to the interred remains.

The HRC found that the failure to show a direct kinship link was not fatal where the burial grounds pre-dated European settlement and were recognised as containing the forbears of the current Polynesian population.[271] Further, the HRC held that the term 'family' must 'be given a broad interpretation so as to include all those comprising the family as understood in the society in question. It follows that cultural traditions should be taken into account when defining the term "family" in a specific situation'.[272] The HRC found that the construction of the hotel unreasonably interfered in the complainant's privacy and family life, with no evidence that France had taken into account the importance of the burial grounds. The HRC did not, however, separately explain its reasoning as to the application of Article 17. Four members of the HRC dissented on the basis that there was no evidence that the complainants' own family members were in the burial ground of the indigenous

260 HRC, *Concluding Observations: El Salvador*, UN Doc CCPR/C/SLV/CO/6 (2010), [11].
261 HRC, *Concluding Observations: Guatemala*, UN Doc CCPR/C/GTM/CO/3 (2012), [3].
262 HRC, *Concluding Observations: Australia*, UN Doc CCPR/C/AUS/CO/5 (2009), [17].
263 HRC, *Concluding Observations: Peru*, UN Doc A/56/40 (2001), vol I, [76(21)].
264 HRC, *Concluding Observations: Honduras*, UN Doc CCPR/C/HND/CO/1 (2006), [18]; HRC, *Concluding Observations: Panama*, UN Doc CCPR/C/PAN/CO/3 (2008), [19].
265 Ibid [26].
266 HRC, *Concluding Observations: Honduras*, UN Doc CCPR/C/HND/CO/1 (2006), [12].
267 HRC, *Concluding Observations: Australia*, UN Doc A/55/40 (28 July 2000), [512]–[513].
268 HRC, *Concluding Observations: Australia*, UN Doc CCPR/C/AUS/CO/5 (2009), [6], [15].
269 *Hopu and Bessert v France*, HRC Communication No 549/1993 (29 July 1997), [10.3].
270 Ibid.
271 Ibid.
272 Ibid.

group as a whole.[273] They also thought that the issues would be more appropriately dealt with as cultural rights under Article 27, which was precluded by a French reservation to that treaty provision.

Social and Economic Rights

Finally, although the HRC is mandated to monitor civil and political rights, it has occasionally emphasised how the denial of socio-economic rights (which are separately governed by the ICESCR) can undermine civil and political rights under the ICCPR. Thus the HRC observed that poverty and lack of education can impair civil and political rights.[274] In this vein it has drawn attention to inadequacies in: healthcare (including sickness and alcoholism);[275] education (including language discrimination, illiteracy and school enrolment and drop-out rates);[276] housing and homelessness;[277] the needs of forcibly displaced persons;[278] and employment[279] (including 'de facto exclusion of indigenous workers in all areas, including land ownership, access to basic services, labour conditions, access to the formal economy and justice, participation in decision-making forums and State institutions and representation in the media and in the public debate'[280]).

The next chapter begins by examining how the UN Committee on Economic, Social and Cultural Rights has more fully considered socio-economic rights in their own right as they apply to indigenous peoples. As is apparent, however, from the foregoing discussion, the HRC has also been able to protect indigenous social, economic and cultural life, including attachment to ancestral lands and resources, through its expansive and group-oriented interpretation of minority cultural rights in Article 27 of the ICCPR, in concert with its application of the right to self-determination to indigenous communities.

CONCLUSION

In the absence of indigenous-specific standards in most major human rights treaties, indigenous peoples have sought to advance their interests by utilising general human rights law. In some areas, the UN Human Rights Committee has tailored the general standards of the ICCPR to address the special circumstances of indigenous peoples. Such adaptation has been most pronounced in respect of the right

[273] Ibid, Individual Opinion of Kretzmer, Buergenthal, Ando and Colville, [4]–[5].

[274] HRC, *Concluding Observations: Paraguay*, UN Doc A/50/40 (1995), [213].

[275] HRC, *Concluding Observations: United States of America*, UN Doc A/50/40 (1995), [290].

[276] HRC, *Concluding Observations: Brazil*, UN Doc A/51/40 (1996), vol I, [337]; HRC, *Concluding Observations: Japan*, UN Doc A/54/40 (1999), vol I, [156].

[277] HRC, *Concluding Observations: Australia*, UN Doc CCPR/C/AUS/CO/5 (2009), [18].

[278] HRC, *Concluding Observations: Colombia*, UN Doc CCPR/C/COL/6 (2010), [23].

[279] HRC, *Concluding Observations: New Zealand*, UN Doc A/50/40 (1995), [182]; HRC, *Concluding Observations: Guatemala*, UN Doc A/51/40 (1996), vol I, [221].

[280] HRC, *Concluding Observations: Guatemala*, UN Doc CCPR/C/GTM/CO/3 (2012), [10].

of self-determination (Article 1) and the right of minorities to take part in cultural life (Article 27). The HRC has extended entitlement to self-determination beyond colonised and occupied peoples to encompass indigenous peoples, while qualifying the content of the right to preclude secession and independent statehood. The HRC has also expansively interpreted minority cultural rights to protect indigenous interests in land and resources—even if its application of such rights has been rather cautious in practice, and even if minority rights are less extensive than those owed to indigenous peoples under general international law. The HRC has also addressed the special circumstances of indigenous peoples in relation to certain other civil and political rights and the socio-economic causes of violations of such rights. The next chapter explores how other UN treaty bodies have considered indigenous peoples' issues and claims.

3

Other UN Human Rights Treaty Bodies and Indigenous Peoples

BEYOND THE UN Human Rights Committee, considered in the previous chapter, most other UN treaty committees have considered indigenous issues when monitoring state compliance with obligations under the respective conventions. Individual complaints can be made under eight of the nine treaties (including the International Covenant on Civil and Political Rights (ICCPR), dealt with in the previous chapter), with the exception being that on migrant workers, which has not yet entered into force. Some of the complaints procedures are relatively new and have yet to produce a body of jurisprudence.[1]

The committees which have dealt most extensively with indigenous issues thus far are the UN Committee on Economic, Social and Cultural Rights (CESCR) (concerning the International Covenant on Economic, Social and Cultural Rights 1966 (ICESCR)) and the UN Committee on the Elimination of Racial Discrimination (CERD) (concerning the International Covenant on the Elimination of All Forms of Racial Discrimination 1965 (ICERD)). The CESCR has given particular attention to self-determination and cultural rights, but also the broader spectrum of economic and social rights. The CERD has focused on racial discrimination, non-recognition of indigenous groups, land and natural resources, and law enforcement and access to justice, and to a lesser extent has also highlighted issues of culture and language, political participation and socio-economic rights.

Significant attention to indigenous issues in more specialised areas has been devoted by a number of other committees. The Committee on the Elimination of Discrimination Against Women (CEDAW Committee) has highlighted issues of gender discrimination, violence against women, access to justice, political participation, and economic and social rights (including property rights). The Committee on the Rights of the Child (CRC) has been concerned with discrimination and violence against children, children's rights in the family, law and justice affecting children, land rights, and economic, social and cultural rights. The Committee Against Torture (CAT) has had a narrower emphasis on torture and ill-treatment of indigenous peoples, including all forms of violence, abuses related to detention, labour exploitation, and the accountability of perpetrators. The remaining UN treaty committees,

[1] For example, the Optional Protocol to the ICESCR entered into force in 2013 (and had only 21 states parties as of 2015) and the Optional Protocol to the Convention on the Rights of the Child entered into force in 2014 (and had 20 states parties as of 2015).

concerning enforced disappearances, disabilities and migrant workers, have thus far given less attention to, or had less opportunity to consider, indigenous issues.

UN COMMITTEE ON ECONOMIC, SOCIAL AND CULTURAL RIGHTS

Economic, social and cultural rights bear special importance for the many indigenous peoples who have been marginalised from economic opportunities and alienated from their ancestral lands and resources. The CESCR has frequently been attentive to indigenous peoples in its general interpretations of ICESCR rights and in monitoring states' reports on implementation. While the CESCR has not defined indigenous peoples, it has repeatedly invoked the International Labour Organization's Convention No 169 concerning Indigenous and Tribal Peoples in Independent Countries as a key normative framework,[2] and encouraged states parties to the ICESCR to ratify it.[3] More recently it has also endorsed the UN Declaration on the Rights of Indigenous Peoples 2007,[4] which may be expected to influence the CESCR over time.

While the CESCR has considered indigenous peoples across the spectrum of social, economic and cultural rights, it has most often focused on the right to take part in cultural life (ICESCR, Article 15) and the right to economic self-determination (Article 1). In general it has also been concerned about the cross-cutting issue of discrimination in respect of all ICESCR rights,[5] given that discrimination often leads to extreme poverty and inadequate access to education, housing and health services.[6] The various grounds of discrimination enumerated in the ICESCR are sufficiently broad to encompass indigenous peoples as a group, namely race, colour, language, religion, national origin, birth, social origin or 'other status'. The CESCR has criticised state non-recognition of an indigenous people as a form of discrimination,[7] including lack of constitutional recognition[8] or formal recognition for participation

[2] CESCR, *Concluding Observations: Colombia*, UN Doc E/C.12/COL/CO/5 (2010), [9].

[3] CESCR, *Concluding Observations: Cambodia*, UN Doc E/C.12/KHM/CO/1 (2009), [16]; CESCR, *Concluding Observations: Democratic Republic of Congo*, UN Doc E/C.12/COD/CO/4 (2009), [14]; CESCR, *Concluding Observations: Sweden*, UN Doc E/C.12/SWE/CO/5 (2008), [15]; CESCR, *Concluding Observations: Japan*, UN Doc E/C.12/1/Add.67 (2001), [45]; CESCR, *Concluding Observations: Morocco*, UN Doc E/C.12/1/Add.55 (2000), [41]; CESCR, *Concluding Observations: Panama*, UN Doc E/2002/22 (2001), [466]; CESCR, *Concluding Observations: Sweden* UN Doc E/2002/22 (2001), [724]; CESCR, *Concluding Observations: Chile*, UN Doc E/2005/22 (2004), [559]. See ILO Convention No 169 concerning Indigenous and Tribal Peoples in Independent Countries (adopted 27 June 1989, entered into force 5 September 1991, 1650 UNTS 383).

[4] CESCR, *General Comment No 21: Right of Everyone to Take Part in Cultural Life (Article 15(1)(a))*, UN Doc E/C.12/GC/21 (21 December 2009), [7]; CESCR, *Concluding Observations: Brazil*, UN Doc E/C.12/BRA/CO/2 (2009).

[5] CESCR, *General Comment No 20: Non-discrimination in Economic, Social and Cultural Rights (Article 2(2))*, UN Doc E/C.12/GC/20 (2 July 2009), [18].

[6] CESCR, *Concluding Observations: Bolivia*, UN Doc E/C.12/1/Add.60 (2001), [14]. See also, for example, CESCR, *Concluding Observations: Chile*, UN Doc E/C.12/1/Add.105 (2004), [13], and [33]–[34]; CESCR, *Concluding Observations: Guatemala*, UN Doc E/1997/22 (1996), [128].

[7] CESCR, *Concluding Observations: Bolivia*, UN Doc E/C.12/1/Add.60 (2001), [14]; see also CESCR, *Concluding Observations: Honduras*, UN Doc E/2002/22 (2001), [140].

[8] CESCR, *Concluding Observations: Chile*, UN Doc E/2005/22 (2004), [540].

in decision-making.[9] It has called generally for affirmative action for indigenous peoples in economic, social and cultural rights.[10]

Right of Self-Determination (ICESCR, Article 1)

More than the HRC under the ICCPR, the CESCR has often addressed the right of indigenous peoples to self-determination under Article 1 of the ICESCR, focusing on its economic aspects. Most commonly this has concerned the adverse impacts on indigenous lands, economic activities and cultural practices of public or private exploitation of natural resources. By way of example, the CESCR found an infringement of Article 1 as a result of the granting of economic land concessions in protected forest areas in Cambodia, resulting in environmental degradation, unsustainable and inequitable development, displacement of indigenous peoples without compensation or resettlement, and loss of livelihoods from land and forest resources.[11] The CESCR has emphasised that development projects must not deprive indigenous peoples of their land and resource rights and should advance their rights and alleviate poverty.[12]

The CESCR has directed much of its criticism at states that have failed to implement existing national laws on indigenous rights. It thus highlighted Cambodia's failure to apply a domestic land law providing communal land title for indigenous peoples, resulting in adverse impacts from mining and oil operations on ancestral lands and resources.[13] The CESCR also raised Article 1 in criticising the Philippines' failure to implement laws protecting indigenous peoples and their lands from the adverse effects of natural resource exploitation, especially mining.[14] It was further concerned that domestic laws conflicted, enabling other property rights to undermine indigenous rights.[15] The CESCR also found that illegal logging in the Democratic Republic of Congo, contrary to forestry laws and a moratorium on concessions (pending the mapping and zoning of forests), engaged Article 1 because it adversely affected the forest environment, resources and lands on which indigenous peoples depended, and their traditional forest management practices.[16]

The CESCR was also concerned at Brazil's slow progress in land reform and demarcation, affecting indigenous self-determination under Article 1.[17] Likewise the 'precarious situation' of indigenous peoples in the Russian Federation was found by the CESCR to raise Article 1 issues, including because existing laws to demarcate

[9] CESCR, *Concluding Observations: Nepal*, UN Doc E/C.12/NPL/CO/2 (2008), [30].
[10] CESCR, *Concluding Observations: Guatemala*, UN Doc E/1997/22 (1996), [140].
[11] CESCR, *Concluding Observations: Cambodia*, UN Doc E/C.12/KHM/CO/1 (2009), [15].
[12] CESCR, *Concluding Observations: Democratic Republic of Congo*, UN Doc E/C.12/COD/CO/4 (2009), [14].
[13] CESCR, *Concluding Observations: Cambodia*, UN Doc E/C.12/KHM/CO/1 (2009), [16].
[14] CESCR, *Concluding Observations: Philippines*, UN Doc E/C.12/PHL/CO/4 (2008), [16].
[15] Ibid.
[16] CESCR, *Concluding Observations: Democratic Republic of Congo*, UN Doc E/C.12/COD/CO/4 (2009), [14].
[17] CESCR, *Concluding Observations: Brazil*, UN Doc E/C.12/BRA/CO/2 (2009), [9].

and protect indigenous territory and lands had not been implemented, in turn risking depriving indigenous peoples of their means of subsistence.[18]

The CESCR has also criticised states where laws to protect indigenous rights are lacking or inadequate. It thus noted Sweden's failure to resolve Sami land rights, and provide for their legislative protection in consultation with them, as adversely affecting Sami culture and way of life, particularly reindeer herding, thus raising self-determination issues under Article 1.[19]

A particular focus has been concern at absent or inadequate laws or practices for consultation with, and the participation of, indigenous peoples in decisions affecting them in areas relevant to self-determination.[20] It thus found Cambodian laws for prior consultation to be insufficient, as well as not being formulated through consultation with indigenous peoples.[21] It specifically called for environmental and social impact assessments and consultations with affected communities as regards proposed resource developments.[22]

The CESCR has also criticised states where consultation and participation opportunities have been inadequate in practice. It thus noted the adverse impacts of infrastructure, development and mega-mining projects on indigenous peoples in Colombia, pursued without accurate information, consultation or free, prior and informed consent, and which prejudiced self-determination.[23] It also highlighted that indigenous representatives in the Democratic Republic of Congo were excluded from a review of illicit logging contracts.[24] It emphasised that future concessions there should only be conducted after comprehensive studies, with indigenous participation, into the social, spiritual, cultural and environmental impacts.[25]

Finally, the CESCR has criticised the effects of a state's economic choices in its international relations where these have adversely affected indigenous self-determination. It thus highlighted the negative impacts of bilateral and multilateral free trade agreements on the ICESCR rights of indigenous people in Colombia.[26] It recommended that the state take into account such rights in trade agreements and mitigate negative impacts.

Cultural Rights (ICESCR, Article 15)

Article 15 of the ICESCR recognises a right of 'everyone' to take part in cultural life and is thus broader in application than minority cultural rights under Article 27 of the ICCPR. The CESCR's most elaborate comments on indigenous peoples are

[18] CESCR, *Concluding Observations: Russian Federation*, UN Doc E/C.12/1/Add.94 (2003), [11], [39].
[19] CESCR, *Concluding Observations: Sweden*, UN Doc E/C.12/SWE/CO/5 (2008), [15].
[20] CESCR, *Concluding Observations: Cambodia*, UN Doc E/C.12/KHM/CO/1 (2009), [15].
[21] Ibid.
[22] Ibid.
[23] CESCR, *Concluding Observations: Colombia*, UN Doc E/C.12/COL/CO/5 (2010), [9].
[24] CESCR, *Concluding Observations: Democratic Republic of Congo*, UN Doc E/C.12/COD/CO/4 (2009), [14].
[25] Ibid.
[26] CESCR, *Concluding Observations: Colombia*, UN Doc E/C.12/COL/CO/5 (2010), [10].

in General Comment No 21 (2009) concerning this right. The CESCR observed that '[t]he decision by a person whether or not to exercise the right to take part in cultural life individually, or in association with others, is a cultural choice and, as such, should be recognized, respected and protected on the basis of equality'.[27] It emphasised that indigenous peoples' cultural life 'may be strongly communal' or 'can only be expressed and enjoyed as a community'.[28] This communal dimension is considered 'indispensable to their existence, well-being and full development, and includes the right to the lands, territories and resources which they have traditionally owned, occupied or otherwise used or acquired'.[29]

In consequence, states must respect and protect indigenous peoples' 'cultural values and rights associated with their ancestral lands and their relationship with nature ... to prevent the degradation of their particular way of life, including their means of subsistence, the loss of their natural resources and, ultimately, their cultural identity'.[30] In particular, states must enable indigenous peoples 'to own, develop, control and use their communal lands, territories and resources, and, where they have been otherwise inhabited or used without their free and informed consent, take steps to return these lands and territories'.[31] States must further respect the free access of indigenous peoples to their culture and heritage and spiritual relationship to land.[32]

The CESCR further acknowledged the right of indigenous peoples to collectively 'maintain, control, protect and develop their cultural heritage, traditional knowledge and traditional cultural expressions'.[33] Also requiring protection is 'the manifestations of their sciences, technologies and cultures, including human and genetic resources, seeds, medicines, knowledge of the properties of fauna and flora, oral traditions, literature, designs, sports and traditional games, and visual and performing arts'.[34] Indigenous peoples must be able to participate in science-related decision-making,[35] including as regards the effect of intellectual property regimes on access to medicines, and the assertion of intellectual property rights over the traditional knowledge of indigenous peoples (known as 'bio-prospecting').[36]

Under Article 15(1)(c) of the ICESCR, states must specifically protect the scientific, literary or artistic productions of indigenous peoples, including their 'knowledge, innovations and practices', which are often expressions of their cultural heritage and traditional knowledge.[37] This includes protection from illegal or unjust

[27] CESCR, *General Comment No 21* (n 4), [7].
[28] Ibid [36].
[29] Ibid.
[30] Ibid.
[31] Ibid.
[32] Ibid [49(d)].
[33] Ibid [37].
[34] Ibid.
[35] Human Rights Council, *Report of the Special Rapporteur in the Field of Cultural Rights on the Right to Enjoy the Benefits of Scientific Progress and its Applications*, UN Doc A/HRC/20/26 (14 May 2012), [22], [43].
[36] Ibid [64].
[37] CESCR, *General Comment No 17: The Right of Everyone to Benefit from the Protection of the Moral and Material Interests Resulting from any Scientific, Literary or Artistic Production of which He or She is the Author (Article 15(1)(c))*, UN Doc E/C.12/GC/17 (12 January 2006), [32].

exploitation of their lands, territories and resources.[38] It also includes intellectual property protection of individual or collective authorship, and prevention of, and compensation for, unauthorised use.[39] States must respect the principle of free, prior and informed consent of indigenous authors and the oral or other customary forms of transmitting scientific, literary or artistic production, and provide for the collective administration of the sharing of benefits of productions.[40] Information about laws and policies to protect authors must also be accessible to indigenous peoples, including in their languages.[41]

In implementing the right to culture under Article 15, the CESCR has observed that it is a 'minimum core obligation' of states to respect the principle of free, prior and informed consent of indigenous peoples in all matters covered by their cultural rights, especially where the preservation of cultural resources is at risk.[42] States must also encourage the participation of indigenous peoples in the design and implementation of laws and policies that affect them.[43] States should further promote education and public awareness about indigenous rights amongst indigenous peoples and the population.[44]

According to the CESCR, the right to take part in cultural life requires the 'appropriateness' of cultural programmes, namely 'the realization of a specific human right in a way that is pertinent and suitable to a given cultural modality or context, that is, respectful of the culture and cultural rights of individuals and communities, including minorities and indigenous peoples'.[45] In this regard states should 'take into account, as far as possible, cultural values attached to, inter alia, food and food consumption, the use of water, the way health and education services are provided and the way housing is designed and constructed'.[46]

Importantly, even in times of 'severe resource constraints, the most disadvantaged and marginalized individuals and groups can and indeed must be protected by the adoption of relatively low-cost targeted programmes'.[47] The obligation to protect cultural rights under Article 15 requires states to prevent third parties from interfering in such rights, including through the illegal or unjust exploitation of their lands, territories and resources by private or transnational enterprises and corporations.[48]

The concerns set out by the CESCR in General Comment No 21 are reflected in various ways in its Concluding Observations on states' reports. The CESCR was thus concerned about the exploitation of forest resources in the Democratic Republic of the Congo, which 'negatively affected the lands and the way of life of numerous indigenous peoples' and impeded 'the enjoyment of their rights as well as their

38 CESCR, *General Comment No 21* (n 4), [50(c)].
39 Ibid [32], [45].
40 CESCR, *General Comment No 17* (n 37), [32].
41 Ibid [18(b)(iii)].
42 CESCR, *General Comment No 21* (n 4), [37], [55].
43 Ibid [55].
44 Ibid [53].
45 Ibid [16(e)].
46 Ibid [16].
47 Ibid [16(b)].
48 Ibid [50]. See also CESCR, *Statement on the Obligations of States Parties Regarding the Corporate Sector and Economic, Social and Cultural Rights*, UN Doc E/C.12/2011/1 (20 May 2011).

material and spiritual relationship with nature and, ultimately their own cultural identity'.[49] It expressed similar concerns about resource exploitation in Chad.[50] In both cases, the CESCR urged the states to adopt laws and measures to protect indigenous lands and cultural identities.[51] As in other areas, decisions or measures affecting indigenous cultural life, including their lands and resources, must only be taken after consultation and with the prior informed consent of indigenous peoples.[52]

The CESCR has often emphasised the need to preserve endangered indigenous languages[53] in order to protect indigenous peoples' cultural life, identity and rights. It has called on states to promote indigenous languages;[54] make available resources for preserving them;[55] and criticised inadequate language programmes.[56] Bilingual education in schools has been identified as a particularly important measure for sustaining indigenous languages and thereby indigenous cultures.[57] In addition, indigenous peoples should have access to judicial and administrative procedures or dealings with public authorities in their own languages.[58] The CESCR has also requested states to disseminate the ICESCR, and to inform indigenous peoples about their rights, in indigenous languages.[59]

The protection of indigenous intellectual property rights under Article 15 has also attracted the CESCR's attention. It has criticised states where collective authorship of indigenous traditional knowledge and cultural heritage is not protected by copyright or other laws.[60] It has accordingly recommended that states adopt legislation to protect collective authorship and to prevent the unauthorised use by third parties of scientific, literary and artistic productions of indigenous peoples.[61] It has further recommended that states 'should develop a special intellectual property regime that protects the collective rights of the indigenous peoples, including their scientific products and traditional knowledge and traditional medicine'.[62] Opening a registry

[49] CESCR, *Concluding Observations: Democratic Republic of the Congo*, UN Doc E/C.12/COD/CO/4 (2009), [36].

[50] CESCR, *Concluding Observations: Chad*, UN Doc E/C.12/TCD/CO/3 (2009), [35]. See also CESCR, *Concluding Observations: Sweden*, UN Doc E/C.12/SWE/CO/5 (2008), [15]; CESCR, *Concluding Observations: Australia*, UN Doc E/C.12/AUS/CO/4 (2009), [32]; CESCR, *Concluding Observations: Madagascar*, UN Doc E/C.12/MDG/CO/2 (2009), [33].

[51] CESCR, *Concluding Observations: Democratic Republic of the Congo*, UN Doc E/C.12/COD/CO/4 (2009), [36]; CESCR, *Concluding Observations: Chad*, UN Doc E/C.12/TCD/CO/3 (2009), [35].

[52] CESCR, *Concluding Observations: Colombia*, UN Doc E/2002/22 (2001), [782]; CESCR, *Concluding Observations: Ecuador*, UN Doc E/2005/22 (2004), [278], [301].

[53] See, eg, CESCR, *Concluding Observations: Canada*, UN Doc E/C.12/CAN/CO/4 (2006), [33]; CESCR, *Concluding Observations: Australia*, UN Doc E/C.12/AUS/CO/4 (1999), [33].

[54] CESCR, *Concluding Observations: Suriname*, UN Doc E/1996/22 (1995), [163].

[55] CESCR, *Concluding Observations: Mexico*, UN Doc E/1994/23 (1993), [236].

[56] Ibid [233].

[57] CESCR, *Concluding Observations: Australia*, UN Doc E/C.12/AUS/CO/4 (2009), [33]; CESCR, *Concluding Observations: Guatemala*, UN Doc E/C.12/1/Add.93 (2003), [45]; CESCR, *Concluding Observations: Cambodia*, UN Doc E/C.12/KHM/CO/1 (2009), [34].

[58] CESCR, *Concluding Observations: Honduras*, UN Doc E/2002/22 (2001), [159]; CESCR, *Concluding Observations: Bolivia*, UN Doc E/2002/22 (2001), [300]; CESCR, *Concluding Observations: Guatemala*, UN Doc E/C.12/1/Add.93 (2003), [45].

[59] CESCR, *Concluding Observations: Paraguay*, UN Doc E/1997/22 (1996), [80]; CESCR, *Concluding Observations: Peru*, UN Doc E/1998/22 (1997), [157].

[60] CESCR, *Concluding Observations: Mexico*, UN Doc E/C.12/MEX/CO/4 (2006), [27].

[61] Ibid [46].

[62] CESCR, *Concluding Observations: Bolivia*, UN Doc E/C.12/BOL/CO/2 (2008), [37].

of indigenous intellectual property rights, with a profit distribution mechanism, is one such step.[63]

More generally, the CESCR has suggested other ways of promoting indigenous cultural life. For example, it has urged states to provide opportunities to create awareness of indigenous cultural heritage,[64] including by enabling indigenous artists to participate in international fora.[65]

Other Economic and Social Rights

Whereas the rights to self-determination and cultural life have provided a focus for the CESCR's concerns about indigenous peoples, the CESCR has occasionally remarked on the application of other ICESCR rights to indigenous peoples. In the area of work rights (ICESCR, Articles 6–8),[66] the CESCR has often been concerned about high rates of unemployment, lack of opportunity, and employment discrimination amongst marginalised and disadvantaged groups generally, amongst which are indigenous peoples.[67] It has also been concerned about inadequate wages[68] and forced child labour.[69] The CESCR has called on states to reduce unemployment through specifically targeted measures, strict application of anti-discrimination laws, quotas and enhancing professional training.[70]

In the related area of social security (ICESCR, Article 9), in General Comment No 19 (2007), the CESCR encouraged states to 'take particular care that indigenous peoples and ethnic and linguistic minorities are not excluded from social security systems through direct or indirect discrimination, particularly through the imposition of unreasonable eligibility conditions or lack of adequate access to information'.[71] In monitoring states, occasionally the CESCR has called for targeted social assistance to indigenous peoples.[72]

63 Ibid.

64 CESCR, *Concluding Observations: Australia*, UN Doc E/1994/23 (1993), [153].

65 Ibid [162].

66 In general the CESCR has been considerably influenced by ILO standards and practice when interpreting the ICESCR's work rights: see Ben Saul, David Kinley and Jacqueline Mowbray, *The International Covenant on Economic, Social and Cultural Rights: Commentary, Cases and Materials* (Oxford University Press, 2014), 'Articles 6–8'.

67 CESCR, *Concluding Observations: Honduras*, UN Doc E/2002/22 (2001), [121]; CESCR, *Concluding Observations: Costa Rica*, UN Doc E/C.12/CRI/CO/4/Corr.1 (2008), [39]; CESCR, *Concluding Observations: Colombia*, UN Doc E/C.12/COL/CO/5 (2010), [11]; CESCR, *Concluding Observations: New Zealand*, UN Doc E/C.12/1993/13 (1994), [14], [17]; CESCR, *Concluding Observations: Canada*, UN Doc E/1999/22 (1998), [392]; CESCR, *Concluding Observations: Mexico*, UN Doc E/2000/22 (1999), [380]; CESCR, *Concluding Observations: Australia*, UN Doc E/2001/22 (2000), [380].

68 CESCR, *Concluding Observations: Mexico*, UN Doc E/C.12/MEX/CO/4 (2006), [14].

69 CERD, *Concluding Observations: Venezuela*, UN Doc A/60/18 (2005); CESCR, *Concluding Observations: Bolivia*, UN Doc E/2002/22 (2001), [274].

70 CESCR, *Concluding Observations: Costa Rica*, UN Doc E/C.12/CRI/CO/4 (2008), [39]; CERD, *Concluding Observations: Guatemala*, UN Doc E/C.12/1/Add.3 (1996), [27]; CERD, *Concluding Observations: Denmark*, UN Doc E/C.12/1/Add.102 (2004), [25]; CERD, *Concluding Observations: Costa Rica*, UN Doc E/C.12/CRI/CO/4/Corr.1 (2008), [36].

71 CESCR, *General Comment No 19: The Right to Social Security (Article 9)*, UN Doc E/C.12/GC/19 (4 February 2008), [35].

72 CESCR, *Concluding Observations: Brazil*, UN Doc E/C.12/BRA/CO/2 (2009), [20(b)]; CERD, *Concluding Observations: Venezuela*, UN Doc E/C.12/1/Add.56 (2001), [20].

The right of indigenous peoples to an adequate standard of living (ICESCR, Article 11, including its component rights to food, water and housing) has also attracted the CESCR's concern. In General Comment No 12 (1999), indigenous people are identified as a disadvantaged or vulnerable group that may need special attention and priority with respect to the accessibility of food, especially where their access to ancestral lands is threatened.[73] In monitoring states, the CESCR has highlighted the impacts of resource exploitation (including agro-fuels) on indigenous subsistence lands and resources as negatively affecting their living standards, particularly regarding food.[74] It has also commented on inadequate nutrition in indigenous communities.[75]

In General Comment No 15 (2002) the CESCR emphasised that states should give special attention to the right to water of indigenous peoples, particularly by protecting their 'access to water resources on their ancestral lands ... from encroachment and unlawful pollution', and providing resources for them to 'design, deliver and control their access to water'.[76] The connection between water and food has also been recognised, with the CESCR noting the need to ensure adequate access to water for subsistence farming and to secure the livelihoods and right to food of indigenous peoples.[77] In monitoring states, the CESCR has highlighted, for instance, unsafe drinking water[78] and concerns about the privatisation of water.[79]

As regards the right to shelter, the CESCR focused in General Comment No 7 (1997) on the disproportionate impacts of forced evictions on indigenous peoples,[80] including because of large development projects financed by international agencies.[81] In monitoring states, the CESCR has been particularly concerned about insufficient or inadequate housing for indigenous people;[82] a lack of low-income housing support;[83] and forced evictions, often due to expropriation of indigenous lands, without adequate compensation or resettlement.[84] A UN Special Rapporteur on

[73] CESCR, *General Comment No 12: The Right to Adequate Food (Article 11)*, UN Doc E/C.12/1999/5 (12 May 1999), [13].

[74] CESCR, *Concluding Observations: Colombia*, UN Doc E/C.12/COL/CO/5 (2010), [21]–[22]; CERD, *Concluding Observations: Cameroon*, UN Doc E/2000/22 (1999), [337], [353].

[75] CESCR, *Concluding Observations: Mexico*, UN Doc E/2000/22 (1999), [380].

[76] CESCR, *General Comment No 15: The Right to Water (Articles 11 and 12 of the Covenant)*, UN Doc E/C.12/2002/11 (20 January 2003), [16(d)].

[77] Ibid [7]; ICESCR, art 1(2) provides that a people may not 'be deprived of its own means of subsistence'.

[78] CESCR, *Concluding Observations: Canada*, UN Doc E/1999/22 (1998), [392].

[79] CESCR, *Concluding Observations: Nepal*, UN Doc E/2002/22 (2001), [576].

[80] CESCR, *General Comment No 7: The Right to Adequate Housing: Forced Evictions (Article 11.1)*, UN Doc E/1998/22 (14 May 1997), Annex IV, [11], [17]–[18].

[81] Ibid [18]–[19].

[82] CESCR, *Concluding Observations: Canada*, UN Doc E/1999/22 (1998), [392]; CESCR, *Concluding Observations: Mexico*, UN Doc E/2000/22 (1999), [380]; CESCR, *Concluding Observations: Australia*, UN Doc E/2001/22 (2000), [380]; CESCR, *Concluding Observations: Bolivia*, UN Doc E/2002/22 (2001), [276]; CESCR, *Concluding Observations: Colombia*, UN Doc E/2002/22 (2001), [771].

[83] CESCR, *Concluding Observations: Bolivia*, UN Doc E/2002/22 (2001), [276].

[84] CESCR, *Concluding Observations: Honduras*, UN Doc E/2002/22 (2001), [130]; CESCR, *Concluding Observations: Bolivia*, UN Doc E/2002/22 (2001), [276]; CESCR, *Concluding Observations: Ecuador*, UN Doc E/2005/22 (2004), [294], [319]; CESCR, *Concluding Observations: Brazil*, UN Doc E/C.12/1/Add.87 (2003), [58]–[59].

the right to housing has further highlighted the life- and health-threatening housing conditions that are disproportionately faced by indigenous peoples, including because of hazardous environmental degradation.[85]

As regards the right to health (ICESCR, Article 12), in General Comment No 14 (2000) the CESCR acknowledged 'emerging international law and practice and the recent measures taken by States' in respect of indigenous peoples.[86] The CESCR recognised a special duty on states to provide 'specific measures' to improve the access of indigenous peoples 'to health services and care [that] should be culturally appropriate, taking into account traditional preventive care, healing practices and medicines'.[87] It also stated that health facilities, goods and services must also be safely physically accessible by indigenous peoples, and accessibility 'also implies that medical services and underlying determinants of health, such as safe and potable water and adequate sanitation facilities, are within safe physical reach, including in rural areas'.[88] It emphasised further that 'States should provide resources for indigenous peoples to design, deliver and control such services so that they may enjoy the highest attainable standard of physical and mental health'.[89] It also called for the protection of the 'vital medicinal plants, animals and minerals' necessary to ensure indigenous health,[90] and for states 'to refrain from prohibiting or impeding traditional preventive care, healing practices and medicines'.[91]

The CESCR also addressed the impact of development on indigenous health. It emphasised that 'the health of the individual is often linked to the health of the society as a whole and has a collective dimension', and thus criticised development-induced displacement: 'development-related activities that lead to the displacement of indigenous peoples against their will from their traditional territories and environment, denying them their sources of nutrition and breaking their symbiotic relationship with their lands, has a deleterious effect on their health'.[92] A UN Special Rapporteur on the right to health has also emphasised concern for indigenous mental health, given that indigenous populations 'are frequently ignored, with no specialist development of psychiatric and support services despite acute needs that are manifest in increasing suicide rates and overrepresentation in high-security mental health facilities'.[93]

[85] UN Commission on Human Rights, Economic, Cultural and Social Rights, *Report of the Special Rapporteur on Adequate Housing as a Component of the Right to an Adequate Standard of Living, Mr Miloon Kothari*, UN Doc E/CN.4/2002/59 (1 March 2002), [46].

[86] CESCR, *General Comment No 14: The Right to the Highest Attainable Standard of Health (Article 12)*, UN Doc E/C.12/2000/4 (11 August 2000), [27], a set of 'special topics of broad application' that relate to Art 12.

[87] *General Comment No 14* (n 86), [27].

[88] Ibid [12(b)(ii)].

[89] Ibid.

[90] Ibid.

[91] Ibid [34].

[92] Ibid [27]; a set of 'special topics of broad application' that relate to Art 12.

[93] UN Commission on Human Rights, *Report of the Special Rapporteur on the Right of Everyone to the Enjoyment of the Highest Attainable Standard of Physical and Mental Health*, UN Doc E/CN.4/2005/51 (11 February 2005), Summary, [12].

In light of its standard setting, in monitoring states the CESCR has commented on high levels of ill-health among indigenous people, in particular women and children,[94] and identified a range of problems, including lower life expectancy,[95] high suicide rates[96] and diseases such as tuberculosis.[97] It has expressed concern about the limited availability and inadequacy of health services for indigenous peoples,[98] including because of discrimination[99] or reductions in state subsidies.[100] The CESCR has urged states to take immediate steps to improve indigenous health, including by implementing a human rights framework that ensures access to the social determinants of health, such as housing, safe drinking water, electricity and effective sanitation.[101] It has asked states to identify health indicators and benchmarks.[102]

In relation to the right to education (ICESCR, Articles 13 and 14), in General Comment No 13 (1990) the CESCR emphasised the obligations of states to 'fulfil (facilitate) the acceptability of education by taking positive measures to ensure that education is culturally appropriate for ... indigenous peoples'.[103] The CESCR has further indicated that indigenous children should have 'adequate opportunities to receive instruction in or of their native language', and that states should take steps to prevent lower educational standards for them, 'their segregation in special classes, and their exclusion from mainstream education'.[104] Educational programmes should incorporate the 'history, knowledge and technologies' and 'social, economic and cultural values and aspirations' of indigenous peoples,[105] particularly since children transmit cultural values inter-generationally.[106] In monitoring states, the CESCR has observed that indigenous people face disadvantage[107] in education, which in turn can affect other socio-economic rights, such as employment.[108] It has specifically criticised lack of education opportunities and funding;[109] high illiteracy

[94] CESCR, *Concluding Observations: Australia*, UN Doc E/C.12/AUS/CO/4 (2009), [28].
[95] CESCR, *Concluding Observations: New Zealand*, UN Doc E/C.12/1/Add.88 (2003), [18]; CESCR, *Concluding Observations: Russia*, UN Doc E/C.12/1/Add.94 (2003), [31].
[96] CESCR, *Concluding Observations: Canada*, UN Doc E/1999/22 (1998), [392].
[97] CESCR, *Concluding Observations: Russia*, UN Doc E/C.12/1/Add.94 (2003), [33].
[98] CECSR, *Concluding Observations: Australia*, UN Doc E/2001/22 (2000), [380]; CESCR, *Concluding Observations: Mexico*, UN Doc E/2000/22 (1999), [380]; CESCR, *Concluding Observations: Costa Rica*, UN Doc E/C.12/CRI/CO/4 (2008), [26]–[27]; CESCR, *Concluding Observations: Australia*, UN Doc E/2001/22 (2000), [380]; CESCR, *Concluding Observations: Australia*, UN Doc E/C.12/AUS/CO/4 (2009), [28].
[99] CESCR, *Concluding Observations: Colombia*, UN Doc E/C.12/COL/CO/5 (2010), [25]; CESCR, *Concluding Observations: Russian Federation*, UN Doc E/C.12/1/Add.94 (2003), [31]; CESCR, *Concluding Observations: Brazil*, UN Doc E/C.12/BRA/CO/2 (2009), [28].
[100] CESCR, *Concluding Observations: Colombia*, UN Doc E/2002/22 (2001), [775].
[101] CESCR, *Concluding Observations: Australia*, UN Doc E/C.12/AUS/CO/4 (2009), [28].
[102] Ibid.
[103] CESCR, *General Comment No 13: The Right to Education (Article 13)*, UN Doc E/C.12/1999/10 (8 December 1990), [50].
[104] CESCR, *Guidelines on Treaty-Specific Documents to be Submitted by States Parties under Articles 16 and 17 of the ICESCR*, UN Doc E/C.12/2008/2 (24 March 2009), [63].
[105] CESCR, *General Comment No 21* (n 4), [27].
[106] Ibid [26].
[107] CECSR, *Concluding Observations: Australia*, UN Doc E/2001/22 (2000), [380]; CESCR, *Concluding Observations: Mexico*, UN Doc E/2000/22 (1999), [380].
[108] CESCR, *Concluding Observations: Australia*, UN Doc E/1994/23 (1993), [150].
[109] CESCR, *Concluding Observations: Peru*, UN Doc E/1998/22 (1997), [144].

rates;[110] the unavailability of education in indigenous languages;[111] and high school drop-out rates.[112]

The rights of families, mothers and children (ICESCR, Article 10) have been addressed by the CESCR in various ways. Concerns about domestic violence against indigenous women has been common.[113] Unequal matrimonial property rights have also been criticised.[114] For indigenous children, difficulties in birth registration have been identified as impairing other ICESCR rights.[115] The CESCR has also been concerned at the over-representation of indigenous children taken into foster care,[116] and child trafficking.[117]

A cross-cutting concern of the CESCR has been violence against indigenous peoples. Indigenous peoples have faced threats of death or execution in connection with forced evictions from their traditional lands for resource projects.[118] Some have been characterised as terrorists and confronted by special security laws because of tensions over land disputes.[119] Their security has been affected by internal displacement due to violence and armed conflict (including because of the spraying of illegal drug crops);[120] the presence of military and paramilitary forces (which interfere with development and economic and social assistance programmes);[121] and insufficient implementation of peace agreements, producing violence, corruption, impunity and lack of reforms.[122]

It should also be mentioned that often when the CESCR mentions indigenous peoples it does not identify specific ICESCR rights. Sometimes this is because the issue in question is pertinent to the realisation of indigenous economic, social and cultural rights as a whole. Indigenous land and natural resources are one such cross-cutting issue. In this respect the CESCR has been concerned about unsettled indigenous land title;[123] inequitable land distribution;[124] extinguishment of indigenous title and treaty rights;[125] regressive amendments to native title laws;[126] agrarian reform;[127] and the privatisation of customary communal land.[128]

110 CESCR, *Concluding Observations: Panama*, UN Doc E/1992/23 (1991), [136]; CESCR, *Concluding Observations: Ecuador*, UN Doc E/2005/22 (2004), [297].

111 CESCR, *Concluding Observations: Honduras*, UN Doc E/2002/22 (2001), [136]; CESCR, *Concluding Observations: Bolivia*, UN Doc E/2002/22 (2001), [279]; CESCR, *Concluding Observations: Suriname*, UN Doc E/1996/22 (1995), [163].

112 CESCR, *Concluding Observations: Suriname*, UN Doc E/1996/22 (1995), [163]; CESCR, *Concluding Observations: New Zealand*, UN Doc E/C.12/1/Add.88 (2003), [20]; CESCR, *Concluding Observations: Ecuador*, UN Doc E/2005/22 (2004), [297].

113 CESCR, *Concluding Observations: New Zealand*, UN Doc E/C.12/1/Add.88 (2003), [15].

114 CESCR, *Concluding Observations: Canada*, UN Doc E/1999/22 (1998), [404].

115 CESCR, *Concluding Observations: Colombia*, UN Doc E/C.12/COL/CO/5 (2010), [19].

116 CESCR, *Concluding Observations: Canada*, UN Doc E/C.12/CAN/CO/4–5 (2006), [24].

117 CESCR, *Concluding Observations: Ecuador*, UN Doc E/2005/22 (2004), [290], [315].

118 CESCR, *Concluding Observations: Brazil*, UN Doc E/C.12/1/Add.87 (2003), [58]–[59].

119 CESCR, *Concluding Observations: Chile*, UN Doc E/2005/22 (2004), [541], [561].

120 CESCR, *Concluding Observations: Colombia*, UN Doc E/2002/22 (2001), [760].

121 CESCR, *Concluding Observations: Mexico*, UN Doc E/2000/22 (1999), [387].

122 CESCR, *Concluding Observations: Guatemala*, UN Doc E/C.12/1/Add.93 (2003), [10].

123 CESCR, *Concluding Observations: Finland*, UN Doc E/2001/22 (2000), [451].

124 CESCR, *Concluding Observations: Guatemala*, UN Doc E/C.12/1/Add.93 (2003), [24].

125 CESCR, *Concluding Observations: Canada*, UN Doc E/1999/22 (1998), [393].

126 CESCR, *Concluding Observations: Australia*, UN Doc E/2001/22 (2000), [381].

127 CESCR, *Concluding Observations: Honduras*, UN Doc E/2002/22 (2001), [151].

128 CESCR, *Concluding Observations: Solomon Islands*, UN Doc E/C.12/1/Add.33 (14 May 1999), [20].

The CESCR has been further concerned about the exploitation of indigenous lands by mining and oil activities, logging and deforestation, cattle ranching and industrial enterprises.[129] The CESCR has found that such activities have adverse effects on the environment, health, economy, way of life and culture of indigenous peoples,[130] sometimes also through forced displacement from ancestral lands.[131] Echoing ILO Convention No 169, the CESCR has often faulted states for pursuing development activities on indigenous lands without informing, consulting and obtaining the free and full consent of indigenous peoples,[132] or involving them in the management and control of natural resources.[133]

Finally, the CESCR has addressed miscellaneous issues affecting indigenous peoples. It has been concerned about the effects of economic crisis and wealth inequality on indigenous peoples,[134] as well as the negative impacts of free trade agreements.[135] It has urged states to enhance domestic monitoring of the situation of indigenous peoples.[136] It has also asked states to involve indigenous peoples in mechanisms for following up its observations.[137]

UN COMMITTEE ON THE ELIMINATION OF RACIAL DISCRIMINATION

The International Convention on the Elimination of All Forms of Racial Discrimination 1966 (ICERD) applies to groups based on 'race, colour, descent, or national or ethnic origin' (Article 1(1)). The CERD has issued a number of interpretive statements confirming that indigenous peoples are covered by the ICERD[138] and this is reflected in its practice.[139] In general it has insisted that 'there is an international standard concerning the specific rights of people belonging to such groups' and criticised states that refuse to recognise indigenous groups as producing different treatment.[140] While the CERD does not itself define indigenous peoples, it

[129] See, eg, CESCR, *Concluding Observations: Paraguay*, UN Doc E/C.12/1/Add.1 (28 May 1996), [9]; CESCR, *Concluding Observations: Venezuela*, UN Doc E/C.12/1/Add.56 (21 May 2001), [12], [22]; CESCR, *Concluding Observations: Panama*, UN Doc E/2002/22 (2001), [450], [466]; CESCR, *Concluding Observations: Colombia*, UN Doc E/2002/22 (2001), [761]; CESCR, *Concluding Observations: Honduras*, UN Doc E/2002/22 (2001), [132].

[130] CESCR, *Concluding Observations: Venezuela*, UN Doc E/C.12/1/Add.56 (2001), [12], [22].

[131] CESCR, *Concluding Observations: Paraguay*, UN Doc E/C.12/1/Add.1 (1996), [9].

[132] CESCR, *Concluding Observations: Ecuador*, UN Doc E/C.12/1/Add.100 (2004), [12], [35].

[133] CESCR, *Concluding Observations: Norway*, UN Doc E/C.12/1/Add.109 (2005), [26].

[134] CESCR, *Concluding Observations: Mexico*, UN Doc E/1994/23 (1993), [233].

[135] Ibid [236] (concerning the North American Free Trade Agreement).

[136] CESCR, *Concluding Observations: Venezuela*, UN Doc E/2002/22 (2001), [83].

[137] CESCR, *Concluding Observations: Canada*, UN Doc E/C.12/CAN/CO/4 (2006), [35].

[138] See CERD, *General Recommendation No 23: Rights of Indigenous Peoples*, UN Doc A/52/18 (18 August 1997), Annex V; *General Recommendation No 24: Concerning Article 1 of the Convention*, UN Doc A/54/18 (1999), [1] ('the Convention relates to all persons who belong to different races, national or ethnic groups or to indigenous peoples').

[139] For early monitoring of indigenous issues by the CERD, see also James Anaya, *Indigenous Peoples in International Law* (2nd edn, Oxford University Press, 2004), 230–32. On the future impact of the UNDRIP on CERD's work, see Patrick Thornberry, 'Integrating the UN Declaration on the Rights of Indigenous Peoples into CERD Practice' in Stephen Allen and Alexandra Xanthaki (eds), *Reflections on the UN Declaration on the Rights of Indigenous Peoples* (Hart, Oxford, 2011), 61.

[140] Ibid [3].

has recommended that 'identification shall, if no justification exists to the contrary, be based upon self-identification by the individual concerned'.[141] In guiding its approach the CERD has also used as a touchstone ILO Convention No 169.[142] It has also recognised indigenous peoples where they occasionally constitute the majority of a state's population, as where they comprise 62 per cent of Bolivians.[143]

The CERD is also the only UN treaty body to have adopted an interpretive statement devoted specifically to indigenous peoples. In General Recommendation 23 (1997) the CERD observed that it has 'consistently affirmed that discrimination against indigenous peoples falls under the scope of the Convention and that all appropriate means must be taken to combat and eliminate' it.[144] It acknowledged historical and contemporary discrimination and deprivation of indigenous rights, particularly in that 'they have lost their land and resources to colonists, commercial companies and State enterprises'.[145] As a result, 'the preservation of their culture and their historical identity has been and still is jeopardized'.[146] The CERD accordingly called on states to ensure freedom from discrimination based on 'indigenous origin or identity'.[147]

While its singular focus on non-discrimination may, at first sight, seem narrow, the ICERD spells out non-discrimination requirements across all civil, political, economic, social and cultural rights, giving the CERD a wide monitoring ambit. Under the periodic reporting procedure, the CERD's examination of racial discrimination against indigenous peoples has thus assessed the full gamut of rights. While it has tended to focus on indigenous peoples in rural and remote areas, where peoples often remain attached to traditional lands, territories and resources, it has occasionally also addressed urban indigenous disadvantage.[148]

In addition to monitoring states' reports, the CERD has occasionally considered individual complaints from indigenous people, and has commonly utilised its early warning and urgent action procedure as a supplementary means to express its concerns about the treatment of indigenous peoples. Those procedures, which culminate in the issuance of decisions, statements or resolutions, aim to prevent existing problems from escalating into larger conflicts, and to respond to problems requiring immediate attention in order to prevent or limit serious harms to indigenous peoples. Such procedures have been utilised in respect of more than 20 states since 1993.

[141] CERD, *General Recommendation No 8: Membership of Racial or Ethnic Groups based on Self-identification*, UN Doc A/45/18 (1990).

[142] CERD, *Concluding Observations: Finland*, UN Doc A/55/18 (2000), [214]; CESCR, *Concluding Observations: Japan*, UN Doc A/56/18 (2001), [175]; CESCR, *Concluding Observations: United States of America*, UN Doc A/56/18 (2001), [400]; CESCR, *Concluding Observations: Guyana*, UN Doc CERD/C/CUY/CO/14 (2006), [23].

[143] CERD, *Concluding Observations: Bolivia*, UN Doc A/58/18 (2003), [335].

[144] CERD, *General Recommendation No 23* (n 138), [1].

[145] Ibid [3].

[146] Ibid.

[147] Ibid [4]. See also CERD, *General Recommendation No 29: Discrimination Based on Descent*, UN Doc A/57/18 (2002), Preamble.

[148] CERD, *Concluding Observations: Peru*, UN Doc A/50/18 (1995), [199]; CESCR, *Concluding Observations: Suriname*, UN Doc CERD/C/SUR/CO/12 (2009), [15].

Discrimination and Recognition

In keeping with its mandate, in monitoring states the CERD has had an over-arching concern for all forms of discrimination against indigenous peoples, whether legal[149] or de facto[150] (as where there is geographical discrimination or underdevelopment).[151] It has been especially concerned where states deny the existence of indigenous peoples.[152] This includes where the state claims that there are no physical distinctions between indigenous and non-indigenous peoples; that indigenous peoples are small in number[153] or experience the same living conditions as others;[154] or where stigmatising legal descriptions of groups are used.[155] It has also been concerned where indigenous people are denied citizenship because of ethnic criteria for nationality,[156] or where their special status can be unilaterally abrogated by a national political institution[157] or impaired by legislation.[158]

The CERD has been further concerned where states discriminatorily recognise some but not other indigenous groups.[159] In this regard it has criticised overly-restrictive laws or practices governing the recognition of indigenous peoples, for instance based on language and ancestral taxation criteria;[160] a predominant ancestry test;[161]

[149] CERD, *Concluding Observations: Brazil*, UN Doc A/51/18 (1996), [301].

[150] CERD, *Concluding Observations: Guatemala*, UN Doc A/50/18 (1995), [304].

[151] CERD, *Concluding Observations: Brazil*, UN Doc A/59/18 (2004), [58]; CESCR, *Concluding Observations: Peru*, UN Doc A/54/18 (1999), [148]; CESCR, *Concluding Observations: Bolivia*, UN Doc A/51/18 (1996), [284].

[152] CERD, *Concluding Observations: Argentina*, UN Doc CERD/C/ARG/CO/19–20 (2010), [27]; CESCR, *Concluding Observations: El Salvador*, UN Doc CERD/C/SLV/CO/13 (2006), [7] (concerning the Nahua-Pipil, the Lencas and the Cacaotera peoples); CESCR, *Concluding Observations: Congo*, UN Doc A/62/18 (2007), [328]; CESCR, *Concluding Observations: Rwanda*, UN Doc CERD/C/RWA/CO/13–17 (2011), [11] (concerning the Batwa people); CESCR, *Concluding Observations: Denmark*, UN Doc CERD/C/DEN/CO/17 (2006), [20] (Thule Tribe of Greenland); CESCR, *Concluding Observations: Panama*, UN Doc CERD/C/PAN/CO/15–20 (2010), [12] (some Ngobe and Emberá communities and the Bri Bri and Naso communities); CESCR, *Concluding Observations: Laos*, UN Doc A/60/18 (2005), [169]; CESCR, *Concluding Observations: Trinidad and Tobago*, UN Doc A/56/18 (2001), [351]; CESCR, *Concluding Observations: Cambodia*, UN Doc A/53/18 (1998), [293].

[153] CERD, *Concluding Observations: El Salvador*, UN Doc A/50/18 (1995), [490].

[154] CERD, *Concluding Observations: Denmark*, UN Doc CERD/C/DEN/CO/17 (2006), [20].

[155] CERD, *Concluding Observations: Cameroon*, UN Doc CERD/C/CMR/CO/15–18 (2010), [15] ('marginal population groups'); CESCR, *Concluding Observations: Guyana*, UN Doc CERD/C/CUY/CO/14 (2006), [10] ('Amerindians').

[156] CERD, *Concluding Observations: Cambodia*, UN Doc A/53/18 (1998), [290].

[157] CERD, *Concluding Observations: United States of America*, UN Doc A/56/18 (2001), [400] (treaties with Indian tribes ('domestic dependent nations') can be unilaterally abrogated by Congress).

[158] CERD, *Concluding Observations: New Zealand*, UN Doc CERD/C/NZL/CO/18–20 (2013), [13] (where marine legislation may restrict the full enjoyment by Māori communities of their rights under the Treaty of Waitangi).

[159] CERD, *Concluding Observations: Denmark*, UN Doc A/57/18 (2002), [123]; CESCR, *Concluding Observations: Botswana*, UN Doc A/57/18 (2002), [301]; CESCR, *Concluding Observations: Panama*, UN Doc CERD/C/PAN/CO/15–20 (2010), [12]; CESCR, *Concluding Observations: Slovenia*, UN Doc A/58/18 (2003), [234], [237] (indigenous and non-indigenous Roma); CESCR, *Concluding Observations: Norway*, UN Doc CERD/C/NOR/CO/18 (2006), [17]; CESCR, *Concluding Observations: Namibia*, UN Doc CERD/C/NAM/CO/12 (2008), [16]; CESCR, *Concluding Observations: Guyana*, UN Doc CERD/C/CUY/CO/14 (2006), [14] (titled and untitled communities).

[160] CERD, *Concluding Observations: Finland*, UN Doc A/58/18 (2003), [404].

[161] CERD, *Concluding Observations: Australia*, UN Doc A/49/18 (1994), [544].

a requirement of continuing existence;[162] the exclusion of indigenous women who marry non-indigenous men;[163] or the non-recognition of essential rights.[164] It has also been concerned where definitions of 'indigenous' may be too expansive or are abused by the state. It questioned how one national definition related to the general concept in international law and to the rights of those classed as non-indigenous.[165] The CERD was concerned where no institution existed to assess applications for recognition independently of the government.[166] It emphasised the importance of self-identification as indigenous,[167] and identified barriers to self-identification, such as the unremedied past mass murders of indigenous people, which deterred group members from asserting their identity.[168] It also asked states to improve their data collection on who is indigenous, based on self-identification.[169]

At a formal legal level, the CERD has called on states to criminalise discrimination,[170] with penalties commensurate with its gravity,[171] and even to constitutionally prohibit it,[172] and provide legal remedies and compensation for it.[173] It has also urged states to criminalise racially motivated violence against indigenous people, incitement to racial discrimination and the dissemination of ideas based on racial superiority or hatred.[174] The CERD noted that a lack of legal complaints or judgments concerning racial discrimination may evidence a lack of awareness of victims of their rights, a lack of confidence in the justice system, insensitivity by law enforcement authorities, or the inappropriate dismissal of cases.[175] States have been further encouraged to collect better data on investigations;[176] raise awareness amongst the population of racial discrimination,[177] including to prevent stereotyping in the media;[178] and adopt a comprehensive national policy against racism and structural racial discrimination.[179]

'Positive discrimination' through 'special measures' (under ICERD, Article 1(4)) for indigenous peoples has also received attention. Where states have objected to the concept of special measures, the CERD has recommended that the state provide for

[162] CERD, *Concluding Observations: Indonesia*, UN Doc A/62/18 (2007), [357].
[163] CERD, *Concluding Observations: Canada*, UN Doc A/57/18 (2002), [332].
[164] CERD, *Concluding Observations: Finland*, UN Doc CERD/C/FIN/CO/20–22 (2012), [12].
[165] CERD, *Concluding Observations: Fiji*, UN Doc CERD/C/FJI/CO/17 (2008), [13].
[166] CERD, *Concluding Observations: Namibia*, UN Doc CERD/C/NAM/CO/12 (2008), [16].
[167] CERD, *Concluding Observations: Finland*, UN Doc A/58/18 (2003), [404]; CESCR, *Concluding Observations: Venezuela*, UN Doc A/60/18 (2005), [377]; CESCR, *Concluding Observations: Indonesia*, UN Doc A/62/18 (2007), [357].
[168] CERD, *Concluding Observations: El Salvador*, UN Doc CERD/C/SLV/CO/13 (2006), [15].
[169] CERD, *Concluding Observations: Costa Rica*, UN Doc A/62/18 (2007), [292].
[170] CERD, *Concluding Observations: Ecuador*, UN Doc A/58/18 (2003), [49].
[171] CERD, *Concluding Observations: Costa Rica*, UN Doc A/62/18 (2007), [299].
[172] CERD, *Concluding Observations: Chile*, UN Doc A/54/18 (1999), [378].
[173] CERD, *Concluding Observations: Venezuela*, UN Doc A/51/18 (1996), [469]; CESCR, *Concluding Observations: Bolivia*, UN Doc CERD/C/BOL/CO/17–20 (2011), [22].
[174] CERD, *Concluding Observations: Mexico*, UN Doc CERD/C/MEX/CO/16–17 (2012), [11].
[175] CERD, *Concluding Observations: Uruguay*, UN Doc CERD/C/URY/CO/14 (2011), [18]; CERD, *Concluding Observations: Ecuador*, UN Doc CERD/C/ECU/CO/20–22 (2012), [18].
[176] CERD, *Concluding Observations: Colombia*, UN Doc CERD/C/COL/CO/14 (2009), [21].
[177] CERD, *Concluding Observations: Argentina*, UN Doc CERD/C/ARG/CO/19–20 (2010), [27].
[178] CERD, *Concluding Observations: Peru*, UN Doc CERD/C/PER/CO/14–17 (2009), [19].
[179] CERD, *Concluding Observations: Peru*, UN Doc CERD/C/PER/CO/14–17 (2009), [10].

the possibility of adopting special measures to promote equal opportunities, address structural discrimination and enhance strategies against inequality and discrimination faced by indigenous groups.[180] The CERD has asked states about the accessibility and effectiveness of special measures available to indigenous peoples.[181] The CERD has, however, warned against using affirmative action to unfairly advantage one group over another and thereby promote a politicised, hegemonic indigenous culture and identity.[182] At a wider political and societal level, the CERD has sometimes encouraged states to pursue remedies of apology, compensation and reconciliation for past structural discrimination and injustice.[183]

The CERD has not shied away from confronting ancient and systemic racial discrimination of global proportions. In its Concluding Observations on the Holy See in 2016, the CERD welcomed Pope Francis' apology in Bolivia for the actions of the Catholic Church against indigenous peoples during colonialism in the Americas.[184] It proceeded to note the concerns of indigenous peoples about the 'current legacy and effects of the Doctrine of Discovery endorsed in the Inter Caetera from 1493 and its related papal bulls'.[185] The Inter Caetera purported to assign rights in newly discovered American territories to Spain. The CERD indicated that these issues engage the non-discrimination obligations under articles 2 and 5 of the ICERD and require remedies and reparation under article 6. To the latter end, the CERD recommended that the state party 'engage in meaningful dialogue with indigenous peoples with the aim of effectively addressing their concerns'.[186] While legally restoring the territory of the Americas to indigenous peoples, or compensating them for over 500 years of lost value, is obviously unrealistic, the CERD has emphasized the burden on the Holy See to discuss, in good faith, a meaningful settlement.

In the individual complaint of *Hagan v Australia* (2003),[187] an Australian indigenous man complained to the CERD that the use of the word 'nigger' in the name and signage of, and public information about, a sports grandstand (the 'E.S. "Nigger" Brown Stand') in the town where the man lived was racially offensive and insulting, contrary to the ICERD.[188] The stand was named in 1960 in honour of a local white personality who was so nicknamed either 'because of his fair skin and blond hair or because he had a penchant for using "Nigger Brown" shoe polish'.[189] The complainant argued that the term, in 2002, was one of the most racially offensive words (regardless of whether it was so in 1960) and that, as a result, he and his family felt unable to attend the area's main sports venue. He also argued that Mr Brown could be honoured without the use of the term.[190] He applied to the CERD after

180 CERD, *Concluding Observations: Sweden*, UN Doc CERD/C/SWE/CO/14 (2013), [8].

181 CERD, *Concluding Observations: Paraguay*, UN Doc CERD/C/PRY/CO/1–3 (2011), [11].

182 CERD, *Concluding Observations: Fiji*, UN Doc A/58/18 (2003), [82]–[85].

183 CERD, *Concluding Observations: Australia*, UN Doc A/49/18 (1994), [547]; CERD, *Concluding Observations: Chile*, UN Doc A/54/18 (1999), [377]; CERD, *Concluding Observations: Australia*, UN Doc A/55/18 (2000), [35]; CERD, *Concluding Observations: Australia*, UN Doc A/60/18 (2005), [45]; CERD, *Concluding Observations: New Zealand*, UN Doc A/57/18 (2002), [415].

184 CERD, Concluding Observations: Holy See, CERD/C/VAT/CO/16-23 (11 January 2016), [16].

185 Ibid.

186 Ibid, [17].

187 *Hagan v Australia*, CERD Communication No 26/2002 (20 March 2003).

188 Specifically, ICERD, arts 2(1)(c), 4, 5(d)(i) and (ix), 5(e)(vi), 5(f), 6 and 7.

189 *Hagan v Australia* (n 184) [2.1].

190 Ibid [3.2].

an Australian federal court found that the use of the name did not breach domestic racial discrimination laws.

Australia responded that the term was not racially discriminatory in its context because it was an integral part of the person's name; its attachment to his name had long ceased to have any racist connotation; there had been consultations with local indigenous people; an indigenous former football personality in the area said it was unproblematic and part of history; and there had been no other complaint over the past 40 years.[191] Australia concluded that it was not objectively likely to offend indigenous people or done 'because of' the race of any person. While the complainant was subjectively offended, Australia argued that the trustees of the sports field were not attempting to justify, promote or incite racial discrimination.[192]

The CERD took account of the context, including the lack of prior objections and that the term originally referred to shoe polish and was 'not designed to demean or diminish its bearer, Mr Brown, who was neither black nor of Aboriginal descent'.[193] It concluded, however, that the 'use and maintenance of the offending term can at the present time be considered offensive and insulting, even if for an extended period it may not have necessarily been so'.[194] It regarded the ICERD as 'a living instrument' that 'must be interpreted and applied taking into the circumstances of contemporary society', which included 'the increased sensitivities in respect of words such as the offending term appertaining today'.[195]

The CERD acknowledged that a public meeting in the town in 1999 had agreed that, in the interest of reconciliation, racially derogatory or offensive terms will not be used or displayed in the future.[196] It found, however, that the memory of Mr Brown 'may be honoured in ways other than by maintaining and displaying a public sign considered to be racially offensive', and accordingly called on Australia to remove the term from the sign.[197] The Australian federal government did not intervene. When the grandstand was demolished in an upgrade to the grounds in 2008, the trustees agreed to the Queensland state government's request not to use the term when honouring Mr Brown in another manner.[198]

Land and Natural Resources

General Recommendation No 23 (1997) gave particular prominence to the right of indigenous peoples 'to own, develop, control and use their communal lands, territories and resources'.[199] Where they have been deprived of these without their consent, the state should make restitution and return them.[200] If that is not possible, indigenous peoples should enjoy a 'right to just, fair and prompt compensation',

[191] Ibid [4.10].
[192] Ibid [4.11].
[193] Ibid [7.2].
[194] Ibid [7.3].
[195] Ibid.
[196] Ibid [8].
[197] Ibid.
[198] 'Toowoomba to drop "Nigger" name from sports ground', *Courier Mail*, 26 September 2008.
[199] Ibid [5].
[200] Ibid.

which 'should as far as possible take the form of [alternative/substitute] lands and territories'.[201] General Recommendation No 23 does not, however, specifically mention a right of self-determination of indigenous peoples, as appears in the UN Declaration on the Rights of Indigenous Peoples 2007. However, in General Comment No 21 (1996) on self-determination, the CERD affirmed the internal aspect of self-determination, including that 'governments should be sensitive towards the rights of persons of ethnic groups [implicitly including indigenous peoples], particularly their right to lead lives of dignity, to preserve their culture, to share equitably in the fruits of national growth, and to play their part in the government of the country of which its members are citizens'.[202] While the CERD rejects any unilateral right of secession in this regard, it does not 'exclude the possibility of arrangements reached by free agreements of all parties concerned'.[203]

In monitoring states under the periodic reporting procedure, the CERD has had an overriding preoccupation with indigenous rights to traditional lands and natural resources. It has been concerned where: states fail to specifically recognise indigenous legal interests in land;[204] indigenous legal interests are insecure, unimplemented, unresolved or delayed;[205] land demarcation and distribution is inequitable;[206] and legal frameworks (including laws and judicial decisions) are inadequate or too restrictive,[207] including because of procedural difficulties (such as high standards of proof[208] or bureaucratic hurdles[209]) or cultural insensitivities.[210]

[201] Ibid.

[202] CERD, *General Recommendation No 21: The Right to Self-determination*, UN Doc A/51/18 (1996), Annex VIII, [5].

[203] Ibid [60].

[204] CERD, *Concluding Observations: Suriname*, UN Doc CERD/C/SUR/CO/12 (2009), [12]; CERD, *Concluding Observations: Ecuador*, UN Doc CERD/C/ECU/CO/19 (2008), [10]; CERD, *Concluding Observations: Cameroon*, UN Doc CERD/C/CMR/CO/15–18 (2010), [15].

[205] CERD, *Concluding Observations: Finland*, UN Doc A/55/18 (2000), [214]; CERD, *Concluding Observations: Colombia*, UN Doc A/54/18 (1999), [473]; CERD, *Concluding Observations: Canada*, UN Doc A/49/18 (1994), [329]; CERD, *Concluding Observations: Argentina*, UN Doc A/52/18 (1997), [548]; CERD, *Concluding Observations: Mexico*, UN Doc CERD/C/MEX/CO/15 (2006), [15]; CERD, *Concluding Observations: Nicaragua*, UN Doc CERD/C/NIC/CO/14 (2008), [21]; CERD, *Concluding Observations: Guatemala*, UN Doc CERD/C/GTM/CO/11, (2006), [17]; CERD, *Concluding Observations: Paraguay*, UN Doc CERD/C/PRY/CO/1–3 (2011), [15].

[206] CERD, *Concluding Observations: Mexico*, UN Doc A/50/18 (1995), [386], [393]; CERD, *Concluding Observations: Brazil*, UN Doc A/51/18 (1996), [309]; CERD, *Concluding Observations: Brazil*, UN Doc A/59/18 (2004), [60].

[207] *CERD, Concluding Observations: Suriname*, UN Doc A/59/18 (2004), [190]; CERD, *Concluding Observations: Australia*, UN Doc A/49/18 (1994), [544]; CERD, *Concluding Observations: Norway*, UN Doc A/58/18 (2003), [481]; CERD, *Concluding Observations: Australia*, UN Doc A/60/18 (2005), [36]; CERD, *Concluding Observations: India*, UN Doc CERD/C/IND/CO/19 (2007), [19].

[208] CERD, *Concluding Observations: Australia*, UN Doc A/60/18, (2005) [37] (where 'continuous observance and acknowledgment of the laws and customs of indigenous peoples since the British acquisition of sovereignty over Australia is required' to establish native title); CERD, *Concluding Observations: Canada*, UN Doc A/57/18 (2002), [330]; CERD, *Concluding Observations: New Zealand*, UN Doc CERD/C/NZL/CO/18–20 (2013), [13] (requiring proof of exclusive use and occupation of marine and coastal areas without interruption since 1840).

[209] CERD, *Concluding Observations: Colombia*, UN Doc CERD/C/COL/CO/14 (2009), [19].

[210] *CERD, Concluding Observations: Cameroon*, UN Doc CERD/C/CMR/CO/15–18 (2010), [18] (where land laws do not take into account the traditions, customs and land tenure systems of indigenous peoples, or their way of life).

The CERD has criticised states for not following their own laws and procedures for the protection of indigenous rights,[211] or not implementing decisions of courts or other legal bodies.[212] It has also denounced state laws that override or conflict with laws protecting indigenous rights,[213] including on compulsory acquisition without compensation,[214] and has called on states to 'ensure that the protection of indigenous rights prevails over commercial and economic interests'.[215] It has highlighted laws which apply differently as between entities within a federal state,[216] and where key national instruments recognising indigenous rights are not regarded as formally binding.[217]

The exploitation or development of natural resources on indigenous lands has often been of concern to the CERD. Examples include mining;[218] oil;[219] pipelines;[220] logging or forestry;[221] industrial plantations;[222] tourism;[223] national parks or game reserves,[224] dams,[225] military bases,[226] nuclear or toxic waste storage,[227] waste dumps and sewage plants;[228] and the sale of land.[229] The CERD has highlighted

211 CERD, *Concluding Observations: Cambodia*, UN Doc CERD/C/KHM/CO/8–13 (2010), [16].

212 CERD, *Concluding Observations: Nicaragua*, UN Doc CERD/C/NIC/CO/14 (2008), [21] (IACtHR in the *Awas Tingni* case); CERD, *Concluding Observations: Colombia*, UN Doc CERD/C/COL/CO/14 (2009), [19] (decisions of the IACtHR and the recommendations of the ILO's Committee of Experts on the Application of Conventions and Recommendations concerning the Curvaradó and Jiguamiandó communities); CERD, *Concluding Observations: Panama*, UN Doc CERD/C/PAN/CO/15–20 (2010), [16] (IACHR precautionary measures for the Naso community in San San and in San San Druy, and of the community in Charco La Pava); CERD, *Concluding Observations: Paraguay*, UN Doc CERD/C/PRY/CO/1–3 (2011), [17] (IACtHR decisions on the Yakye Axa, Sawhoyamaxa and Xamok Kasek communities); CERD, *Concluding Observations: Suriname*, UN Doc CERD/C/SUR/CO/12 (2009), [18] (IACtHR in the *Saramaka People* case and the *Moiwana Village* case).

213 CERD, *Concluding Observations: Argentina*, UN Doc A/56/18 (2001), [51]; CERD, *Concluding Observations: Peru*, UN Doc A/54/18 (1999), [157]; CERD, *Concluding Observations: Sweden*, UN Doc A/49/18 (1994), [200].

214 CERD, *Concluding Observations: Guyana*, UN Doc CERD/C/CUY/CO/14 (2006), [17].

215 CERD, *Concluding Observations: Chile*, UN Doc CERD/C/CHL/CO/15–18 (2009), [23].

216 CERD, *Concluding Observations: Mexico*, UN Doc CERD/C/MEX/CO/16–17 (2012), [11].

217 CERD, *Concluding Observations: New Zealand*, UN Doc CERD/C/NZL/CO/18–20 (2013), [7] (where the Treaty of Waitangi is not a formal part of domestic law, 'even though the State party considers it the founding document of the nation', and decisions of the Waitangi Tribunal are not binding).

218 CERD, *Concluding Observations: Nicaragua*, UN Doc A/50/18 (1995), [535]; CERD, *Concluding Observations: Finland*, UN Doc CERD/C/304/Add.7 (1996), [11]; CERD, *Concluding Observations: Panama*, UN Doc A/32/18 (1977), [338]; CERD, *Concluding Observations: Suriname*, UN Doc A/59/18 (2004), [194].

219 CERD, *Concluding Observations: Nigeria*, UN Doc A/60/18 (2005), [294].

220 CERD, *Concluding Observations: Cameroon*, UN Doc CERD/C/CMR/CO/15–18 (2010), [18].

221 CERD, *Concluding Observations: Suriname*, UN Doc A/59/18 (2004), [192]; CERD, *Concluding Observations: Cameroon*, UN Doc CERD/C/304/Add.53 (1998), [17].

222 CERD, *Concluding Observations: Cambodia*, UN Doc CERD/C/304/Add.54 (1998), [13]; CERD, *Concluding Observations: Indonesia*, UN Doc A/62/18 (2007), [359] (oil palm).

223 CERD, *Concluding Observations: Panama*, UN Doc A/32/18 (1977), [338].

224 CERD, *Concluding Observations: Sri Lanka*, UN Doc A/56/18 (2001), [335]; CERD, *Concluding Observations: Botswana*, UN Doc A/57/18 (2002), [304]; CERD, *Concluding Observations: Namibia*, UN Doc CERD/C/NAM/CO/12 (2008), [16]; CERD, *Concluding Observations: Cameroon*, UN Doc CERD/C/CMR/CO/15–18 (2010), [18].

225 CERD, *Concluding Observations: India*, UN Doc CERD/C/IND/CO/19 (2007), [19].

226 CERD, *Concluding Observations: Denmark*, UN Doc A/56/18 (1996), [72].

227 CERD, *Concluding Observations: United States of America*, UN Doc A/56/18 (2001), [400]; CERD, *Concluding Observations: United States of America*, UN Doc CERD/C/USA/CO/6 (2008), [29].

228 CERD, *Concluding Observations: Chile*, UN Doc CERD/C/CHL/CO/15–18 (2009), [23].

229 CERD, *Concluding Observations: United States of America*, UN Doc A/56/18 (2001), [400].

the negative impacts of such activities on the environment,[230] spiritual practices and cultural identity,[231] health, education, economy and way of life of indigenous peoples.[232] It has called on states to respect international environmental standards; develop policies for environmental impacts on indigenous peoples; conduct environmental impact assessments; and undertake inspections and investigations.[233]

The overriding substantive principle guiding the CERD's review of state reporting in this area, stemming from ILO Convention No 169, is that indigenous peoples have a right to own, develop, control and use their communal lands, territories and resources.[234] A related procedural principle, also from ILO Convention No 169, is that indigenous peoples have a right to participate in decision-making affecting them, namely by being informed and consulted on proposed development projects, and by giving their free, prior and informed consent.[235] These obligations apply to both public and private development, and the CERD has further called on states to regulate the extra-territorial activities of their companies when involved in natural resource exploitation on indigenous land abroad.[236]

The CERD has thus frequently been concerned where states failed to provide information, consult or obtain indigenous peoples' consent, in practice[237] and law.[238] It has been concerned about inadequate consultations,[239] including where private developers conducted the consultations (leading to an imbalance of power in negotiations),[240] or where consultations were unregulated or not carried out systematically and in good faith.[241] The CERD further objected where indigenous resource decisions are subject to ministerial approval,[242] or diluted by the voting power of non-indigenous resource users.[243] Where projects are developed, the CERD has

230 CERD, *Concluding Observations: Colombia*, UN Doc CERD/C/304/Add.1 (1996), [8]; CERD, *Concluding Observations: Suriname*, UN Doc A/59/18 (2004), [194]; CERD, *Concluding Observations: Nigeria*, UN Doc A/60/18 (2005), [294] ('environmental racism').

231 CERD, *Concluding Observations: Argentina*, UN Doc A/59/18 (2004), [246]; CERD, *Concluding Observations: Guatemala*, UN Doc A/52/18 (1997), [93]; CERD, *Concluding Observations: Costa Rica* UN Doc CERD/C/304/Add.71 (1999), [18].

232 CERD, *Concluding Observations: Chile*, UN Doc CERD/C/CHL/CO/15–18 (2009), [23]; CERD, *Concluding Observations: Nigeria*, UN Doc A/60/18 (2005), [294]; CERD, *Concluding Observations: Peru*, UN Doc CERD/C/PER/CO/14–17 (2009), [14].

233 CERD, *Concluding Observations: Suriname*, UN Doc A/59/18 (2004), [194]; CERD, *Concluding Observations: Nigeria*, UN Doc A/60/18 (2005), [294]; CERD, *Concluding Observations: Chile*, UN Doc CERD/C/CHL/CO/15–18 (2009), [23].

234 CERD, *Concluding Observations: Guatemala*, UN Doc CERD/C/GTM/CO/11 (2006), [17]; CERD, *Concluding Observations: Brazil*, UN Doc A/59/18 (2004), [60].

235 CERD, *Concluding Observations: El Salvador*, UN Doc A/50/18 (1995), [491].

236 CERD, *Concluding Observations: Canada*, UN Doc CERD/C/CAN/CO/18 (2007), [17]; CERD, *Concluding Observations: Australia*, UN Doc CERD/C/AUS/CO/15–17 (2010), [13].

237 CERD, *Concluding Observations: Suriname*, UN Doc CERD/C/SUR/CO/12 (2009), [14]; CERD, *Concluding Observations: Sweden*, UN Doc CERD/C/SWE/CO/14 (2013), [17]; CERD, *Concluding Observations: Peru*, UN Doc CERD/C/PER/CO/14–17 (2009), [14].

238 CERD, *Concluding Observations: Ecuador*, UN Doc CERD/C/ECU/CO/20–22 (2012), [17].

239 CERD, *Concluding Observations: New Zealand*, UN Doc CERD/C/NZL/CO/18–20 (2013), [18]; CERD, *Concluding Observations: Bolivia*, UN Doc CERD/C/BOL/CO/17–20 (2011), [20].

240 CERD, *Concluding Observations: Panama*, UN Doc CERD/C/PAN/CO/15–20 (2010), [14].

241 CERD, *Concluding Observations: Bolivia*, UN Doc CERD/C/BOL/CO/17–20 (2011), [20].

242 CERD, *Concluding Observations: Guyana*, UN Doc CERD/C/CUY/CO/14 (2006), [14].

243 CERD, *Concluding Observations: Finland*, UN Doc CERD/C/FIN/CO/20–22 (2012), [13] (where Finnish reindeer cooperatives, the majority of whose members practice modern reindeer farming rather than traditional Sámi reindeer husbandry, take decisions by majority vote).

emphasised that indigenous peoples have a right to participate in the management of projects,[244] and to receive compensation for damage where restitution of land is not possible.[245] The duty to make reparation extends to the taking of resources, as where indigenous reindeer herds are taken by predators protected by the state's wildlife protection laws.[246]

The exploitation of indigenous lands and resources has often involved the forced eviction, displacement or relocation of indigenous peoples,[247] including by home demolitions[248] and non-renewal of leases.[249] In addition, indigenous peoples have been sometimes forcibly resettled,[250] disproportionately displaced by armed conflict (particularly indigenous women and children, and without adequate humanitarian assistance),[251] or displaced by population transfers or the migration of others to their lands.[252] Some indigenous refugees have also been forcibly repatriated to unsafe home states.[253] The CERD has called on states to inform and consult indigenous peoples on the reasons for displacement, obtain their free and informed consent, provide compensation and resettlement, and assist them to maintain cultural ties.[254]

The CERD has also condemned the use of intimidation[255] or violence in the exploitation of indigenous lands and resources and/or the forced displacement of indigenous peoples. This has included arbitrary arrests and detention,[256] false charges,[257] excessive use of force, disappearances, and murders and summary executions.[258] The CERD has identified the perpetrators as variously including public authorities

[244] CERD, *Concluding Observations: Namibia*, UN Doc CERD/C/NAM/CO/12 (2008), [16].

[245] CERD, *Concluding Observations: Peru*, UN Doc CERD/C/PER/CO/14–17 (2009), [20]; CERD, *Concluding Observations: Cameroon*, UN Doc CERD/C/CMR/CO/15–18 (2010), [18]; CERD, *Concluding Observations: Guatemala*, UN Doc A/52/18 (1997), [93].

[246] CERD, *Concluding Observations: Sweden*, UN Doc CERD/C/SWE/CO/14 (2013), [18].

[247] CERD, *Concluding Observations: Denmark*, UN Doc A/56/18 (1996), [72] (military base); CERD, *Concluding Observations: Philippines*, UN Doc A/52/18 (1997), [425] (development zones); CERD, *Concluding Observations: Nepal*, UN Doc A/59/18 (2004), [128] (wildlife preservation); CERD, *Concluding Observations: Panama*, UN Doc CERD/C/PAN/CO/15–20 (2010), [13] (energy, resources and tourism); CERD, *Concluding Observations: India*, UN Doc CERD/C/IND/CO/19 (2007), [19] (dams).

[248] CERD, *Concluding Observations: Israel*, UN Doc CERD/C/ISR/CO/14–16 (2012), [20] (Bedouin communities in the Negev).

[249] CERD, *Concluding Observations: Fiji*, UN Doc A/58/18 (2003), [88].

[250] CERD, *Concluding Observations: Laos*, UN Doc A/60/18 (2005), [170] (highlanders moved to the plains).

[251] CERD, *Concluding Observations: Colombia*, UN Doc CERD/C/COL/CO/14 (2009), [16].

[252] CERD, *Concluding Observations: Vietnam*, UN Doc A/56/18(SUPP) (2001), [421]; CERD, *Concluding Observations: Costa Rica*, UN Doc A/57/18 (2002), [74]; CERD, *Concluding Observations: Nicaragua*, UN Doc CERD/C/NIC/CO/14 (2008), [21].

[253] CERD, *Concluding Observations: Viet Nam*, UN Doc CERD/C/VNM/CO/10–14 (2012), [18].

[254] CERD, *Concluding Observations: Laos*, UN Doc A/60/18 (2005), [170]; CERD, *Concluding Observations: Guatemala*, UN Doc CERD/C/GTM/CO/11 (2006), [17] (restitution of lands for displacement by armed conflict or development).

[255] CERD, *Concluding Observations: Argentina*, UN Doc A/52/18 (1997), [548]; CERD, *Concluding Observations: Cambodia*, UN Doc CERD/C/KHM/CO/8–13 (2010), [19].

[256] CERD, *Concluding Observations: Chile*, UN Doc A/54/18 (1999), [375]; CERD, *Concluding Observations: Guatemala*, UN Doc A/52/18 (1997), [81].

[257] CERD, *Concluding Observations: Cambodia*, UN Doc CERD/C/KHM/CO/8–13 (2010), [19].

[258] CERD, *Concluding Observations: Nigeria*, UN Doc A/60/18 (2005), [294]; CERD, *Concluding Observations: Mexico*, UN Doc A/52/18 (1997), [307]; CERD, *Concluding Observations: Venezuela*, UN Doc A/60/18 (2005), [380].

(such as law enforcement, military police, and paramilitary groups)[259] and private groups (such as big landowners, private armed groups or militias, and oil company personnel).[260] According to the CERD such violence violates the right to security of person and it has called on states to independently monitor, investigate and punish perpetrators.[261] It has also welcomed national state of emergency laws aimed at stopping the forced eviction of indigenous peoples.[262]

Broader economic developments which impact on indigenous lands and resources have also been identified by the CERD. These include economic crises,[263] structural adjustment and privatisation,[264] economic internationalisation[265] and free trade agreements.[266]

Under its early warning and urgent action procedure, the CERD has often focused on activities threatening indigenous land and natural resources. For example, the CERD was concerned that amendments to Australia's native title legislation were discriminatory and inconsistent with ICERD obligations. Whereas the original law of 1993, adopted to implement a landmark High Court decision in *Mabo (No 2) v Commonwealth* (1992),[267] 'delicately balanced' the rights of indigenous and non-indigenous title holders, the amendments regressively created 'legal certainty for Governments and third parties at the expense of indigenous title'.[268] Indigenous people had also not been effectively consulted.[269]

The CERD was similarly concerned at a New Zealand law, the Foreshore and Seabed Act 2004, that was adopted in response to a Court of Appeal decision in the *Ngati Apa* case.[270] The CERD observed that the law appeared to discriminate against the Maori, particularly by extinguishing customary titles over the foreshore and seabed and failing to provide a right of remedy.[271] The CERD was further concerned that the law was adopted hastily and without sufficient consultation, resulting in a failure to consider alternatives that may have better accommodated the

259 CERD, *Concluding Observations: Brazil*, UN Doc A/51/18 (1996), [303]; CERD, *Concluding Observations: Mexico*, UN Doc A/52/18 (1997), [307]; CERD, *Concluding Observations: Panama*, UN Doc CERD/C/PAN/CO/15–20 (2010), [13].

260 CERD, *Concluding Observations: Venezuela*, UN Doc A/60/18 (2005), [380]; CERD, *Concluding Observations: Brazil*, UN Doc A/51/18 (1996), [303]; CERD, *Concluding Observations: Mexico*, UN Doc A/52/18 (1997), [307].

261 CERD, *Concluding Observations: Venezuela*, UN Doc A/60/18 (2005), [380]; CERD, *Concluding Observations: Paraguay*, UN Doc CERD/C/PRY/CO/1–3 (2011), [15]; CERD, *Concluding Observations: Argentina*, UN Doc CERD/C/ARG/CO/19–20 (2010), [21].

262 CERD, *Concluding Observations: Argentina*, UN Doc CERD/C/ARG/CO/19–20 (2010), [21].

263 CERD, *Concluding Observations: Argentina*, UN Doc A/56/18 (2001), [49].

264 CERD, *Concluding Observations: Nicaragua*, UN Doc A/50/18 (1995), [533]; CERD, *Concluding Observations: Sweden*, UN Doc CERD/C/304/Add.103 (2000), [13].

265 CERD, *Concluding Observations: Mexico*, UN Doc A/50/18 (1995), [380].

266 CERD, *Concluding Observations: New Zealand*, UN Doc CERD/C/NZL/CO/18–20 (2013), [18].

267 *Mabo (No 2) v Commonwealth* (1992) 175 CLR 1.

268 CERD, *Decision 2(54) on Australia*, A/54/18 (18 March 1999), [6] (specific concerns included: 'the Act's "validation" provisions; the "confirmation of extinguishment" provisions; the primary production upgrade provisions; and restrictions concerning the right of indigenous title holders to negotiate non-indigenous land uses': [7].

269 Ibid [9].

270 *Ngati Apa v Attorney General* [2003] 3 NZLR 643.

271 CERD, *Decision 1(66), New Zealand Foreshore and Seabed Act 2004*, UN Doc CERD/C/DEC/NZL/1 (11 March 2005), [6].

competing interests.[272] It noted widespread Maori opposition to the law and their perception that it was discriminatory.[273] It urged the authorities to avoid 'exploiting racial tensions for their own political advantage'.[274] It also urged the state to resume dialogue, 'in a spirit of goodwill and in accordance with the ideals of the Waitangi Treaty', to mitigate the discriminatory effects, including by applying the law flexibly or amending the law.[275]

The CERD cautioned Suriname for authorising, despite the CERD's previous protests, additional resource exploitation and infrastructure projects that threatened irreparable harm to indigenous and tribal peoples.[276] The affected communities had not been notified and had not consented. The CERD called on Suriname to ensure that its mining law acknowledged indigenous rights in land and resources; required indigenous peoples' agreement before granting concessions; and ensured effective remedies and compensation.[277]

The CERD was concerned about irreparable harm to the Western Shoshone peoples in the United States, as a result of the accelerated exploitation of, and encroachment upon, their traditional lands, and the extinguishment of traditional land and resource rights.[278] In particular, the CERD was concerned about the privatisation of ancestral lands for transfer to multinational extractive industries and energy developers; destructive activities in areas of spiritual and cultural significance (including a nuclear waste repository, use of explosives and open pit gold mining, and geothermal energy leases at hot springs); and underground nuclear testing.[279]

Such activities occurred or were planned without consultation with, and against the protests of, the indigenous communities, who also faced difficulties in challenging them in court.[280] Alienation of land had also taken place under an 'Indian Claims Commission' which did not comply with human rights standards.[281] The CERD found that the Western Shoshone had been intimidated and harassed by state authorities, such as through 'the imposition of grazing fees, trespass and collection notices, impounding of horse and livestock, restrictions on hunting, fishing and gathering, as well as arrests, which gravely disturb the enjoyment of their ancestral lands'.[282]

Consequently, the CERD found that the United States was not respecting its ICERD obligations, in particular to guarantee equality before the law and the non-discriminatory enjoyment of civil, political, economic, social and cultural rights.[283]

[272] Ibid [4].
[273] Ibid [5].
[274] Ibid [3].
[275] Ibid [7]–[8].
[276] CERD, *Decision 1(67) on Suriname*, UN Doc CERD/C/DEC/SUR/4 (1 November 2005), [3]; see also earlier CERD, *Decision 3(66) on Suriname*, UN Doc CERD/C/DEC/SUR/1 (9 March 2005).
[277] Ibid [4].
[278] CERD, *Decision 1(68): United States of America*, UN Doc CERD/C/USA/DEC/1 (11 April 2006), [4], [6].
[279] Ibid [7].
[280] Ibid.
[281] Ibid [6] (citing the finding to this effect in *Mary and Carrie Dann v United States*, Case 11.140, IACtHR, 27 December 2002).
[282] Ibid [7].
[283] Ibid.

It requested the United States to respect and protect such rights, especially the right to health and cultural rights that were threatened by environmental harm and damage to spiritually and culturally significant places.[284] The CERD urged the United States to initiate a dialogue with indigenous representatives to find an acceptable solution, respecting their right to own, develop, control and use their communal lands, territories and resources.[285] It urged the United States to freeze any privatization of land; desist from extractive and harmful activities; cease measures of intimidation or harassment; and rescind the measures already imposed.[286]

Culture and Language

In General Comment No 23 (1997) the CERD emphasised that states must recognise, respect and promote indigenous culture, history, language and way of life as an enrichment of the state's cultural identity.[287] States must specifically ensure that indigenous peoples can practice their cultural traditions, customs and languages,[288] and provide them with 'conditions allowing for a sustainable economic and social development compatible with their cultural characteristics'.[289]

As noted above, in monitoring states the CERD has often highlighted the links between indigenous lands and resources and their cultural and spiritual beliefs, practices and identities. In addition, the protection of indigenous languages has been a focus, particularly where they are endangered.[290] The CERD has been concerned at the inability to use indigenous languages in administrative and judicial matters,[291] including because of a lack of interpreters.[292] It has been concerned about a lack of, or deficiencies in, bilingual education,[293] including where only some indigenous languages are used,[294] or where languages are taught only in the early years of school.[295] The CERD has found that this contributes to high illiteracy rates.[296] Illiteracy in the national language can also disadvantage indigenous peoples in defending their rights.[297] The CERD has pointed out where laws have not been translated

284 Ibid [8].
285 Ibid [9].
286 Ibid [10].
287 CERD, *General Recommendation No 23* (n 138), [4].
288 Ibid.
289 Ibid.
290 CERD, *Concluding Observations: Peru*, UN Doc CERD/C/PER/CO/14–17 (2009), [13]; CERD, *Concluding Observations: Suriname*, UN Doc A/59/18 (2004), [200].
291 CERD, *Concluding Observations: Russia*, UN Doc A/51/18 (1996), [138]; CERD, *Concluding Observations: Guatemala*, UN Doc A/50/18 (1995), [309]; CERD, *Concluding Observations: Mexico*, UN Doc A/52/18 (1997), [306].
292 CERD, *Concluding Observations: Guatemala*, UN Doc A/52/18 (1997), [79].
293 CERD, *Concluding Observations: Mexico*, UN Doc A/50/18 (1995), [386]; CERD, *Concluding Observations: Russia*, UN Doc A/51/18 (1996), [138]; CERD, *Concluding Observations: Venezuela*, UN Doc A/51/18 (1996), [471]; CERD, *Concluding Observations: Ecuador*, UN Doc CERD/C/ECU/CO/19 (2008), [20]; CERD, *Concluding Observations: Paraguay*, UN Doc CERD/C/PRY/CO/1–3 (2011), [19].
294 CERD, *Concluding Observations: El Salvador*, UN Doc CERD/C/SLV/CO/14–15 (2010), [21].
295 CERD, *Concluding Observations: Chile*, UN Doc CERD/C/CHL/CO/19–21 (2013), [15].
296 CERD, *Concluding Observations: Guatemala*, UN Doc A/50/18 (1995), [311].
297 CERD, *Concluding Observations: Bolivia*, UN Doc A/51/18 (1996), [269].

into indigenous languages,[298] and where the media is inaccessible in indigenous languages.[299] The CERD has indicated that its own concluding observations on states' performance should be translated.[300] It has called on states to take measures and adopt plans to preserve indigenous languages.[301]

Other aspects of indigenous culture have been highlighted by the CERD. It has called on states to protect indigenous peoples' cultural heritage,[302] including sacred and cultural sites and objects, and enable access to them and participation in their management.[303] It has endorsed laws for the protection of indigenous intellectual and cultural property rights, including in relation to traditional knowledge, genetic and biological resources, and on the relationship of indigenous communities with the environment in connection with conservation, language, cultural heritage, traditional healing and medicine.[304]

As regards religion, the CERD has been concerned by laws and practices which differentiate between or establish a hierarchy among religions, adversely affecting indigenous freedom of thought, conscience and religion.[305] In this connection it has criticised requirements on individuals to mention their faith on legal documents such as identity cards and birth certificates, leading to discrimination and harassment.[306] It noted where people of minority religions face difficulties in registering marriages or births,[307] or are impeded from accessing their places of worship.[308]

Political Rights

In General Comment No 23 (1997), the CERD observed that indigenous peoples must have equal rights of participation in public life, and decisions relating to their rights and interests must not be taken without their informed consent.[309] In monitoring states, the CERD has often commented on the lack of participation or under-representation of indigenous peoples in politics and public life, including in parliament, government and public service,[310] the military,[311] and in public inquiries

[298] CERD, *Concluding Observations: Peru*, UN Doc A/54/18 (1999), [152]; CERD, *Concluding Observations: New Zealand*, UN Doc A/57/18 (2002), [420]; CERD, *Concluding Observations: Peru*, UN Doc CERD/C/PER/CO/14–17 (2009), [13].

[299] CERD, *Concluding Observations: Botswana*, UN Doc A/57/18 (2002), [305].

[300] CERD, *Concluding Observations: Guyana*, UN Doc CERD/C/CUY/CO/14 (2006), [27].

[301] CERD, *Concluding Observations: Suriname*, UN Doc A/59/18 (2004), [200]; CERD, *Concluding Observations: Costa Rica*, UN Doc A/62/18 (2007), [308].

[302] CERD, *Concluding Observations: Costa Rica*, UN Doc A/62/18 (2007), [308]; CERD, *Concluding Observations: Venezuela*, UN Doc A/51/18 (1996), [471].

[303] CERD, *Concluding Observations: Saint Lucia*, UN A/59/18 (2004), [450], [447]; CERD, *Concluding Observations: Guatemala*, UN Doc CERD/C/GTM/CO/11 (2006), [18].

[304] CERD, *Concluding Observations: New Zealand*, UN Doc CERD/C/NZL/CO/18–20 (2013), [13].

[305] CERD, *Concluding Observations: Indonesia*, UN Doc A/62/18 (2007), [363].

[306] Ibid.

[307] Ibid.

[308] CERD, *Concluding Observations: El Salvador*, UN Doc CERD/C/SLV/CO/13 (2006), [14].

[309] CERD, *General Recommendation No 23* (n 138), [4].

[310] CERD, *Concluding Observations: Australia*, UN Doc A/49/18 (1994), [548]; CERD, *Concluding Observations: Guatemala*, UN Doc A/50/18 (1995), [305]; CERD, *Concluding Observations: Guatemala*, UN Doc A/52/18 (1997), [83]; CERD, *Concluding Observations: Guyana*, UN Doc CERD/C/CUY/CO/14 (2006), [13].

[311] CERD, *Concluding Observations: Guyana*, UN Doc CERD/C/CUY/CO/14 (2006), [18].

on indigenous issues.[312] It has identified specific barriers to participation, including the lack of identity papers and illiteracy;[313] a prohibition on illiterates being elected;[314] low education levels;[315] and multiple and intersectional discrimination against women.[316] It has supported special measures or affirmative action through electoral quotas for indigenous peoples in parliament,[317] and criticised quotas that are too limited[318] or that were abrogated.[319]

The CERD has also been concerned where indigenous representative bodies have been abolished,[320] are not representative or have only advisory functions.[321] It has urged states to speed up implementation of the principle of indigenous peoples exercising meaningful control over their affairs, as well as constitutional recognition of indigenous peoples.[322]

Law Enforcement and Access to Justice

The over-incarceration of indigenous people has concerned the CERD,[323] including as a result of racially discriminatory mandatory minimum sentencing for minor property offences.[324] It has been concerned about growing imprisonment rates for indigenous women,[325] inadequate detention conditions,[326] separate prisons for indigenous peoples[327] and deaths in custody.[328] It has called on states to pursue alternatives to imprisonment wherever possible, including by allowing offenders to serve their sentences in their communities.[329] It has supported diversionary and preventive programmes in juvenile justice and culturally sensitive procedures and practices among the police and judiciary.[330]

312 CERD, *Concluding Observations: Japan*, UN Doc CERD/C/JPN/CO/3–6 (2010), [20] (insufficient representation of Ainu people in consultation forums and in the Advisory Panel of Eminent Persons conducting a survey on the status of Ainu outside of Hokkaido).

313 CERD, *Concluding Observations: Peru*, UN Doc A/54/18 (1999), [154].

314 CERD, *Concluding Observations: Brazil*, UN Doc A/51/18 (1996), [302].

315 CERD, *Concluding Observations: Congo*, UN Doc CERD/C/COG/CO/9 (2009), [16].

316 CERD, *Concluding Observations: Bolivia*, UN Doc CERD/C/BOL/CO/17–20 (2011), [13].

317 CERD, *Concluding Observations: New Zealand*, UN Doc A/57/18 (2002), [419].

318 CERD, *Concluding Observations: Bolivia*, UN Doc CERD/C/BOL/CO/17–20 (2011), [13] (where only 7 of 130 seats were reserved).

319 CERD, *Concluding Observations: Russia*, UN Doc CERD/C/RUS/CO/19 (2008), [20].

320 CERD, *Concluding Observations: Australia*, UN Doc A/60/18 (2005), [31].

321 CERD, *Concluding Observations: Australia*, UN Doc CERD/C/AUS/CO/15–17 (2010), [15].

322 Ibid.

323 CERD, *Concluding Observations: Canada*, UN Doc A/49/18 (1994), [326]; CERD, *Concluding Observations: Australia*, UN Doc A/49/18 (1994), [545]; CERD, *Concluding Observations: Australia*, UN Doc A/55/18 (2000), [38]; CERD, *Concluding Observations: Canada*, UN Doc A/57/18 (2002), [333]; CERD, *Concluding Observations: Canada*, UN Doc CERD/C/CAN/CO/19–20 (2012), [12].

324 CERD, *Concluding Observations: Australia*, UN Doc A/55/18 (2000), [39].

325 CERD, *Concluding Observations: Australia*, UN Doc CERD/C/AUS/CO/15–17 (2010), [20].

326 Ibid.

327 CERD, *Concluding Observations: Venezuela*, UN Doc A/51/18 (1996), [472].

328 CERD, *Concluding Observations: Australia*, UN Doc A/49/18 (1994), [543]; CERD, *Concluding Observations: Canada*, UN Doc A/57/18 (2002), [333].

329 CERD, *Concluding Observations: Canada*, UN Doc CERD/C/CAN/CO/19–20 (2012), [12].

330 CERD, *Concluding Observations: Australia*, UN Doc A/60/18 (2005), [25].

Intimidation and violence against indigenous people (and their human rights defenders)[331] has been amongst the most frequent concerns of the CERD, whether by state authorities (such as the police, military[332] and 'eco-guards'[333]) or private groups (such as armed groups, civilian self-defence patrols[334] and racist[335] or totalitarian groups[336]). As noted earlier, violence has often occurred in the context of land and natural resource disputes, but also in relation to organised crime,[337] the drug trade,[338] counter-terrorism[339] and armed conflict.[340] Acts have included threats and harassment;[341] ill-treatment and abuse;[342] excessive use of force during demonstrations and civil unrest;[343] forcible arbitrary arrests and detention;[344] cruel, inhuman or degrading treatment;[345] forced recruitment;[346] killing and summary or extra-judicial executions;[347] and enforced disappearances.[348] In some cases, indigenous peoples have been brought to 'the brink of extinction due to armed conflict and related consequences'.[349] It also has been noted that in some cases impunity has led to lynchings and vigilantism in retaliation.[350]

To remedy violence against indigenous peoples, the CERD has called on states to investigate, prosecute and punish offenders and compensate the victims,[351] including for the mass murder of indigenous peoples.[352] It has called for the repeal of amnesty laws that shield perpetrators.[353] It has also called for the training of law enforcement officials and the military to protect human rights;[354] the raising of awareness

331 CERD, *Concluding Observations: Mexico*, UN Doc CERD/C/MEX/CO/16–17 (2012), [15].
332 CERD, *Concluding Observations: Ecuador*, UN Doc CERD/C/ECU/CO/19 (2008), [14].
333 CERD, *Concluding Observations: Congo*, UN Doc CERD/C/COG/CO/9 (2009), [13].
334 CERD, *Concluding Observations: Guatemala*, UN Doc A/50/18 (1995), [307].
335 CERD, *Concluding Observations: Bolivia*, UN Doc CERD/C/BOL/CO/17–20 (2011), [17].
336 CERD, *Concluding Observations: Chile*, UN Doc CERD/C/CHL/CO/15–18 (2009), [18].
337 CERD, *Concluding Observations: Mexico*, UN Doc CERD/C/MEX/CO/16–17 (2012), [13].
338 CERD, *Concluding Observations: Colombia*, UN Doc A/54/18 (1999), [463].
339 CERD, *Concluding Observations: Peru*, UN Doc A/50/18 (1995), [201], [203]; CERD, *Concluding Observations: Chile*, UN Doc CERD/C/CHL/CO/15–18 (2009), [15]; CERD, *Concluding Observations: Chile*, UN Doc CERD/C/CHL/CO/19–21 (2013), [14]; CERD, *Concluding Observations: Russia*, UN Doc CERD/C/RUS/CO/20–22 (2013), [13].
340 CERD, *Concluding Observations: Colombia*, UN Doc CERD/C/COL/CO/14 (2009), [25].
341 CERD, *Concluding Observations: Bolivia*, UN Doc A/58/18 (2003), [340].
342 CERD, *Concluding Observations: Chile*, UN Doc CERD/C/CHL/CO/15–18 (2009), [19].
343 CERD, *Concluding Observations: Ecuador*, UN Doc A/58/18 (2003), [58].
344 CERD, *Concluding Observations: Bangladesh*, UN Doc A/56/18 (2001), [71].
345 Ibid.
346 CERD, *Concluding Observations: Colombia*, UN Doc CERD/C/COL/CO/14 (2009), [14].
347 CERD, *Concluding Observations: Bangladesh*, UN Doc A/56/18 (2001), [71].
348 CERD, *Concluding Observations: Colombia*, UN Doc CERD/C/COL/CO/14 (2009), [14].
349 Ibid [25].
350 CERD, *Concluding Observations: Guatemala*, UN Doc A/52/18 (1997), [80].
351 CERD, *Concluding Observations: Mexico*, UN Doc A/50/18 (1995), [395]; CERD, *Concluding Observations: Brazil*, UN Doc A/51/18 (1996), [308]; CERD, *Concluding Observations: Chile*, UN Doc CERD/C/CHL/CO/15–18 (2009), [19]; CERD, *Concluding Observations: El Salvador*, UN Doc CERD/C/SLV/CO/14–15 (2010), [18].
352 CERD, *Concluding Observations: El Salvador*, UN Doc CERD/C/SLV/CO/13 (2006), [15].
353 CERD, *Concluding Observations: El Salvador*, UN Doc CERD/C/SLV/CO/14–15 (2010), [18].
354 CERD, *Concluding Observations: Australia*, UN Doc A/49/18 (1994), [548]; CERD, *Concluding Observations: Brazil*, UN Doc A/51/18 (1996), [308]; CERD, *Concluding Observations: Ecuador*, UN Doc A/58/18 (2003), [58]; CERD, *Concluding Observations: Chile*, UN Doc CERD/C/CHL/CO/15–18 (2009), [19]; CERD, *Concluding Observations: Colombia*, UN Doc CERD/C/COL/CO/14 (2009), [17].

about human rights amongst the public and in schools;[355] and information campaigns about their rights for indigenous peoples.[356] The CERD has further called for the strengthening of the judiciary;[357] more funding for ombudsperson offices;[358] and laws and mechanisms to protect human rights defenders.[359]

In relation to access to justice, the CERD has noted that barriers for indigenous peoples include non-recognition as legal persons before the courts;[360] ineffective remedies for collective rights;[361] insufficient public defenders;[362] and the inability to use indigenous languages,[363] and unavailability of interpreters or bilingual counsel,[364] in court. The CERD has recommended that states provide training to judges, public prosecutors and justice system staff to ensure indigenous peoples have effective and equal access to justice.[365] It has also supported diversionary, preventive and restorative justice strategies. It has encouraged the accessibility of courts by asking states to reduce the distance between courts and where indigenous peoples live.[366]

Indigenous law and justice systems have also been considered by the CERD. It has noted that the non-recognition of indigenous legal systems can impair access to justice.[367] Accordingly it has called on states to respect and ensure respect for and recognition of the traditional systems of justice, 'in conformity with international human rights law',[368] including by establishing special indigenous courts.[369] It has criticised the slow adoption of laws governing the authority, jurisdiction and responsibilities of indigenous justice systems,[370] and called on states to harmonise indigenous customs with the positive legal order.[371]

Where indigenous justice systems are recognised by state law, the CERD has been concerned where national legal systems do not include certain personal, material and territorial matters within the scope of the indigenous justice system, such that reality does not correspond to the situation of coexistence between indigenous and non-indigenous persons.[372] It has also been concerned about a lack of clarity in jurisdictional demarcation, coordination and cooperation between indigenous and

355 CERD, *Concluding Observations: Chile*, UN Doc A/54/18 (1999), [380].
356 CERD, *Concluding Observations: Suriname*, UN Doc A/59/18 (2004), [197].
357 CERD, *Concluding Observations: Guatemala*, UN Doc A/50/18 (1995), [309].
358 CERD, *Concluding Observations: Panama*, UN Doc CERD/C/PAN/CO/15–20 (2010), [7]–[14], [16], [19]–[22].
359 CERD, *Concluding Observations: Mexico*, UN Doc CERD/C/MEX/CO/16–17 (2012), [15].
360 CERD, *Concluding Observations: Suriname*, UN Doc A/59/18 (2004), [193]; CERD, *Concluding Observations: Argentina*, UN Doc A/59/18 (2004), [246].
361 CERD, *Concluding Observations: Suriname*, UN Doc CERD/C/SUR/CO/12 (2009), [18].
362 CERD, *Concluding Observations: Guatemala*, UN Doc A/52/18 (1997), [79].
363 CERD, *Concluding Observations: Nicaragua*, UN Doc CERD/C/NIC/CO/14 (2008), [19].
364 CERD, *Concluding Observations: Guatemala*, UN Doc CERD/C/GTM/CO/11 (2006), [14]; CERD, *Concluding Observations: Mexico*, UN Doc CERD/C/MEX/CO/15 (2006), [13].
365 CERD, *Concluding Observations: Guatemala*, UN Doc CERD/C/GTM/CO/12–13 (2010), [8].
366 CERD, *Concluding Observations: Cameroon*, UN Doc CERD/C/CMR/CO/15–18 (2010), [17].
367 CERD, *Concluding Observations: Guatemala*, UN Doc CERD/C/GTM/CO/11 (2006), [14].
368 Ibid [14].
369 CERD, *Concluding Observations: Mexico*, UN Doc CERD/C/MEX/CO/16–17 (2012), [12].
370 CERD, *Concluding Observations: Ecuador*, UN Doc CERD/C/ECU/CO/20–22 (2012), [19].
371 CERD, *Concluding Observations: Mexico*, UN Doc A/50/18 (1995), [388].
372 CERD, *Concluding Observations: Bolivia*, UN Doc CERD/C/BOL/CO/17–20 (2011), [22].

non-indigenous justice systems.[373] The CERD has further criticised customary traditional courts which do not equitably represent indigenous customs.[374]

Economic and Social Rights

The CERD has often expressed concern that indigenous peoples are discriminated against or disadvantaged across the spectrum of socio-economic rights, including rights to education, health, employment, social security, an adequate standard of living (including food, water and shelter) and in access to basic services.[375] As a result they often live in extreme and multidimensional poverty.[376] Sometimes they are forced to leave their ancestral lands in search of better opportunities,[377] further impacting on their culture and identity. In consequence, the CERD has called on states to ensure effective protection against discrimination,[378] and provide affirmative action, in these areas,[379] within the shortest possible time and by allocating sufficient resources.[380]

Concerning indigenous health, the CERD has been concerned about high infant and maternal mortality;[381] high suicide rates;[382] life expectancy gaps;[383] chronic malnutrition;[384] substance abuse;[385] the forced sterilisation of women;[386] diseases (including malaria,[387] HIV/AIDS,[388] water-borne diseases[389] and sexually

373 Ibid.

374 CERD, *Concluding Observations: Cameroon*, UN Doc CERD/C/CMR/CO/15–18 (2010), [17] (where Bantu customs predominate over others).

375 CERD, *Concluding Observations: Panama*, UN Doc CERD/C/PAN/CO/15–20 (2010), [12]; CERD, *Concluding Observations: Congo*, UN Doc CERD/C/COG/CO/9 (2009), [15]; CERD, *Concluding Observations: Guatemala*, UN Doc A/50/18 (1995), [313]; CERD, *Concluding Observations: Viet Nam*, UN Doc CERD/C/VNM/CO/10–14 (2012), [13]; CERD, *Concluding Observations: Mexico*, UN Doc CERD/C/MEX/CO/16–17 (2012), [18]; CERD, *Concluding Observations: Canada*, UN Doc CERD/C/CAN/CO/19–20 (2012), [19].

376 CERD, *Concluding Observations: Argentina*, UN Doc CERD/C/ARG/CO/19–20 (2010), [29]; CERD, *Concluding Observations: Canada*, UN Doc CERD/C/CAN/CO/19–20 (2012), [19]; CERD, *Concluding Observations: Guatemala*, UN Doc CERD/C/GTM/CO/12–13 (2010), [12]; CERD, *Concluding Observations: Viet Nam*, UN Doc CERD/C/VNM/CO/10–14 (2012), [13].

377 CERD, *Concluding Observations: Costa Rica*, UN Doc A/62/18 (2007), [300].

378 CERD, *Concluding Observations: Argentina*, UN Doc CERD/C/ARG/CO/19–20 (2010), [29].

379 CERD, *Concluding Observations: Australia*, UN Doc A/46/18 (1991), [245]; CERD, *Concluding Observations: Bangladesh*, UN Doc A/56/18 (2001), [66].

380 CERD, *Concluding Observations: Australia*, UN Doc A/55/18 (2000), [41].

381 CERD, *Concluding Observations: Costa Rica*, UN Doc A/57/18 (2002), [74]; CERD, *Concluding Observations: Guatemala*, UN Doc CERD/C/GTM/CO/12–13 (2010), [13].

382 CERD, *Concluding Observations: Canada*, UN Doc A/49/18 (1994), [326]; CERD, *Concluding Observations: Australia*, UN Doc A/49/18 (1994), [545].

383 CERD, *Concluding Observations: Peru*, UN Doc A/54/18 (1999), [155]; CERD, *Concluding Observations: Guyana*, UN Doc CERD/C/CUY/CO/14 (2006), [19].

384 CERD, *Concluding Observations: Guatemala*, UN Doc CERD/C/GTM/CO/12–13 (2010), [12].

385 CERD, *Concluding Observations: Canada*, UN Doc A/49/18 (1994), [326]; CERD, *Concluding Observations: Australia*, UN Doc A/49/18 (1994), [545].

386 CERD, *Concluding Observations: Peru*, UN Doc A/54/18 (1999), [155]; CERD, *Concluding Observations: Mexico*, UN Doc CERD/C/MEX/CO/15 (2006), [17].

387 CERD, *Concluding Observations: Guyana*, UN Doc CERD/C/CUY/CO/14 (2006), [19].

388 CERD, *Concluding Observations: Panama*, UN Doc CERD/C/PAN/CO/15–20 (2010), [19]; CERD, *Concluding Observations: Namibia*, UN Doc CERD/C/NAM/CO/12 (2008), [21].

389 CERD, *Concluding Observations: Guatemala*, UN Doc CERD/C/GTM/CO/12–13 (2010), [14].

transmitted diseases in mining and forestry areas[390]); the adverse effects of environmental pollution (such as mercury and bacterial contamination of rivers caused by mining[391]); lack of safe drinking water;[392] mental health;[393] sexual and reproductive health services;[394] and the inaccessibility of health services and infrastructure.[395] The CERD has recommended that states develop and implement a comprehensive and culturally sensitive strategy to ensure that indigenous peoples receive quality healthcare, with particular attention to indigenous women and children, and can access interpreter services.[396]

In the area of education, the CERD has been concerned about the lack of free primary education;[397] low school and university enrolments and/or attendance;[398] difficulties in obtaining birth certificates that are necessary for enrolment;[399] high repetition and drop out rates;[400] lack of qualified teachers, textbooks and classrooms;[401] lack of culturally relevant curricula and schools;[402] lack of bilingual education; high illiteracy rates;[403] and insults and bullying.[404] The CERD has called on states to use their maximum available resources to assist indigenous peoples by building schools, training teachers, providing culturally appropriate textbooks, using indigenous languages and extending scholarship programmes.[405]

In relation to work rights, the CERD has called for equal opportunities in employment for indigenous people,[406] including in recruitment and promotion,[407] equal pay,[408] and the right to form and join trade unions.[409] It has condemned slavery[410] and debt servitude,[411] and drawn attention to the vulnerability of indigenous migrant workers.[412] It has encouraged states to adopt special measures to guarantee work

390 CERD, *Concluding Observations: Suriname*, UN Doc A/59/18 (2004), [196].
391 CERD, *Concluding Observations: Guyana*, UN Doc CERD/C/CUY/CO/14 (2006), [19].
392 CERD, *Concluding Observations: Bolivia*, UN Doc A/51/18 (1996), [268].
393 CERD, *Concluding Observations: New Zealand*, UN Doc A/57/18 (2002), [422].
394 CERD, *Concluding Observations: Panama*, UN Doc CERD/C/PAN/CO/15–20 (2010), [19].
395 CERD, *Concluding Observations: Nicaragua*, UN Doc CERD/C/NIC/CO/14 (2008), [22].
396 CERD, *Concluding Observations: Mexico*, UN Doc CERD/C/MEX/CO/16–17 (2012), [19].
397 CERD, Concluding Observations: Colombia (2009), UN Doc CERD/C/COL/CO/14, [23].
398 CERD, *Concluding Observations: Guyana*, UN Doc CERD/C/CUY/CO/14 (2006), [20]; CERD, *Concluding Observations: Namibia*, UN Doc CERD/C/NAM/CO/12 (2008), [21]; CERD, *Concluding Observations: Guatemala*, UN Doc CERD/C/GTM/CO/11 (2006), [20].
399 CERD, *Concluding Observations: Cameroon*, UN Doc CERD/C/CMR/CO/15–18 (2010), [16].
400 CERD, *Concluding Observations: Cambodia*, UN Doc CERD/C/KHM/CO/8–13 (2010), [20].
401 CERD, *Concluding Observations: Guyana*, UN Doc CERD/C/CUY/CO/14 (2006), [20].
402 CERD, *Concluding Observations: Guatemala*, UN Doc CERD/C/GTM/CO/11 (2006), [20]; CERD, *Concluding Observations: Cameroon*, UN Doc CERD/C/CMR/CO/15–18 (2010), [16].
403 CERD, *Concluding Observations: Guatemala*, UN Doc CERD/C/GTM/CO/12–13 (2010), [13]; CERD, *Concluding Observations: Colombia*, UN Doc CERD/C/COL/CO/14 (2009), [23]; CERD, *Concluding Observations: Guatemala*, UN Doc CERD/C/GTM/CO/11 (2006), [20]; CERD, *Concluding Observations: Cameroon*, UN Doc CERD/C/CMR/CO/15–18 (2010), [16].
404 CERD, *Concluding Observations: Cameroon*, UN Doc CERD/C/CMR/CO/15–18 (2010), [16].
405 CERD, *Concluding Observations: Guyana*, UN Doc CERD/C/CUY/CO/14 (2006), [20].
406 CERD, *Concluding Observations: Canada*, UN Doc A/49/18 (1994), [325].
407 CERD, *Concluding Observations: Peru*, UN Doc A/54/18 (1999), [156].
408 CERD, *Concluding Observations: Costa Rica*, UN Doc A/62/18 (2007), [301].
409 CERD, *Concluding Observations: Guatemala*, UN Doc A/50/18 (1995), [310].
410 CERD, *Concluding Observations: Congo*, UN Doc CERD/C/COG/CO/9 (2009), [15].
411 CERD, *Concluding Observations: Paraguay*, UN Doc CERD/C/PRY/CO/1–3 (2011), [16].
412 CERD, *Concluding Observations: Mexico*, UN Doc CERD/C/MEX/CO/16–17 (2012), [20].

rights and conditions of work.[413] In the related area of social security, the CERD has asked states to take into account the specific needs of indigenous peoples.[414] It criticised as racially discriminatory measures which restricted how indigenous people could spend welfare payments, ostensibly to promote child welfare.[415]

An individual complaint to the CERD, *Moylan v Australia* (2013),[416] concerned alleged discrimination in social security entitlements. The complainant was an Aboriginal Australian man, aged 61 at the time of making the complaint, who wished to retire at the age of 60 years. He had no savings and little superannuation and needed to rely on the state's aged pension. Under Australia's social security laws, he was eligible to receive the pension at 65 years of age. The complainant submitted that, according to official data, Aboriginal men had a life expectancy of 59 years, roughly 17 years less than all Australian men, yet the qualifying age for the pension was the same. Accordingly he argued that the law had discriminatory effects on Aboriginal Australians, contrary to Articles 5 and 6 of the ICERD. On the facts, the CERD found the complaint inadmissible for failure to exhaust domestic remedies, namely a claim in court under racial discrimination legislation.[417] The CERD explicitly qualified its inadmissibility decision by stating that it was 'without prejudice to the question of the merits regarding the alleged structural discrimination related to pension entitlements'.[418]

Vulnerable Groups

The CERD has been attentive to the double discrimination, on the basis of sex/gender and ethnicity, faced by indigenous women, and has encouraged states to counter it by adopting gender plans and policies, with indigenous participation.[419] Domestic violence (including murder), sexual harassment[420] and coerced sterilisation[421] have also been highlighted.

As regards indigenous children, the CERD has condemned their sexual exploitation, as well as child labour,[422] child servitude and slavery, prostitution, and trafficking and sale, often in areas of natural resource exploitation.[423] The failure of states

[413] CERD, *Concluding Observations: Suriname*, UN Doc CERD/C/SUR/CO/12 (2009), [17].

[414] CERD, *Concluding Observations: Argentina*, UN Doc A/56/18 (2001), [52]. ICERD art 5(e)(iv) requires states to eliminate race discrimination in the right to social security and social services.

[415] CERD, *Concluding Observations: Australia*, UN Doc CERD/C/AUS/CO/15–17 (2010), [16].

[416] *Moylan v Australia*, CERD Communication No 47/2010 (27 August 2013).

[417] Ibid [6.3]–[6.6]. The complainant argued unsuccessfully that this remedy would be ineffective because any court decision would be unable to change the discriminatory legislation itself.

[418] Ibid [6.6].

[419] CERD, *Concluding Observations: Costa Rica*, UN Doc A/62/18 (2007), [305]; CERD, *Concluding Observations: Ecuador*, UN Doc CERD/C/ECU/CO/19 (2008), [13].

[420] CERD, *Concluding Observations: New Zealand*, UN Doc A/57/18 (2002), [423]; CERD, *Concluding Observations: Ecuador*, UN Doc CERD/C/ECU/CO/19 (2008), [13]; CERD, *Concluding Observations: Guatemala*, UN Doc CERD/C/GTM/CO/11 (2006), [15].

[421] CERD, *General Recommendation No 25: Gender Related Dimensions of Racial Discrimination*, UN Doc A/55/18 (2000), Annex V, [2].

[422] CERD, *Concluding Observations: Paraguay*, UN Doc CERD/C/PRY/CO/1–3 (2011), [16].

[423] CERD, *Concluding Observations: Suriname*, UN Doc A/59/18 (2004), [195] (mining and forestry areas); CERD, *Concluding Observations: Venezuela (Bolivarian Republic of)*, UN Doc A/60/18 (2005), [381] (illegal gold prospecting).

to register indigenous births (and consequently to provide identity documents) has been noted.[424] The failure of states to remedy past policies of racially discriminatory indigenous child removals from their families has been criticised, including where a state refused an apology or compensation because removals were lawful at the time and purportedly intended to assist the children.[425]

Implementation Issues

Finally, to aid states in implementation of their ICERD obligations towards indigenous peoples, the CERD has encouraged states to adopt specific plans[426] and effective monitoring mechanisms for assessing progress,[427] such as indicators[428] and benchmarks[429] to evaluate policies and programmes. It has also encouraged states to support national institutions for advancing indigenous rights, from the courts and representative bodies to ombudspersons and human rights commissions.[430] As regards the latter, in an early warning and urgent action decision, the CERD criticised Australia's abolition of the position of Aboriginal and Torres Strait Islander Social Justice Commissioner and the assignation of those functions to a generalist deputy president of the national human rights commission.[431]

UN COMMITTEE ON THE ELIMINATION OF DISCRIMINATION AGAINST WOMEN

Indigenous issues have generally not been raised thus far in individual complaints decided by CEDAW, since the entry into force of the Optional Protocol in 2000. At the standard setting level, indigenous peoples have also scarcely been mentioned in the 32 General Recommendations adopted by the CEDAW Committee up to 2015. In the few references in interpretive statements, the CEDAW Committee has noted that societal factors can determine women's health and as such, special attention should be given to the health needs and rights of women belonging to vulnerable and disadvantaged groups, including indigenous women.[432] It has highlighted that discrimination against older women is often multidimensional, with indigenous women often experiencing a disproportionate degree of age discrimination.[433] The CEDAW

424 CERD, *Concluding Observations: Congo*, UN Doc CERD/C/COG/CO/9 (2009), [17]; CERD, *Concluding Observations: Panama*, UN Doc CERD/C/PAN/CO/15–20 (2010), [12].

425 CERD, *Concluding Observations: Australia*, UN Doc CERD/C/304/Add.101 (2000), [13]; CERD, *Concluding Observations: Australia*, UN Doc A/60/18 (2005), [45].

426 CERD, *Concluding Observations: Costa Rica*, UN Doc A/57/18 (2002), [76].

427 CERD, *Concluding Observations: Peru*, UN Doc A/50/18 (1995), [202].

428 CERD, *Concluding Observations: Mexico*, UN Doc A/50/18 (1995), [389].

429 CERD, *Concluding Observations: Australia*, UN Doc A/60/18 (2005), [39].

430 CERD, *Concluding Observations: Ecuador*, UN Doc A/58/18 (2003), [51].

431 CERD, *Decision 2(54) on Australia*, UN Doc A/54/18 (18 March 1999), [10].

432 CEDAW, *General Recommendation No 24: Article 12: Women and Health*, UN Doc A/54/38/Rev.1 (1999), [6].

433 CEDAW, *General Recommendation No 27: Older Women and Protection of their Human Rights*, UN Doc CEDAW/C/GC/27 (16 December 2010), [13].

Committee has recommended that states provide protection against the displacement of indigenous women with special dependency on land, and address the risks to, and particular needs of, internally displaced indigenous women.[434]

Discrimination

In monitoring states under the periodic reporting procedure, the CEDAW Committee has been concerned about how human rights violations distinctively affect indigenous women. It has emphasised that they experience 'double' or 'multiple and intersectoral' discrimination, based on their sex, ethnic origin and social status, which impedes their enjoyment of human rights and full participation in all spheres of life.[435] This includes, for example discrimination in property rights, where only indigenous men but not indigenous women are entitled to build residences in certain areas,[436] or in matrimonial property rights.[437] It also includes discrimination that emanates from within indigenous legal systems, as in 'harmful cultural practices' based on 'gender-stereotyped roles for men and women, such as the "bride price"';[438] strong gender stereotypes in indigenous communities generally;[439] or questions of indigenous status and group membership.[440] In general the CEDAW Committee has called on states to take concrete, targeted, evaluated and efficient temporary measures to promote substantive equality for indigenous women in all fields, including political participation, health, education and employment.[441] It has also called on states to sensitise indigenous communities about women's rights and to combat patriarchal attitudes.[442]

Political Rights

The CEDAW Committee has been especially concerned about low levels of participation in public life by, and inadequate political representation of, indigenous women,[443] including in government, parliament, the judiciary, councils and the diplomatic service.[444] It has noted the negative impacts of patriarchal attitudes and stereotypes in this regard.[445] States have been encouraged to establish electoral and

[434] CEDAW, *General Recommendation No 30: Women in Conflict Prevention, Conflict and Post-Conflict Situations*, UN Doc CEDAW/C/GC/30 (18 October 2013), [57].
[435] CEDAW, *Concluding Observations: Ecuador*, UN Doc CEDAW/C/ECU/CO/7 (2008), [24]–[25]; CERD, *Concluding Observations: Guatemala*, UN Doc CEDAW/C/GUA/CO/7 (2009), [41].
[436] CEDAW, *Concluding Observations: China*, UN Doc CEDAW/C/CHN/CO/6 (2006), [37] –[38].
[437] CEDAW, *Concluding Observations: Canada*, UN Doc A/58/38 (2003), Part I, [361].
[438] CEDAW, *Concluding Observations: Mexico*, UN Doc CEDAW/C/MEX/CO/7–8 (2012), [34].
[439] CEDAW, *Concluding Observations: Guatemala*, UN Doc A/57/38 (2002), Part III, [188].
[440] CEDAW, *Concluding Observations: Canada*, UN Doc A/58/38 (2003), Part I, [361].
[441] CEDAW, *Concluding Observations: Ecuador*, UN Doc CEDAW/C/ECU/CO/7 (2008), [24]–[25]; CEDAW, *Concluding Observations: Brazil*, UN Doc CEDAW/C/BRA/CO/3 (2012), [26]–[27].
[442] CEDAW, *Concluding Observations: Canada*, UN Doc A/58/38 (2003), Part I, [362].
[443] CEDAW, *Concluding Observations: Ecuador*, UN Doc CEDAW/C/ECU/CO/7 (2008), [13], [42].
[444] CEDAW, *Concluding Observations: Chile*, UN Doc CEDAW/C/HL/CO/5–6 (2012), [24].
[445] Ibid.

other quotas to increase the participation and representation of indigenous women in public life.[446]

Violence Against Women

The CEDAW Committee has also been concerned about violence against indigenous women,[447] including sexual violence, trafficking and exploitation.[448] Violence by security forces has been of concern, including 'feminicide' in the context of law enforcement against organised crime,[449] rape in 'emergency zones',[450] and sexual abuse by military units (and gold miners) on indigenous lands.[451] It has been further concerned about domestic violence in indigenous communities, as in Australia where indigenous women are 35 times as likely to be hospitalised as a result of family violence-related assaults as non-indigenous females.[452] Arranged marriages have also been of concern.[453] The CEDAW Committee has been concerned where incestual sexual abuse was not considered a crime.[454] Barriers to justice for victims have been identified as including discrimination by health workers;[455] language barriers (including lack of interpreters for indigenous women in prison);[456] lack of enforcement and impunity, permissive social attitudes, and lack of data;[457] and changes to the prosecution of domestic violence and cuts in support for victims.[458]

Access to Justice

Specific obstacles to access to justice for indigenous people identified by the CEDAW Committee include illiteracy, lack of information about rights, lack of tailored legal assistance, the length of legal proceedings and high costs, gender stereotyping, and insufficient understanding of women's rights by the judiciary.[459] The CEDAW Committee has urged states to enhance access to justice, including by disseminating information about rights and remedies in indigenous languages, and training prosecutors,

446 CEDAW, *Concluding Observations: Australia*, UN Doc CEDAW/C/AUS/CO/5 (2006), [16]; CEDAW, *Concluding Observations: Costa Rica*, UN Doc CEDAW/C/CRI/CO/5–6 (2011), [24]–[25]; CEDAW, *Concluding Observations: Chile*, UN Doc CEDAW/C/HL/CO/5–6 (2012), [24].

447 CEDAW, *Concluding Observations: Ecuador*, UN Doc CEDAW/C/ECU/CO/7 (2008), [24]–[25].

448 Ibid [22]; CEDAW, *Concluding Observations: Indonesia*, UN Doc CEDAW/C/IDN/CO/6–7 (2012), [45]; CEDAW, *Concluding Observations: Congo*, UN Doc CEDAW/C/COG/CO/6 (2012), [41]–[42].

449 CEDAW, *Concluding Observations: Mexico*, UN Doc CEDAW/C/MEX/CO/7–8 (2012), [34].

450 CEDAW, *Concluding Observations: Peru*, UN Doc A/50/38 (1995), [438].

451 CEDAW, *Concluding Observations: Brazil*, UN Doc A/58/38 (2003), Part II, [114].

452 CEDAW, *Concluding Observations: Australia*, UN Doc CEDAW/C/AUS/CO/7 (2010), [40]–[41].

453 CEDAW, *Concluding Observations: New Zealand*, UN Doc A/58/38 (2003), Part II, [423].

454 CEDAW, *Concluding Observations: Peru*, UN Doc CEDAW/C/PER/CO/6 (2007), [18].

455 CEDAW, *Concluding Observations: Congo*, UN Doc CEDAW/C/COG/CO/6 (2012), [41]–[42].

456 CEDAW, *Concluding Observations: Brazil*, UN Doc CEDAW/C/BRA/CO/3 (2012), [32]–[33].

457 CEDAW, *Concluding Observations: Nicaragua*, UN Doc CEDAW/C/NIC/CO/6 (2007), [19].

458 CEDAW, *Concluding Observations: Canada*, UN Doc A/58/38 (2003), Part I, [359].

459 CEDAW, *Concluding Observations: Bolivia*, UN Doc CEDAW/C/BOL/CO/4 (2008), [16]–[17]; CEDAW, *Concluding Observations: Argentina*, UN Doc CEDAW/C/ARG/CO/6 (2010), [15].

judges and lawyers.[460] The CEDAW Committee has, however, cautioned that too much emphasis on indigenous cultural specificities might undermine the principles of non-discrimination and formal and substantive gender equality, for instance where recognition of community justice makes justice more accessible but perpetuates stereotypes and prejudices that discriminate against women.[461]

Economic and Social Rights

The CEDAW Committee has frequently been concerned about indigenous women living in poverty, social exclusion and poor socio-economic conditions, thus impairing the spectrum of economic, social and cultural rights, including access to housing, healthcare, education, credit facilities, employment and vocational training, and social services.[462] Sometimes this is because indigenous women lack identity documents and cannot access public institutions, services and benefits.[463] Access by women to indigenous land, water and natural resources has also been a concern.[464] The CEDAW Committee has called on states to emphasise indigenous women's rights and address the causes of discrimination in development plans, programmes and cooperation.[465]

In the area of education, the CEDAW Committee has been concerned about high illiteracy rates and low school enrolment and completion rates affecting indigenous girls.[466] As regards employment, the CEDAW Committee has been concerned by gender discrimination against indigenous women, including in recruitment;[467] access to vocational training;[468] stereotyping that leads to segregation in lower quality jobs;[469] dismissals for pregnancy;[470] bonded labour;[471] child labour;[472] wage gaps;[473] and sexual harassment. While welcoming income-generating opportunities for indigenous women, the CEDAW Committee has cautioned that a focus on entrepreneurship may not lead to indigenous women's economic independence.[474] In the

460 CEDAW, *Concluding Observations: Bolivia*, UN Doc CEDAW/C/BOL/CO/4 (2008), [16]–[17].
461 Ibid [22].
462 CEDAW, *Concluding Observations: Peru*, UN Doc CEDAW/C/PER/CO/6 (2007), [36]–[37]; CEDAW, *Concluding Observations: Ecuador*, UN Doc CEDAW/C/ECU/CO/7 (2008), [18]; CEDAW, *Concluding Observations: Bolivia*, UN Doc CEDAW/C/BOL/CO/4 (2008), [11]; CEDAW, *Concluding Observations: Peru*, UN Doc CEDAW/C/PER/CO/6 (2007), [36].
463 CEDAW, *Concluding Observations: Bolivia*, UN Doc CEDAW/C/BOL/CO/4 (2008), [18].
464 CEDAW, *Concluding Observations: Indonesia*, UN Doc CEDAW/C/IDN/CO/6–7 (2012), [45].
465 CEDAW, *Concluding Observations: Peru*, UN Doc CEDAW/C/PER/CO/6 (2007), [36]–[37]; CEDAW, *Concluding Observations: Ecuador*, UN Doc CEDAW/C/ECU/CO/7 (2008), [18].
466 CEDAW, *Concluding Observations: Bolivia*, UN Doc CEDAW/C/BOL/CO/4 (2008), [11]; CEDAW, *Concluding Observations: Ecuador*, UN Doc CEDAW/C/ECU/CO/7 (2008), [30]; CEDAW, *Concluding Observations: Nepal*, UN Doc CEDAW/C/NPL/CO/4–5 (2011), [27].
467 CEDAW, *Concluding Observations: Australia*, UN Doc CEDAW/C/AUS/CO/7 (2010), [38]–[39].
468 CEDAW, *Concluding Observations: Surinam*, UN Doc CEDAW/C/SUR/CO/3 (2007), [28].
469 CEDAW, *Concluding Observations: Brazil*, UN Doc CEDAW/C/BRA/CO/3 (2012), [22].
470 CEDAW, *Concluding Observations: Ecuador*, UN Doc CEDAW/C/ECU/CO/7 (2008), [36].
471 CEDAW, *Concluding Observations: Nepal*, UN Doc CEDAW/C/NPL/CO/4–5 (2011), [29].
472 Ibid.
473 CEDAW, *Concluding Observations: Brazil*, UN Doc CEDAW/C/BRA/CO/3 (2012), [22].
474 CEDAW, *Concluding Observations: Canada*, UN Doc A/58/38 (2003), Part I, [377].

related area of social security, the CEDAW Committee has been concerned about budget cuts in social services affecting indigenous women,[475] and called for indigenous women to have access to social security and employment benefits, including paid maternity leave.[476]

In the area of health, the CEDAW Committee has commented on the poor access of indigenous women to healthcare, including sexual and reproductive health, leading to high rates of maternal mortality,[477] and deaths from illegal and unsafe abortions.[478] The CEDAW Committee has been concerned about teenage pregnancy;[479] and where there are no special programmes for indigenous women to address the situation of children and adolescents living in situations of risk or abandonment.[480] The high rate of HIV/AIDS (and other sexually transmitted diseases[481]) among some indigenous women has also been noted, including where it results from a power differential between women and men, which often prevents women from insisting on safe and responsible sex practices.[482] It has been concerned about lower life expectancy for indigenous women,[483] and environmental pollution.[484]

Property Rights

One individual communication before the CEDAW Committee concerned discrimination against an indigenous woman in relation to property. In *Kell v Canada* (2012),[485] an aboriginal woman alleged discrimination on the basis of sex, marital status and cultural heritage[486] in her treatment by a local housing authority in its decisions on the allocation of housing reserved for indigenous people, in the Northwest Territories in Canada. She and her non-indigenous partner were issued an Agreement for Purchase and Sale for a house on leasehold land in 1991. She was subsequently the victim of domestic violence, resulting in her losing jobs and being admitted to a battered women's shelter. Her partner successfully requested the housing authority (of which he was a board member) to direct the housing corporation to remove her name from a document certifying co-ownership. Her partner also denied her access to return to the house and threatened legal action to evict her, and her legal aid lawyer did not contest this but urged her to comply with the evacuation request. The complainant sought domestic remedies against her partner, but he died from cancer, so she proceeded against his estate and the housing corporation. Despite the insistence of her legal aid lawyer, she rejected an offer of monetary compensation to

475 Ibid [357], [359].
476 CEDAW, *Concluding Observations: Costa Rica*, UN Doc A/58/38 (2003), Part II, [63].
477 CEDAW, *Concluding Observations: Bolivia*, UN Doc CEDAW/C/BOL/CO/4 (2008), [11]; CEDAW, *Concluding Observations: Nicaragua*, UN Doc CEDAW/C/NIC/CO/6 (2007), [17]–[18].
478 CEDAW, *Concluding Observations: Nicaragua*, UN Doc CEDAW/C/NIC/CO/6 (2007), [17]–[18].
479 CEDAW, *Concluding Observations: New Zealand*, UN Doc A/53/38/Rev.1 (1998), Part II, [279].
480 CEDAW, *Concluding Observations: Peru*, UN Doc A/57/38 (2002), Part III, [494].
481 CEDAW, *Concluding Observations: Suriname*, UN Doc A/57/38 (2002), Part II, [65].
482 CEDAW, *Concluding Observations: Panama*, UN Doc CEDAW/C/PAN/CO/7 (2010), [44]–[45].
483 CEDAW, *Concluding Observations: Australia*, UN Doc A/52/38/Rev.1 (1997), Part II, [397].
484 CEDAW, *Concluding Observations: Suriname*, UN Doc A/57/38 (2002), Part II, [65].
485 *Kell v Canada*, CEDAW Committee Communication No 19/2008 (28 February 2012).
486 She alleged violations of CEDAW, arts 1, 2(d), 14(2)(h), 15(1)–(3) and 16(1)(h): ibid [3.1]–[3.6].

settle the case, insisting she wished to return to her home. Further proceedings led to the dismissal of her claim and she was ordered to pay costs.

The CEDAW Committee found that the complainant's property rights were prejudiced as a result of the actions taken by the housing authority acting in concert with her partner, and the related actions of the housing corporation and legal aid lawyers.[487] It held that she suffered 'intersectional discrimination' on the basis of her status as an aboriginal woman victim of domestic violence, contrary to Article 1 of the CEDAW.[488] The Committee also found consequential or related violations of the CEDAW provisions requiring Canada to eliminate discrimination and provide effective legal protection (Article 2(d) and (e)), and to afford her the same rights in property as her partner (Article 16(1)(h)).[489] There was, however, no evidence of discrimination related to her coming from a rural area, or that she was prevented from residing elsewhere in her community.[490] The CEDAW Committee recommended that Canada provide her with housing of an equivalent quality, location and size to that she was deprived of, and appropriately compensate her.[491] It also recommended the recruitment and training of more aboriginal women to provide legal aid to aboriginal women, including on domestic violence and property rights; and the review of legal aid and effective access to justice.[492]

UN COMMITTEE ON THE RIGHTS OF THE CHILD

As mentioned in the introductory chapter, the Convention on the Rights of the Child is the only international human rights treaty that expressly mentions the rights of indigenous people, in the contexts of children's rights to media and language (Article 17(d)), education (Article 29), and culture, religion and language (Article 30). As discussed below, a few of the CRC's General Comments have elaborated on aspects of indigenous children's rights, and numerous issues have arisen in monitoring states' reports. As of 2015 there is not yet any jurisprudence in individual cases since the Optional Protocol only entered into force in 2014.

Discrimination

The CRC has often been concerned where indigenous children suffer racism, stigmatisation or racial discrimination in law or practice.[493] At a formal level, the CRC

487 Ibid [10.2].
488 Ibid [10.2].
489 Ibid [10.3]–[10.5] and [10.7].
490 Ibid [10.6].
491 Ibid [11].
492 Ibid [11].
493 CRC, *Concluding Observations: Ecuador*, UN Doc CRC/C/ECU/CO/4 (2010), [34]; CRC, *Concluding Observations: Argentina*, UN Doc CRC/C/ARG/CO/3–4 (2010), [31]; CRC, *Concluding Observations: Thailand*, UN Doc CRC/C/THA/CO/3–4 (2012), [33]; CRC, *Concluding Observations: Myanmar*, UN Doc CRC/C/MMR/CO/3–4 (2012), [96]; CRC, *Concluding Observations: Guatemala*, UN Doc CRC/C/GTM/CO/3–4 (2010), [40]; CRC, *Concluding Observations: Congo*, UN Doc CRC/C/COG/CO/1 (2006), [88].

has been concerned where indigenous groups are not recognised by the state,[494] are subject to assimilation or integration,[495] or where laws on indigenous people do not explicitly address indigenous children's rights.[496] It has been concerned where significant numbers of indigenous children are stateless or potentially stateless,[497] and where children's citizenship can be revoked if a parent renounces or loses their citizenship.[498] It has identified a lack of birth registration of indigenous children as a major barrier to the realisation of their rights in domestic legal systems, including because of inaccessible or poorly implemented procedures[499] or a lack of knowledge of procedures.[500] Sometimes this has led to the recruitment of child soldiers due to uncertainties about age.[501] The CRC has called on states to tailor birth registration procedures to indigenous needs, for instance through mobile units to reach children, and based on respect for their cultures.[502] Discrimination in socio-economic rights is discussed further below.

Violence Against Indigenous Children

The CRC has identified various forms of violence against indigenous children, including torture and cruel, inhuman or degrading treatment by the police and military in detention.[503] Other forms of mental and physical abuse of children have been highlighted,[504] such as domestic violence, including where it is believed to be an 'educative measure'.[505] The CRC has criticised punishments such as 'public shaming' and corporal punishment.[506] Most commonly the CRC has focused on sexual violence, including rape,[507] whether committed by state authorities[508] or in the context of development projects such as mining and forestry.[509] Concern has been expressed about sexual exploitation and abuse, such as in domestic service,[510] trafficking,[511] the sale of children, child prostitution and child pornography.[512]

494 CRC, *Concluding Observations: Denmark*, UN Doc CRC/C/DNK/CO/4 (2011), [67].
495 CRC, *Concluding Observations: Viet Nam*, UN Doc CRC/C/VNM/CO/3–4 (2012), [39]–[40]; CRC, *Concluding Observations: Brazil*, UN Doc CRC/C/143 (2004), [96].
496 CRC, *Concluding Observations: Congo*, UN Doc CRC/C/COG/CO/1 (2006), [88].
497 CRC, *Concluding Observations: Thailand*, UN Doc CRC/C/THA/CO/3–4 (2012), [41].
498 CRC, *Concluding Observations: Australia*, UN Doc CRC/C/AUS/CO/4 (2012), [37]–[38].
499 CRC, *Concluding Observations: Argentina*, UN Doc CRC/C/ARG/CO/3–4 (2010), [40]–[41].
500 CRC, *Concluding Observations: Paraguay*, UN Doc CRC/C/PRY/CO/3 (2010), [33].
501 CRC, *Concluding Observations: Philippines*, UN Doc CRC/C/PHL/CO/1 (2008), [17].
502 CRC, *Concluding Observations: Argentina*, UN Doc CRC/C/ARG/CO/3–4 (2010), [40]–[41].
503 CRC, *Concluding Observations: Congo*, UN Doc CRC/C/COG/CO/1 (2006), [40]–[41].
504 CRC, *Concluding Observations: Bolivia*, UN Doc CRC/C/BOL/CO/4 (2009), [49]–[50]; CRC, *Concluding Observations: Argentina*, UN Doc CRC/C/ARG/CO/3–4 (2010), [31].
505 CRC, *Concluding Observations: Bolivia*, UN Doc CRC/C/BOL/CO/4 (2009), [49]–[50].
506 CRC, *Concluding Observations: Ecuador*, UN Doc CRC/C/150 (2005), [459]–[460].
507 CRC, *Concluding Observations: Congo*, UN Doc CRC/C/COG/CO/1 (2006), [40]–[41].
508 Ibid.
509 CRC, *Concluding Observations: Suriname*, UN Doc CRC/C/SUR/CO/2 (2007), [67]–[68].
510 CRC, *Concluding Observations: Bolivia*, UN Doc CRC/C/BOL/CO/4 (2009), [77].
511 CRC, *Concluding Observations: Thailand*, UN Doc CRC/C/THA/CO/2 (2006), [73].
512 CRC, *Concluding Observations: United States*, UN Doc CRC/C/USA/CO/1 (2008), [20].

In responding to violence and sexual abuse, the CRC has been concerned about impunity[513] and called on states to investigate, prosecute and punish perpetrators.[514] It has asked states to criminalise offences such as gang rape[515] and legislate against sexual exploitation.[516] It has demanded that states not punish victims,[517] and urged them to provide victims with access to physical and psychological recovery, social reintegration and compensation.[518] States have been asked to strengthen public awareness campaigns and provide information, parental guidance and counselling concerning domestic violence; and train professionals working with children to report and act in suspected cases of domestic violence, taking into account the cultural diversity of indigenous communities.[519] The CRC has encouraged states to study the root causes of sexual violence against children, including through technical assistance from the UN Children's Fund (UNICEF).[520] It has suggested that the root causes include poverty, gender discrimination, unsafe migration, and the lack of a comprehensive child protection system.[521]

Law and Justice

In the related area of law and justice, the CRC has been concerned about the routine refusal of bail for juveniles;[522] over-incarceration of indigenous children;[523] lack of legal assistance and interpreters;[524] and indigenous deaths in custody.[525] It has consequently asked states to take measures to prevent children entering into contact with the criminal justice system or traditional indigenous justice systems, including by supporting families and communities to address social determinants of crime.[526] It has called on states to develop alternatives to detention in both state and indigenous justice systems, such as probation, mediation, community service orders, or suspended sentences.[527] It has noted conflicts between positive law and indigenous customary law, called for a clearer separation of competencies and requested that both legal systems respect children's rights.[528] It has emphasised that the best interests of the indigenous child should always be taken into account in family and

513 CRC, *Concluding Observations: Honduras*, UN Doc CRC/C/HND/CO/3 (2007), [83]–[84].
514 CRC, *Concluding Observations: Congo*, UN Doc CRC/C/COG/CO/1 (2006), [40]–[41].
515 Ibid.
516 CRC, *Concluding Observations: Suriname*, UN Doc CRC/C/SUR/CO/2 (2007), [67]–[68].
517 Ibid.
518 CRC, *Concluding Observations: Congo*, UN Doc CRC/C/COG/CO/1 (2006), [40]–[41]; CRC, *Concluding Observations: Suriname*, UN Doc CRC/C/SUR/CO/2 (2007), [67]–[68].
519 CRC, *Concluding Observations: Bolivia*, UN Doc CRC/C/BOL/CO/4 (2009), [49]–[50].
520 CRC, *Concluding Observations: Congo*, UN Doc CRC/C/COG/CO/1 (2006), [40]–[41].
521 CRC, *Concluding Observations: Nepal*, UN Doc CRC/C/NPL/CO/1 (2012), [20].
522 CRC, *Concluding Observations: Australia*, UN Doc CRC/C/69 (1997), [104].
523 Ibid [114].
524 CRC, *Concluding Observations: Guatemala*, UN Doc CRC/C/108 (2001), [283].
525 CRC, *Concluding Observations: Canada*, UN Doc CRC/C/113 (2003), [71].
526 CRC, *Concluding Observations: Bolivia*, UN Doc CRC/C/BOL/CO/4 (2009), [81]–[82].
527 Ibid.
528 Ibid.

criminal law.[529] The CRC has criticised law enforcement authorities for perceiving urban indigenous children as potential delinquents and targeting them with curfews or media campaigns.[530]

Family Life

The CRC has placed substantial emphasis on the family rights of indigenous children as well as children's rights within the family. In General Comment No 11 (2009), the CRC indicated that special measures may be needed 'to safeguard the integrity of indigenous families and communities by assisting them in their child-rearing responsibilities'.[531] Further, states should collect data on their family situation, including on foster care and adoption processes, and use it to design family and alternative care policies in a culturally sensitive way.[532] The CRC has emphasised that '[m]aintaining the best interests of the child and the integrity of indigenous families and communities should be primary considerations in development, social services, health and education programmes'.[533] State activities should respect and support traditional extended family structures.[534]

This includes in alternative care placements, where due regard should be paid to the child's ethnic, religious, cultural and linguistic background.[535] Where indigenous children are over-represented among children separated from their families, 'specially targeted policy measures should be developed in consultation with indigenous communities in order to reduce the number of indigenous children in alternative care and prevent the loss of their cultural identity'.[536] Where children are in care outside their communities, special measures should be taken to ensure that the child can maintain his or her cultural identity.[537]

In monitoring states, the CRC has been concerned where indigenous children are separated from their families and placed into care that does not adequately preserve their cultural and linguistic identity.[538] It has called for the reduction of children in care, measures to support them to stay with their families,[539] and the need for more indigenous care service providers.[540] More generally, the CRC has called on states to support families in parenting skills; in their struggle against poverty; and to make accessible psychological, social and legal services and day care.[541]

[529] CRC, *Concluding Observations: Congo*, UN Doc CRC/C/COG/CO/1 (2006), [28].
[530] CRC, *Concluding Observations: Panama*, UN Doc CRC/C/PAN/CO/3–4 (2011), [33].
[531] CRC, *General Comment No 11: Indigenous Children and their Rights under the Convention*, UN Doc CRC/C/GC/11 (12 February 2009), [46].
[532] Ibid [47].
[533] Ibid.
[534] CRC, *Concluding Observations: New Zealand*, UN Doc CRC/C/133 (2003), [154].
[535] Ibid [48].
[536] Ibid.
[537] CRC, *General Comment No 11* (n 528), [46]–[48].
[538] CRC, *Concluding Observations: Australia*, UN Doc CRC/C/AUS/CO/4 (2012), [37]–[38].
[539] CRC, *Concluding Observations: Chile*, UN Doc CRC/C/CHL/CO/3 (2007), [44]–[45].
[540] CRC, *Concluding Observations: Australia*, UN Doc CRC/C/AUS/CO/4 (2012), [51]–[52].
[541] CRC, *Concluding Observations: Argentina*, UN Doc CRC/C/ARG/CO/3–4 (2010), [51].

Indigenous Land Rights

The CRC has noted the difficulties indigenous children face in access to and respect for their traditional lands.[542] It has expressed concern where states allow the continuing dispossession of indigenous peoples from their historical lands,[543] and where new forced displacement occurs, such as because of corporate activity and the destruction of natural resources.[544] It has been alarmed by the effects on indigenous children and families forcibly evicted from their ancestral lands,[545] including as a result of highly polluting oil, gas and mining technologies by foreign companies.[546] It has criticised the lack of clear social and environmental standards for such developments, including corporate obligations to protect children's rights.[547]

The CRC has been further concerned about a lack of prior consultation with indigenous children and communities, and called for social impact studies of investment projects likely to affect children's rights, such as forced displacement and dispossession and damage to cultural heritage.[548] The CRC has been concerned about the environmental and health impacts on children of aerial fumigation of drug plantations.[549] It has called for independent, rights-based environmental and social impact assessments of such activities, prior consultation with indigenous communities, and precautions to protect children's health.[550]

Economic, Social and Cultural Rights

The CRC has been concerned about the full gamut of indigenous children's economic, social and cultural rights. It has often noted the prevalence of poverty affecting them,[551] which adversely affects their life opportunities and impedes the full enjoyment of their rights, including access to basic social and health services, food, water and sanitation, and education,[552] as well as their survival, development and culture.[553] It has criticised the 'cultural invisibility' of indigenous children and the lack of policies to promote their development and well-being, leading, for instance, to indigenous adolescents emigrating.[554]

542 CRC, *Concluding Observations: Guatemala*, UN Doc CRC/C/GTM/CO/3–4 (2010), [101].
543 Ibid.
544 CRC, *Concluding Observations: Honduras*, UN Doc CRC/C/HND/CO/3 (2007), [83]–[84].
545 CRC, *Concluding Observations: Bolivia*, UN Doc CRC/C/BOL/CO/4 (2009), [61].
546 CRC, *Concluding Observations: Philippines*, UN Doc CRC/C/PHL/CO/3–4 (2009), [21].
547 CRC, *Concluding Observations: Ecuador*, UN Doc CRC/C/ECU/CO/4 (2010), [30]–[31].
548 CRC, *Concluding Observations: Panama*, UN Doc CRC/C/PAN/CO/3–4 (2011), [27].
549 CRC, *Concluding Observations: Colombia*, UN Doc CRC/C/COL/CO/3 (2006), [73].
550 Ibid.
551 CRC, *Concluding Observations: Thailand*, UN Doc CRC/C/THA/CO/3–4 (2012), [82]; CRC, *Concluding Observations: Guatemala*, UN Doc CRC/C/GTM/CO/3–4 (2010), [40]; CRC, *Concluding Observations: Honduras*, UN Doc CRC/C/HND/CO/3 (2007), [83]–[84].
552 CRC, *Concluding Observations: Thailand*, UN Doc CRC/C/THA/CO/2 (2006), [60]; CRC, *Concluding Observations: Kenya*, UN Doc CRC/C/KEN/CO/2 (2007), [69]–[70]; CRC, *Concluding Observations: Thailand*, UN Doc CRC/C/THA/CO/3–4 (2012), [33].
553 CRC, *Concluding Observations: Myanmar*, UN Doc CRC/C/MMR/CO/3–4 (2012), [96]; CRC, *Concluding Observations: Burundi*, UN Doc CRC/C/BDI/CO/2 (2010), [78].
554 CRC, *Concluding Observations: El Salvador*, UN Doc CRC/C/SLV/CO/3–4 (2010), [91].

At a budgetary level, the CRC has criticised states for reducing spending on children or misspending funds allocated for children,[555] and condemned corruption.[556] It has urged states to prioritise allocations to ensure the implementation of economic, social and cultural rights of indigenous children, 'to the maximum extent of available resources and, where needed, within the framework of international cooperation'.[557] It has objected where states are performing well economically yet fail to adequately fund programmes for vulnerable children.[558]

In the area of health, the CRC has been concerned about high infant and maternal mortality;[559] sudden infant death and foetal alcohol syndromes;[560] malnutrition;[561] diseases (particularly HIV/AIDS,[562] and Hepatitis B[563]); harmful traditional practices like female genital mutilation;[564] disabilities;[565] substance abuse;[566] and suicides.[567] It has highlighted teenage pregnancies and sexually transmitted infections and the lack of information and programmes on sexual and reproductive health,[568] including in schools.[569] The CRC has often been concerned about access to health services,[570] including immunisation,[571] and for mental health,[572] and provided in indigenous languages.[573] Structural determinants of ill health have also been identified, such as poor sanitation and lack of clean water.[574] The CRC has called for more targeted information, services and preventive strategies,[575] as well as better data collection on indigenous children's health.[576] It has noted that low cost actions can, for instance, dramatically improve infant mortality rates.[577]

555 CRC, *Concluding Observations: Peru*, UN Doc CRC/C/PER/CO/3 (2006), [81]–[82].

556 CRC, *Concluding Observations: Congo*, UN Doc CRC/C/COG/CO/1 (2006), [15].

557 Ibid.

558 CRC, *Concluding Observations: Colombia*, UN Doc CRC/C/24 (1994), [74].

559 CRC, *Concluding Observations: Ecuador*, UN Doc CRC/C/ECU/CO/4 (2010), [34]; CRC, *Concluding Observations: Bolivia*, UN Doc CRC/C/BOL/CO/4 (2009), [53]; CRC, *Concluding Observations: Paraguay*, UN Doc CRC/C/PRY/CO/3 (2010), [79]; CRC, *Concluding Observations: Panama*, UN Doc CRC/C/PAN/CO/3–4 (2011), [54].

560 CRC, *Concluding Observations: Canada*, UN Doc CRC/C/113 (2003), [84].

561 CRC, *Concluding Observations: Paraguay*, UN Doc CRC/C/PRY/CO/3 (2010), [79]; CRC, *Concluding Observations: Ecuador*, UN Doc CRC/C/ECU/CO/4 (2010), [34]; CRC, *Concluding Observations: Bolivia*, UN Doc CRC/C/BOL/CO/4 (2009), [59]–[60]; CRC, *Concluding Observations: Guatemala*, UN Doc CRC/C/GTM/CO/3–4 (2010), [40]; CRC, *Concluding Observations: Panama*, UN Doc CRC/C/PAN/CO/3–4 (2011), [54].

562 CRC, *General Comment No 3 (2003): HIV/AIDS and the Rights of the Child*, UN Doc CRC/GC/2003/3 (17 March 2003), [21], [30].

563 CRC, *Concluding Observations: Peru*, UN Doc CRC/C/PER/CO/3 (2006), [46].

564 CRC, *Concluding Observations: Kenya*, UN Doc CRC/C/KEN/CO/2 (2007), [53], [69]–[70].

565 CRC, *Concluding Observations: Chile*, UN Doc CRC/C/114 (2002), [367].

566 CRC, *Concluding Observations: Canada*, UN Doc CRC/C/113 (2003), [86].

567 CRC, *Concluding Observations: Mexico*, UN Doc CRC/C/MEX/CO/3 (2006), [50].

568 Ibid.

569 CRC, *Concluding Observations: Panama*, UN Doc CRC/C/PAN/CO/3–4 (2011), [56].

570 CRC, *Concluding Observations: Congo*, UN Doc CRC/C/COG/CO/1 (2006), [88]; CRC, *Concluding Observations: Panama*, UN Doc CRC/C/PAN/CO/3–4 (2011), [54].

571 CRC, *Concluding Observations: India*, UN Doc CRC/C/137 (2004), [459].

572 CRC, *Concluding Observations: Mexico*, UN Doc CRC/C/MEX/CO/3 (2006), [50].

573 CRC, *Concluding Observations: Finland*, UN Doc CRC/C/FIN/CO/4 (2011), [63].

574 CRC, *Concluding Observations: Bolivia*, UN Doc CRC/C/BOL/CO/4 (2009), [61].

575 CRC, *Concluding Observations: Panama*, UN Doc CRC/C/PAN/CO/3–4 (2011), [58].

576 CRC, *General Comment No 4: Adolescent Health and Development in the Context of the Convention on the Rights of the Child*, UN Doc CRC/GC/2003/4 (2003), [13].

577 CRC, *Concluding Observations: Argentina*, UN Doc CRC/C/121 (2002), [71].

In the field of education, the CRC has been concerned about inadequate access to schooling;[578] low enrolment rates;[579] high drop out rates; illiteracy;[580] and poor quality education (including weak teacher training[581] and inadequate infrastructure[582]). It has been particularly concerned about the lack of, or inadequate education in, indigenous languages or bilingual education,[583] and the related lack of opportunities for the expression of indigenous culture and practices.[584] In this respect it has highlighted the lack of indigenous teachers, relevant teacher training, and textbooks in indigenous languages.[585] It has identified barriers to education, such as poverty or lack of financial resources of parents;[586] education maladapted to indigenous lifestyles;[587] and harmful traditional practices such as early marriages and child labour.[588] The CRC has also highlighted the discrimination faced by girls who do not attend or complete school.[589]

Concerning labour rights, the CRC has condemned child labour, particularly in its worst forms,[590] such as servitude[591] or forced labour, and other forms of economic exploitation.[592] It has identified high numbers of indigenous working children in some areas,[593] including in very hazardous situations such as manually cleaning sewers and latrines,[594] mining[595] and deep sea fishing.[596] It has called on states to develop and implement comprehensive plans to prevent and combat child labour, in accordance with ILO standards.[597]

Finally, the CRC has addressed some miscellaneous matters. It has called on states to take into account the 'best interests' of the child in all decisions affecting them, and to enable the participation and right to be heard of children in such decisions.[598] It has called for national human rights institutions to be physically accessible to all children and to reach out to 'the most vulnerable and disadvantaged', including

578 CRC, *Concluding Observations: Chile*, UN Doc CRC/C/CHL/CO/3 (2007), [61]; CRC, *Concluding Observations: Kenya*, UN Doc CRC/C/KEN/CO/2 (2007), [69]–[70]; CRC, *Concluding Observations: Paraguay*, UN Doc CRC/C/PRY/CO/3 (2010), [60].

579 CRC, *Concluding Observations: Kenya*, UN Doc CRC/C/KEN/CO/2 (2007), [69]–[70].

580 CRC, *Concluding Observations: Kenya*, UN Doc CRC/C/KEN/CO/2 (2007), [69]–[70]; CRC, *Concluding Observations: Argentina*, UN Doc CRC/C/ARG/CO/3–4 (2010), [31].

581 CRC, *Concluding Observations: Kenya*, UN Doc CRC/C/KEN/CO/2 (2007), [69]–[70]; CRC, *Concluding Observations: Paraguay*, UN Doc CRC/C/PRY/CO/3 (2010), [60].

582 CRC, *Concluding Observations: Costa Rica*, UN Doc CRC/C/150 (2005), [714].

583 CRC, *Concluding Observations: Finland*, UN Doc CRC/C/FIN/CO/4 (2011), [63].

584 CRC, *Concluding Observations: El Salvador*, UN Doc CRC/C/SLV/CO/3–4 (2010), [91].

585 CRC, *Concluding Observations: Viet Nam*, UN Doc CRC/C/VNM/CO/3–4 (2012), [67]; CRC, *Concluding Observations: Costa Rica*, UN Doc CRC/C/CRI/CO/4 (2011), [69].

586 CRC, *Concluding Observations: Paraguay*, UN Doc CRC/C/PRY/CO/3 (2010), [60].

587 CRC, *Concluding Observations: Kenya*, UN Doc CRC/C/KEN/CO/2 (2007), [69]–[70].

588 Ibid.

589 CRC, *Concluding Observations: Burundi*, UN Doc CRC/C/BDI/CO/2 (2010), [78].

590 CRC, *Concluding Observations: Suriname*, UN Doc CRC/C/SUR/CO/2 (2007), [65].

591 CRC, *Concluding Observations: Bolivia*, UN Doc CRC/C/BOL/CO/4 (2009), [73].

592 CRC, *Concluding Observations: Congo*, UN Doc CRC/C/COG/CO/1 (2006), [88].

593 CRC, *Concluding Observations: Paraguay*, UN Doc CRC/C/PRY/CO/3 (2010), [79].

594 CRC, *Concluding Observations: Congo*, UN Doc CRC/C/COG/CO/1 (2006), [79]–[80].

595 CRC, *Concluding Observations: Bolivia*, UN Doc CRC/C/BOL/CO/4 (2009), [73].

596 CRC, *Concluding Observations: Honduras*, UN Doc CRC/C/HND/CO/3 (2007), [72].

597 CRC, *Concluding Observations: Congo*, UN Doc CRC/C/COG/CO/1 (2006), [79]–[80].

598 CRC, *Concluding Observations: Belize*, UN Doc CRC/C/146 (2005), [364].

indigenous groups.[599] It also called for greater cooperation between states and civil society, including indigenous leaders and communities, in implementing children's rights.[600] It has asked states to translate and disseminate the Convention on the Rights of the Child into indigenous languages, and to train those working for and with children about it.[601] It has requested states to collect better data on the challenges facing indigenous children.[602]

UN COMMITTEE AGAINST TORTURE

As might be expected given its mandate, the CAT has focused on torture or ill-treatment of indigenous peoples[603] and related issues. To date, individual complaints have not tended to raise indigenous-specific issues. In monitoring states, the CAT has been concerned about all forms of violence against indigenous people, including threats and attacks against, or killings of, indigenous human rights defenders;[604] and excessive and disproportionate use of force (including firearms) during social protests,[605] including those in defence of land rights.[606] The CAT has often focused on violence by public authorities (including the police, prison authorities, the military and paramilitaries), and where the military is used in civil security tasks to counter social protests.[607] It has also been concerned about attacks by private actors, including private security officers[608] and armed groups (as where they threaten victims of forced displacement seeking the return of land,[609] or abduct and forcibly recruit child soldiers[610]). It has condemned gender violence, including domestic and sexual violence.[611]

The CAT has commented further on a number of issues surrounding detention. It has been concerned about arbitrary arrests, particularly preventive administrative detention and warrants issued without sufficient evidence.[612] It has objected to the misapplication of counter-terrorism laws to social protests by indigenous peoples;[613] the use of the criminal law to persecute indigenous people;[614] and the

[599] CRC, *General Comment No 2: The Role of Independent National Human Rights Institutions in the Promotion and Protection of the Rights of the Child*, UN Doc CRC/GC/2002/2 (2002), [15].

[600] CRC, *Concluding Observations: Guatemala*, UN Doc CRC/C/GTM/CO/3–4 (2010), [32]–[33]; CRC, *Concluding Observations: Nicaragua*, UN Doc CRC/C/NIC/CO/4 (2010), [28]–[29].

[601] CRC, *Concluding Observations: Argentina*, UN Doc CRC/C/ARG/CO/3–4 (2010), [25]–[26].

[602] CRC, *Concluding Observations: Colombia*, UN Doc CRC/C/COL/CO/3 (2006), [26]–[27].

[603] CAT, *Concluding Observations: Ecuador*, UN Doc CAT/C/ECU/CO/3 (2006), [17].

[604] CAT, *Concluding Observations: Guatemala*, UN Doc CAT/C/GTM/CO/5–6 (2013), [14]; CAT, *Concluding Observations: Philippines*, UN Doc CAT/C/PHL/CO/2 (2009), [11].

[605] CAT, *Concluding Observations: Peru*, UN Doc CAT/C/PER/CO/5–6 (2013), [12].

[606] CAT, *Concluding Observations: Canada*, UN Doc CAT/C/CAN/CO/6 (2012), [22].

[607] CAT, *Concluding Observations: Guatemala*, UN Doc CAT/C/GTM/CO/5–6 (2013), [16].

[608] Ibid.

[609] CAT, *Concluding Observations: Colombia*, UN Doc CAT/C/COL/CO/4 (2010), [26].

[610] CAT, *Concluding Observations: Philippines*, UN Doc CAT/C/PHL/CO/2 (2009), [24].

[611] CAT, *Concluding Observations: Bolivia*, UN Doc CAT/C/BOL/CO/2 (2013), [15].

[612] CAT, *Concluding Observations: Colombia*, UN Doc CAT/C/COL/CO/4 (2010), [20].

[613] CAT, *Concluding Observations: Chile*, UN Doc CAT/C/CHL/CO/5 (2009), [23].

[614] CAT, *Concluding Observations: Guatemala*, UN Doc CAT/C/GTM/CO/5–6 (2013), [14].

misuse of arrests to stigmatise indigenous people.[615] It has highlighted inhumane prison conditions,[616] and the over-incarceration of indigenous people (including because of disproportionate and discriminatory mandatory minimum sentences for minor offences); over-crowding in prisons; inadequate mental health services; and indigenous deaths in custody.[617]

Impunity for perpetrators of violence against indigenous people has often been criticised by the CAT, whether for lack of law or its enforcement, and including for mass atrocities such as the deaths or disappearances of 200,000 mostly indigenous people in Guatemala,[618] or the 250,000 victims (again, many indigenous) of armed conflict in Colombia.[619] The CAT has accordingly urged states to promptly and effectively investigate, prosecute and punish perpetrators.[620] States should also provide reparations for victims, including restitution, compensation, rehabilitation (including psychological and social care), satisfaction and guarantees of non-repetition.[621] The CAT has further encouraged states to provide training for public officials (including, for instance, police, army and prison officers, public servants, migration officials, prosecutors and judges) on matters such as the prohibition (and investigation and documentation) of torture, international standards on the use of force and firearms, and liabilities for excessive force.[622]

A final concern of the CAT has been labour exploitation of indigenous people.[623] This has included forced labour practices amounting to slavery; debt bondage and serfdom (in areas such as agriculture, stock-raising and forestry); domestic servitude; and child labour (as in mining, brick-making and saw mills).[624] The CAT has also been concerned about human trafficking for labour and sexual exploitation, particularly women and girls coerced into prostitution in brothels, for example in mining shanty towns in poor rural areas.[625]

CONCLUSION

As with the practice of the HRC under the ICCPR, discussed in the previous chapter, discrimination against indigenous peoples has been a cross-cutting concern of all of the key UN human rights treaty bodies, whether in relation to a broad spectrum of rights (the CERD and CESCR), a narrower set of rights (the CAT), or in relation to

615 CAT, *Concluding Observations: Colombia*, UN Doc CAT/C/COL/CO/4 (2010), [20].
616 CAT, *Concluding Observations: Canada*, UN Doc CAT/C/CAN/CO/6 (2012), [22].
617 CAT, *Concluding Observations: Australia*, UN Doc CAT/C/AUS/CO/3 (2008), [23].
618 CAT, *Concluding Observations: Guatemala*, UN Doc CAT/C/GTM/CO/5–6 (2013), [10].
619 CAT, *Concluding Observations: Colombia*, UN Doc CAT/C/COL/CO/4 (2010), [25].
620 CAT, *Concluding Observations: Chile*, UN Doc CAT/C/CHL/CO/5 (2009), [23]; CAT, *Concluding Observations: Peru*, UN Doc CAT/C/PER/CO/5–6 (2013), [12].
621 CAT, *Concluding Observations: Colombia*, UN Doc CAT/C/COL/CO/4 (2010), [25] (invoking the UN Basic Principles and Guidelines on the Right to a Remedy and Reparation for Victims of Gross Violations of International Human Rights Law and Serious Violations of International Humanitarian Law).
622 CAT, *Concluding Observations: Peru*, UN Doc CAT/C/PER/CO/5–6 (2013), [12]; CAT, *Concluding Observations: Guatemala*, UN Doc CAT/C/GTM/CO/5–6 (2013), [24].
623 CAT, *Concluding Observations: Paraguay*, UN Doc CAT/C/PRY/CO/4–6 (2011), [27].
624 CAT, *Concluding Observations: Peru*, UN Doc CAT/C/PER/CO/5–6 (2013), [21].
625 Ibid.

vulnerable groups (the CEDAW Committee and CRC). Like the HRC, the CESCR has shared a concern for the self-determination and cultural rights of indigenous peoples. The CESCR's broader emphasis on indigenous economic, social and cultural rights has been shared to varying degrees by the CERD, CEDAW Committee and CRC. Also like the HRC, some of the other committees have acknowledged the significance of land and resources in securing indigenous rights (including the CERD, CEDAW Committee and CRC).

Various committees have also shared the HRC's concerns about violence against indigenous peoples and wider law and justice considerations (including detention) (CERD, CEDAW Committee, CRC and CAT). Indigenous political participation has been of special interest to the CERD and CEDAW Committee, while family rights and child rights in the family have concerned the CRC. Indigenous peoples have featured less prominently in the practice of treaty bodies devoted to disabilities (established in 2008), enforced disappearances (created in 2010) and migrant workers (2003, but still with only 48 parties), although this may be expected to change over time as these committees become more established.

The next two chapters move from the international to the regional plane. Chapter 4 explores how regional human rights systems in the Americas and Africa have developed a distinctive rights jurisprudence concerning indigenous land and natural resources. Chapter 5 then considers how these regional systems have dealt with cultural, socio-economic and physical integrity rights in relation to indigenous peoples. These chapters suggest that regional human rights systems have gone further than the UN treaty bodies in protecting indigenous interests through expansively interpreting human rights norms in certain areas. This is partly because the constituent instruments of those regional systems sometimes provide greater latitude for regional bodies to protect such interests, but it is also because of dynamic, creative and culturally sensitive interpretation of rights.

4

Regional Human Rights Systems: Indigenous Property Rights in Land and Natural Resources

LIKE THE MAJOR international human rights treaties, most regional human rights instruments do not expressly address indigenous rights. Instead, regional courts have progressively interpreted general human rights standards to take into account the specific circumstances, cultural characteristics and distinctive experiences of indigenous peoples. This chapter considers the Inter-American and African regional human rights systems, where regional human rights instruments have been applied to indigenous peoples in a significant number of cases. Brief attention is also given to the more limited ways that European human rights bodies have considered indigenous issues in some contexts.

The American continents have a long history of dispossession of indigenous peoples, including of Native American and Inuit peoples in North America and the many indigenous groups in South America affected by Spanish and Portuguese colonisation. At the regional level, American states expressed concern about the situation of indigenous peoples as early as 1922 at the International Conference of American States, and later at the Conferences of the Pan American Union in the 1930s and the First Inter-American Indian Congress in 1940.[1]

In 1948, the (then) Conference of American States (now the Organization of American States (OAS)) addressed indigenous rights in its Inter-American Charter of Social Guarantees.[2] Article 39 of that non-binding instrument provided that states must take measures 'to provide the Indian protection and assistance, protecting his life, liberty, and property, and defending him from extermination, and safeguarding him from oppression and exploitation, protecting him from poverty, and providing adequate education'. It further required states 'to preserve, maintain, and develop the assets of the Indians or their tribes, and ... promote the exploitation of the natural, industrial, and extractive wealth or other sources of income from such assets or related to it, so as to ensure ... the economic emancipation of the indigenous groups'. States were also encouraged to create institutions or services 'to protect the Indians, and in particular to ensure respect for their lands, to legalize their possession by

[1] Inter-American Commission on Human Rights (IACHR), *The Human Rights Situation of the Indigenous People in the Americas*, OEA/Ser.L/V/II.108, Doc 62 (20 October 2000), Introduction.

[2] Ninth International Conference of American States, Resolution XXIX: Final Act of the Ninth International Conference of American States (1948).

them, and to prevent the invasion of such lands by outsiders'. The instrument was well-intentioned, albeit reflecting a paternalistic view of indigenous peoples as passive objects of external protection.

The modern Inter-American human rights system, belonging to the 35 member states of the OAS, is built around the American Declaration on Rights and Duties of Man 1948 and the American Convention on Human Rights 1969. Where an OAS member state is not a party to the American Convention, the American Declaration, though not a treaty, is now regarded as imposing binding obligations. In interpreting these standards the Inter-American system also commonly refers to ILO Convention No 169 concerning Indigenous and Tribal Peoples in Independent Countries 1989 as the more specialised law (*lex specialis*).[3] Institutionally, the Inter-American instruments are overseen by the Inter-American Commission on Human Rights, established in 1959, and the Inter-American Court of Human Rights, created in 1979. A Special Rapporteur on the Rights of Indigenous Peoples was created in 1990. Since 1989, the Commission has been drafting a Proposed Declaration on the Rights of Indigenous Peoples, at the request of the OAS.[4] The Commission has also sought to advance 'soft' law standards in other areas, as through its recommendations on the rights of indigenous peoples in voluntary isolation and initial contact in the Americas.[5]

In monitoring states, the Inter-American Commission considered indigenous issues from as early as 1970,[6] being initially concerned with severe racial discrimination,[7] and issuing a thematic resolution on the special protection of indigenous peoples in 1972.[8] It has issued numerous country and special reports on indigenous peoples;[9]

[3] IACHR, *The Human Rights Situation of the Indigenous People in the Americas* (n 1), Introduction.

[4] Approved by the IACHR on 26 February 1997, at its 1333rd Session, 95th Regular Session. See also IACHR, *Authorities and Precedents in International and Domestic Law for the Proposed American Declaration on the Rights of Indigenous Peoples*, OEA/Ser.L/V/II.110, Doc 22 (1 March 2001).

[5] IACHR, *Indigenous Peoples in Voluntary Isolation and Initial Contact in the Americas: Recommendations for Full Respect of their Human Rights*, OEA/Ser.L/V/II, Doc 47/13 (30 December 2013).

[6] IACHR, *Guahibo Indians v Colombia*, Case No 1690, OEA/Ser.L/V/II.30, Doc 45 rev 1, 21 (26 February 1973).

[7] IACHR, *The Human Rights Situation of the Indigenous People in the Americas* (n 1), Introduction, ch 3. On Inter-American system monitoring of indigenous issues, see also James Anaya, *Indigenous Peoples in International Law* (2nd edn, Oxford University Press, 2004), 232–34 and 258–71. For a theoretical appraisal, see James Hopkins, 'The Inter-American System and the Rights of Indigenous Peoples: Human Rights and the Realist Model' in Stephen Allen and Alexandra Xanthaki (eds), *Reflections on the UN Declaration on the Rights of Indigenous Peoples* (Hart Publishing, 2011), 135.

[8] IACHR, *Resolution on Special Protection for Indigenous Populations: Action to Combat Racism and Racial Discrimination*, OEA/Ser.L/V/II.29, Doc 41 rev 2 (13 March 1973), cited in IACHR, *Yanomani v Brazil*, Case No 7615, Resolution No 12/1985 (5 March 1985).

[9] IACHR, *Fourth Report on the Situation of Human Rights in Guatemala*, OEA/Ser.L/V/II.83, Doc 16 rev (1 June 1993); IACHR, *Second Report on the Situation of Human Rights in Colombia*, OEA/Ser.L/V/II.84, Doc 39 rev (14 October 1993); IACHR, *Third Report on the Situation of Human Rights in Colombia*, OEA/Ser.L/V/II.102, Doc 9 rev 1 (26 February 1999); IACHR, *Report on the Situation of Human Rights in Ecuador*, OEA/Ser.L/V/II.96, Doc 10 rev 1 (24 April 1997); IACHR, *Report on the Situation of Human Rights in Brazil*, OEA/Ser.L/V/II.97, Doc 29 rev 1 (29 September 1997); IACHR, *Report on the Situation of Human Rights in Mexico*, OEA/Ser.L/V/II.100, Doc 7 rev 1 (24 September 1998); IACHR, *Second Report on the Situation of Human Rights in Peru*, OEA/Ser.L/V/II.106, Doc 59 rev (2 June 2000); IACHR, *Report on the Situation of Human Rights of a Segment of the Nicaraguan Population of Miskito Origin*, OEA/Ser.L./V.II.62, Doc 10 rev 3 (29 November 1983); IACHR, *Special Report on the Human Rights Situation in the so-called 'Communities in Resistance' in Guatemala*, OEA/Ser/L/V/II.86, Doc 5 rev 1 (16 June 1994) (recommending that the state resolve land ownership conflicts resulting from the resettlement of indigenous communities who were forcibly displaced during the armed conflict in the early 1980s, and to meet their basic needs).

considered hundreds of individual petitions;[10] issued reports preceding, and participated in, litigation before the Inter-American Court; requested states to adopt 'precautionary measures' to prevent irreparable harm to individuals or the subject matter of pending proceedings;[11] and facilitated a 'friendly settlement' procedure between states and aggrieved indigenous groups.

While consideration of indigenous issues has been more developed over a longer period in the Inter-American system, the African human rights system has also increasingly dealt with indigenous issues, particularly since 2001. As discussed in chapter 1, most African states have been reluctant to recognise the concept of indigenous peoples, unlike in the Americas. Largely this is because of a perception that all Africans are 'indigenous' and that acknowledging only some minorities as indigenous would be divisive. This political reluctance has constrained the legal recognition of indigenous issues in the African system.

The African system is a creature of the 54 member states of the African Union (formerly the Organization of African Unity) and is based on the standards in the African Charter on Human and Peoples' Rights 1981. It is supervised by the African Commission on Human and Peoples' Rights, established in 1987, and an African Court of Human and Peoples' Rights, created in 2006. While to date the African Court has not decided any cases dealing with indigenous peoples, the African Commission has issued a number of important standard setting decisions since 2001. In addition, the African Commission sought to clarify standards on indigenous peoples in Africa through its 2007 Advisory Opinion on the UN Declaration on the Rights of Indigenous Peoples 2007 (UNDRIP).[12]

In both regional systems, in the absence of specific indigenous rights, a few key general rights have been interpreted and applied in ways that recognise indigenous interests. The ordinary right to property has been especially significant in both systems. In the African system, the related but more specialised collective rights of peoples to control wealth and resources, and to development, have also featured prominently—and in some ways have gone further than the Inter-American system in recognising the breadth of indigenous interests in land and resources. Explicit cultural rights in the African Charter have also been relevant, while the Inter-American system has indirectly taken culture into account in interpreting property rights. In other cases, rights to life, food, housing, health and environment have been invoked in particularised ways to protect indigenous peoples. Both systems have also addressed various forms of severe violence against indigenous peoples.

The regional jurisprudence has proved significant not only in interpreting regional standards, but in providing detail and clarity in respect of international standards which, for various reasons, remain abstract or ambiguous in international law.[13] As will be seen, the African and Inter-American regional systems have also

[10] IACHR, *The Human Rights Situation of the Indigenous People in the Americas* (n 1), Introduction.

[11] Under IACHR's Rules of Procedure, art 25.

[12] ACHPR, *Advisory Opinion on the United Nations Declaration on the Rights of Indigenous Peoples*, 41st Session (May 2007).

[13] Gaetano Pentassuglia, 'Towards a Jurisprudential Articulation of Indigenous Land Rights' (2011) 22 *European Journal of International Law* 165, 177–82.

cross-pollinated one another in a productive judicial dialogue about underlying principles relating to indigenous peoples and their rights.[14] This in turn has helped to stimulate the evolution of wider international standards, including principles reflected in the UN Declaration on the Rights of Indigenous Peoples of 2007.

INDIGENOUS RIGHTS IN PROPERTY: LAND AND NATURAL RESOURCES

One of the most important ways that regional human rights bodies have protected indigenous peoples is through the creative interpretation and application of property rights. The American Convention on Human Rights 1969 guarantees a 'right to the use and enjoyment of ... property' in Article 21(1), and any deprivation of property, for reasons of public utility or social interest, must be according to law and justly compensated (Article 21(2)).[15] The African Charter on Human and Peoples' Rights 1981 similarly guarantees a 'right to property' in Article 14, which may only be encroached upon in the public or community interest and in accordance with law. In addition, Article 21 of the African Charter recognises a people's collective right to freely dispose of their wealth and natural resources, in their exclusive interest; not to be deprived of such resources; and to lawfully recover and be adequately compensated for despoiled property.[16] Article 22(2) of the African Charter uniquely requires states 'to ensure the exercise of the right to development'.

INTER-AMERICAN COMMISSION ON HUMAN RIGHTS

The Inter-American Commission considered indigenous issues from as early as 1970,[17] being initially concerned with severe racial discrimination,[18] and issuing a thematic resolution on the special protection of indigenous peoples in 1972.[19] It has

[14] Ibid 187–88.

[15] American Convention on Human Rights, art 21 (adopted 22 November 1969, entered into force 18 July 1978, 1144 UNTS 143): 'Right to Property: 1. Everyone has the right to the use and enjoyment of his property. The law may subordinate such use and enjoyment to the interest of society. 2. No one shall be deprived of his property except upon payment of just compensation, for reasons of public utility or social interest, and in the cases and according to the forms established by law. 3. Usury and any other form of exploitation of man by man shall be prohibited by law.'

[16] Art 21(5) further requires states to eliminate all forms of foreign economic exploitation, so as to enable their peoples to fully benefit from national resources.

[17] IACHR, *Guahibo Indians v Colombia*, Case No 1690, OEA/Ser.L/V/II.30, Doc 45 rev 1 (26 February 1973), 21.

[18] IACHR, *The Human Rights Situation of the Indigenous People in the Americas* (n 1), Introduction, ch 3. For early monitoring of indigenous issues by the HRC, see also Anaya, *Indigenous Peoples in International Law* (n 7) 232–34 and 258–71. For a theoretical appraisal, see James Hopkins, 'The Inter-American System and the Rights of Indigenous Peoples: Human Rights and the Realist Model' in Stephen Allen and Alexandra Xanthaki (eds), *Reflections on the UN Declaration on the Rights of Indigenous Peoples* (Hart Publishing, 2011), 135.

[19] IACHR, *Resolution on Special Protection for Indigenous Populations: Action to Combat Racism and Racial Discrimination* (n 8), cited in IACHR, *Yanomani v Brazil* (n 8).

issued numerous country and special reports on indigenous peoples;[20] considered hundreds of individual petitions;[21] issued reports preceding, and participated in, litigation before the Inter-American Court; requested states to adopt 'precautionary measures' to prevent irreparable harm to individuals or the subject matter of pending proceedings;[22] and facilitated a 'friendly settlement' procedure between states and aggrieved indigenous groups. Property rights have been central to the Inter-American system's efforts to protect indigenous lands and resources, as the key cases discussed below indicate. The Commission has also issued a thematic compilation of norms and jurisprudence on indigenous rights to traditional lands and resources.[23]

The Yanomami Indians in Brazil

Among the Commission's early cases, some of its more detailed findings stemmed from a complaint brought in 1980 by a coalition of non-governmental organisations (NGOs) on behalf of the Yanomami Indians in Brazil. Around 12,000 Yanomami lived in the Amazon forest near the Venezuelan border. In the 1960s, Brazil approved plans to develop and exploit the Amazon, including building a highway through Yanomami territory in 1973, which was followed by the discovery and exploitation of minerals by companies and prospectors and an influx of farmer-settlers.

These activities and the mass influx of outsiders had grave physical and psychological consequences for the Yanomami, including the disintegration of their culture and society, prostitution, begging, epidemics and deaths from infectious diseases (including influenza, tuberculosis, measles and venereal diseases), violence by miners and prospectors, and dislocation from their traditional lands. While Brazilian law formally recognised some of their rights, and declared a reserved territory of 7 million hectares in 1982, these measures were not effective in practice. Agricultural projects purportedly for their benefit resulted in further loss of their lands. The authorities also encouraged their integration, undermining their communities. The law treated the Yanomami as incompetent to perform certain acts and established guardianship over them. Medical care was inadequate. Hundreds of Yanomami disappeared or died and they risked extinction.

[20] IACHR, *Fourth Report on the Situation of Human Rights in Guatemala* (n 9); IACHR, *Second Report on the Situation of Human Rights in Colombia* (n 9); IACHR, *Third Report on the Situation of Human Rights in Colombia* (n 9); IACHR, *Report on the Situation of Human Rights in Ecuador* (n 9); IACHR, *Report on the Situation of Human Rights in Brazil* (n 9); IACHR, *Report on the Situation of Human Rights in Mexico* (n 9); IACHR, *Second Report on the Situation of Human Rights in Peru* (n 9); IACHR, *Report on the Situation of Human Rights of a Segment of the Nicaraguan Population of Miskito Origin* (n 9); IACHR, *Special Report on the Human Rights Situation in the so-called 'Communities in Resistance' in Guatemala* (n 9) (recommending that the state resolve land ownership conflicts resulting from the resettlement of indigenous communities who were forcibly displaced during the armed conflict in the early 1980s, and to meet their basic needs).

[21] IACHR, *The Human Rights Situation of the Indigenous People in the Americas* (n 1), Introduction.

[22] Under IACHR's Rules of Procedure, art 25.

[23] IACHR, *Indigenous and Tribal Peoples' Rights over their Ancestral Lands and Natural Resources: Norms and Jurisprudence of the Inter-American Human Rights System*, OEA/Ser.L/V/II. Doc 56/09 (30 December 2009).

In its report in 1985, the Inter-American Commission found that, by allowing these activities and failing to ensure their safety and health, Brazil failed to take timely and effective measures to protect the Yanomami, their ancestral lands and culture. The Commission identified violations of their rights, under the American Declaration, to life, liberty and personal security (Article 1); residence and movement (Article 8); and health and well-being (Article 11). It also recalled that Article 27 of the International Covenant on Civil and Political Rights (ICCPR) protects the right of ethnic groups to special protection in the use of their own language, the practice of their own religion, and in all the characteristics necessary for the preservation of their cultural identity. The Commission further stated that 'for historical reasons and because of moral and humanitarian principles, special protection for indigenous populations constitutes a sacred commitment of the [American] states'.[24] As such, the failure of Brazil to protect those whom it was responsible to protect was considered all the more reprehensible. The Commission noted that the OAS had already made it a priority for states to preserve and strengthen the cultural heritage of ethnic groups and to strengthen non-discrimination.

The Commission recommended wide-ranging remedies. It urged Brazil to take preventive and curative health measures to protect the lives and health of Indians exposed to infectious or contagious diseases. It further recommended that programmes of education, medical protection and social integration be carried out in consultation with the Yanomami and experts, and that state officials receive training in indigenous rights and non-discrimination. Most importantly, it recommended that Brazil set and demarcate the boundaries of Yanomami lands—the first time an inter-governmental organisation had made such a proposal.[25]

The Miskitos in Nicaragua

In another early case, in 1984 the Commission reported on the situation of the Miskitos in Nicaragua,[26] an indigenous people living on the Pacific coast. The Miskitos had lived under a British protectorate from the late seventeenth century until 1860, when a treaty between Britain and Nicaragua recognised the latter's sovereignty over the Miskitos' territories, while preserving the Miskitos' customs and internal self-government.[27] Subsequent agreements provided for Nicaragua's recognition of the Miskitos' legal title to some traditional lands.[28] Chronic underdevelopment of the region, the exploitation of natural resources by foreign and domestic companies, and a growth in ethnic identity, led to the formation in the 1970s of organisations for the defence of indigenous rights.[29]

[24] Ibid.
[25] IACHR, *The Human Rights Situation of the Indigenous People in the Americas* (n 1), ch 3.
[26] IACHR, *Report on the Situation of Human Rights of a Segment of the Nicaraguan Population of Miskito Origin* (n 9).
[27] Ibid [A(7)].
[28] Ibid [A(8)–(9)].
[29] Ibid [A(10)–(12)].

Tensions grew under the government of the Frente Sandinista de Liberación Nacional (FSLN) from 1979, with the Miskitos resisting the government's attempt to change their way of life and tribal organisation to follow the government's socio-political objectives.[30] Nicaragua responded with drastic measures to control what it saw as an anti-revolutionary, secessionist movement, including mass arrests of indigenous leaders and military control over the indigenous organisation, Misurasata.[31] Around 3,000 Miskitos fled to Honduras in 1981. Conflict was fuelled by Nicaragua's agrarian reforms, which did not take into account indigenous rights to land and compensation,[32] and incursions into Nicaragua by anti-Sandinista armed groups on the Honduran border.[33] The increasing militarisation of the area saw violence against the Miskitos, including threats of group extermination; arbitrary mass arrests; torture; disappearances; murders; aerial bombardment of villages; burning of homes, temples and schools; religious persecution; appropriation of cattle and other assets; the forced relocation of 8,500 villagers; and an exodus of 10,000 refugees into Honduras.[34]

In its report in 1983, the Inter-American Commission found violations of the rights to life, personal freedom, personal integrity, due process, freedom of residence and transit, and property under the American Convention. In examining the right to property under Article 21, the Commission considered two types of claim: first, the destruction of the Miskitos' housing, personal belongings, crops and livestock; and secondly, their dispossession from ancestral lands.[35] Nicaragua originally justified such destruction as necessary to deny resources to subversive armed groups. In the proceedings, however, Nicaragua admitted the destruction of property so the issue was no longer in dispute, and the Commission recommended that procedures be established to pay just compensation. In its ongoing effort to facilitate a friendly settlement, the Commission observed that Nicaragua had not complied with its recommendations, with the state arguing that its provision of housing, food, healthcare, land and farming tools to the people in new settlements was sufficient compensation.[36]

As regards the dispute over ancestral lands, the Commission did not wish to limit the sovereign rights of Nicaragua and found itself 'not in a position to pronounce on the strictly legal validity of the claim of indigenous peoples on their ancestral lands'.[37] It nonetheless emphasised that this was 'one of the most serious problems' between the Miskitos and Nicaragua, and recommended that Nicaragua study fair solutions to the problem, taking into account indigenous aspirations, economic

[30] Ibid [B(2)].
[31] Ibid [B(3)].
[32] Ibid [B(4)].
[33] Ibid [B(5)].
[34] Ibid [B(6)–(7)], [D].
[35] Ibid [F].
[36] IACHR, *Resolution on the Friendly Settlement Procedure in the Situation of Human Rights in a Sector of the Nicaraguan Population of Miskito Origin*, Case No 7964, OEA/Ser.L/V.II.62, Doc 26 (16 May 1984), [7(h)].
[37] IACHR, *Report on the Situation of Human Rights of a Segment of the Nicaraguan Population of Miskito Origin* (n 9) Part II, [F(6)].

interests and territorial unity.[38] The Commission observed that the Miskitos were economically dependent on the government because they had been deprived of their traditional means of subsistence and their land claims remained unresolved.[39] It also noted the lack of participation by the Miskitos in decisions affecting them. In the friendly settlement process, the Commission noted that Nicaragua was unwilling to comply with its recommendations, and was further violating Miskito rights through harmful changes to land tenure and exploitative agrarian reforms.[40]

The Maya in Belize

In *Maya Indigenous Communities v Belize* (2004),[41] indigenous people in Southern Belize were adversely affected by Belize granting logging and oil concessions on traditional lands, which harmed the environment on which they depended for subsistence and jeopardised their culture and survival. The complainants argued that Belize violated Article 23 of the American Declaration by failing to recognise and establish mechanisms to protect their communal property rights, and granting concessions without effective consultation or informed consent. They claimed further that Belize violated the right to equality before the law, equal protection and non-discrimination (Article 2) by failing to provide them with the protections necessary to exercise their property rights. They also argued that Belize violated the right to judicial protection (Article 18) by rendering domestic judicial proceedings brought by the Maya people ineffective through unreasonable delay.

As regards the right to property, after invoking its own and international jurisprudence,[42] the Commission held that the Maya had traditionally occupied the territories through their traditional agriculture, hunting, fishing and other land and resource use practices, regardless of the dates that particular villages were established.[43] The Commission left it to Belize to fulfil its obligation to define and demarcate the territory, in full collaboration with the Maya people and according to their customary land use practices.[44] Under Article 23, Belize was required to take special measures to recognise and guarantee the interest that indigenous people have in the occupation and use of their traditional lands and resources.[45] This required Belize to effectively delimit and demarcate their territory, protect it and officially recognise it. Such steps further required effective and informed consultations with the Maya people concerning the boundaries of their territory, taking into account their traditional

[38] Ibid Part III, Recommendations, [3(j)].

[39] Ibid Part III(A), Conclusions, [10].

[40] IACHR, *Resolution on the Friendly Settlement Procedure in the Situation of Human Rights in a Sector of the Nicaraguan Population of Miskito Origin* (n 36) [7(i)].

[41] IACHR, *Maya Indigenous Communities v Belize (Merits)*, Case No 12.053, Report No 40/2004 (12 October 2004); *(Admissibility)* Case No 12.053, Report No 78/2000 (5 October 2000).

[42] Ibid [113]–[120].

[43] Ibid [130].

[44] Ibid.

[45] Ibid [131]–[132].

land use practices and customary land tenure system.[46] The Commission found that Belize had failed to discharge these obligations in domestic law.[47]

Concerning the concessions, the Commission found that Belize had granted oil and logging concessions to third parties on the Maya's lands without undertaking effective, participatory and fully and accurately informed consultations.[48] It further held that Belize's failure to respect communal property rights was exacerbated by the environmental damage from the logging concessions.[49] In this respect, Belize had failed to put into place adequate safeguards, mechanisms and staff to supervise and monitor the concessions.[50] The Commission acknowledged the importance of economic development, but insisted that it must not harm the basic rights of indigenous communities and the environment on which they depend for their physical, cultural and spiritual well-being.[51]

Dann Case in the United States

The case of *Mary and Carrie Dann v United States* (2002)[52] involved two members of the Dann band who lived on and occupied a ranch in Nevada, which was part of the ancestral territory of the Western Shoshone indigenous people. They argued that the United States had interfered with their traditional land by appropriating it as federal property through an unfair procedure (an Indian Claims Commission), removing their livestock, and permitting gold prospecting. Their subsistence hunting had been impeded by state officials and trespass actions taken against them for accessing their land.

Because the United States was not a party to the American Convention, the complainants alleged violations of the American Declaration,[53] including the rights to equality before the law (Article 2); religious freedom (Article 3); family rights (Article 6); the right to work (Article 14); fair trial (Article 18); and property (Article 23). The United States responded that the Danns still enjoyed title, ownership and possession of their ranch; they were permitted to graze stock on public lands under licence; they had lost interests in the lands because of encroachment by non-Native Americans from the late nineteenth century, whose title had been recognised in fair proceedings at the Indian Claims Commission; and the Western Shoshone had been awarded US$26 million in compensation, held in trust until its distribution was agreed with them.

[46] Ibid [132].

[47] Ibid [133].

[48] Ibid [140]–[143] (also citing the Inter-American Court decision in *Awas Tingni v Nicaragua* (n 92); and the UN HRC case of *Chief Bernard Ominayak and Lubicon Lake Band v Canada*, HRC Communication No 167/1984, UN Doc CCPR/C/38/D/167/1984 (26 March 1990)).

[49] Ibid [148].

[50] Ibid [147].

[51] Ibid [150] (also invoking the African Commission in the *Ogoni* case: *Social and Economic Rights Action Center and the Center for Economic and Social Rights v Nigeria*, ACHPR Communication No 155/1996, 2001 AHRLR 60 (27 October 2001), [149]).

[52] IACHR, *Mary and Carrie Dann v United States*, Case No 11.140, Report No 75/2002 (27 December 2002).

[53] Ibid [95].

The Inter-American Commission interpreted the American Declaration in light of international human rights law on indigenous peoples.[54] The Commission emphasised the importance of land to the survival of indigenous peoples, their culture, and the realisation of their human rights.[55] International law was found to recognise a right to legal recognition of indigenous territories and property; alteration of title only by informed consent under conditions of equality; and fair compensation for loss of property.[56] Articles 18 (fair trial) and 23 (property) of the Declaration were duly interpreted to require that indigenous peoples are fully and accurately informed of the nature and consequences of land determination processes, and given an effective opportunity to participate individually or collectively.[57]

On the facts, the Commission found that land claims were pursued by one Western Shoshone band without a mandate from other bands (including the Danns), and that no appropriate consultations with the Western Shoshone were held at the relevant time.[58] Further, property rights in traditional lands were extinguished through the Indian Claims Commission process, without being accorded the ordinary US constitutional protections that require expropriation to be for a valid public purpose, and with notice, just compensation and judicial review.[59] The United States had not justified their differential treatment, the Danns were not effectively represented in the process, and the merits were not reviewed by the courts. The value of compensation awarded was also inappropriate because it was based on an average extinguishment date (which did not relate to specific lands) and excluded interest.[60] Their treatment was further regarded as unequal, contrary to Article 2 of the Declaration.[61] The Commission did not accept the US argument that extinguishment was justified to encourage settlement and agricultural development, particularly given that the lands in question were occupied until recently by the Western Shoshone.[62]

The Los Cimientos in Guatemala

A friendly settlement involving ancestral lands was facilitated by the Commission in 2003 in a case lodged in 1993 by the Los Cimientos indigenous community in Guatemala. The community was granted legal title in 1909 to lands they had occupied since before that time.[63] The complainants alleged that, during an armed conflict in 1981, the Guatemalan Army occupied an area inhabited by 672 indigenous families, ostensibly for counter-insurgency operations against the Guerrilla Army of

[54] Ibid [97], [131].
[55] Ibid [128], [131].
[56] Ibid [130]–[131]. See also Art XVIII of the Proposed American Declaration on the Rights of Indigenous Peoples, approved by the IACHR on 26 February 1997, at its 1333rd Session, 95th Regular Session.
[57] Ibid [140].
[58] Ibid.
[59] Ibid [144].
[60] Ibid.
[61] Ibid [145].
[62] Ibid.
[63] IACHR, *Community of San Vicente los Cimientos v Guatemala (Friendly Settlement)*, Petition 11.197, Report No 68/2003 (10 October 2003), [25].

the Poor (EGP). After threats of shelling and the murder of two of its members, the community was forced to flee its land in early 1982, abandoning livestock and crops of corn, beans and coffee. They lived as internally displaced persons in precarious conditions and under threat of further attack. Some families returned to find their homes had been burned down and their possessions stolen. In 1985, the community began negotiating with Guatemala to return and have their legal title recognised, but found it necessary to commence legal action in 1990. The community was expelled again in 1994, and in 2001 their lands were violently taken by outsiders, with government support.

A friendly settlement facilitated by the Commission was reached in 2002, by which Guatemala agreed to purchase and transfer 845 hectares of land to 233 indigenous families and to provide transport, food, healthcare, housing, humanitarian assistance and services during their relocation. It was also agreed to identify and negotiate urgent projects to reactivate the community's productive, economic and social capacities, to foster the community's development and well-being. The arrangements were to be monitored over time by a multi-party commission.

The Garífuna in Honduras

The Commission has decided a number of cases involving the Garífuna indigenous communities living on the Atlantic or Caribbean coast of Honduras, and in 2013 filed two cases before the Inter-American Court to enforce its findings.[64] The Garífuna emerged in the eighteenth century from the intermingling of indigenous (Arawak Indian and Kalinagu) peoples and Africans, involving deportation and migration from Caribbean islands. Honduras did not challenge that the Garífuna are indigenous. The Commission accepted that they are 'the product of cultural syncretism between indigenous and African peoples'; self-identify as indigenous; have a collective notion of ancestral property; and have preserved their own unique culture and ethnicity (based on their 'cultural forms, organizations, and social and cultural institutions, way of life, cosmovision, habits, customs, ceremonial rights, language, clothing, and special relationship to the land').[65] The beach and the sea are an important part of their ethnic and cultural identity, and their livelihoods involve small-scale fishing, subsistence cropping (rice, cassava, bananas and yucca), and hunting small marine and forest animals (such as deer, agoutis, turtles and manatees).[66] Their language, dance and music was recognised by UNESCO in 2001 as part of the oral and intangible heritage of humanity.

In *Garífuna Community of 'Triunfo de la Cruz' v Honduras* (2012), the Commission found that Honduras had violated the right to property in Article 21 of the American Convention because it did not provide effective access to collective

[64] *Garífuna Community of 'Triunfo de la Cruz' and Its Members v Honduras*, Case 12.548, IACtHR Application, filed 21 February 2013; *Garífuna Community of Punta Piedra and Its Members v Honduras*, IACtHR Application, Case No 12.761, filed 11 October 2013.

[65] *Garífuna Community of 'Triunfo de la Cruz' and Its Members v Honduras (Merits)*, Case 12.548, IACHR Report No 76/12 (7 November 2012), [190].

[66] Ibid [53]–[58].

indigenous property title to ancestral territory.[67] Specifically, Honduras lacked a culturally appropriate legal framework to recognise indigenous ancestral property, and its ordinary agrarian law framework was insufficient to protect areas used for traditional subsistence activities and cultural practices.[68]

In addition, even where title was granted, the Commission found that Honduras failed to promptly delimit, demarcate and effectively protect indigenous territory.[69] In particular, the legal titles granted were too uncertain and overlapping (including allowing tourism leases and other investments); access to ancestral land was restricted by the creation of protected areas; and their land was not protected against occupation by third parties (*mestizos* peasants (*ladinos*) and other non-Garífunas). In dealing with conflicting titles, Honduras did not prioritise indigenous attachments to land, make restitution of their lands, or provide other lands of equal extent and quality. It also allowed urban expansion, through private land sales, to encroach on their lands, disregarding their customary land law.[70] This exacerbated conflict, harassment, violence and anxiety, including threats and use of firearms, arrests, destruction of crops, and denial of access to subsistence resources.

Procedurally, the Commission found that Article 21 was further violated because Honduras failed to ensure that prior, free and informed consultation with the Garífuna, in accordance with their customs and traditions, took place in relation to decisions affecting their territory and resources (including as regards tourism projects, the creation of the protected area, and the sale of their land).[71] Environmental and social impact assessments were also deficient. Beyond Article 21, the Commission found violations of the due legal process protections in Articles 8 and 25 of the American Convention in relation to Garífuna communal property rights.[72]

In a second case, *Garífuna Community of Punta Piedra v Honduras* (2013),[73] the Commission found that Honduras had failed to ensure the community's effective and peaceful enjoyment of its (titled) territory by not preventing the intrusion of, and dispossession by, non-indigenous peasants (*ladinos*) since 1993, and by not clearing their property title after 20 years of dispute.[74] The result was continuing violence and insecurity, including threats, assaults, killings, the intensification of racism and discrimination by mestizos towards them, burning of forests, and impunity for perpetrators. This was despite the community already enjoying legal title to their lands, albeit subject to other conflicting national laws which Honduras had not resolved.[75] The Commission noted further that Honduras must also respect the rights of the third parties in resettling them, including through compensation. A lack of effective judicial protection under Article 25 of the American Convention was also identified in connection with the violation of property rights.

[67] Ibid [294].

[68] Ibid [210]–[217].

[69] Ibid [218]–[233].

[70] Ibid [234]–[249].

[71] Ibid [250]–[266].

[72] Ibid [267]–[293].

[73] *Garífuna Community of Punta Piedra and Its Members v Honduras (Merits)*, Case 12.761, IACHR Report No 3/13 (21 March 2013).

[74] Ibid [86]–[110].

[75] Ibid [82]–[83].

The Kaliña and Lokono Peoples in Suriname

Following the Inter-American Court's case law on Suriname, discussed below, the Inter-American Commission has also found violations of indigenous property rights under Article 21 in a case involving eight villages of indigenous peoples in Suriname.[76] The Kaliña and Lokono peoples have traditionally occupied the lands and territories on the northeast coast for thousands of years, with their territorial boundaries recorded in their oral histories and recognised by neighbouring groups,[77] and their customary law acknowledging collective ownership.[78] They have a close material and spiritual relationship with their lands and resources and a tradition of sustainably using them in their subsistence livelihoods, which rely on hunting, fishing, swidden agriculture, and collecting forest products (for food, building materials, medicines, utensils and fuel).[79] The Commission observed that their 'notion of their own freedom as peoples depends on their ability to continue their traditional uses of their lands, territories and natural resources'.[80]

In the first place, the Commission found that Suriname violated Article 21 by failing to adopt effective measures to recognise their collective property rights to the lands, territories and natural resources they had traditionally occupied and used.[81] Suriname's domestic law did not adequately recognise indigenous collective property rights, as the Court had already found in a number of cases,[82] and Suriname had not yet reformed its laws. Secondly, Suriname further violated their collective property rights because it granted land titles to non-indigenous people,[83] authorised mining[84] and established three nature reserves,[85] all on their ancestral lands and territories, and without consultation aimed at obtaining their free, prior and informed consent.

The Commission acknowledged the importance of environmental preservation, but not at the cost of indigenous rights.[86] Suriname had not shown the unavailability of alternative, less intrusive means of protecting the nature reserves, taking into account indigenous rights; nor had it conducted sufficient environmental and social impact assessments. The reserves were also excessive because indigenous peoples were sometimes prevented from accessing them. Suriname had also authorised an environmentally damaging bauxite mine in one reserve, undercutting its argument that the reserves were necessary to protect the environment.

Finally, the Commission found that Suriname violated the right to juridical personality under Article 3 of the American Convention, because there was no

76 *Kaliña and Lokono Peoples v Suriname (Merits)*, Case 12.639, IACHR Report No 79/13 (18 July 2013).
77 Ibid [34].
78 Ibid [94].
79 Ibid [36], [94].
80 Ibid.
81 Ibid [91]–[99].
82 *Moiwana Community v Suriname (Preliminary Objections, Merits, Reparations and Costs)* (2005) IACtHR (Ser C) No 145 (15 June 2005); *Saramaka v Suriname (Preliminary Objections, Merits, Reparations and Costs)* (2007) IACtHR (Ser C) No 172 (28 November 2007).
83 *Kaliña and Lokono Peoples v Suriname (Merits)* (n 76) [101]–[116].
84 Ibid [117]–[132].
85 Ibid [133]–[156].
86 Ibid [134].

effective recourse to prevent or remedy violations of their collective property rights. Dissatisfied with Suriname's response to its findings, the Commission commenced proceedings in the Inter-American Court in 2014.[87]

Precautionary Measures

As mentioned, the Commission has also recommended that states issue precautionary measures (PM) to prevent irreparable harm and these include cases where the lives or physical integrity of indigenous communities are threatened on account of intrusions on their land. Other notable examples include the adverse impacts of development on indigenous lands, particularly hydroelectricity dams[88] and mining concessions.[89] The Commission has been variously concerned about environmental pollution and degradation, including the adverse effects on water and food sources necessary for survival; the spread of diseases and epidemics, and other adverse effects on indigenous health; the influx of outside settlers; mass forced displacement; interference in property rights; adverse impacts on cultural and livelihood activities, including hunting, fishing, agriculture and livestock; and interference in communities living in voluntary isolation. The Commission has been further concerned about the lack of prior, free and informed consultation about development projects, including access to information such as environmental and social impact assessments. Some of these concerns arose in cases later decided by the Inter-American Court and discussed below.[90]

INTER-AMERICAN COURT OF HUMAN RIGHTS

The Inter-American Commission has referred an increasing number of cases involving indigenous issues to the Inter-American Court since the 1990s,[91] with comprehensive, standard setting judgments being issued since 2001. Building on the earlier work of the Commission, the jurisprudence on indigenous communal property rights has been considerably elaborated by the Inter-American Court in a series of cases from 2001.

[87] *Kaliña and Lokono Peoples v Suriname*, Case No 12.639, IACtHR Application, filed 4 February 2014.

[88] *Indigenous Communities of the Xingu River Basin, Pará, Brazil*, IACHR PM 382/10 (1 April 2011); *Ngöbe Indigenous Communities et al, Panama*, IACHR PM 56/08 (18 June 2009).

[89] *Communities of the Maya People (Sipakepense and Mam) of the Sipacapa and San Miguel Ixtahuacán Municipalities in the Department of San Marcos, Guatemala*, IACHR PM 260-07 (20 May 2010); *Community of San Mateo de Huanchor, Peru*, IACHR PM (17 August 2004).

[90] See, eg, *Yakye Axa Indigenous Community v Paraguay (Merits, Reparations and Costs)* (2005) IACtHR (Ser C) No 125 (17 June 2005) and *Saramaka v Suriname (Preliminary Objections, Merits, Reparations and Costs)* (2007) IACtHR (Ser C) No 172 (28 November 2007).

[91] *Aloeboetoe v Suriname (Merits)* (1991) IACtHR (Ser C) No 11 (4 December 1991).

The Awas Tingni in Nicaragua

Awas Tingni Community v Nicaragua (2001)[92] involved an indigenous community of 600 people on the Atlantic Coast of Nicaragua who subsisted on family farming and communal agriculture, gathering fruit and medicinal plants, hunting and fishing. The community had no real property title to the traditional lands it claimed, which partly overlapped with other indigenous claimants. The Nicaraguan forestry authorities had authorised a private corporation to commence logging on their lands without their consent.

Adopting an 'evolutionary interpretation' of Article 21 of the American Convention, the Inter-American Court found that the right to property included the rights of members of indigenous communities within the framework of communal property (which was also recognised by Nicaragua's Constitution).[93] Such a right was characterised by a communitarian tradition of community not individual land ownership.[94] The Court held further that the very existence of indigenous groups conferred upon them the right to live freely in their territory; and the close ties of indigenous people with the land must be recognised and understood as the fundamental basis of their cultures, spiritual life, integrity and economic survival.[95] Land for them was not a matter of mere possession and production but 'a material and spiritual element which they must fully enjoy, even to preserve their cultural legacy and transmit it to future generations'.[96]

Although the community lacked formal legal title to their lands, the Court found that indigenous customary law must be taken into account, by which possession of the land may be regarded as sufficient for indigenous interests to be officially recognised and registered.[97] Nicaragua recognised communal title in principle but had not regulated the procedure for identifying particular titles, and in this case had not objected to the Awas Tingni's claim.[98] The Court thus found that the community had 'a communal property right to the lands they currently inhabit, without detriment to the rights of other indigenous communities'.[99]

Because Nicaragua had not demarcated their land, the community was uncertain about its limits and hence its ability to use it.[100] As a result, the Court ordered Nicaragua to delimit, demarcate and title their land, and prevent state or private agents from affecting the existence, value, use or enjoyment of the claimed land pending its titling.[101] The Court concluded that Nicaragua had violated the community's right to use and enjoy its property, in particular by granting concessions to third parties to

[92] *Awas Tingni Community v Nicaragua (Merits, Reparations and Costs)* (2001) IACtHR (Ser C) No 79 (31 August 2001).
[93] Ibid [148].
[94] Ibid [149].
[95] Ibid.
[96] Ibid.
[97] Ibid [151].
[98] Ibid [152].
[99] Ibid [153].
[100] Ibid [154].
[101] Ibid.

exploit their land and resources.[102] The Court found a separate violation of the right to judicial protection under Article 25 of the American Convention, because Nicaragua had failed to adopt domestic legal measures to delimit, demarcate and title their lands, or process their court challenge within a reasonable time.[103]

The Paraguayan Chaco Cases

The Inter-American Court has made similar findings about communal property rights in subsequent cases. Quite a few have involved indigenous peoples from the Paraguayan Chaco, a large, sparsely populated, arid region bordering Bolivia and Brazil. *Yakye Axa Indigenous Community v Paraguay* (2005)[104] concerned an indigenous community of 319 people, in 90 families, that was part of the Southern Lengua Enxet people of the Paraguayan Chaco. Their traditional economy was based on seasonal hunting, gathering and fishing, as well as farming and livestock-raising.[105] The Chaco was occupied from the late nineteenth century by non-indigenous settlers, with much land sold on the London stock exchange, and accompanied by Anglican evangelisation and 'pacification'.[106] The Yakye Axa experienced very bad living conditions and lack of services on livestock estates, with no wages or very low wages, and sexual exploitation of women. Their resettlement by the church in the 1980s failed to improve their living conditions, and a lack of water and food led to many deaths.

From 1993, the Yakye Axa commenced steps in Paraguay to reclaim their traditional lands, while living precariously along a public road. There, they experienced constant threats and harassment and suffered 'extreme' and 'destitute living conditions'.[107] They could not practice their traditional subsistence activities on their lands; few had jobs or income; there were no basic services (including medical facilities); dwellings were poor; there was no clean, reliable water, sanitation or electricity; malnutrition and disease was widespread; there was scarce transportation; and the local school was inadequate.

The Inter-American Court took a dynamic, evolutionary approach to the interpretation of the right to property in Article 21 of the American Convention,[108] by taking into account the recognition of communal property in ILO Convention No 169 (which Paraguay had ratified).[109] As a result, the Court acknowledged the close relationship of indigenous peoples to their land as the fundamental basis for their culture,

[102] Ibid.
[103] Ibid [137]–[139].
[104] *Yakye Axa Indigenous Community v Paraguay (Merits, Reparations and Costs)* (2005) IACtHR (Ser C) No 125 (17 June 2005), [124], [131], [135]–[137]. The IACHR had issued precautionary measures in 2002 requesting the state to suspend their eviction, refrain from affecting their property rights, and provide for their basic needs: *Yakye Axa Indigenous Community, Paraguay*, IACHR PM (26 September 2002).
[105] Ibid [50].
[106] Ibid.
[107] Ibid [50(93)].
[108] Ibid [125].
[109] Ibid [127], [130], [136].

spiritual life, wholeness, economic survival and preservation and transmission of culture to future generations.[110] It stated further that indigenous culture:

> directly relates to a specific way of being, seeing, and acting in the world, developed on the basis of their close relationship with their traditional territories and the resources therein, not only because they are their main means of subsistence, but also because they are part of their worldview, their religiosity, and therefore, of their cultural identity.[111]

The Court found that these cultural ties must be safeguarded by Article 21.[112] It noted that the term 'property' includes material things but also 'any right which may be part of a person's patrimony; that concept includes all movables and immovables, corporeal and incorporeal elements and any other intangible object capable of having value'.[113]

Paraguay's Constitution recognised the cultural identity of indigenous peoples and their rights in communal lands, and Paraguay did not dispute the cultural and economic ties of the Yakye Axa to their claimed lands.[114] Paraguay had, not, however, made such rights effective, in part because it claimed that the Yakye Axa's claim conflicted with private property rights.[115] The Court held that where private and communal property rights conflict, restrictions on rights are permissible where they are established by law, necessary, proportional, and pursue a legitimate aim in a democratic society.[116] The Court emphasised that indigenous territorial rights 'encompass a broader and different concept that relates to the collective right to survival as an organized people, with control over their habitat as a necessary condition for reproduction of their culture, for their own development and to carry out their life aspirations'.[117] It found that the restriction of property rights may be necessary to preserve indigenous cultural identities, and proportional if fair compensation is paid to those affected.[118] Further, it held that if land cannot be returned to indigenous communities 'for concrete and justified reasons', alternative suitable lands and fair compensation could be paid to the indigenous community, where a consensus has been reached and in accordance with the community's own mechanism of consultation, values, customs and customary law.[119] Here, the Yakye Axa had not agreed to Paraguay's offer of alternative lands.[120]

Consequently, the Court found that Paraguay had violated Article 21 by not giving effective domestic legal protection to the right of the Yakye Axa to use and enjoy their traditional lands, thus threatening the development and transmission

[110] Ibid [131].
[111] Ibid [135].
[112] Ibid [137].
[113] Ibid.
[114] Ibid [138], [140].
[115] Ibid [141]–[142].
[116] Ibid [144].
[117] Ibid [146].
[118] Ibid [148].
[119] Ibid [149]–[151] (also invoking Art 16(4) of ILO Convention No 169 concerning Indigenous and Tribal Peoples in Independent Countries (adopted 27 June 1989, entered into force 5 September 1991, 1650 UNTS 383)).
[120] Ibid [152].

of their traditional practices and culture.[121] The Court noted that it was not its role to define the Yakye Axa's traditional territory, but ordered Paraguay to delimit, demarcate, title and transfer their land within three years.[122] If traditional territory was privately owned, the Court ordered Paraguay to assess the legality, necessity and proportionality of its expropriation, in the light of the land's importance to the Yakye Axa's culture and survival.[123] If restitution was not possible, Paraguay was required to provide alternative land by consensus with the Yakye Axa, in accordance with their methods of consultation and decision-making, practices and customs.[124] Paraguay was further required to establish a consultation fund to purchase necessary lands and pay compensation.[125]

In the year following that decision, *Sawhoyamaxa Indigenous Community v Paraguay* (2006)[126] involved similar historical circumstances affecting another sedentary indigenous community, of around 400 people in 80 families, living on the Paraguayan Chaco. The Sawhoyamaxa are part of the South Enxet and North Enhelt Lengua ethnic groups, living along a public road outside the cattle estates they had left after they sought to reclaim them as their traditional lands from 1991 onwards. The community was deprived of its traditional means of subsistence and lived in extreme poverty and poor health, without basic services, despite the authorities legally acknowledging its precarious conditions.[127] Thirty members of the community died as a result.[128]

The Inter-American Court closely followed its interpretation of the right to property in the *Awas Tingni* and *Yakye Axa* cases. Paraguay recognised the Sawhoyamaxa's attachments to land, but as in *Yakye Axa* objected that these interests conflicted with private property rights. More generally Paraguay protested that recognising their claim would convict the state 'for the "sins" committed during the [Spanish] conquest', leading to the 'absurd situation in which the whole country could be claimed by indigenous peoples'.[129]

The Court found that indigenous peoples who unwillingly lost possession of their lands, when they were lawfully transferred to innocent third parties, were entitled to restitution, or to obtain other lands of equal extent and quality.[130] The Court found further that the right to restitution persists as long as the indigenous community's unique spiritual and material relationship with their traditional lands endures, or else lapses.[131] Such relationship can be expressed in different ways, depending on the

[121] Ibid [155]–[156].
[122] Ibid [215], [217].
[123] Ibid [217].
[124] Ibid.
[125] Ibid [218].
[126] *Sawhoyamaxa Indigenous Community v Paraguay (Merits, Reparations and Costs)* (2006) IACtHR (Ser C) No 146 (29 March 2006), [118]–[121], [131]; *Pueblo Indígena de Sarayaku v Ecuador (Provisional Measures)* (2005) IACtHR (Ser E) No 21 (17 June 2005), [2]. See also, *Maya Indigenous Community of the Toledo District v Belize*, Case 12.053, IACHR Report No 40/2004 (12 October 2004).
[127] Ibid [73(62)].
[128] Ibid [73(74)].
[129] Ibid [125].
[130] Ibid [128].
[131] Ibid [131].

circumstances, and may include: traditional use or presence, as through spiritual or ceremonial ties; settlements or sporadic cultivation; seasonal or nomadic gathering, hunting and fishing; and customary use of natural resources. Where such activities and relationship have been impeded by loss of land or other reasons beyond their control (such as violence), the Court held that the right of restitution survives until such hindrances disappear.[132] On the facts, despite their dispossession and denial of access, the Court found that the Sawhoyamaxa continued to carry out traditional activities and their right of restitution had not lapsed.[133]

The Court acknowledged that it was not its role to determine whether the Sawhoyamaxa's communal rights prevailed over private owners, but rejected Paraguay's arguments against their enforcement.[134] The mere existence of long held, lawful private ownership was not regarded as an objective and reasonable ground for dismissing indigenous claims, nor was the fact that the existing owners were productively exploiting the lands. The Court also found that a bilateral investment treaty did not preclude indigenous claims because it allowed for public purpose expropriation, and in any event could not be enforced inconsistently with the American Convention.[135] Consequently, the Court ordered restitution of the lands within three years, with Paraguay required to consider purchasing or expropriating them.[136] If restitution were not possible, Paraguay was required to offer alternative equivalent lands, in agreement with the community in accordance with its decision-making and consultation procedures.[137]

Yet another case concerning the property of indigenous people on the Paraguayan Chaco is *Xákmok Kásek Indigenous Community v Paraguay* (2010).[138] The community comprised 66 families with 268 individuals whose claim to 10,700 hectares of traditional land under domestic legal procedures had been frustrated by prolonged delays since 1990. The use of their traditional lands had been disrupted since the late nineteenth century by the sale and development of their lands for agriculture (including the extermination of wild animals, the fencing of cattle ranches, and restrictions on traditional hunting, cropping, herding, fishing and gathering); 'religious pacification' through Christian missions; and the 'sedentarisation' of nomadic peoples.[139] In 2008, they were further affected by Paraguay's creation, without consultation, of a private nature reserve over part of their lands.[140] They were thus deprived of ownership of, and access to, their land, leaving them in a vulnerable situation regarding food, medicine and sanitation, in turn threatening their integrity and survival as a community.

132 Ibid [132].
133 Ibid [134].
134 Ibid [135]–[140].
135 Ibid [140].
136 Ibid [210]–[212].
137 Ibid [212].
138 *Xákmok Kásek Indigenous Community v Paraguay (Merits, Reparations and Costs)* (2010) IACtHR (Ser C) No 214 (24 August 2010).
139 Ibid [58]–[75].
140 Ibid [79]–[82].

Paraguay recognised the community's right to communal ownership of their traditional lands and subsistence activities essential to their culture, but disputed their right to the return of the specific lands claimed.[141] In particular, Paraguay argued that, traditionally, the community had been nomadic across a vast area, and the claimed lands within that area held no special significance. It further objected that their claim could not override conflicting private property rights, by which the land was already productively utilised.[142] It maintained that it intended to transfer 1,500 hectares of alternative land to the community to fulfil its needs.

As in its previous cases, the Inter-American Court recognised that Article 21 of the American Convention protects the close relationship of indigenous peoples to their traditional communal lands and the natural resources relevant to their culture, as well as the resulting intangible elements.[143] It reiterated that such relationship is essential to their culture, spiritual life, integrity and economic survival.[144]

In deciding the dispute, the Court found that the specific area of 10,700 hectares claimed by the community was indeed part of its (admittedly larger) traditional lands, even if the precise boundaries were uncertain.[145] It based its conclusion on community and expert evidence as to the history of its settlement and displacement, including the locations of villages, hunting and fishing grounds, burial grounds and medicinal plants, and the indigenous language names given to particular places (such as settlement sites, wells, lakes, woods, palm groves, spartina (cord-grass) plantations, areas for gathering and fishing, and cemeteries). The Court further found that the lands claimed were appropriate and the most suitable for the community's way of life.

While the community did not own the lands, it had a right to recover them under Paraguay's laws.[146] Its right to land persisted because the community continued to carry out its traditional activities (despite the restrictions it faced) including by secretly hunting, gathering medicine plants and customarily burying their dead.[147] To the extent that it was prevented from continuing its activities, it was because of circumstances outside of its control, namely the creation of the nature reserve.[148] The Court found further that the alternative land offered by Paraguay was unacceptable because of its limited size (only 1,500 hectares, when 66 families required a minimum of 100 hectares each); its location outside the traditional territorial range; and the community had already rejected it.[149]

The Court emphasised the adverse cultural impacts of restricted access to traditional lands and the violation of communal property rights under Article 21.[150] In particular, there were severe negative effects on the Xákmok Kásek's languages, shamanistic

141 Ibid [88]–[89].
142 Ibid [53].
143 Ibid [85].
144 Ibid [86].
145 Ibid [95]–[107].
146 Ibid [111].
147 Ibid [114]–[115].
148 Ibid [115].
149 Ibid [118]–[121].
150 Ibid [174]–[181].

rituals and ancestral knowledge, initiation rituals, the way they commemorate their dead, their relationship with the land, and their 'cosmovision' and way of life.[151] For example, the Court noted that languages had been lost by younger generations, shamanism was disappearing, and people could not be buried in chosen sacred places. Their traditional means of subsistence had also been impeded, including hunting, fishing and gathering.[152] In these respects the Court highlighted the insufficiency of the 'productive' conception of the land when considering conflicting communal and private property rights.[153]

Finally, the Court concluded that Paraguay had not processed the community's land claim with due diligence and thus had separately violated other provisions of the American Convention, namely Article 8(1) (the principle of reasonable time in administrative proceedings); Article 25(1) (the right to judicial protection); and Article 2 (the right to an effective remedy).[154] The domestic proceedings did not offer the community a real possibility to recover its traditional lands. They had considered the issues exclusively from the perspective of the productivity of land, thus discriminatorily disregarding the particularities of the community's culture and its special relationship with its traditional lands.[155]

It should be mentioned that the Inter-American Commission also brokered a 'friendly settlement' in an earlier Paraguayan Chaco case, thus obviating the need for litigation in the Court and illustrating the ability of the Commission to constructively mediate disputes. In *Enxet-Lamenxay and Kayleyphapopyet (Riachito) Indigenous Communities v Paraguay* (1999),[156] the complainants were indigenous communities of 16,000 people who traditionally subsisted on hunting, fishing and gathering, as well as small cultivation and animal breeding. All of their lands were privatised by the state between the late nineteenth century and 1950, and numerous domestic efforts to secure legal recognition of their lands had failed. Under an agreement facilitated and monitored by the Commission, Paraguay agreed to hand over almost 22,000 hectares of land and allow the occupation and use of the land pending titling. In addition, Paraguay undertook to provide food, medicine, tools and transport to relocate them, and to remove the existing private landowners. The new settlements would also be supplied with sanitary, medical and educational assistance and road works. The Commission was to be consulted in the event of disputes. The Commission continued to monitor the arrangement through meetings and on-site visits. Title deeds were issued in 1999.

151 Ibid [176].
152 Ibid [180].
153 Ibid [182].
154 Ibid [131]–[170].
155 Ibid [170].
156 *Enxet-Lamenxay and Kayleyphapopyet (Riachito) Indigenous Communities v Paraguay*, IACHR Case No 11.713, Report No. 90/1999 (1 January 1999).

Other Inter-American Court Cases

The Kichwa/Sarayaku in Ecuador

The right to property was also central in *Kichwa Indigenous People of Sarayaku v Ecuador* (2012),[157] where Ecuador had permitted a private company to explore for oil in the traditional Amazon forest territories of the 1,200 Kichwa indigenous people of Sarayaku.[158] The Kichwa subsisted on family-based, customary farming, hunting, fishing and gathering in their territory.[159] According to their world-view, 'the jungle is alive and nature's elements have spirits (*Supay*), which are interconnected and whose presence makes places sacred'.[160] The Kichwa and their decision-making structures had been politically recognised by Ecuador since 1979,[161] and they were awarded land title in 1992.[162] Ecuador recognised the collective rights of indigenous peoples in its Constitution in 1998 and ratified ILO Convention No 169 in the same year. As such, there was no dispute over their right to communal property.[163]

However, Ecuador granted oil concessions over large parts of the Kichwa's territories in 1995–96.[164] The Kichwa claimed that they were not consulted and did not consent. The oil company sought the support of the community by offering jobs and payments, and attempting to divide the Kichwa's leaders.[165] The Kichwa commenced domestic proceedings. They also resorted to direct actions to block the development, by deploying their population in 'peace and life' camps on their land's borders to block the company's access.[166] The Kichwa were threatened and harassed, and a group of 120 was attacked with machetes, sticks, stones and firearms by another indigenous group in the presence of police.[167] The company's activities proceeded in some places, including the use of explosives, which denied the Kichwa access to subsistence resources and limited their freedom of movement and cultural rights.

Following its earlier jurisprudence,[168] the Inter-American Court found that Ecuador had violated the Kichwa's communal right to property and natural resources.[169] Ecuador had failed to consult with, and guarantee the participation of the Kichwa (through their own institutions and mechanisms and in accordance with their values, practices, customs and forms of organisation) in decisions affecting their territory, communal property rights, life and cultural identity.[170]

157 *Kichwa Indigenous People of Sarayaku v Ecuador (Merits and Reparations)* (2012) IACtHR (Ser C) No 245 (27 June 2012).
158 Ibid [2], [52].
159 Ibid [54].
160 Ibid [58].
161 Ibid [55].
162 Ibid [61]–[62].
163 Ibid [149].
164 Ibid [63]–[65].
165 Ibid [73]–[78].
166 Ibid [100].
167 Ibid [107]–[108].
168 Ibid [145]–[176].
169 Ibid [145]–[220].
170 Ibid [232].

Specifically, none of the five elements of the right to consultation was fulfilled.[171] First, the Kichwa had not been consulted in advance. Secondly, the consultations were not undertaken in good faith with the aim of reaching an agreement. This was because the process was delegated to a private company and not monitored by the state; military and private security were oppressively present in the area; indigenous political structures were not respected; and meetings produced tension and dispute rather than a climate of respect conducive to consensus.

Thirdly, the consultation was not appropriate and accessible because the company had attempted to negotiate with the Kichwa without respecting their political organisation. Fourthly, the environmental impact plan was prepared without the Kichwa's participation; was implemented by a private entity sub-contracted by the developer, without state monitoring; and did not take into account the social, spiritual and cultural impacts. Fifthly, consultation was not informed because it did not provide the Kichwa with the necessary environmental impact information, allow them to discuss those matters, or inform them of the advantages and disadvantages of the project in relation to their culture and way of life.

The Inter-American Court also interpreted the Kichwa's rights to property and consultation in light of an implied 'right to cultural identity'.[172] The Court emphasised that disregard for indigenous land rights could affect other basic rights such as the right to cultural identity and survival.[173] Invoking non-discrimination in Article 1(1) of the Convention, the Court held that recognition of the right to cultural identity is necessary to understand, respect and guarantee human rights under the Convention.[174] States must accordingly ensure that indigenous peoples are properly consulted on matters that affect or could affect their cultural and social life, in accordance with their values, traditions, customs and forms of organisation.[175]

On the facts, the Court found that company had damaged areas of great environmental, cultural and subsistence food value for the Kichwa.[176] This resulted in the suspension of ancestral events and spiritual ceremonies, and interrupted youth initiation ceremonies. Such disruptions, as well as the diversion of the adults into defending their territorial borders, 'had an impact on teaching children and young people about their traditions and cultural rituals, and on perpetuating the spiritual knowledge of the sages'.[177] Further, the use of explosives destroyed forests, water sources, caves, underground rivers and sacred sites, and caused animals to migrate.[178] Harm to symbolic sites and the natural world had a profound impact on the community's social and spiritual relationships.[179] The Kichwa had not been consulted on matters affecting their cultural identity, and the destruction of their cultural heritage entailed a significant lack of respect for their social and cultural identity, customs,

171 Ibid [180]–[220].
172 Ibid [212]–[220].
173 Ibid [212].
174 Ibid [213].
175 Ibid [217].
176 Ibid [218].
177 Ibid.
178 Ibid.
179 Ibid [219].

traditions, worldview and way of life, which caused them 'great concern, sadness and suffering'.[180] There was thus a violation of Article 21 property rights in relation to 'the right to cultural identity'.[181]

The Kuna in Panama

The Inter-American Court also considered indigenous communal property rights in *Kuna Indigenous People of Madungandí and the Emberá Indigenous People of Bayano and their Members v Panama* (2014).[182] The case was brought by indigenous peoples whose ancestral lands were flooded, and who were forced to relocate, as a result of the construction of the Bayano hydroelectric dam and reservoir in the 1970s. The Kuna people had lived in tropical rainforest areas since the sixteenth century, and their 80,000 members mainly practised slash and burn, subsistence swidden agriculture, reforestation, hunting and fishing. The 31,000 Emberá people migrated from Colombia to river areas in Panama in the seventeenth and eighteenth centuries and engaged in hunting, fishing and crafts. Non-indigenous farmers or settlers had also migrated to these areas as a result of the hydroelectricity project. While indigenous collective property rights were recognised in Panama's Constitution and other national laws,[183] Panama's agreements with the indigenous peoples to provide them with more and better land, and compensation, for the loss of their lands were never adequately or effectively implemented. The complainants argued that Panama had failed to recognise, title and demarcate the alternative lands on which they had settled; not protected their territories and natural resources from invasion and illegal logging; and not provided effective procedures for collective land ownership and to vindicate their rights.

The Inter-American Court reiterated its jurisprudence that Article 21 protects not only classical property rights but also indigenous communal property rights in traditional lands and natural resources.[184] This includes obligations on the state to recognise legal title, ownership and registration based on traditional possession; and to delimit, demarcate and title such lands.[185] Critically, the Court found that where restitution of traditional lands is impossible (as it was here, due to the permanent flooding of the land), the above principles equally apply to alternative lands allocated by the state as a result of relocation.[186] Otherwise indigenous peoples who had been forcibly dispossessed from their ancestral lands would be unable to enjoy security of tenure due to causes outside of their control.[187]

[180] Ibid [220].
[181] Ibid [232].
[182] *Kuna Indigenous People of Madungandí and the Emberá Indigenous People of Bayano and their Members v Panama (Preliminary Objections, Merits, Reparations and Costs)* (2014) IACtHR (Ser C) No 284 (14 October 2014).
[183] Ibid [114]–[115].
[184] Ibid [111]–[124].
[185] Ibid [117], [119].
[186] Ibid [122].
[187] Ibid.

The Court then examined Panama's treatment of a series of parcels of land in respect of each indigenous community.[188] It found that Panama had violated Article 21 because it had either unreasonably delayed, or failed, to delimit, demarcate and title the various lands. Abstract legal recognition of indigenous land rights was considered insufficient and resulted in prolonged indigenous uncertainty about where they could freely use and enjoy their lands and resources.[189] Panama further violated Article 21 by granting and not revoking a private title on collective lands.[190] In addition, the Court found that Panama's failure to provide for internal rules to delimit, demarcate and title land violated its obligations to take measures to give effect to Convention rights (under Article 2); to provide effective judicial remedies for violations (Article 25); and to guarantee due process of law (Article 8).[191] Moreover, certain domestic proceedings related to the dispute were found to involve further breaches of Articles 8 and 25.[192] The Court could not conclude, however, that Panama's inadequate land title procedures discriminated against indigenous peoples.[193]

'Tribal' Peoples in Suriname: The Moiwana

The Inter-American Court similarly recognised the communal property rights, under Article 21 of the American Convention, of a 'tribal' people in *Moiwana Community v Suriname* (2005).[194] The distinction between 'tribal' and 'indigenous' peoples, stemming from ILO Convention No 169, was discussed in chapter 1. The *Moiwana* case was brought by the N'djuka people of Moiwana village, who are a Maroon tribe descended from African slaves who escaped from Dutch colonists in the seventeenth century.[195] Moiwana village was settled in the late nineteenth century and its members engaged in traditional hunting, farming and fishing in their territories. The case concerned the consequences of a supposed counter-insurgency operation by Suriname's military regime, which killed 40 (of 170) villagers, destroyed the village, and displaced its members. While the American Convention had not entered into force at the time of the attack, the complainants argued that the attack's continuing consequences, namely impunity for the perpetrators, and continuing displacement, presently violated the Convention. The surviving villagers had escaped into the forest, thereafter became refugees in French Guiana, and suffered continuing poverty and deprivation. Most were unable or unwilling to return to their village and lands for fear of further attacks and because of the prevailing impunity for the perpetrators.[196] They had been unable to practise their customary means

[188] Ibid [125]–[146].
[189] Ibid [135]–[136].
[190] Ibid [145].
[191] Ibid [157].
[192] Ibid [173], [187].
[193] Ibid [203].
[194] *Moiwana Community v Suriname (Preliminary Objections, Merits, Reparations and Costs)* (2005) IACtHR (Ser C) No 145 (15 June 2005), [132]–[133].
[195] Ibid [86].
[196] Ibid [86(43)].

of subsistence and livelihood,[197] or to recover the remains of relatives killed in the attack and perform customary burial rites for them.[198]

Earlier in its decision, the Inter-American Court had found that Suriname's failure to investigate the attack prevented the Moiwana from voluntarily returning to live safely on their traditional lands.[199] The Court then found that while formal legal title to their land rested with the state,[200] mere possession of ancestral land, held according to customary cultural, spiritual and economic ties and practices, should suffice to obtain official recognition of communal ownership.[201] Although the Moiwana community was not indigenous, the Court accepted that it had lived in the area in strict adherence to N'djuka customs since the late nineteenth century; possessed an 'all-encompassing relationship' to its traditional lands; had a communal concept of property ownership; and its occupancy was recognised by other N'djuka clans and indigenous communities.[202] As such, the Court applied its earlier jurisprudence on the communal property rights of indigenous peoples to use and enjoy their traditional territories to a similarly situated tribal people.[203] The precise boundaries of its territory, however, had to be determined in consultation with neighbouring communities.[204]

'Tribal' Peoples in Suriname: The Saramaka

The case of *Saramaka People v Suriname* (2007) was brought by another Maroon tribal people whose use of traditional lands was adversely affected by the state's granting of logging and mining concessions.[205] As noted in chapter 1, while they are not strictly 'indigenous', the Inter-American Court drew an analogy between the legal situation of tribal and indigenous peoples under the American Convention to recognise communal tribal property rights. Unlike in the *Awas Tingni* case, here the domestic law did not recognise a right to communal property and the state was not a party to ILO Convention No 169.[206]

In interpreting the right to property in Article 21 of the American Convention, the Inter-American Court noted that, pursuant to Article 29(b) of the Convention, the Court cannot interpret it to restrict rights in the ICCPR and International Covenant

197 Ibid [86(18)].
198 Ibid [86(20)].
199 Ibid [128].
200 Ibid [130].
201 Ibid [131].
202 Ibid [132]–[133].
203 Ibid [133]–[135].
204 Ibid [133].
205 *Saramaka v Suriname (Preliminary Objections, Merits, Reparations and Costs)* (2007) IACtHR (Ser C) No 172 (28 November 2007), [92]–[96]. Precautionary measures were issued by the IACtHR on 8 August 2002, requesting the state to suspend all concession activity: *De Vereninig van Saramakaanse (Twelve Saramaka Clans), Suriname*, IACHR PM (8 August 2002). See also Lisl Brunner, 'The Rise of Peoples' Rights in the Americas: The Saramaka People Decision of the Inter-American Court of Human Rights' (2008) 7 *Chinese Journal of International Law* 699.
206 *Saramaka v Suriname* (n 205) [93].

on Economic, Social and Cultural Rights (ICESCR).[207] Accordingly, the Court invoked the right of self-determination in common Article 1 of the twin Covenants as giving indigenous and tribal peoples the right to 'freely pursue their economic, social and cultural development' and 'freely dispose of their natural wealth and resources', so as not to be 'deprived of [their] own means of subsistence'.[208] The Court further observed that under Article 27 of the ICCPR, indigenous communities constituting a minority must not be denied their right, in community with the other group members, to enjoy their own culture, which may consist in a way of life which is closely associated with territory and use of its resources.[209]

The Court concluded that the right to property in Article 21 entitles indigenous and tribal communities to freely determine and enjoy their own social, cultural and economic development, which includes the right to enjoy their spiritual relationship with the territory they have traditionally used and occupied.[210] Article 21 thus 'grants to the members of the Saramaka community the right to enjoy property in accordance with their communal tradition'.[211] On the facts the Court found that the Saramaka enjoyed communal property rights to the territory they traditionally used and occupied, derived from their longstanding use and occupation of the land and resources necessary for their physical and cultural survival.[212]

Suriname accordingly had an obligation to adopt special measures to recognise, respect, protect and guarantee those rights.[213] The Court found that Suriname had not fulfilled its obligation, because its law only permitted indigenous people to exercise privileges in land but not to effectively control and own it.[214] It rejected Suriname's arguments that the Saramaka's traditional land tenure system was unclear; that it would be discriminatory to recognise special rights for them; or that existing laws and judicial remedies were sufficient.[215]

Also at issue was whether the Saramaka's right to traditional territories encompassed the natural resources in and on the land. Suriname disputed that such rights encompassed ownership of minerals in the subsoil (which were owned by the state)[216] or extended to resources (such as gold) not traditionally used by the tribe for subsistence (traditional uses being agriculture, hunting, fishing, and so on). The Court invoked its earlier cases[217] to find that tribal and indigenous peoples have a right to the natural resources in land for the same reason that they enjoy a right to the land itself: to ensure their physical and cultural survival as a community and to preserve their way of life.[218] The right to territory would be 'meaningless' if it were

207 Ibid.
208 Ibid.
209 Ibid [94].
210 Ibid [95].
211 Ibid.
212 Ibid [96].
213 Ibid.
214 Ibid [116].
215 Ibid [97]–[114].
216 Ibid [119], [125].
217 Namely the *Yakye Axa v Paraguay* (n 104) and *Sawhoyamaxa v Paraguay* (n 126) cases, discussed above.
218 *Saramaka v Suriname* (n 205) [121].

not connected to the land's resources.[219] As a result, it was necessary to protect their lands and resources to prevent their extinction as a people.[220] Article 21 was found to protect 'those natural resources traditionally used and necessary for the very survival, development and continuation of such people's way of life'.[221] The state was accordingly required to take special measures to guarantee their survival and to ensure they could continue to live their traditional way of life, and maintain their distinct cultural identity, social structure, economic system, customs, beliefs and traditions.[222]

The Court acknowledged that tribal and indigenous rights over land and natural resources are not absolute but, like other rights, are subject to limitations, including 'the interest of society' under Article 21.[223] The Court noted that a state may restrict the right to property where restrictions are previously established by law, necessary, proportional, and aim to achieve a legitimate objective in a democratic society.[224] Another 'crucial factor' is whether a restriction would deny indigenous traditions and customs in a way that endangered the very survival of the group and its members.[225]

The Court further demanded that the state comply with procedural safeguards in issuing concessions over natural resources in indigenous territory.[226] First, the indigenous community must effectively participate, from the early stages, in any development plans. This means that the state must, in good faith, actively consult the community in conformity with their customs and traditions, including by the giving and receiving of information (particularly as to environmental and health risks), with the objective of reaching an agreement knowingly and voluntarily.[227] Large-scale projects with major impacts additionally require the free, prior and informed consent of the community.[228] Secondly, the community must receive a reasonable benefit from development, which encompasses the right to compensation for deprivation of property, its resources, and their use.[229] Thirdly, no development may be granted without a prior environmental and social impact assessment.

On the facts, the Court found that the concessions granted by Suriname did not comply with these safeguards. The Saramaka traditionally used timber and forest products for boats, roofing, cooking, fuel, trade and sale.[230] While they did not traditionally use gold or have a cultural relationship with it, the Court held that its exploitation would affect their other natural resources.[231] When issuing the logging and mining concessions, Suriname had failed to: ensure the effective participation

219 Ibid [122].
220 Ibid [121].
221 Ibid [122].
222 Ibid.
223 Ibid [127].
224 Ibid.
225 Ibid.
226 Ibid [129].
227 Ibid [133].
228 Ibid [134].
229 Ibid [138]–[139].
230 Ibid [144]–[146].
231 Ibid [155].

of the Saramaka through their traditional decision-making processes; conduct prior environmental and social impact studies of harmful activities which ruined forests, blocked creeks, flooded land and contaminated water supplies; and share the economic benefits with, or compensate, the Saramaka.[232]

AFRICAN SYSTEM: AFRICAN COMMISSION ON HUMAN AND PEOPLES' RIGHTS

While the Inter-American jurisprudence concerning indigenous land and resources has centred on the right to property, the African regional jurisprudence has protected such interests through a combination of an orthodox right to property (in Article 14 of the African Charter), the more unusual collective right of a people to freely dispose of their wealth and natural resources (Article 21), and the right to development (Article 22(2)).

The Ogoni in Nigeria

In *Social and Economic Action Rights Centre (SERAC) v Nigeria* (2001),[233] the complainants alleged a violation of Article 21 of the African Charter,[234] namely a people's right to freely dispose of its wealth and natural resources. The case was brought by the Ogoni communities from the Niger Delta, who were adversely affected by oil exploitation by Nigeria and its commercial partners, including Shell Petroleum Development Corporation. Such activities contaminated the environment (including water, soil and air) and harmed human health (including through skin infections, gastrointestinal and respiratory ailments, cancer risks, and neurological and reproductive problems). Nigeria was allegedly negligent in failing to conduct health and environmental impact studies, require companies to consult the people, monitor oil operations or enforce environmental standards. In response to non-violent opposition, Nigerian security forces had attacked the Ogoni, killing people, destroying villages and displacing thousands of people. Ogoni food sources (including crops, animals and fish) were also harmed by the attacks and the pollution.

The African Commission did not explicitly characterise the Ogoni as 'indigenous' or 'tribal' but implicitly accepted, without explanation, that the Ogoni were a 'people' entitled to the rights in Article 21, whether because they were a distinct group or simply a part of the Nigerian population. On the facts, in a brief decision, the African Commission found a violation of Article 21 because, 'despite its obligation to protect persons against interferences in the enjoyment of their rights ... Nigeria facilitated the destruction of Ogoniland'.[235] Specifically, Nigeria had given

232 Ibid [147]–[153], [155]–[158].

233 *SERAC v Nigeria* (n 51).

234 Other allegations are considered further below, namely violations regarding the rights to life, health and non-discrimination, and a 'satisfactory environment'.

235 *SERAC v Nigeria* (n 51) [58].

'the green light to private actors, and the oil companies in particular, to devastatingly affect the well-being of the Ogonis'.[236] The complainants also alleged that property rights under Article 14 of the African Charter were violated, but this argument was confined to issues of housing and evictions, considered in the next chapter.

The Endorois in Kenya

The right to property (Article 14), the right to freely dispose of natural resources (Article 21) and the right to development (Article 22) were considered at length in the later case of *Endorois Welfare Council v Kenya* (2010).[237] The case was brought by the Endorois, an indigenous community forcibly evicted from traditional lands by Kenya's creation of a game reserve in 1973, and denied access to those lands after 1978. This denied them vital economic resources (namely medicinal salt licks, fertile soil, traditional herbs and unpolluted water in the Lake Bogoria region) which kept their cattle healthy and sustained their livelihoods. It also disrupted their religious and traditional practices, including their prayer sites, places for circumcision rituals and other ceremonial cultural sites. Promised compensation and benefits did not materialise. From 2000, some of their ancestral lands were demarcated and sold by Kenya to third parties, and in 2002 a gold mining concession (with associated road works) was granted to a private company, risking water pollution. While some access to the reserve was later reinstated, it was at the discretion of the game reserve and uncertain, and the community had no say in the land's management.

Concerning the right to property under Article 14, the African Commission noted that Kenya did not dispute that the area was the Endorois' ancestral land.[238] The Commission accepted that the community accordingly had a right to property with regard to its ancestral land, the possessions attached to it, and its animals.[239] The right to property included the rights to access it; not have it invaded or encroached upon; undisturbed possession, use and control; and its economic resources.[240] The Commission also indicated that special measures may have to be taken to protect the rights, interests and benefits of indigenous communities in their traditional lands.[241]

The Commission held that Kenya was obliged to recognise and give legal effect to the Endorois' communal property rights, even if it presented difficulties for domestic land law, or was (wrongly) perceived as discriminatory.[242] The Endorois' property rights were found to have been encroached upon by the expropriation and denial of ownership.[243] It was not sufficient to confer mere privileges in land, as through a

[236] Ibid.

[237] *Centre for Minority Rights Development (Kenya) and Minority Rights Group International on behalf of Endorois Welfare Council v Kenya*, ACHPR Communication No 276/2003, 2009 AHRLR 75 (4 February 2010).

[238] Ibid [183] (although as noted in chapter 1, Kenya did dispute whether they were a distinct community).

[239] Ibid [184].

[240] Ibid [186].

[241] Ibid [187].

[242] Ibid [194]–[196].

[243] Ibid [199].

trust which gave them access to land and beneficial but not actual title, and which had proved inadequate to protect their rights.[244] *De jure*, permanent ownership, not de facto ownership or mere access, was required.[245]

Where the right to property is violated, the Commission held that the state must make restitution, by returning the land, or, where that is not possible on objective and reasonable grounds, by providing alternative lands of equal extent and quality, in agreement with the indigenous community.[246] Kenya had not provided substitute land of equal quality.[247] In any event, the state's arguments were not reasonably and objectively grounded. The Commission found that, although their ancestral land was now a game reserve, the Endorois were its ancestral guardians and thus best equipped to maintain its delicate ecosystem.[248] They were prepared to undertake such conservation work; no other community had settled there in the meantime; the land was not spoliated and was still inhabitable; and their alienation from it threatened their cultural survival and way of life.[249] The encroachment was thus not proportionate to any public need.[250]

Finally, the Commission observed that fair compensation must be paid, and the amount of £30 thus far provided flew 'in the face of common sense and fairness'.[251] Compensation for loss of land must take into account: (a) the full replacement cost prior to displacement; (b) costs of moving and transitional support during resettlement; and (c) assistance to improve or restore former living standards, income earning capacity, and production levels.[252]

The African Commission additionally found that Kenya had violated the Endorois' right as a people to freely dispose of its wealth and natural resources under Article 21 of the African Charter. Kenya argued that the Endorois had benefited from the tourism and mining projects,[253] but the Commission found these claims to be unsubstantiated. The Commission accepted that the right to natural resources in traditional lands vested in the Endorois.[254] This included rubies, which they did not traditionally use as part of their economy or cultural identity, because mining them would affect other resources, such as water, which were necessary for survival.[255] On this point the Commission reasoned by analogy from the Inter-American Court's decision in *Saramaka People v Suriname* (2005), discussed earlier (concerning the non-traditional resource of gold), which also identified a duty on the state to consult indigenous communities in conformity with their traditions, share any benefits, and conduct environmental and social assessments. The Commission then found that

244 Ibid [199].
245 Ibid [205]–[206].
246 Ibid [234].
247 Ibid.
248 Ibid [235].
249 Ibid.
250 Ibid [238].
251 Ibid [236].
252 Ibid [237].
253 Ibid [253]. It also claimed that the Endorois were consulted and had reached agreement on some projects.
254 Ibid [267].
255 Ibid [263]–[266].

Kenya had not evaluated whether it was necessary to restrict private property rights to preserve the survival of the Endorois.[256] As such, it had violated Article 21(1). Further, it had not provided restitution or adequate compensation as required under Article 21(2).

The African Commission also found that Kenya had violated the right to development under Article 22 of the African Charter. It defined development as both a means (constitutive) and an end (instrumental), with minimum criteria of equity, choice, non-discrimination, participation, accountability and transparency.[257] Development was said to aim to empower communities and improve their capabilities and choices.[258] Forced evictions, for instance, violate the freedom to choose where one lives and thus infringes the right to development.[259] Procedurally, the Commission held that Kenya had a duty to actively consult, in good faith and through constant communication, with the community according to its customs and traditions.[260] It was further required to obtain the community's free, prior and informed consent on a project such as this, which had a major impact on traditional territory.[261]

The Commission found that Kenya had violated the participation requirement of the right to development because its consultations were inadequate, did not adequately inform the Endorois, and did not enable them to shape the game reserve project or take part in it.[262] Kenya also did not obtain their free and informed consent.[263] The community representatives were in an unequal bargaining position, being illiterate and having a different understanding of property use and ownership.[264] As a result, the Endorois believed that their pastoralist way of life and access to land could continue alongside the game reserve. Because Kenya had not informed them that the reserve would deny them all rights of return and access to their lands, the complainants legitimately expected that, after eviction, they could continue to access their land for religious ceremonies and medicinal purposes.

The Commission further found that equitable benefit sharing is vital to the right to development, and would be violated if projects decrease the well-being of the community, or fail to provide just compensation.[265] Kenya was thus required to ensure that the Endorois were not left out of the development process.[266] Instead, Kenya had not provided land of equal value, providing only semi-arid substitute land that was unsuitable for pastoralism.[267] Nor were the Endorois adequately compensated. They were left in precarious state, with their access to clean drinking water

256 Ibid [267]–[268] (by applying the tests, in Art 14 of the African Charter, for whether a restriction is 'in the interest of public need or in the general interest of the community' and 'in accordance with appropriate laws').
257 Ibid [277].
258 Ibid [283].
259 Ibid [278]–[279].
260 Ibid [289].
261 Ibid [290].
262 Ibid [281], [290].
263 Ibid [291]–[292].
264 Ibid [282].
265 Ibid [294]–[296].
266 Ibid [298].
267 Ibid [286].

severely undermined and their traditional means of subsistence (through grazing) curtailed.[268] The right to development in Article 22 was thus violated.

CONCLUSION

The normative instruments of the African and Inter-American human rights systems do not explicitly protect indigenous rights. In both systems, however, the right to property has been expansively interpreted to recognise indigenous rights in land and natural resources. In the Inter-American system, Article 21 of the American Convention requires states to protect the communal property rights of the territories that indigenous communities have traditionally used and occupied, as being essential to the foundations of their cultures, spirituality, integrity and economic survival. Also protected are natural resources that have been traditionally used and are necessary for the survival of indigenous ways of life; while non-traditional resources must not be disturbed if this would interfere in the traditional resources upon which indigenous survival depends. Notably, the Inter-American system has further acknowledged that the violation of indigenous property rights can affect other rights, such as an implied right to cultural identity and survival also arising under Article 21.[269]

The Inter-American system has articulated the content of indigenous property rights as follows. First, traditional indigenous possession of lands, absent formal title to property, is regarded as equivalent to full ownership.[270] Secondly, traditional possession entitles indigenous people to demand state recognition of ownership and the registration of property title.[271] Thirdly, the state must delimit, demarcate and grant collective title to indigenous lands.[272] Fourthly, indigenous communities which have unwillingly left their lands, or lost possession of them, for reasons outside their control, retain ownership rights, even absent formal title.[273] The right to recover traditional lands persists as long as an indigenous community maintains its unique relationship to such lands.[274] Fifthly, where the land from which indigenous peoples were dispossessed has been legitimately transferred, in good faith, to innocent third parties, indigenous people still have a right of restitution to recover them. This could involve the state purchasing back lands from private owners, at no cost to the indigenous people, or providing them with other lands of the same extent and quality.[275]

The Inter-American system has further required that states comply with procedural safeguards when issuing concessions over resources in indigenous territory.[276] First, the indigenous community must effectively participate from the inception

[268] Ibid [288].

[269] *Kichwa Indigenous People of Sarayaku v Ecuador* (n 157) [212].

[270] *Awas Tingni v Nicaragua* (n 92) [151]; *Sawhoyamaxa v Paraguay* (n 126) [128].

[271] *Awas Tingni v Nicaragua* (n 92) [151].

[272] Ibid [164]; *Yakye Axa v Paraguay* (n 104) [215]; *Saramaka v Suriname* (n 205) [194].

[273] *Moiwana v Suriname* (n 194) [133]; *Sawhoyamaxa v Paraguay* (n 126) [128].

[274] *Xákmok Kásek v Paraguay* (n 138) [112].

[275] *Sawhoyamaxa v Paraguay* (n 126) [128]–[130]; *Xákmok Kásek v Paraguay* (n 138) [109], [128].

[276] *Saramaka v Suriname* (n 205) [129]–[139].

of any development. This requires the state to actively consult the community, in good faith and according to its customs and traditions, by providing and receiving information on environmental and health risks, and aiming to reach a voluntary, informed agreement. Large-scale projects with major impacts additionally require the community's free, prior and informed consent. This is equally true of 'green' developments (such as nature reserves or eco-tourism) as it is of more obviously destructive industries such as logging, mining or commercial agriculture. Secondly, the community must receive a reasonable benefit from development, which encompasses the right to compensation for deprivation of property, its resources and their use. Thirdly, no development may be granted without a prior environmental and social impact assessment.

In the African system, the right to property in Article 14 of the African Charter has also been interpreted to recognise that indigenous communities enjoy a communal property right to their ancestral land and the possessions and animals attached to it. It includes rights to access, possess, use and control the land and its resources, and a freedom from external invasion or encroachment upon it (such as by expropriation). States are required to specially protect and give legal effect to these rights. In cases of violation (including by forced displacement), states must make restitution, by returning the land, or where that is not possible, by providing alternative lands of equal extent and quality, in agreement with the indigenous community, and fair compensation. Compensation must cover the full replacement value of land, the costs of resettlement and the restoration of living standards and livelihoods.

In the African system, related but more specialised collective rights under the African Charter have also been interpreted to protect indigenous lands and resources. The right of peoples to control wealth and resources (in Article 21 of the African Charter) has been held to require states to protect indigenous land and resources from destructive external interference by state and private actors.[277] This includes protection against interference (such as by mining) with non-traditional, non-culturally significant resources which would affect other survival resources (such as water). Further, the forced eviction of indigenous peoples from their land and homes, and the consequent violation of the freedom to choose where one lives, has been found to violate indigenous peoples' right to development under Article 22 of the Charter.

Procedurally, proposed interferences with indigenous land and resources (whether under Articles 14, 21 or 22) require states to consult indigenous communities, in good faith and in conformity with their traditions, and conduct environmental and social assessments. A community's free, prior and informed consent is required for projects that would have major impacts on indigenous territory. A project's benefits must also be equitably shared, meaning that indigenous well-being must not decrease or just compensation must be provided.

The next chapter moves beyond property and resource rights to consider how regional human rights systems have protected other critical indigenous interests.

[277] *SERAC v Nigeria* (n 51) [58].

5

Regional Human Rights Systems: Indigenous Cultural, Socio-economic and Physical Integrity Rights

THIS CHAPTER EXPLORES three further critical themes in the regional jurisprudence that have been particularly prominent in cases involving indigenous peoples: cultural rights, socio-economic rights and civil rights to life, liberty and physical integrity. As will be apparent, often these issues are closely linked to the indigenous land and resource rights considered in the previous chapter, including because of the connections between traditional lands and culture and socio-economic well-being, and because violence against indigenous people is often related to their dispossession and disputes over land. The chapter concludes by briefly charting the very limited cases in which indigenous issues have featured in the European regional human rights system, under the Council of Europe's European Convention on Human Rights 1950 and Framework Convention on the Protection of National Minorities 1995. Some cases have considered issues such as indigenous culture, land, resources and housing, albeit without recognising explicit indigenous rights.

CULTURAL RIGHTS IN REGIONAL JURISPRUDENCE

African System

As discussed in the previous chapter, African system cases dealing with property (Article 14) and resource (Article 21) rights have often recognised the cultural significance of attachments to traditional lands and resources. In addition, the express right to culture in Article 17(2)–(3) of the African Charter has been considered by the African Commission. Article 17(2) provides that '[e]very individual may freely take part in the cultural life of his community' (and thus resembles Article 15 of the International Covenant on Economic, Social and Cultural Rights (ICESCR), albeit with greater emphasis on its communal aspect). Article 17(3) provides further that '[t]he promotion and protection of morals and traditional values recognised by the community shall be the duty of the State'.

The case of *Endorois Welfare Council v Kenya* (2010)[1] was brought on behalf of the Endorois, an indigenous community that was forcibly removed from its ancestral

[1] *Centre for Minority Rights Development (Kenya) and Minority Rights Group International on behalf of Endorois Welfare Council v Kenya*, ACHPR Communication No 276/2003, 2009 AHRLR 75 (4 February 2010).

pastoral lands (used for cattle-raising) around Lake Bogoria when Kenya established a game reserve. The complainants argued that this violated their right to cultural life under Article 17(2) and (3), because it restricted access to cultural sites and damaged their pastoralist way of life.[2] Specifically, the Endorois argued that the lands were central to their regular religious and traditional practices, including places for prayer, circumcision rituals, festivals, and other cultural ceremonies.[3] They believed that the spirits of their people lived on the Lake, and that the nearby forest was the birthplace and first settlement of their people. Moreover, they held the land in high esteem as 'sacred' and believed it was inextricably linked to the cultural integrity of the community and its traditional way of life.[4] They saw land as belonging to the community not the individual, and as essential to their health, livelihood, religion, culture and preservation and survival as a traditional people. The land was also a source of traditional medicinal plants.[5] Kenya countered that the Endorois were still permitted to access forest areas, and that the complainants were disguising political claims as cultural practices.[6]

In interpreting cultural rights under Article 17, the African Commission observed that states must refrain from destroying minorities but also respect and protect the religious and cultural heritage (such as sacred buildings or sites) that is essential to group identity.[7] It emphasised that Article 17 has a dual nature, protecting both individual participation in the cultural life of the community as well as requiring the state to protect the community's traditional values.[8] The Commission understood culture broadly to include 'a spiritual and physical association with one's ancestral land, knowledge, belief, art, law, morals, customs, and any other capabilities and habits acquired by humankind as a member of' a distinct society, and including religion and language.[9] It emphasised that association with ancestral land was critical to the cultural survival of indigenous pastoralist and hunter-gatherer communities.[10] It also noted the importance of states protecting and promoting cultural diversity, including by addressing challenges such as exclusion, exploitation, discrimination, poverty, displacement, lack of participation in decision-making, forced assimilation and violence.[11]

The Commission observed that, unlike certain other rights under the African Charter (including the right to property), Article 17 contains no express limitations clause.[12] It interpreted this to mean that the drafters 'envisaged few, if any, circumstances in which it would be appropriate to limit a people's right to culture'.[13] Further,

[2] Ibid [239].
[3] Ibid [6].
[4] Ibid [16].
[5] Ibid [16].
[6] Ibid [240].
[7] Ibid [241].
[8] Ibid.
[9] Ibid. The Commission also cited the African Cultural Charter 1976: [242].
[10] Ibid [243]–[245] (citing the UN HRC, the ACHPR's Working Group on Indigenous Populations/Communities, and the UN Special Rapporteur on the Situation of Human Rights and Fundamental Freedoms of Indigenous People in Kenya).
[11] Ibid [246]–[248].
[12] Ibid [249].
[13] Ibid.

even if limitations were admissible, the Commission held that they would need to be proportionate to a legitimate aim and not adversely interfere in the exercise of the community's cultural rights. Thus, on the facts, even if the creation of a game reserve was a legitimate aim, Kenya's failure to allow a right of access to the Endorois to celebrate cultural festivals and rituals would not be proportionate.[14] Further, the Commission noted that their cultural activities did not threaten the reserve's ecosystem. The Commission concluded that Kenya's laws and actions 'denied community access to an integrated system of beliefs, values, norms, mores, traditions and artifacts closely linked to access to the Lake'.[15] Further, it seriously threatened their pastoralist way of life by forcing them to live on semi-arid lands without access to medicinal salt licks and other resources vital to their livestock.[16] As such, Kenya violated Article 17(2) and (3) because it denied 'the very essence of the Endorois' right to culture ... rendering the right, to all intents and purposes, illusory'.[17]

The complainants mounted a related argument that Kenya violated their right to freely practice religion under Article 8 of the African Charter, by evicting them from their land, denying them access to religious sites, and failing to demarcate and protect sites within the game reserve.[18] Access to perform rituals such as circumcisions, marriage, initiation and annual seasonal festivals had been denied, and they had also not been able to visit the spiritual home of the living and dead Endorois around the lake.[19] Kenya responded that its conservation measures had protected these areas while still enabling access.[20]

The African Commission accepted that the Endorois' spiritual beliefs and ceremonial practices constituted a religion under the African Charter and international law.[21] Worshipping or assembling in connection with a belief, maintaining places for these purposes, and celebrating ceremonies or rituals were all found to be characteristics of religion.[22] Religion could also be linked with land and cultural beliefs and practices.[23] The Commission found that the cultural and religious practices centred on Lake Bogoria were 'of prime significance to all Endorois'.[24] The Endorois prayed there, their ancestors were buried there, and they regarded it as the spiritual home of the living and dead. They also believed that their Great Ancestor, Dorios, came from the heavens and settled in the adjacent Mochongoi Forest.[25] Further, they believed that each season the lake water turned red and its hot springs emitted a strong odour, signalling the time to perform ceremonies to appease the ancestors who drowned when the Lake formed.[26]

14 Ibid [249].
15 Ibid [250].
16 Ibid [251].
17 Ibid.
18 Ibid [163].
19 Ibid [164].
20 Ibid.
21 Ibid [165]–[168].
22 Ibid [165].
23 Ibid [166].
24 Ibid.
25 Ibid [167].
26 Ibid.

The Commission acknowledged that religious practices could be restricted by law where such provisions pursue a legitimate aim, are proportionate and reasonable, and do not vitiate the right.[27] Harsh restrictions, such as those affecting the Endorois, require 'exceptionally good reasons'.[28] On the facts, the Commission found that denial of access to the Lake restricted the Endorois' freedom to practice religion and was not justified by any significant public security or other interest, such as economic development or ecological protection.[29] It believed that allowing the Endorois to access the land for religious purposes would not detract from conservation or development goals.[30] Article 8 was consequently held to be violated.

A violation of Article 17 was unsuccessfully alleged in *Malawi African Association and others v Mauritania* (2000).[31] The case was brought by representatives of the black population of southern Mauritania, who had suffered arbitrary arrests and detention, inhumane prison conditions, torture, death sentences, massacres, extra-judicial executions, and slavery or servitude, at the hands of the government and the majority ethnic group (Beidane). The complainants alleged a violation of their linguistic rights under Article 17 on the basis that the state denied them the right to speak their own languages. Mauritania argued that it maintained an institute of national languages which taught their languages, and that difficulties arose because many of the languages were exclusively oral and only spoken in small parts of the country. The Commission found that the complainants had not provided evidence to substantiate their allegations and thus could not find a violation of Article 17.[32]

Inter-American System

While the non-binding American Declaration 1948 recognises a right to take part in the cultural life of the community,[33] such right was not included in the American Convention 1969. The right does appear in Article 14 of the Additional Protocol to the American Convention on Human Rights in the Area of Economic, Social and Cultural Rights 1988 ('Protocol of San Salvador') but is not justiciable before the Inter-American Commission or the Inter-American Court of Human Rights.[34]

[27] Ibid [172].
[28] Ibid.
[29] Ibid [173].
[30] Ibid.
[31] *Malawi African Association and Others v Mauritania*, ACHPR Communications Nos 54/1991, 61/1991, 96/1993, 98/1993, 164/1997, 196/1997, 210/1998 (11 May 2000).
[32] Ibid [138].
[33] American Declaration, art 13: 'Every person has the right to take part in the cultural life of the community, to enjoy the arts, and to participate in the benefits that result from intellectual progress, especially scientific discoveries. He likewise has the right to the protection of his moral and material interests as regards his inventions or any literary, scientific or artistic works of which he is the author'.
[34] See Additional Protocol to the American Convention on Human Rights in the Area of Economic, Social and Cultural Rights ('San Salvador Protocol'), A-52, (adopted 17 November 1988, entered into force 16 November 1999, OAS Treaty Series No 69) art 19(6) (providing that only trade union rights (Art 8) and the right to education (Art 13) are justiciable). Art 14 of the Protocol recognises a right of everyone to take part in the cultural and artistic life of the community and to enjoy the benefits of scientific and technological progress, and stipulates various state obligations of protection and cooperation.

The Inter-American Commission and Court have, however, protected indigenous cultural interests by: referencing international standards (such as the International Covenant on Civil and Political Rights (ICCPR) and ILO Convention No 169); applying Article 13 of the American Declaration; and taking into account cultural considerations when interpreting the American Convention rights, including the right to property, right to life, freedom of conscience and religion, freedom of movement and residence, and the rights of the child.

In the early case of the *Miskitos* in Nicaragua in 1983, discussed in the previous chapter, the Commission rejected a claim than indigenous or minority groups enjoyed a group right of political autonomy or self-determination under international law (as it then stood).[35] It emphasised, however, that individuals enjoy a right of non-discrimination (under Article 1 of the American Convention), while ethnic minority groups enjoy a right to culture under Article 27 of the ICCPR[36] (which informs regional interpretation). As such, Nicaragua did not enjoy 'an unrestricted right to impose a total assimilation of these indigenous peoples'.[37] The Commission observed that the fulfilment of American Convention rights is essential to the survival and functioning of an indigenous community as a group and the preservation of its cultural values.[38] It found further that indigenous groups have a right to use their language, exercise their religion, and enjoy other aspects linked to the preservation of their cultural identity, including their ancestral and communal lands.[39] The Commission recommended that Nicaragua establish appropriate state institutions to protect such rights, designed through extensive consultation with, and implemented through the direct participation of, indigenous ethnic minorities and their freely appointed representatives.[40]

As is apparent from the land cases discussed in the previous chapter, the Inter-American Court has often recognised cultural identity as an integral aspect of the right to communal property and natural resources under Article 21 of the American Convention.[41] Thus, to recall, in the *Yakye Axa* case the Court emphasised that indigenous culture 'directly relates to a specific way of being, seeing, and acting in the world, developed on the basis of their close relationship with their traditional territories and the resources therein, not only because they are their main means of

[35] IACHR, *Report on the Situation of Human Rights of a Segment of the Nicaraguan Population of Miskito Origin*, OEA/Ser.L./V.II.62, Doc 10 rev 3 (29 November 1983), Part II, [B].

[36] Ibid Part II, [B(1)–(2)].

[37] Ibid Part II, [B(11)].

[38] Ibid Part II, [B(14)] (particularly, the right to protection of honour and dignity; freedoms of thought and expression, assembly and association, and movement and residence; and the right to choose their authorities).

[39] Ibid Part II, [B(15)].

[40] Ibid.

[41] *Yakye Axa Indigenous Community v Paraguay (Merits, Reparations and Costs)* (2005) IACtHR (Ser C) No 125 (17 June 2005), [131]–[137]. See also *Moiwana Community v Suriname (Preliminary Objections, Merits, Reparations and Costs)* (2005) IACtHR (Ser C) No 145 (15 June 2005), [130]–[134]; *Sawhoyamaxa Indigenous Community v Paraguay (Merits, Reparations and Costs)* (2006) IACtHR (Ser C) No 146 (29 March 2006), [118]; *Saramaka v Suriname (Preliminary Objections, Merits, Reparations and Costs)* (2007) IACtHR (Ser C) No 172 (28 November 2007); *Kichwa Indigenous People of Sarayaku v Ecuador (Merits and Reparations)* (2012) IACtHR (Ser C) 245 (27 June 2012), [212]–[220].

subsistence, but also because they are part of their worldview, their religiosity, and therefore, of their cultural identity'.[42] It also invoked Article 13 of ILO Convention No 169, which requires states to respect 'the special importance for the cultures and spiritual values of the peoples concerned of their relationship with the lands or territories', individually and collectively.[43]

The Inter-American system has also highlighted the cultural dimensions of other rights recognised in the American Convention. In *Bámaca Velásquez v Guatemala* (2002),[44] a Maya indigenous leader and guerrilla commander disappeared after an encounter with the military and was secretly imprisoned, tortured and executed. Guatemala did not investigate or punish those responsible, who were state agents, or locate and return his remains to his family. The Court found a violation of the right to life (Article 4) (among other violations) in its merits judgment in 2000.[45] In its later reparations decision, the Court required Guatemala to locate his remains and return them, at no cost, to his next of kin, so that he could be buried in accordance with Maya customs and religious beliefs.[46] The Court observed that 'care for the mortal remains of a person is a form of observance of the right to human dignity' and that '[r]espect for those remains, observed in all cultures, acquires a very special significance in the Mayan culture'.[47] For the Maya:

> funeral ceremonies ensure the possibility of the generations of the living, the deceased person, and the deceased ancestors meeting anew. Thus, the cycle between life and death closes with these funeral ceremonies, allowing them to 'express their respect for Efraín, have him near and return him or take him to live with the ancestors', as well as for the new generations to share and learn about his life, something that is traditional in his indigenous culture.[48]

The cultural aspects of other rights were recognised in *Río Negro Massacres v Guatemala* (2012),[49] which concerned the massacre of Maya communities by the Guatemalan army and civil self-defence patrols in 1980 and 1982, and consequent violations against the survivors (such as a failure to investigate and punish perpetrators). Violations included forced disappearances, forced displacement, destruction of the community's social fabric, failure to identify executed persons, failure to bury the victims in keeping with traditions, and discrimination. The Court acknowledged that there is no express right to 'bury the dead' in the American Convention, but emphasised the importance of farewell rites in Maya culture[50] as coming within freedom of conscience and religion in Article 12. Maya funeral rites could not be

[42] *Yakye Axa v Paraguay* (n 41) [135].
[43] Ibid [136].
[44] *Bámaca Velásquez v Guatemala (Reparations and Costs)* (2002) IACtHR (Ser C) No 91 (22 February 2002).
[45] *Bámaca Velásquez v Guatemala (Merits)* (2000) IACtHR (Ser C) No 70 (25 November 2000) (also finding violations of art 7 (right to personal liberty); art 5(1) and (2) (right to humane treatment) as relates to both the victim and his next of kin; and arts 8 and 25 (right to fair trail and judicial protection)).
[46] *Bámaca Velásquez v Guatemala (Reparations and Costs)* (n 44) [79], [82].
[47] Ibid [81].
[48] Ibid.
[49] *Río Negro Massacres v Guatemala* (2012) IACtHR (Ser C) No 250 (4 September 2012).
[50] Ibid [155]–[156].

celebrated because Guatemala had not found or identified most of the remains of those massacred and disappeared.[51] In addition, other rites could not be performed because sacred locations had been flooded by a hydroelectricity plant, disrupting the Maya 'cosmovision, religious beliefs and, consequently, their cultural identity or integrity, which is a fundamental and collect right of the indigenous communities that must be respected in a multicultural, pluralist, and democratic society'.[52] The Court also found that displacement resulting from the massacres led to the destruction of their social structure, the disintegration of families, and the loss of cultural and traditional practices and the Maya Achí language.[53]

In the same case, the Court discussed the cultural aspects of freedom of movement and residence in Article 22 of the American Convention. The Court recognised that, because of their special cultural and material relationship with their traditional lands, indigenous people are rendered especially vulnerable by forced displacement.[54] The destructive effect of displacement 'generates a clear risk of the cultural or physical extinction of the indigenous peoples' and so requires the state to adopt measures of protection taking into account indigenous characteristics, customary law, values, practices and customs.[55]

Further in this case, in interpreting the rights of the child in Article 19, the Court held that states must protect the right of indigenous children to live according to their own culture, religion and language.[56] According to the Court, the 'full and harmonious development of their personality' required that indigenous children, 'in keeping with their cosmovision, need to grow and develop preferably within their own natural and cultural environment, because they possess a distinctive identity that connects them to their land, culture, religion, and language'.[57] On the facts, child survivors of a massacre had been forcibly taken to live with their aggressors, perform child labour, and were forbidden from contacting their relatives. The Court found that their cultural rights as indigenous children were violated because they were forced to live in foreign and hostile communities and to work for members of the civil self-defence patrols that had attacked them.[58]

An autonomous right to culture was pleaded in the Commission case of *Grand Chief Michael Mitchell v Canada* (2008).[59] The complainant was a Canadian citizen and resident and a member of the Mohawk First Nations community. Upon re-entering Canada from the United States, he refused to pay a customs duty that was charged on goods he intended to bring into Mohawk territory. He argued that the right to take part in the cultural life of the community in Article 13 of the American Declaration encompassed an Aboriginal right to trade with other indigenous First

[51] Ibid [160].
[52] Ibid.
[53] Ibid [162].
[54] Ibid [177].
[55] Ibid.
[56] Ibid [143].
[57] Ibid [144].
[58] Ibid [146], [150].
[59] IACHR, *Grand Chief Michael Mitchell v Canada*, Case No 12.435, Report No 61/2008 (25 July 2008).

Nations (on both sides of the Canada/United States border) without having to pay customs duties to either country. The goods included a washing machine, blankets, bibles, clothing, motor oil and food (bread, butter, milk, cookies and soup). The complainant argued that the goods were not culturally significant but cross-border trade was.[60]

The Commission noted that its jurisprudence on indigenous peoples had been grounded in rights other than culture (such as property, life, liberty, personal security, residence and movement, health and equality).[61] It then drew upon the UN Human Rights Committee's interpretation of minority cultural rights under Article 27 of the ICCPR, while noting that Article 13 of the American Declaration guarantees cultural rights for all, not only minorities.[62] In particular, it endorsed the HRC's view that economic activities may be protected as cultural activities if they are essential to the culture of the community.[63] Further, it accepted the limitation, but not the denial, of cultural rights.[64]

On this basis, the Commission acknowledged that cross-border trade in specific cultural goods (such as those manufactured by indigenous people), or culturally distinctive practices associated with cross-border trading that are peculiar and integral to indigenous culture, may be protected by Article 13 of the American Declaration.[65] Article 13 was further found to protect against disproportionate or discriminatory restrictions on cultural trade.[66] The complainant argued that tariffs both limited trade and made business unprofitable, and that their removal would not jeopardise protected industries in Canada given the small size of the Iroquois population (55,000 people, compared to 20 million people in Ontario and Quebec).[67]

The Commission found it unnecessary to determine whether the trade was protected cultural activity. Instead, it held that the complainant had not proven that the taxes, tariffs and restrictions disproportionately or discriminatorily affected trade.[68] The tariffs were applied on a non-discriminatory basis, did not prevent the complainant from trading within the Mohawk/Iroquois culture within Canada, and did not impede or prevent internal trading.[69] The Commission affirmed that non-discriminatory taxes, tariffs and restrictions on imports were reasonable limitations open to states in controlling their borders,[70] as long as they did not have discriminatory or disproportionate impacts. As such, Article 13 was not violated.[71]

[60] Ibid [79].
[61] Ibid [72].
[62] Ibid [73].
[63] Ibid [75]–[76] (citing HRC, *Mahuika and Others v New Zealand*, HRC Communication No 547/1993 (27 October 2000) and *Länsman and Others v Finland*, HRC Communication No 511/1992 (8 November 1994)).
[64] Ibid [77].
[65] Ibid [78].
[66] Ibid.
[67] Ibid [80].
[68] Ibid [79].
[69] Ibid [81].
[70] Ibid [82].
[71] Ibid [83].

SOCIO-ECONOMIC RIGHTS

Neither the American Convention nor the African Charter expressly protects most internationally recognised social, economic and cultural rights, and instead both focus on civil and political rights. The latter include freedom from slavery,[72] which has obvious socio-economic implications; the Inter-American Commission, for instance, extensively investigated the plight of 600 Guaraní indigenous families on agricultural estates in the Bolivian Chaco subjected to debt bondage, forced labour and contemporary slavery[73] and denied access to justice and their ancestral territory. The denial of political rights can also severely impact on the capacity of indigenous peoples to direct and control their own development and resources. In another case, the Commission identified discriminatory forced conscription of Maya-Quichés indigenous youth in Guatemala.[74]

One political rights case with socio-economic implications was *YATAMA v Nicaragua* (2005),[75] where Nicaragua had denied electoral registration to members of YATAMA ('the organisation of the people of Mother Earth'), an indigenous organisation that emerged in the 1970s to defend indigenous territories and natural resources, and promote development and self-government, on the Atlantic coast. The Inter-American Court found that this violated the complainants' rights to participate in government (Article 23) and equal protection (Article 24). Although the registration requirements applied to all groups, they disproportionately and discriminatorily affected indigenous communities by imposing a form of political organisation that was alien to indigenous practices, customs and traditions.[76] YATAMA had its own organisational structure, inherited from its ancestors, called 'community democracy', which was based on territorial, district, community and regional assemblies in indigenous territories.[77] Nicaraguan law itself required respect for indigenous forms of organisation.

The Court found that indigenous communities had a right to 'participate directly and proportionately to their population in the conduct of public affairs, and also do this from within their own institutions and according to their values, practices, customs and forms of organization, provided these are compatible with the human rights embodied in the Convention'.[78] The registration requirements impeded the exercise of the right of indigenous people to be elected and take part in public affairs, and such restriction was unnecessary and disproportionate.[79] The Court also found violations of the rights to a fair trial (Article 8) and judicial protection (Article 25).

[72] American Convention, art 6; African Charter, art 5.

[73] IACHR, *Captive Communities: Situation of the Guaraní Indigenous People and Contemporary Forms of Slavery in the Bolivian Chaco*, OEA/Ser.L/V/II. Doc 58 (24 December 2009).

[74] IACHR, *Alejandro Piché Cuca v Guatemala*, Case No 10.975, Report on the Merits No 36/93 (6 October 1993), [27] (violating the right to personal liberty (art 7), the protection of human dignity (Art 11) and the right to freedom of movement (art 22)).

[75] *YATAMA v Nicaragua* (2005) IACtHR (Ser C) No 127 (25 June 2005).

[76] Ibid [218].

[77] Ibid [124(13)].

[78] Ibid [225].

[79] Ibid [218]–[220].

Paradoxically, while both the Inter-American and African systems have more explicit mandates to protect civil and political rights, in practice both systems have often managed to creatively interpret aspects of socio-economic rights into their mandates when addressing indigenous issues. Only a few socio-economic rights are expressly recognised in regional instruments, such as the right to health (Article 16) and the right to a clean environment (Article 24) under the African Charter (additional collective rights to natural resources and development were discussed in the previous chapter). In the Inter-American system, while social and economic rights are embodied in the San Salvador Protocol 1988, only its right to education and trade union rights are justiciable before the Inter-American Court. Nonetheless, as the next section shows, both regional systems have, to a considerable extent, implicitly protected socio-economic rights when interpreting rights within their mandates. This is particularly the case in relation to the right to life (potentially encompassing implicit rights to food, water, health, education, culture and housing) and the right to property (including housing and protection against forced evictions).

Socio-economic Dimensions of the Right to Life

Cases in both the African and Inter-American systems have recognised the socio-economic dimensions of the right to life. In *SERAC v Nigeria* (2001), the African Commission held that Nigeria violated the right to life (under Article 4 of the African Charter) of the Ogoni people by terrorising and killing them on a widespread scale, and allowing oil companies to attack them.[80] In addition, the Commission recognised that the life of individuals and Ogoni society as a whole was affected by 'pollution and environmental degradation to a level humanly unacceptable [that] has made living in the Ogoni land a nightmare'.[81] It noted that the destruction of their land and farms prejudiced their survival, thereby violating the right to life.

Food and Water Rights

African System

In the same case, the African Commission also implied a right to food into the cumulative rights to life (Article 4), health (Article 16) and development (Article 22).[82] Nigeria had destroyed and threatened Ogoni food sources through oil development that polluted the soil and water on which Ogoni farming and fishing depended.[83] Raids on villages destroyed crops and farm animals, while the prevailing terror and insecurity made it impossible for villagers to return to their lands.

[80] *Social and Economic Rights Action Center and the Center for Economic and Social Rights v Nigeria*, ACHPR Communication No 155/1996, 2001 AHRLR 60 (27 October 2001), [67].
[81] Ibid [67].
[82] Ibid [64].
[83] Ibid [9].

Malnutrition and starvation resulted. The Commission found that the 'right to food is inseparably linked to the dignity of human beings and is therefore essential for the enjoyment and fulfilment of such other rights as health, education, work and political participation'.[84] Nigeria was obligated to protect and improve food sources and to ensure access to adequate food for all citizens.[85] At a minimum, Nigeria was required not to destroy or contaminate food sources, or allow private actors to do so, or to prevent people's efforts to feed themselves.[86] On the facts, Nigeria was found to have violated all three of these duties.[87]

Implied rights to food and water were raised in another African case, *COHRE v Sudan* (2009),[88] brought by indigenous Black African tribes in Darfur who were victims of violence by the Sudanese armed forces and pro-regime Janjaweed militias. Seeking to build on the decision in *SERAC v Nigeria* (2001) discussed above, the complainants argued that forced evictions violated not only their implied right to food but also a right to water that is equally implicit in the rights to life (Article 4), health (Article 16) and development (Article 22) under the African Charter.[89] In its decision, the Commission did not directly consider rights to food and water in discussing the rights to life and development. However, as discussed below, it found that the destruction of food, crops and livestock, and the poisoning of water wells, violated the right to health.

In its implementation guidelines on economic, social and cultural rights in the African Charter, the African Commission has also suggested that 'the right to water and sanitation' requires states to ensure that there is adequate access to water for subsistence farming and for securing the livelihoods of indigenous communities.[90]

Inter-American System

The right to food and other socio-economic rights have also been recognised as implicit in the right to life under Article 4 of the American Convention on Human Rights 1969. In *Yakye Axa Indigenous Community v Paraguay* (2005), the complainants argued that denial of access to traditional lands prevented them from accessing conditions that would enable them to live a decent life. As a result they lived in precarious material conditions with poor access to basic rights to health, food and education.[91] They argued that their right to life was consequently impaired because it depended on the realisation of these other basic rights.[92]

[84] Ibid [65].
[85] Ibid.
[86] Ibid.
[87] Ibid [66].
[88] *Sudan Human Rights Organisation and Centre on Housing Rights and Evictions (COHRE) v Sudan*, ACHPR Communications No 279/2003-296/2005, (2009) AHRLR 154 (May 2009).
[89] Ibid [124]–[125] (also invoking CESCR, *General Comment No 12: The Right to Adequate Food (Article 11)*, UN Doc E/C.12/1999/5 (12 May 1999)).
[90] ACHPR, *Principles and Guidelines on the Implementation of Economic, Social and Cultural Rights in the African Charter on Human and Peoples' Rights* (November 2010), 51–54.
[91] *Yakye Axa v Paraguay* (n 41) [158(e)].
[92] Ibid.

The Inter-American Court found that the right to life 'includes not only the right of every human being not to be arbitrarily deprived of his life, but also the right that conditions that impede or obstruct access to a decent existence should not be generated'.[93] Accordingly it held that states must generate 'minimum living conditions that are compatible with the dignity of the human person and of not creating conditions that hinder or impede it'.[94] States must therefore take positive, concrete measures to fulfil the right to decent life, giving priority to the vulnerable and taking into account the different indigenous way of life.[95] It interpreted such obligations as informed by states' duties concerning socio-economic rights under the San Salvador Protocol 1988 and ILO Convention No 169.[96]

On the facts, the Court recalled that the Yakye Axa lived in 'extremely destitute conditions as a consequence of lack of land and access to natural resources', pending the resolution of their land claim.[97] Deprivation of land had 'caused special and grave difficulties to obtain food', because their temporary settlement was not appropriate for cultivation or traditional subsistence activities such as hunting, fishing and gathering.[98] The settlements also lacked appropriate housing with minimum services like clean water and toilets.[99] These conditions adversely affected nutrition. Education and healthcare were also deficient.[100]

The Court found that the impairment of such rights had a major impact on the right to a decent existence and the basic conditions necessary to exercise other human rights, such as education and cultural identity.[101] Paraguay's denial of the right to communal property had also negatively affected the community's right to a decent life, by depriving it of access to traditional means of subsistence and natural resources, clean water and traditional medicines.[102] Although Paraguay had taken some measures to provide the community with services and assistance,[103] and had offered alternative lands,[104] these were insufficient and the current living conditions were incompatible with dignity.[105] Paraguay also failed to take special measures to protect children and the elderly (who were responsible for orally transmitting the group's culture to younger generations).[106] Paraguay accordingly violated their right to life.[107] There was not, however, sufficient evidence to find further that 16 individuals had died as a result of the lack of food and medical care.[108]

93 Ibid [161].
94 Ibid [162].
95 Ibid [162]–[163].
96 Ibid [163].
97 Ibid [164].
98 Ibid.
99 Ibid.
100 Ibid [165]–[166].
101 Ibid [167].
102 Ibid [168].
103 Ibid [169].
104 Ibid [170]–[171].
105 Ibid [168].
106 Ibid [172], [175].
107 Ibid [176].
108 Ibid [177]–[178].

In terms of remedies, the Court ordered Paraguay to identify and grant to the Yakye Axa suitable traditional lands within three years.[109] Once the land was provided, Paraguay was required to create a community development fund and programme to supply drinking water and sanitary infrastructure, and education, housing, agricultural and health programmes.[110] In the meantime, or for as long as the community remained landless, Paraguay had to provide the basic services and goods required for subsistence, including sufficient water for drinking and hygiene; regular medical care and medicine (including for children, the elderly and pregnant women); food in sufficient quantities, variety and quality to enable the minimum conditions for a decent life; latrines; and bilingual education material.[111]

In *Río Negro Massacres v Guatemala* (2012), the Court similarly ordered Guatemala to improve living conditions in a settlement of forcibly displaced indigenous Maya survivors of massacres,[112] after finding violations of the right to personal integrity (Article 5) in combination with violations of freedoms of conscience and religion (Article 12) and movement and residence (Article 22) (discussed below). In particular, it ordered Guatemala to design and implement food security and nutrition programmes; provide systems for drainage, sewage and potable water; improve the health centre by providing permanent staff for physical, psychological and dental care, as well as medicines and ambulances; and reconstruct or improve elementary schools and establish bilingual higher education.

Housing Rights

African System

A number of regional cases have implied housing rights into express rights, such as rights to life, health, property and family rights. In *SERAC v Nigeria* (2001), Nigeria had caused or allowed the razing of Ogoni villages, leaving thousands homeless and unable to sustain themselves.[113] The African Commission acknowledged that the right to housing or shelter is not explicitly provided under the African Charter.[114] It declared, however, that the wanton destruction of shelter is prohibited because it adversely affects African Charter rights to health (Article 16), property (Article 14), and the protection of the family (Article 18(1)).[115] The Commission held that, as a minimum, the obligation to respect the right to shelter requires states not to destroy housing and not to obstruct others from rebuilding lost homes.[116] The obligation to protect housing further requires states to prevent non-state actors (including landlords, property developers, and land owners) from infringing on housing rights and

[109] *Yakye Axa v Paraguay* (n 41) [211]–[217].
[110] Ibid [205].
[111] Ibid [221].
[112] *Río Negro Massacres v Guatemala* (n 49) [284].
[113] *SERAC v Nigeria* (n 80) [7]–[8].
[114] Ibid [60].
[115] Ibid.
[116] Ibid [61].

to provide remedies for infringements.[117] The Commission observed that the right to shelter 'goes further than a roof over one's head. It extends to embody the individual's right to be let alone and to live in peace, whether under a roof or not'.[118]

The Commission found that Nigeria failed to fulfil its obligations because it destroyed Ogoni houses and villages, and obstructed, harassed, beat, shot and killed innocent citizens who attempted to rebuild their homes.[119] Nigeria also violated the ancillary housing rights to protection against forced evictions and to security of tenure.[120] It described forced evictions as 'extremely traumatic' and causing 'physical, psychological and emotional distress', loss of economic sustenance, poverty, family disintegration, homelessness, injury and even death.[121]

Sudan Human Rights Organisation and Centre on Housing Rights and Evictions (COHRE) v Sudan (2009)[122] concerned an armed conflict between rebel groups in the Darfur region of western Sudan and Sudan's armed forces, as well as the Janjaweed Arab militia forces sponsored by Sudan. A US non-governmental organisation (NGO), COHRE, argued that Sudan and the Janjaweed attacked not only rebel forces but also the Black indigenous civilian tribal population, including by forcibly evicting the residents of hundreds of villages and destroying their homes, displacing a million people.[123] It was argued that the impacts on housing violated the rights to freedom from cruel, inhumane or degrading treatment (Article 5); liberty and security (Article 6); freedom of movement and residence (Article 12); property (Article 14); health (Article 16); and family rights (Article 18). The forced evictions and destruction of housing were also alleged to violate the right to housing that was implicit in Articles 14, 16 and 18,[124] and the rights to adequate food and water implicit in Articles 4, 16 and 22.[125] Sudan also allegedly violated Article 7 by failing to investigate and prosecute those responsible for forced evictions and destroying houses.[126] Sudan responded, without admitting responsibility, that a 2006 peace agreement addressed these concerns.[127]

As regards Article 5, influenced by precedents of the UN Committee Against Torture and the European Court of Human Rights,[128] the African Commission accepted that forced evictions and destruction of housing by non-state actors may amount to cruel, inhuman and degrading treatment or punishment if the state fails to protect the victims.[129] On the facts, the Commission found that Sudan and the Janjaweed

[117] Ibid [61].
[118] Ibid.
[119] Ibid [62].
[120] Ibid [63] (citing CESCR, *General Comment No 4: The Right to Adequate Housing (Article 11(1))*, UN Doc E/1992/23 (13 December 1991)).
[121] Ibid [63].
[122] *COHRE v Sudan* (n 88).
[123] Ibid [14].
[124] Ibid [115]–[116].
[125] Ibid [124].
[126] Ibid [120].
[127] Ibid [127]–[144].
[128] Ibid [159]–[162] (citing *Hijrizi v Yugoslavia*, CAT Communication No 161/2000 (2 December 2002) (eviction of Roma residents by non-Roma residents, in the presence of police); *Selçuk and Asker v Turkey (Judgment)*, ECtHR, Application Nos 23184/1994; 23185/1994 (24 April 1998) (burning of a Kurdish village by Turkish security forces).
[129] Ibid [159].

actively participated in the forced eviction of civilians as part of a counter-insurgency strategy, and that 'this kind of treatment was cruel and inhuman and threatened the very essence of human dignity'.[130] No derogation is permitted from the African Charter, and evictions were not justifiable limitations on rights (under Article 27) where the evicted civilians did not benefit from public security objectives, but suffered insecurity in internally displaced person (IDP) camps.[131] Sudan was found to have violated Article 5 by not diligently protecting civilians from violations by its forces or third parties, and by failing to provide remedies.[132]

The Commission found that the forced evictions and destruction of housing further violated the right to liberty and security of person in Article 6 of the Charter.[133] The right to liberty was infringed because most of the IDPs and refugees were unable to freely return to their homes, because of the continuing insecurity or the destruction of their houses,[134] and Sudan had failed to take appropriate measures of protection.[135] The Commission noted that IDPs could not even venture outside the IDP camps for fear of being killed or of women being raped by Janjaweed militia when fetching water or firewood.[136]

The right to liberty and security was seen by the Commission to complement the freedom of movement and residence in Article 12, which was also violated by Sudan.[137] The Commission held that the latter right includes the freedom to reside in any part of the state that a citizen wishes, without interference from the state,[138] and that the 'right to protection from displacement' derives from freedom of movement and residence.[139] The forced displacement of thousands of civilians, their confinement in IDP camps or as refugees, and the prevailing insecurity, deprived them of their freedom of movement and residence, contrary to Article 12.[140] These restrictions on rights were not justified as necessary or proportionate.[141]

Concerning the right to property under Article 14, the Commission found that states have a duty to establish conditions and provide the means to protect property even during armed conflict, including by resettling those unavoidably displaced in safety and with dignity.[142] Following European jurisprudence, the Commission found that the right to property extends to ancestral lands that are not formally registered or titled, and to the economic resources in such lands which peoples depend upon for their livelihood.[143] States must also protect against violations by non-state

130 Ibid [164].
131 Ibid [165]–[166].
132 Ibid [168].
133 Ibid [179].
134 Ibid [176]–[177].
135 Ibid [179].
136 Ibid [177].
137 Ibid [186]–[190].
138 Ibid [187].
139 Ibid [189] (also citing, at [188], the duty to prevent displacement under Principle 5 of the HRC, *UN Guiding Principles on Internal Displacement*, UN Doc E/CN.4/1998/53/Add.2 (11 February 1998)).
140 Ibid [190].
141 Ibid [188].
142 Ibid [201].
143 Ibid [195]–[200] (citing *Dogan v Turkey (Judgment)*, ECtHR Applications Nos 8803/2002–8811/2002, 8813/2002 and 8815/2002–8819/2002 (29 June 2004)).

forces.[144] Further, the Commission noted that the UN's *Pinhero Principles* (2005) were relevant in interpreting Article 14 and require states, during armed conflict, to prohibit punitive forced evictions, demolition of houses, destruction of agricultural areas, and arbitrary confiscation or expropriation of lands.[145] On the facts, the Commission found that Sudan had forcibly evicted and demolished the houses of the victims, and did not protect them from Janjaweed attacks.[146] Irrespective of whether they possessed legal titles to land, the victims were unlawfully deprived of their property under Article 14 because they could no longer derive their livelihood from the land and resources they had possessed for generations.[147]

As regards the right to health in Article 16, the Commission found, following the approach of the UN Committee on Economic, Social and Cultural Rights (CESCR), that the right to health extended beyond healthcare to include the underlying determinants or conditions of health, including water, food, nutrition, housing, and protection against pollution.[148] The right thus requires states not to interfere in health rights, and to prevent third parties from interfering in them,[149] but also to provide basic services such as medicine, safe drinking water and electricity.[150] On the facts the Commission found that the destruction of homes, livestock and farms, and the poisoning of water sources such as wells, exposed the victims to serious health risks, in violation of Article 16.[151]

Concerning the obligation to protect the family under Article 18 of the Charter, the Commission indicated that states must refrain from actions that arbitrarily or unlawfully interfere in the family unit, such as the separation of family members and forced displacement of families,[152] including through forced expulsions in peace or war.[153] On the facts, the Commission found that forced evictions by Sudan and the Janjaweed, and killing and separating family members, threatened the very foundation of the family and rendered the right to family life difficult.[154] Article 18 was violated because Sudan failed to protect the victims from its own forces or third parties.

Finally, the Commission found that the attacks and forced evictions suffered by the Darfurian people violated their collective right to economic, social and cultural development under Article 22 of the African Charter.[155] This was because these

[144] Ibid [202] (citing *Akdivar v Turkey (Judgment)*, ECtHR Application No 21893/1993 (16 September 1996)).

[145] Ibid [203]–[204] (citing HRC and UN Sub-Commission on the Promotion and Protection of Human Rights, *Principles on Housing and Property Restitution for Refugees and Displaced Persons: 'Pinheiro Principles'*, UN Doc E/CN.4/Sub.2/2005/17 (28 June 2005)).

[146] Ibid [205].

[147] Ibid.

[148] Ibid [208]–[209] (citing CESCR, *General Comment No 14: The Right to the Highest Attainable Standard of Health (Article 12)*, UN Doc E/C.12/2000/4 (11 August 2000)).

[149] Ibid [210].

[150] Ibid [211] (citing *Free Legal Assistance Group v Zaire (Merits)*, ACHPR Communications Nos 25/1989, 47/90, 56/1991, 100/1993 (4 April 1996)).

[151] Ibid [212].

[152] Ibid [213]–[214].

[153] Ibid [215] (citing *Union inter africaine des droits de l'Homme, Fédération internationale des ligues des droits de l'Homme and others v Angola*, ACHPR Communication No 159/96 (1997)).

[154] Ibid [216].

[155] Ibid [224]. Their status as a 'people' was discussed in chapter 1.

actions denied them the opportunity to engage in economic, social and cultural activities, including by interfering in children's education.[156] The Commission observed that the conflict in Darfur arose because of underdevelopment and marginalisation of Black Africans, and instead of addressing those causes Sudan collectively punished the civilian population through its military campaign.[157]

Inter-American System

While the Inter-American system has dealt extensively with indigenous land and property rights, it has focused less on housing rights. As noted earlier, in the *Yakye Axa* case, the Inter-American Court found that the lack of appropriate housing with minimum services (like clean water and toilets) contributed to the violation of the right to life under Article 4 of the American Convention.[158] In the *Sawhoyamaxa* case,[159] concerning rights violations resulting from displacement from traditional lands, the Court ordered Paraguay to provide adequate housing and services, especially medical care and sanitation 'necessary for survival'.[160]

In *Río Negro Massacres v Guatemala* (2012),[161] the forced displacement and state-sponsored resettlement of survivors of massacres of indigenous Mayan communities were found to violate their freedom of movement and residence under Article 22 of the American Convention. Article 22 was interpreted to include a right against forced displacement, including in armed conflict.[162] States must guarantee freedom of movement and residence, positively protect the displaced (including from private actors), and facilitate the return, resettlement and reintegration of the displaced.[163] The Court emphasised that displaced indigenous peoples are especially vulnerable because of their cultural and material dependence for survival on ancestral lands and the consequent risks of their cultural or physical extinction.[164]

On the facts, the Court found that the Maya were unable to return to their ancestral lands because of a well-founded fear of violations of their rights to life and personal integrity if they returned, and because the land was flooded by a hydroelectricity reservoir.[165] While Guatemala had taken steps to resettle the survivors, the Court found that it had not created the conditions or provided the means that were essential to repair or mitigate the effects of displacement.[166] The settlement did not enable the survivors to resume their traditional economic activities or earn a stable income, resulting in the disintegration of the community's social structure and

[156] Ibid [224].
[157] Ibid [223]–[224].
[158] *Yakye Axa v Paraguay* (n 41) [164].
[159] *Sawhoyamaxa v Paraguay* (n 41).
[160] Ibid [248(12)]. A similar order was made by the Court in *Yakye Axa v Paraguay* (n 41) [242(6)–(14)].
[161] *Río Negro Massacres v Guatemala* (n 49) [184].
[162] Ibid [172]–[173] (citing the *UN Guiding Principles on Internal Displacement*, UN Doc E/CN.4/1998/53/Add.2 (11 February 1998)).
[163] Ibid [174]–[176].
[164] Ibid [177].
[165] Ibid [180]–[181].
[166] Ibid [183].

its cultural and spiritual life.[167] Further, living conditions were precarious, with basic needs in health, education, electricity and water not being fully met. In addition to this violation of freedom of movement and residence under Article 22, the Court found that their forced displacement violated, in combination, their right to personal integrity (Article 5) and freedom of conscience and religion (Article 12), because it led to the destruction of their social structure, the disintegration of families, and loss of cultural and traditional practices and language.[168]

The Inter-American system has also often recommended or ordered the provision of housing by way of reparations. For example, in *Río Negro Massacres v Guatemala* (2012) the Court ordered Guatemala to improve the streets and avenues in the settlement and implement a drainage system, treat sewage and waste water, and supply potable water.[169] In the friendly settlement facilitated by the Commission in *Los Cimientos v Guatemala* (2003), the state agreed to provide 'minimal housing' and services during the resettlement of almost 700 indigenous families displaced by conflicts in the 1980s and 1990s.[170] Another settlement, *Mercedes Julia Huenteao Beroiza and others v Chile* (2004), remedied the expulsion of the Mapuche Pehuenche people from traditional lands by the construction of a hydroelectricity project. Chile agreed to subsidise the construction of homes for those relocated.[171]

Health Rights

In Africa, as noted earlier, in *COHRE v Sudan* (2009), the African Commission found that the destruction of homes, livestock and farms, and the poisoning of water sources such as wells, exposed the victims to serious health risks, in violation of Article 16.[172] The Commission made more elaborate findings on health in *SERAC v Nigeria* (2001), where the Ogoni argued that oil activities violated their individual 'right to enjoy the best attainable state of physical and mental health' (under Article 16 of the African Charter) and their right as a people to a 'general satisfactory environment favourable to their development' (under Article 24). They alleged that Nigeria had directly participated in polluting activities, failed to protect them from harm by private companies, facilitated harm by companies by providing them with security forces, and failed to provide or permit studies of environmental and health risks.[173]

The African Commission noted that the right to a clean and safe environment is closely linked to the fulfilment of social and economic rights.[174] It held that the right

[167] Ibid [183].
[168] Ibid [162].
[169] Ibid [284].
[170] Section 9 of the Agreement, as appended to IACHR, *Community of San Vicente Los Cimientos v Guatemala (Friendly Settlement)*, Petition No 11.197, Report No 68/2003 (10 October 2003), [36].
[171] IACHR, *Mercedes Julia Huenteao Beroiza and others v Chile (Friendly Settlement)*, Petition No 4617/02, Report No 30/2004 (11 March 2004), [34(7)].
[172] Ibid [212].
[173] *SERAC v Nigeria* (n 80) [50].
[174] Ibid [51].

to a healthy environment requires the state to take reasonable measures to prevent pollution or ecological degradation, promote conservation, and secure ecologically sustainable development and use of natural resources.[175] The state must also refrain from directly threatening the rights to health and a clean environment.[176] It must further order or permit independent scientific monitoring of environmental impacts, and provide affected communities with information and meaningful opportunities to be heard and participate in development decision-making.[177] The Commission acknowledged that Nigeria had a right to produce oil, including to fulfil its population's economic and social rights.[178] It found, however, that Nigeria had not fulfilled its obligations to protect health and environmental rights, and exacerbated the situation by its security forces attacking, burning and destroying villages.[179]

The Inter-American system has occasionally addressed health concerns in relation to indigenous people but without elaborating an extensive jurisprudence. As noted earlier, for instance, in *Yakye Axa v Paraguay* the Inter-American Court was concerned that the denial of traditional lands and resources (including traditional medicines), and poor alternative living conditions (including inadequate healthcare) impaired the health rights of displaced indigenous peoples and thus impaired the right to life under Article 4 of the American Convention.[180] There was not, however, sufficient evidence to find further that 16 particular individuals had died as a result of (inter alia) deficient medical care.[181]

Family Rights

As noted earlier, in *SERAC v Nigeria* (2001) the African Commission observed that the destruction of housing could violate the protection of the family under Article 18(1) of the African Charter.[182] Likewise, in *COHRE v Sudan* (2009) the African Commission found a violation of family rights due to the state's failure to protect families against displacement and separation arising from forced evictions and the destruction of housing.[183]

In a different context, the Inter-American system has addressed the cultural particularities of indigenous family life. In *Aloeboetoe v Suriname (Merits)* (1991),[184] Surinamese soldiers had beaten with rifle butts a group of over 20 unarmed maroons ('bush negroes'), who were falsely suspected of being members of the insurgent group Jungle Commando. Some were seriously wounded with bayonets and knives, and were stepped and urinated upon. Seven were taken away and killed. Before

175 Ibid [52].
176 Ibid.
177 Ibid [53].
178 Ibid [54].
179 Ibid.
180 *Yakye Axa v Paraguay* (n 41) [158(e)], [165]–[168].
181 Ibid [177]–[178].
182 Ibid [60].
183 *COHRE v Sudan* (n 88).
184 *Aloeboetoe v Suriname (Merits)* (1991) IACtHR (Ser C) No 11 (4 December 1991).

the Inter-American Court, Suriname accepted responsibility for violations of the obligation to respect rights (Article 1) and the rights to life (Article 4), humane treatment (Article 5), personal liberty (Article 7) and judicial protection (Article 25). The Court ordered Suriname to pay adequate reparations to the next of kin and to investigate and punish the perpetrators.

In its later reparations decision, *Aloeboetoe v Suriname (Reparations and Costs)* (1993),[185] a dispute arose about identifying the successors of the victims, with the Commission arguing that it should be decided by reference to Saramaka customs, while Suriname argued for the application of national civil law.[186] The Court observed that reparation and compensation is governed by international law; that international treaty and customary law could identify who are a person's successors; and that national family law may also be relevant.[187]

On the facts, the Court found that Surinamese family law did not effectively apply to the Saramaka, who were unaware of it, adhered to their own rules, and did not utilise the state's tribunals.[188] Suriname had also failed to provide the prerequisites for the enforcement of Surinamese law, namely facilities to register births, marriages and deaths. Surinamese law also recognised Saramaka customary law. Under Saramaka customs, tribal families are matriarchal and commonly polygamous, with the principal group of relatives (the '*bêè*') comprising all of a woman's descendants.[189] In theory, compensation owed to a person would thus be payable to the *bêè*, whose representative would distribute it amongst its members.

The Court found, however, that the Inter-American Commission had requested compensation and its distribution in pragmatic ways that did not follow Saramaka custom.[190] In the absence of directly applicable international or national law, the Court found that it had 'no alternative but to apply general principles of law'.[191] The Court found that in most legal systems it is generally accepted that a person's successors are his or her children; that spouses generally have a share in marital assets and sometime inheritance rights; and, absent a spouse or children, ascendants are heirs.[192] The Court then held that the categories of 'children', 'spouse' and 'ascendants' were to be interpreted according to local law, namely Saramaka custom (given the ineffectiveness of Surinamese national law).[193] Customary law was, however, only be taken into account to the extent that it did not contradict the American Convention, such that no distinction on the basis of sex could be made in identifying 'ascendants', 'even if that might be contrary to Saramaka custom'.[194] Recognising customary law was significant because it allowed multiple wives of a victim to receive compensation as successors, given that the Saramaka accepted polygamy.

[185] *Aloeboetoe v Suriname (Reparations and Costs)* (1993) IACtHR (Ser (10) Series C No 15 (10 September 1993).
[186] Ibid [55].
[187] Ibid [55], [61].
[188] Ibid [58].
[189] Ibid [59].
[190] Ibid [60].
[191] Ibid [61] (citing Statute of the International Court of Justice, art 38(1)(c)).
[192] Ibid [62].
[193] Ibid.
[194] Ibid.

VIOLENCE AND EXCESSIVE LAW ENFORCEMENT AGAINST INDIGENOUS PEOPLES

Many cases in the African and Inter-American systems have dealt with violence against indigenous peoples, for instance as violations of the rights to life, liberty, personal integrity, humane treatment and freedom from torture. In most cases, the human rights in question were interpreted and applied in their ordinary manner and not in ways specific to indigenous peoples. However, in quite a few cases, the victims were targeted either because of their status as indigenous peoples, or because indigenous attachments to traditional lands and resources stood in the way of aggressive development activities. Violence has also targeted those assisting or defending indigenous peoples. This section briefly discusses some of the typical kinds of violence experienced by indigenous peoples in cases before regional bodies.

Inter-American System

Inter-American Commission

The Inter-American system has examined violence against indigenous peoples since the early 1970s. This includes, for instance, Inter-American Commission cases concerning violent incursions from 1960 by security forces and settlers into the ancestral lands of the indigenous Guahibo people in Colombia;[195] and killings, inhumane treatment, enforced malnutrition, enslavement, disappearances, suppression of culture, denial of ancestral lands and alleged genocide against the Aché people of Paraguay.[196] In the case of the Miskitos of Nicaragua, mentioned earlier, the situation involved murders, aerial bombardment and destruction of villages, and threats of racial elimination. Eventually a friendly settlement was facilitated by the Commission, by which Nicaragua undertook to provide a process and mechanism for compensating the close relatives of those who died and those who were physically injured.

Since the 1980s to the present, the Commission has dealt with hundreds of cases of alleged killings, including massacres, of indigenous peoples by state agents during the repression of dissident movements,[197] especially in Peru, Guatemala and Colombia. Indigenous peoples were targeted on suspicion of being insurgents[198] or supporting guerrillas;[199] or were violently injured or displaced in counter-insurgency

[195] *Guahibo Indians v Colombia*, IACHR, Case No 1690, OEA/Ser.L/V/II.30, Doc 45 rev 1 (26 February 1973), 21.

[196] IACHR, *Resolution on Case No 1802 (Paraguay)* (27 May 1977).

[197] IACHR, *The Human Rights Situation of the Indigenous People in the Americas*, OEA/Ser.L/V/II.108, Doc 62 (20 October 2000), ch 3.

[198] *Aloeboetoe v Suriname (Merits)* (1991) IACtHR (Ser C) No 11 (4 December 1991) (seven deaths); *Remigio Domingo Morales and Rafael Sánchez and Others v Guatemala*, IACHR, Cases Nos 10.626, 10.627, 11.198(A), 10.799, 10.751 and 10.901, Report on the Merit No 59/01 (4 April 2001) (nine of 15 killed were indigenous).

[199] IACHR, *Report on the Situation of Human Rights in the Republic of Guatemala*, OEA/Ser.L/V/II.61, Doc 47 rev 1 (5 October 1983), 70.

operations.[200] Some were killed or executed by state-sponsored 'civil self-defence patrols',[201] sometimes on the pretext of combating subversion. Others were killed or threatened for refusing to join 'civilian self-defence patrols' in the context of forced resettlement and the eradication of 'suspicious' persons.[202] Other cases concerned the murder of indigenous people defending indigenous communities,[203] or other human rights defenders working with indigenous peoples;[204] the massacre of indigenous peoples by security forces and landowners in land disputes;[205] or violence and threats in such disputes.[206] Unlawful detention, torture and forced disappearance have also been confronted by the Commission,[207] including against indigenous human rights defenders.[208] The Commission has further dealt with the aftermath of violent conflict, as when addressing resettlement difficulties encountered, decades later, by thousands of indigenous 'Communities of Peoples in Resistance' who were terrorised and forcibly displaced in the Guatemalan conflict in the 1980s and had lived in 'subhuman' conditions in the jungles and mountains.[209]

[200] IACHR, *Community of San Vicente Los Cimientos v Guatemala (Friendly Settlement)*, Petition No 11.197, Report No 68/2003 (10 October 2003); *Severiano Santiz Gomez v Mexico*, IACHR, Case No 11.411, Report No 43/1997 (18 February 1998) (three killed by the Mexican Army in the indigenous community of Morelia).

[201] *Juan Chanay Pablo and Others v Guatemala (Colotenango Case)*, IACHR, Case No 11.212, Friendly Settlement Report No 19/97 (13 March 1997) (protesters killed in a Mayan community); *Remigio Domingo Morales and Rafael Sánchez and Others v Guatemala*, IACHR, Cases Nos 10.626, 10.627, 11.198(A), 10.799, 10.751 and 10.901, Report on the Merit No. 59/01 (4 April 2001) (killing of 15 persons, nine of whom were indigenous); *Martín Pelicó Coxic and Others v Guatemala*, IACHR, Case No 11.658, Report on the Merit No 80/07 (15 October 2007) (killing of a Mayan NGO worker opposed to conscription into civilian self-defence patrols, by members of such a patrol, within a pattern of extra-judicial executions of indigenous defenders).

[202] *María Mejía v Guatemala*, IACHR, Case No 10.553, Report No 32/96 (16 October 1996) (a husband and wife were killed, and 39 other family and community members threatened with death unless they moved within 10 days).

[203] *Martín Pelicó Coxic and Others v Guatemala*, IACHR, Case No 11.658, Report on the Merit No 80/07, 15 October 2007.

[204] IACHR, *The Human Rights Situation of the Indigenous People in the Americas*, Press Release No 5/1999, 'Murder in the Indigenous Community "Menominee" (Colombia)', Inter-Am. OEA/Ser.L/V/II.108, Doc 62 (8 March 1999) (three environmental activists killed in connection with their work for the U'wa indigenous community of Colombia, in violation of the right to personal integrity of civilians and prohibition of extra-judicial execution); IACHR, *Dianna Ortiz v Guatemala*, Case No 10.526, Report No 31/19S96 (16 October 1996) (where a Catholic nun with US citizenship was kidnapped, tortured and sexually abused by Guatemalan state agents and questioned about her relationship with 'subversives', namely indigenous people).

[205] *Caloto Massacre v Colombia*, IACHR, Case No 11.101, Report No 36/2000 (13 April 2000) (20 leaders and members of the Paez indigenous community were killed when lured to a meeting with an agricultural company, violating their rights to life, physical integrity and judicial protection).

[206] IWGIA, *The Indigenous World 2013* (Copenhagen, 2013), 511 (concerning precautionary measures issued by the Commission on 29 May 2012 to protect 76 displaced members of the Triqui community in Oaxaca, Mexico).

[207] *Gerónimo Gómez López v Mexico*, IACHR, Friendly Settlement Report No 68/12, Petition No 318-05 (17 July 2012) (unlawful detention, torture and forced disappearance of a Tsotsil indigenous man in Chiapas state).

[208] *Samuel de la Cruz Gómez v Guatemala*, IACHR, Case No 10.606, Report on the Merit No 11/98 (7 April 1998) (detention and disappearance of a Mayan human rights defender, who opposed conscription into civilian self-defence patrols, by state agents, in violation of rights to juridical personality, life, humane treatment, personal liberty and judicial guarantees and protection, under Arts 3, 4, 5, 7, 8 and 25 of the American Convention).

[209] IACHR, *Special Report on the Human Rights Situation in the so-called 'Communities of Peoples in Resistance' in Guatemala*, OEA/Ser/L/V/II.86, Doc 5 rev 1 (16 June 1994). See also the IACHR's earlier

Violence has also included arbitrary arrest, assault and death in police custody[210] or at the hands of unknown state agents;[211] and abduction, beatings and detention by the military.[212] Violence against indigenous women on account of their ethnicity and perceived political affiliation has also occurred. For example, in a Mexican case, three sisters from the Tzeltal ethnic group were detained, interrogated (in Spanish, not their own language) and raped by military personnel, who falsely accused them of being members of the *Zapatista* National Liberation Army.[213] Their targeting as alleged *Zapatistas*[214] was closely linked to their indigenous identity.

In many of the Commission's resolutions and recommendations in these cases, and in its requests for precautionary measures, the Commission variously identified violations of the rights to life (Article 4); humane treatment (Article 5); freedom from slavery and involuntary servitude (Article 6); liberty and security (Article 7); due process (Article 8); freedom of conscience and religion (Article 12); freedom of association (Article 16); freedom of movement and residence (Article 22); and judicial protection (Article 25). It has also occasionally found violations of the American Declaration, as well as the Inter-American Convention to Prevent and Punish Torture 1985.[215] It has typically called for the investigation and prosecution of perpetrators, and recommended reparations for victims and relatives.[216]

One of the most common ways that the Commission has confronted violence against indigenous peoples is by requesting states to issue 'precautionary measures' to prevent irreparable harm, pending the resolution of a case on the merits. These typically aim to avert threats to the life and physical integrity of individuals (especially indigenous leaders and human rights defenders,[217] women's

reports: OEA/Ser. L/V/II.53, Doc 21 rev 2 (October 1981) (First Report); OEA/ Ser. L/V./ II.512, Doc 47 (October 1983) (Second Report); OEA/Ser. L/V/ II.66 (September 1985) (Third Report); and OEA/Ser. L/V/ II.83, Doc 16 rev 1 (1 June 1992) (Fourth Report).

210 *Ovelário Tames v Brazil*, IACHR, Case No 11.516, Report on the Merit 60/99 (13 April 1999) (following the arbitrary detention of a Macuxi Indian for 'suspiciously' climbing on a truck).

211 *Rolando and Atanasio Hernández Hernández v Mexico*, IACHR, Case No 11.543, Report on the Merit No 1/98, (5 May 1998) (killing of two indigenous Otomi men who had been threatened by a local political boss).

212 *Ceferino Ul Musicue and Leonel Coicue v Colombia*, IACHR, Case No 9.853, Report on the Merit No 4/98 (7 April 1998) (members of the Paez indigenous community forced to act as guides by the Army).

213 *Ana, Beatriz and Celia González Pérez v Mexico*, IACHR, Case No 11.565, Report on the Merit 53/01 (4 April 2001).

214 Ibid [51].

215 See, eg, *Severiano Santiz Gomez v Mexico* (n 200) (where the Mexican Army assaulted and tortured in the Indian Community of Morelia).

216 IACHR, *The Human Rights Situation of the Indigenous People in the Americas*, OEA/Ser.L/V/ II.108, Doc 62 (20 October 2000), ch 3.

217 IACHR Precautionary Measures (PMs): *Hernán Henry Díaz, Colombia*, PM 131/12 (11 June 2012); *Qom Navogoh Indigenous Community of 'La Primavera', Argentina*, PM 404/10 (21 April 2011); *Jesús Tecú Osorio and his Family, Guatemala*, PM 290/09 (6 October 2009); *Leaders of the Indigenous Regional Council of Cauca (CRIC) and their Advisers, Colombia*, PM 301/08 (14 January 2009); *Tacana Indigenous Community of Miraflores, Riberalta, Bolivia* (11 March 2005); *Wiwa Indigenous People of the Sierra Nevada of Santa Marta, Colombia* (4 February 2005); *Obtilia Eugenio Manuel and Others, Mexico* (14 January 2005); *Holmes Enrique Fernández, Jorge Salazar and Other Members of the Cauca Association of Persons Displaced from the Naya (Asociación Caucana de Desplazados del Naya, ASOCAIDENA), Colombia* (14 October 2004); *Raúl Javier Gatica Bautista, Mexico* (27 September 2004); *Leonidas Iza, Ecuador* (27 February 2004); *Amílcar Mendez, Guatemala* (3 October 2003);

representatives,[218] the disappeared,[219] and witnesses to violence[220]), families[221] or communities (including those living in voluntary isolation[222]). Such cases are often linked to land disputes[223] (including encroachment and resource exploitation by outsiders,[224] and disputes between[225] or within[226] indigenous communities); forced

Zenilda Maria de Araujo and Marcos Luidson de Araujo (Cacique Marquinhos), Indigenous Leaders of the Xucuru People, Brazil (29 October 2002); *Members of the Rigoberta Menchú Foundation, Guatemala* (29 July 2002); *Members of the Embera Chamí People, Colombia* (15 March 2002); *Aldo González Rojas and Melina Hernández Sosa, Mexico* (29 November 2001); *Anselmo Roldan Aguilar, Guatemala* (31 July 2001); *Lombardo Lacayo Sambula and Horacio Martínez Calix, Honduras* (6 May 1999); *José Rentería Pérez and 14 Persons from La Humedad, Oaxaca, Mexico* (13 April 1999); *Pablo Tiguilá Mendoza, Pedro Tiguilá Hernández and Manuela Tiguilá Hernández, Guatemala* (27 January 1998); *Maximiliano Campo and 11 Other Leaders of the Paez Indigenous People, Colombia* (7 January 1998); *Brenda Mayol and Others, Guatemala* (30 July 1996); *Community of the Zenu Indigenous People, Colombia* (18 June 1996); *Rosalina Tuyuc, Manuela Alvarado, Amilcar Méndez and Nineth Montenegro, Guatemala* (19 March 1996); *Union of Communities of the Northern Zone of Isthmus AC (UCIZONI), México* (18 December 1995); *César Ovidio Sánchez Aguilar and Members of Indigenous Peoples' Organization in Santa Barbara, Huehuetenango, Guatemala* (30 November 1995).

218 IACHR PMs: *Aura Lolita Chávez Ixcaquic, Guatemala* (7 November 2005); *Women Leaders of the Wayúu Indigenous People, Colombia* (23 September 2004); *Members of 15 Cabildos and Resguardos of the Pijao Indigenous People, Colombia* (2 October 2003); *Rosalina Tuyuc, Guatemala* (11 August 2003); *National Association of Peasant and Indigenous Women of Colombia (ANMUCIC), Colombia* (2 March 2001).

219 IACHR PMs: *Hernán Henry Díaz, Colombia*, PM 131/12 (11 June 2012); *Members of the Sarayacu Indigenous Community* (5 May 2003); *Kimi Domicó and Other Members of the Embera Katio Indigenous Communities of Alto Sinú, Colombia* (4 June 2001).

220 IACHR PMs: *Marcos Bonifacio Castillo, Member of the Garifuna Community of Punta Piedras, Honduras* (20 August 2007); *Rosario Hernández Grave, Manuel Hernández Ajbac, Manuel Mendoza Jolomocox, Jesus Chaperón Marroquín, Gustavo Vásquez Peralta and Rogelio Cansi, Guatemala* (23 August 1996).

221 IACHR PMs: *Lorenzo Santos Torres and Family, Mexico*, PM 338/13 (8 November 2013); *Qom Navogoh Indigenous Community of 'La Primavera', Argentina*, PM 404/10 (21 April 2011).

222 IACHR PMs: *Indigenous Communities of the Xingu River Basin, Pará, Brazil*, PM 382/10 (1 April 2011); *Indigenous Peoples of Mashco Piro, Yora, and Amahuaca in Voluntary Isolation, Peru* (22 March 2007); *The Tagaeri and Taromenami Indigenous Peoples, Ecuador* (10 May 2006).

223 IACHR PMs: *Teribe and Bribri of Salitre Indigenous People, Costa Rica*, PM 321/12 (30 April 2015); *Lorenzo Santos Torres and Family, Mexico*, PM 338/13 (8 November 2013); *Members of the Lof Paichil Antriao Community of the Mapuche Indigenous People*, Argentina, PM 269/08 (6 April 2011); *Naso Indigenous People of the Bocas del Toro Region, Panama*, PM 118/09 (30 November 2009); *Garifuna Community of San Juan, Honduras* (7 July 2006); *Garifuna Community of Triunfo de la Cruz, Honduras* (28 April 2006); *Indigenous Peoples of Ingaricó, Macuxi, Wapichana, Patamona and Taurepang in Raposa Serra do Sol, Roraima State, Brazil* (6 December 2004); *Zenilda Maria de Araujo and Marcos Luidson de Araujo (Cacique Marquinhos), Indigenous Leaders of the Xucuru People, Brazil* (29 October 2002); *Yakye Axa Indigenous Community, Paraguay* (26 September 2001); *Lombardo Lacayo Sambula and Horacio Martínez Calix, Honduras* (6 May 1999); *Mary and Carrie Dann, USA* (28 June 1999); *Union of Communities of the Northern Zone of Isthmus AC (UCIZONI), México* (18 December 1995).

224 IACHR PMs: *Communities of the Kuna of Madungandí and Emberá of Bayano Peoples, Panama*, PM 105/11 (5 April 2011); *Indigenous Communities of the Xingu River Basin, Pará, Brazil*, PM 382/10 (1 April 2011); *Maho Indigenous Community, Suriname*, PM 395-09 (27 October 2010); *Community of Alto Guayabal–Coredocito of the Emberá People, Colombia*, PM 12-09 (25 February 2010); *Ngöbe Indigenous Communities and others, Panama*, PM 56/08 (18 June 2009); *Indigenous Peoples of Mashco Piro, Yora, and Amahuaca in Voluntary Isolation, Peru* (22 March 2007); *The Tagaeri and Taromenami Indigenous Peoples, Ecuador* (10 May 2006).

225 IACHR PMs: *Inhabitants of the Mixteca Indigenous Community of Lázaro Cárdenas, Putla, Oaxaca, Mexico*, PM 102-10 (4 August 2010); *The Union of Guarayo Native Peoples (COPNAG), Bolivia* (27 November 2006).

226 IACHR PM, *The Union of Guarayo Native Peoples (COPNAG), Bolivia* (27 November 2006).

evictions or displacement[227] (including by armed actors[228]); armed conflict;[229] non-consensual development activities,[230] including those causing environmental degradation;[231] inadequate access to basic needs;[232] the spread of diseases and epidemics;[233] denial of access or harm to cultural sites;[234] corruption;[235] and excessive responses to demonstrations.[236]

In requesting precautionary measures, the Commission usually urges the state in general terms to take the necessary measures to prevent harm, but it also often makes more specific requests. For instance, it has asked states to investigate and punish the perpetrators of violence; provide police protection for communities or the premises of human rights defenders;[237] suspend evictions or displacement;[238]

[227] IACHR PMs: *14 Q'echi Indigenous Communities of the Municipality of Panzós, Guatemala*, PM 121-11 (20 June 2011); *Members of the Lof Paichil Antriao Community of the Mapuche Indigenous People, Argentina*, PM 269/08 (6 April 2011); *Rapa Nui Indigenous People, Chile*, PM 321/10 (7 April 2011); *Naso Indigenous People of the Bocas del Toro Region, Panama*, PM 118/09 (30 November 2009); *Mercedes Julia Huenteao and Others, Chile* (1 August 2003); *Yakye Axa Indigenous Community, Paraguay* (26 September 2001).

[228] IACHR PMs: *Members of the Triqui Indigenous Community in the San Pedro River Valley, San Juan Cópala, Putla de Guerrero, Oaxaca, Mexico*, PM 60/12 (29 May 2012); *21 Families of the Nonam Community of the Wounaan Indigenous People, Colombia*, PM 355/10 (3 June 2011); *135 Inhabitants of San Juan Copala, Mexico*, PM 197-10 (7 October 2010); *Tacana Indigenous Community of Miraflores, Riberalta, Bolivia* (11 March 2005); *Wiwa Indigenous People of the Sierra Nevada of Santa Marta, Colombia* (4 February 2005); *Indigenous Peoples of Ingaricó, Macuxi, Wapichana, Patamona and Taurepang in Raposa Serra do Sol, Roraima State, Brazil* (6 December 2004); *Holmes Enrique Fernández, Jorge Salazar and Other Members of the Cauca Association of Persons Displaced from the Naya (Asociación Caucana de Desplazados del Naya, ASOCAIDENA), Colombia* (14 October 2004); *Indigenous Community Kelyenmagategma of the Enxet People, Paraguay* (12 October 2004); *Kankuamo Indigenous People, Colombia* (24 September 2003); *Survivors of the Massacre in Acteal in 1997, Mexico* (24 December 1997).

[229] IACHR PMs: *Nasa People of Toribio, San Francisco, Tacueyo, and Jambalo Reservations, Colombia*, PM 255/11 (14 November 2011); *Members of the Awá Indigenous People of the Departments of Nariño and Putumayo, Colombia*, PM 61/11 (16 March 2011); *Members of 15 Cabildos and Resguardos of the Pijao Indigenous People, Colombia* (2 October 2003); *Kankuamo Indigenous People, Colombia* (24 September 2003); *Members of the Embera Chamí People, Colombia* (15 March 2002).

[230] IACHR PMs: *Maya Indigenous Communities, Belize* (20 October 2000); *Awas Tingni Indigenous Community, Nicaragua* (30 October 1997).

[231] IACHR PMs: *Communities of the Maya People (Sipakepense and Mam) of the Sipacapa and San Miguel Ixtahuacán Municipalities in the Department of San Marcos, Guatemala*, PM 260-07 (20 May 2010); *Community of San Mateo de Huanchor, Peru* (17 August 2004); *De Vereninig van Saramakaanse (12 Saramaka Clans), Suriname* (8 August 2012).

[232] IACHR PMs: *21 Families of the Nonam Community of the Wounaan Indigenous People, Colombia*, PM 355/10 (3 June 2011); *Members of the Lof Paichil Antriao Community of the Mapuche Indigenous People, Argentina*, PM 269/08 (6 April 2011); *Yakye Axa Indigenous Community, Paraguay* (26 September 2001).

[233] IACHR PM, *Indigenous Communities of the Xingu River Basin, Pará, Brazil*, PM 382/10 (1 April 2011).

[234] IACHR PMs: *Members of the Lof Paichil Antriao Community of the Mapuche Indigenous People, Argentina*, PM 269/08 (6 April 2011); *Maya Sitio El Rosario-Naranjo Comunity, Guatemala* (14 July 2006).

[235] IACHR PM, *Aura Lolita Chávez Ixcaquic, Guatemala* (7 November 2005).

[236] IACHR PMs: *Rapa Nui Indigenous People, Chile*, PM 321/10 (7 April 2011); *Naso Indigenous People of the Bocas del Toro Region, Panama*, PM 118/09 (30 November 2009); *Patricia Ballestero Vidal, Lee Pope and Arnold Fuentes, Chile* (3 March 1999).

[237] IACHR PM, *Tacana Indigenous Community of Miraflores, Riberalta, Bolivia* (11 March 2005).

[238] IACHR PM, *Yakye Axa Indigenous Community, Paraguay* (26 September 2002).

suspend development projects;[239] conduct prior, free, informed consultations with indigenous communities on development proposals;[240] recognise indigenous land title and protect land from intrusion;[241] protect indigenous cultural identity and their special relationship to land, and appoint a community defender;[242] provide humanitarian assistance and basic needs (such as healthcare and food) to communities displaced[243] or affected by development activities;[244] enable communities to return to their land;[245] prevent and remedy pollution from development activities;[246] and remove landmines from ancestral lands, and provide landmine risk education.[247]

As noted earlier, while indigenous identity was often a direct or indirect reason why an individual was targeted for violence, in most instances the Commission has applied American Convention rights to indigenous peoples in a manner similar to how it would apply them in non-indigenous cases. Occasionally, however, it has adopted interpretations specific to indigenous peoples, as where it emphasised that states have a duty to afford special protection to indigenous peoples when protecting the right to life.[248] The Commission has also highlighted that the harm suffered by some victims was aggravated by their indigenous identity, for example because of their lack of knowledge of the language of their aggressors and the other authorities, or because they were repudiated by their own community's customs as a result of shame and humiliation, forcing them to abandon their homes.[249] The Commission has thus reminded states of their obligation to respect indigenous cultures.[250]

The Commission has sometimes been able to deal with the socio-economic causes of serious violence against indigenous peoples. For example, in 2012 the Commission approved a friendly settlement reached in 1999 between Venezuela and Yanomami indigenous people on the border with Brazil.[251] The settlement stemmed

239 IACHR PM, *Ngöbe Indigenous Communities and Others, Panama*, PM 56/08 (18 June 2009).

240 IACHR PM, *Indigenous Communities of the Xingu River Basin, Pará, Brazil*, PM 382/10 (1 April 2011).

241 Ibid.

242 IACHR PM, *Wiwa Indigenous People of the Sierra Nevada of Santa Marta, Colombia* (4 February 2005).

243 IACHR PMs: *21 Families of the Nonam Community of the Wounaan Indigenous People, Colombia*, PM 355/10 (3 June 2011); *Members of the Lof Paichil Antriao Community of the Mapuche Indigenous People, Argentina*, PM 269/08 (6 April 2011); *Yakye Axa Indigenous Community, Paraguay* (26 September 2002).

244 IACHR PMs: *Communities of the Maya People (Sipakepense and Mam) of the Sipacapa and San Miguel Ixtahuacán Municipalities in the Department of San Marcos, Guatemala*, PM 260-07 (20 May 2010).

245 IACHR PM, *21 Families of the Nonam Community of the Wounaan Indigenous People, Colombia*, PM 355/10 (3 June 2011).

246 IACHR PMs: *Community of San Mateo de Huanchor, Peru* (17 August 2004); *Communities of the Maya People (Sipakepense and Mam) of the Sipacapa and San Miguel Ixtahuacán Municipalities in the Department of San Marcos, Guatemala*, PM 260-07 (20 May 2010).

247 IACHR PM, *Members of the Awá Indigenous People of the Departments of Nariño and Putumayo, Colombia*, PM 61/11 (16 March 2011).

248 Ibid [44].

249 IACHR, *Ana, Beatriz and Celia González Pérez v Mexico*, Case No 11.565, Report on the Merit 53/01 (4 April 2001), [95].

250 Ibid.

251 IACHR, *Yanomani Indigenous People of Xaximu v Venezuela (Friendly Settlement)*, Petition No 11.706, IACHR Report No 32/12 (20 March 2012).

from a petition lodged with the Commission in 1996 concerning the murder of 16 Yanomami (including women and children) in 1993 by private Brazilian mining prospectors (*garimpeiros*). Venezuela had failed to prevent the intrusion of up to 2,000 *garimpeiros* onto Yanomami territory, which had led to conflict, violence (including plots to exterminate the Yanomami), and environmental harm. Venezuela also failed to investigate, prosecute and punish the alleged killers. The petitioners alleged violations by Venezuela of the right to life, humane treatment, a fair trial, property, equal protection and judicial protection.

As part of the settlement, Venezuela undertook to monitor and control the entry of *garimpeiros* and illegal mining in the Yanomami area; improve indigenous health services; improve legislative protection of indigenous people (which ultimately included ratification of ILO Convention No 169 and its constitutional incorporation); and appoint an expert in indigenous issues to monitor the settlement. As regards justice for the victims, Venezuela agreed to monitor prosecutions of the perpetrators that were then continuing in Brazil. In 1996 five *garimpeiros* had been convicted for 20 years and six months in prison for the crimes of genocide, running contraband and illegal prospecting (*garimpo*); the decision was upheld on appeal in 2006.

Other Commission cases (not involving violence) have also involved a denial of justice. In one friendly settlement involving Mexico, a Maya accused was not assisted by an interpreter and thus could not properly defend himself or make himself understood in his own language.[252] His grasp of the language of the proceedings, Spanish, was limited to everyday activities and he could not understand technical and scientific terms. As part of the settlement, Mexico agreed to strengthen access to justice and human rights for indigenous communities.[253]

Inter-American Court

Massacres and Other Threats In addition to Commission cases, the Inter-American Court has considered many cases of violence against indigenous peoples. At the most aggravated level are situations involving massacres. For example, in *Plan de Sanchéz Massacre v Guatemala* (2004),[254] 268 people, mostly Maya, were massacred by the Guatemalan Army and civilian collaborators in 1982. The massacre was part of a campaign of terror, scorched earth operations and forced displacement directed against indigenous communities, who were considered supporters of guerrilla forces.[255] Attacks targeted indigenous houses, livestock, harvests, and other means of survival, social, economic, and political institutions and cultural and religious practices. The massacre was alleged to be part of a genocidal state policy intended to destroy the Maya people. For years after the massacre, a climate of fear, threats and persecution prevented the survivors and next of kin from seeking justice. Some survivors were unable to return to their homes to resume their livelihoods. A judicial

[252] *Ricardo Ucan Seca v Mexico (Friendly Settlement)*, Petition No 12.660, IACHR Report No 91/10 (15 July 2010).

[253] Ibid [25(e)].

[254] *Plan de Sanchéz Massacre v Guatemala (Merits)* (2004) IACtHR (Ser C) No 145 (29 April 2004).

[255] Ibid [42].

complaint was lodged in 1992, after peace agreements, but Guatemala allegedly did not seriously investigate or punish the perpetrators.

In the proceedings before the Inter-American Court, Guatemala accepted the alleged facts and acknowledged its international legal responsibility.[256] As such, the Court deemed that Guatemala had violated the rights to humane treatment (Article 5); fair trial (Article 8); privacy (Article 11); freedom of conscience and expression (Article 12); freedom of association (Article 16); property (Article 21); equal protection (Article 24); judicial protection (Article 25); and the obligation to respect American Convention rights (Article 1).[257] The Court found that it had no jurisdiction to decide if genocide had occurred (because its competence was limited to the American Convention and regional instruments).[258] It declared, however, that when later deciding upon reparations it would take into account that 'facts such as those stated, which gravely affected the members of the Maya Achí people in their identity and values and that took place within a pattern of massacres, constitute an aggravated impact'.[259]

Río Negro Massacres v Guatemala (2012)[260] similarly concerned a series of massacres of over 450 Maya, including babies and children, by the Guatemalan Army and civil self-defence patrols between 1980 and 1982. Some of the Maya had earlier been forcibly displaced by the flooding of their ancestral lands by a hydroelectricity dam. The violence included rape; torture; the abduction, forced labour and denial of identity of indigenous children; forced displacement; destruction of property and denial of ancestral lands and resources; and the loss of the Maya's social, cultural, religious, economic and political values and institutions. The violence was part of a security strategy by Guatemala to target Maya communities (including through a 'scorched earth' policy) as subversives or 'internal enemies' supporting guerrilla forces, and was part of a pattern of discrimination and racism. Violations against the survivors and relatives were also alleged, such as a failure to identify executed persons, bury them according to Maya customs, and investigate and punish the perpetrators.

As regards the massacres, the Inter-American Court found violations of the rights to life (Article 4); personal integrity (Article 5); humane treatment (Article 5); personal liberty (Article 7); child rights (Article 19); and, in the case of the disappeared, juridical personality (Article 3). Rape was viewed as a violation of rights to personal integrity (Article 5) and privacy (Article 11). Forced labour was seen to violate freedom from slavery (Article 6), family rights (Article 17) and child rights (Article 19). The Court was, however, unable to find that the violence was motivated by discrimination, while the claim of genocide was outside its jurisdiction.[261]

Development activities which threaten the right to life of indigenous communities have also been considered by the Court. In *Kichwa Indigenous People of Sarayaku v*

[256] Ibid [46].
[257] Ibid [47].
[258] Ibid [51].
[259] Ibid.
[260] *Río Negro Massacres v Guatemala* (n 49).
[261] Ibid [233]–[234].

Ecuador (2012),[262] the Court held that Ecuador put at grave risk the rights to life and physical integrity of the Sarayaku by allowing an oil company to place 1,400 kilograms of explosives on their territory, and failing to deactivate them.[263] This also denied the Sarayaku safe access to their sacred areas and hunting grounds, infringing their right to communal property.[264]

Violence Against Indigenous Leaders Other cases in the Inter-American Court have dealt with violence against indigenous leaders, and the Court has often found violations of, for example, the rights to life (Article 4); humane treatment (Article 5); liberty (Article 7); fair trial (Article 8); freedom from retrospective punishment (Article 9); family rights (Article 17); non-discrimination and equal protection (Article 24); and judicial protection (Article 25). In *Bámaca Velásquez v Guatemala* (2000),[265] an indigenous leader and guerrilla commander disappeared in an encounter with the Guatemalan Army, was secretly imprisoned for four months, and was tortured and executed. Guatemala failed to investigate or punish those responsible. In *Escué Zapata v Colombia* (2007),[266] a governor of indigenous protection was beaten and shot by the Colombian Army, allegedly as part of a pattern of violence against indigenous people (through which 500 leaders had been murdered in the past 25 years). In *Tiu Tojín v Guatemala* (2008),[267] a mother and her daughter disappeared at the hands of the Guatemalan Army and civil self-defence patrols, on suspicion of her being a guerrilla. In some cases, the Court was unable to find that the individuals were targeted because they were indigenous leaders.[268] In one case, however, it found that the victims' relatives faced discriminatory obstacles in accessing justice and a fair trial because they were indigenous.[269]

A stark example of the deliberate targeting of indigenous leaders is the case of *Chitay Nech v Guatemala* (2010),[270] which concerned the forced disappearance of a Maya indigenous political leader during the internal conflict in Guatemala in the early 1980s, and the state's failure to diligently investigate and provide justice to his next of kin. The Court observed that indigenous communities and their leaders were specifically targeted by the state as the purported 'internal enemy' and supporters of the guerrillas, with Maya accounting for over 83 per cent of those forcibly

[262] *Kichwa Indigenous People of Sarayaku v Ecuador (Merits and Reparations)* (2012) IACtHR (Ser C) No 245 (27 June 2012).

[263] Ibid [248]–[249].

[264] Ibid [246].

[265] *Bámaca Velásquez v Guatemala (Merits)* (2000) IACtHR (Ser C) No 70 (25 November 2000); *(Reparations and Costs)* (2002) IACtHR (Ser C) No 91 (22 February 2002).

[266] *Escué Zapata v Colombia (Merits, Reparations and Costs)* (2007) IACtHR (Ser C) No 165 (5 May 2008).

[267] *Tiu Tojín v Guatemala (Merits, Reparations and Costs)* (2008) IACtHR (Ser C) No 190 (26 November 2008).

[268] *Escué Zapata v Colombia* (n 266); *López Álvarez v Honduras (Merits, Reparations and Costs)* (2006) IACtHR (Ser C) No 141 (1 February 2006).

[269] *Tiu Tojín v Guatemala* (n 267) [97], [100].

[270] *Chitay Nech and others v Guatemala (Preliminary Objections, Merits, Reparations, and Costs)* (2010) IACtHR (Ser C) No 212 (25 May 2010).

disappeared between 1980 and 1983.[271] Forced disappearances aimed to punish not only the victim but their family and community. The Court found that forced disappearance deprived the victim of his right to political participation as a representative of the indigenous community that elected him to serve their vision and tradition, pursue their self-determination, and participate in development decision-making.[272] It also deprived the community of its right to be represented.

Further, his forced disappearance, ongoing threats, and continuing impunity resulted in his family fleeing the area in fear, in violation of the freedom from forced displacement that is an implied aspect of freedom of movement and residence.[273] The Court found that this had a particularly grave effect on his Maya family because it 'provoked a rupture with his cultural identity, which signified the total eradication of any reference to the life that he had before the persecution, including his culture, language and his ancestral past'.[274] It accordingly made the family vulnerable to cultural extinction and physical rootlessness.[275] In addition, the forced disappearance and displacement disrupted their nuclear and extended family life in a particularly grave manner because of their Maya indigenous identity.[276] It also deprived the indigenous children in the family of their right to live in accordance with their own culture, religion and language, and in connection with their lands.[277]

Denial of Justice for Indigenous Peoples The Inter-American Court has also confronted cases where states have apparently targeted indigenous leaders through excessive or irregular criminal justice measures. In *Norín Catrimán and others v Chile* (2014),[278] seven Mapuche indigenous leaders, and a non-indigenous activist, were convicted of excessive terrorism offences for social protests over ancestral land claims, despite their damage to property not harming anyone's physical integrity or life. The Court found that Chile had violated their freedom of expression (Article 12) because the criminal penalties included restrictions on communicating with the media, which prevented them from representing the political, social and spiritual interests of their communities.[279] The Court further held that the application of terrorism offences to the Mapuche 'could have instilled a reasonable fear in other members of this people involved in actions related to the social protest and the claim for their territorial rights, or who would eventually want to participate in this'.[280]

271 Ibid [66]–[67], [108].
272 Ibid [113]–[117] (American Convention, art 23(1)(a)).
273 Ibid [139].
274 Ibid [146]; see also [145].
275 Ibid [147].
276 Ibid [159]–[163].
277 Ibid [167]–[170].
278 *Norín Catrimán v Chile (Merits, Reparations and Costs)* (2014) IACtHR (Ser C) No 279 (29 May 2014).
279 Ibid [375]–[376].
280 Ibid [376]. See also *Report of the Special Rapporteur on Human Rights and Terrorism, Ben Emmerson, Mission to Chile*, UN Doc A/HRC/25/59/Add.2 (14 April 2014), [47]–[79]. For the impact of counter-terrorism on indigenous rights in another context, see Javaid Rehman, 'Between the Devil and the Deep Blue Sea: Indigenous Peoples as the Pawns in the US "War on Terror" and the Jihad of Osama Bin Laden' in Stephen Allen and Alexandra Xanthaki (eds), *Reflections on the UN Declaration on the Rights of Indigenous Peoples* (Hart, Oxford, 2011), 561.

The penalties also violated their political rights under Article 23 by preventing them from acting to protect their communities, which affected both individual and community rights.[281] In the case of one prisoner confined 250 kilometres from his community and family, the Court found that the distance involved a violation of family rights, especially given the significance of indigenous ties to their place of origin and community.[282]

Other cases involve violence against, and consequent denial of justice to, indigenous peoples on account of their indigenous identity. Both the cases of *Ortega v Mexico* (2010)[283] and *Cantú v Mexico* (2010)[284] concerned the rape of an indigenous woman by military personnel deployed to combat organised crime, in the context of a pattern of 'institutional military violence' against indigenous women.[285] The cases also involved a lack of due diligence by the authorities in investigating and punishing the perpetrators, and difficulties faced by indigenous women in accessing justice (including language barriers, physical inaccessibility, social stigma, distrust and fear of reprisals). The women came from areas where indigenous people were marginalised, impoverished and extremely vulnerable.

The case of *Ortega* is illustrative. The Court took into account the indigenous characteristics of the victim in a number of different ways. First, it recognised language (she spoke Me'paa) and interpretation (into Spanish) difficulties as relevant to dismiss challenges to the consistency of her allegations.[286] Secondly, her complaint was seen as more credible precisely because it was persistently made despite the obstacles facing her as an indigenous woman, including language, social and cultural stigma, geographical remoteness and the ongoing presence of the military.[287] Thirdly, in interpreting the 'severe pain or suffering' element of the definition of torture, the Court accepted that 'according to her indigenous worldview ... [her] suffering was experienced as a "loss of the spirit"'.[288]

Fourthly, concerning the state's lack of due diligence in investigating, the Court found that the failure to provide her with an interpreter 'was inappropriate to respect her cultural diversity'.[289] Further, her inability to be able to file a claim in her language was found to be discriminatory unequal treatment in the light of her language and ethnicity.[290] The Court affirmed that 'in order to guarantee access to justice to

281 Ibid [384]–[385].

282 Ibid [403], [408].

283 *Fernández Ortega and Others v Mexico (Preliminary Objections, Merits, Reparations and Costs)* (2010) IACtHR (Ser C) No 215 (30 August 2010).

284 *Rosendo Cantú and Others v Mexico (Preliminary Objection, Merits, Reparations, and Costs)* (2010) IACtHR (Ser C) No 216 (31 August 2010).

285 *Ortega v Mexico* (n 283) [79]; *Cantú v Mexico* (284) [70]–[71]. However, in Ortega the Court was unable to find, for lack of evidence, that the victim was targeted because of her participation in an indigenous women's organisation and hence that her freedom of association was violated: [219].

286 *Ortega v Mexico* (n 283) [105]: 'the differences in the story, rather than relating to a problem of consistency, may be due to the alleged victim's difficulties in expressing herself or to the intervention of third parties, or result from the use of different languages or interpretations in the translations'.

287 Ibid [107].

288 Ibid [126].

289 Ibid [195].

290 Ibid [201].

members of indigenous communities, it is indispensable that States offer effective protection that considers the particularities, social and economic characteristics, as well as the situation of special vulnerability, customary law, values, customs, and traditions'.[291]

Fifthly, the Court considered the vulnerability of indigenous women in ordering reparations;[292] and the need for measures encompassing the wider indigenous community, so that the victim can 'reincorporate herself into her living space and cultural identity, as well as re-establishing the fabric of the community'.[293] Accordingly, the Court required that an interpreter must be provided in proceedings;[294] that the state train officials on the investigation of sexual abuse in a manner that considers gender and ethnicity;[295] and that the state improve the accessibility of services in indigenous areas dealing with violence against women.[296]

Additionally, the Court found that public acknowledgement of wrongdoing was particularly important in indigenous communities as the first step in 'healing' the effects of the wrong in the community.[297] More broadly, the Court required Mexico to furnish the resources for her community to establish a women's centre, run by the community's women, to provide education on human rights and women's rights in a manner 'adapted to the indigenous community's view of the world'.[298] Further, Mexico was required to support the housing and food needs of the community's indigenous girls studying in a city away from home, so that they can continue their studies, or otherwise establish a high school in the community.[299]

Many of the issues and findings were similar in *Cantú v Mexico* (2010). In addition, in that case the victim's family's right to personal integrity was violated because she and her young daughter were forced into exile after the rape and thus separated from their community, culture and family members.[300] The child was also unable to be educated in her mother tongue. As regards reparations, for procedural reasons the Court was unable to consider arguments that Mexico should be required to obtain the prior, free and informed consent of indigenous peoples before the entry of security forces onto their territory.[301] For the same reason the Court did not consider an argument that the state should establish adequate conditions for the victims to return to their native community (including property restitution, psycho-emotional support and measures to address risks and threats).[302]

291 Ibid [200].
292 Ibid [223].
293 Ibid [267].
294 Ibid [230].
295 Ibid [260].
296 Ibid [278]. The Court was, however, unable to rule on the Commission's request that Mexico design a culturally respectful policy on access to justice for indigenous women, because the Commission had not pointed to defects in the existing programmes: [271]–[274].
297 Ibid [243]–[244].
298 Ibid [267].
299 Ibid [270].
300 *Cantú v Mexico* (n 284) [138].
301 Ibid [268].
302 Ibid [269].

African System

The African system has also dealt with violence against indigenous people. *Malawi African Association and others v Mauritania* (2000)[303] involved violations against the Black population and protest groups of southern Mauritania by an Arab military government that had marginalised them. Repression included mass political arrests and arbitrary detention, unfair trials resulting in the death penalty and inhumane detention conditions, the mass expulsion of villagers, torture, extra-judicial executions and massacres. It was alleged that 339 people died in prison and over 100,000 Black slaves were serving in Beidane (majority ethnic group) houses.

The African Commission found violations of the right to life (Article 4) as a result of executions following unfair trials, as well as the lack of respect for life manifest in the denial of food and medical care to prisoners, and torture.[304] Freedom from torture or inhumane treatment (Article 5) was violated because of the poor detention conditions, including denial of food and medical care and chaining and locking up prisoners in overpopulated cells lacking hygiene. In addition, the state inflicted slow deaths through burning or burying people in sand; administered electric shocks or tied weights to genitals; used water torture; burnt bodies with various instruments; used stress positions (such as the 'jaguar'); put pepper in eyes; raped women; and permanently deprived people of light or exposed them to cold temperatures.[305] Forced labour analogous to slavery was found to violate Article 5.[306] The poor prison conditions, including lack of food, medical care, blankets and hygiene, even resulting in death, also violated the right to health in Article 16.[307] The political arrests and arbitrary detentions violated Article 6 and family rights under Article 18, while irregular, unfair trials infringed Article 7 and the requirement of judicial independence in Article 26.

The campaign of political repression was found to violate the political freedoms of information and expression (Article 9), association (Article 10), assembly (Article 11) and movement and residence (Article 12). The latter violation included the eviction of Black Mauritanians from their houses, expulsion abroad and denial of citizenship. The confiscation and looting of property, and the expropriation or destruction of land and houses, violated the right to property in Article 14.[308] In general, the Commission found that the violence and repression amounted to discrimination contrary to Article 2.[309] Black Mauritanians were forcibly displaced, detained, tortured or killed 'because of the colour of their skin' in the context of the extreme francophone and arabophone factions that opposed one another.[310]

[303] *Malawi African Association and Others v Mauritania*, ACHPR Communications Nos 54/1991, 61/1991, 96/1993, 98/1993, 164/1997, 196/1997, 210/1998 (11 May 2000).

[304] Ibid [120].

[305] Ibid [116]–[117].

[306] Ibid [135].

[307] Ibid [122].

[308] Ibid [128].

[309] Ibid [130]–[131] (also invoking the UN General Assembly's Declaration of the Rights of People Belonging to National, Ethnic, Religious or Linguistic Minorities, UN Doc A/RES/47/135 (18 December 1992)).

[310] Ibid [130].

In *Social and Economic Action Rights Centre (SERAC) v Nigeria* (2001), mentioned earlier, Nigerian security forces attacked, burned and destroyed Ogoni villages and homes to dislodge officials and supporters of the Movement of the Survival of Ogoni People, which opposed environmental destruction by oil companies.[311] Some of the attacks involved combined uniformed forces of police, army, airforce and navy, including weapons such as tanks, while others involved uniformed gunmen using military weapons, also suggesting state involvement. The attacks deliberately left thousands of villagers homeless. Nigeria also destroyed Ogoni food sources (such as crops and animals) and allowed their soil and water to be polluted, threatening their farming and fishing, and producing malnutrition and starvation. The security forces created a state of terror and insecurity that made it impossible for many Ogoni villagers to return. Nigeria also failed to investigate and punish the perpetrators. The African Commission found that these acts violated the right to life and personal integrity under Article 4 of the African Charter.[312] It noted that the security forces 'were given the green light to decisively deal with the Ogonis, which was illustrated by the wide spread terrorisations and killings'.[313] The pollution and environmental destruction made living in Ogoniland 'a nightmare' and prejudiced their survival individually and as a community.

Congo v Burundi (2003)[314] involved large-scale violence by the armed forces of Burundi, Rwanda and Uganda in Congolese territory in 1998. It included the massacre of thousands of civilians; mass rape of women and girls, and the intentional spreading of sexually transmitted diseases; mutilations; the deportation of civilians to concentration camps; looting of civilian property; and the systematic plunder of natural resources. The siege of a hydroelectricity dam also cut off electricity to hospitals, resulting in deaths and disrupting the economy. It was alleged that a goal of these operations was 'to make the indigenous people disappear from these regions and thus, to establish … "Tutsiland"'.[315] The case did not, however, consider specific impacts on issues such as indigenous land or cultural rights, but rather the impact of the violence on the whole population of eastern Congo.

Pursuant to Articles 60 and 61 of the African Charter, the African Commission interpreted the African Charter in the light of international law, including the UN Charter and international humanitarian law.[316] The Commission found that the killings, massacres, rapes, mutilations and other abuses committed during the foreign occupation violated the right to life and personal integrity (Article 4), as well as Part III of the Fourth Geneva Convention 1949 and Article 75 of Additional Protocol I of 1977 to those Conventions.[317] Such acts were also found to be directed against the victims because of their national origin and were discriminatory, contrary to Article 2.[318] Looting, killing, mass transfers of civilians, and the siege of the hydroelectricity dam

311 *SERAC v Nigeria* (n 80) [7].

312 Ibid [67].

313 Ibid.

314 *Congo v Burundi*, ACHPR Communication No 277/1999 IHRL 3031 (15–29 May 2003).

315 Ibid [6].

316 Ibid [69], [70], [78].

317 Ibid [79]–[80]. Rape was additionally found to violate the Convention on the Elimination of All Forms of Discrimination Against Women (CEDAW): [86]; see also [89].

318 Ibid [80].

and interruption of essential services in the hospital, leading to deaths of patients, and the general disruption of life and state of war, were held to violate the rights to health (Article 16) and education (Article 17).[319] The mass transfer of civilians to Rwandan camps violated family rights (Article 18(1)), freedom of movement and the right to leave and return (Article 12(1)–(2)).[320] Indiscriminate dumping, or mass burial, of victims was held to violate the Congolese people's right to cultural development under Article 22.[321]

The Commission also addressed interferences in property as a result of the conflict.[322] It found that the right to property (Article 14) was violated as a result of the looting, killing, mass and indiscriminate transfers of civilians, the siege and damage of the hydro dam, stopping of essential services in the hospital (leading to deaths of patients), and the general disruption of life by the state of war.[323] The siege of the hydro dam was further found to violate international humanitarian law prohibitions on attacking installations containing dangerous forces, and on the destruction or seizure of enemy property unless militarily necessary.[324] The Commission also noted violations of the prohibition on pillage of private property.[325] More generally, the Commission regarded the occupation of eastern Congo as a violation of a people's right of self-determination under Article 20 of the African Charter.[326]

In *COHRE v Sudan* (2009),[327] mentioned earlier, Sudan was found responsible for committing, and aiding state-sponsored Janjaweed militias to commit, violence against the Black African tribes in Darfur, including the mass killings and bombings of thousands of civilians, forced displacement of a million people, destruction of property (including villages, markets and wells) and rape, in an internal armed conflict. The violence also prevented Darfurians from farming, collecting firewood for cooking, and collecting grass for livestock.

The African Commission found that Sudan violated the right to life (Article 4), which includes rights to dignity and livelihood, by failing to promptly, independently and effectively investigate arbitrary killings and extra-judicial executions allegedly committed by its forces and the non-state Janjaweed militias.[328] Many cases were not investigated; investigations were prematurely terminated without identifying perpetrators; victims and witnesses were intimidated; law enforcement authorities

[319] Ibid [88].
[320] Ibid [81].
[321] Ibid [87] (as well as Additional Protocol I, art 34).
[322] The Commission also found that the invasion of Congo violated UN Charter prohibitions on the use of force and intervention [68] and the right to peace and security, and peaceful dispute settlement, in Art 23 of the African Charter [73]–[76].
[323] Ibid [88].
[324] Ibid [82]–[84] (respectively citing Protocol I Additional to the Geneva Conventions of 12 August 1949, and Relating to the Protection of Victims of International Armed Conflicts, Art 56 (adopted 8 June 1977, entered into force 7 December 1978, (1979) 1125 UNTS 3); and The Hague Convention (II) with respect to the Laws and Customs of War on Land, Annex: Regulations Concerning the Laws and Customs of War on Land, art 23 (adopted 29 July 1899, entered into force 4 September 1900)).
[325] *Congo v Burundi* (n 314) [85] (citing *Prosecutor v Delalić and Others*, IT-96-21-T, ICTY Trial Chamber Judgment (16 November 1998), [587]).
[326] Ibid [77].
[327] *COHRE v Sudan* (n 88).
[328] Ibid [145]–[153].

were not independent and judicial authorities were weak; the few prosecutions brought did not deal with major crimes or high-ranking perpetrators; and impunity prevailed.

The Commission also found that Sudan violated the prohibition on torture and cruel, inhuman or degrading punishment or treatment under Article 5.[329] Psychological and physical torture and degrading and inhuman treatment, involving intimidation, coercion and violence, was inflicted by military and militia attacks, forced eviction and displacement, destruction of property and survival resources, and rape.[330] Sudan was held not to have acted diligently to protect civilians against such attacks by its forces or the Janjaweed.[331]

The right to liberty and security of person (Article 6) was found to be infringed by Sudan's failure to protect the hundreds of victims of arbitrary arrest and detention.[332] It was also violated because most of the displaced persons were unable to return to their homes (due to insecurity or destruction of property), and the right to liberty was found to complement freedom of movement (under Article 12).[333] Leaving displaced persons camps left men vulnerable to death and women to rape, notwithstanding the deployment of African Union and UN forces. As noted in the previous section, the Commission also found violations of the rights to health (Article 16), family (Article 18) and development (Article 22), in the latter respect because Sudan targeted civilians to collectively punish them.[334]

Finally, Sudan violated Article 7 by failing to investigate and prosecute the perpetrators and provide the complainants with access to a competent tribunal.[335] The victims were displaced by their fear of constant bombing, violence, and the burning of housing and evidence. Under these circumstances 'it would be an affront to common sense and justice to expect the victims to bring their plights to the courts'[336] and justice was 'illusory and impractical'.[337]

INDIGENOUS PEOPLES IN THE EUROPEAN HUMAN RIGHTS SYSTEMS

European Convention on Human Rights

Indigenous issues have been more prevalent and visible in regional human rights systems in the Americas and Africa than in Europe. Under the European Convention on Human Rights 1950 (ECHR), the case law has generally focused on minorities rather than indigenous peoples, including, for example, Roma/Travellers, Kurds, Greek and Turkish Cypriots, Chechens, ethnic Russians and other national

329 Ibid [154]–[168].
330 Ibid [157].
331 Ibid [168].
332 Ibid [169]–[179].
333 Ibid [177].
334 Ibid [223]–[224].
335 Ibid [180]–[185].
336 Ibid [182].
337 Ibid [185].

minorities. Such cases have addressed a wide range of ECHR rights, but especially non-discrimination and political, language and cultural rights. The many Roma cases have often addressed housing rights and the adverse cultural impacts of planning laws and forced evictions, for instance in relation to the right to respect for (a minority's) private and family life and the home under Article 8 of the ECHR.[338]

For example, the European Court of Human Rights (ECtHR) has accepted that a travelling lifestyle, and occupation of caravans, is an integral part of Gypsy ethnic identity and traditional lifestyle, even if total nomadism is no longer followed.[339] Measures affecting the stationing of caravans thus impact not only on respect for the home but the ability to maintain Gypsy identity and to lead private and family life in accordance with it. States must protect the security, identity and lifestyle of such minorities, including within the regulatory planning and decision-making processes. A similar approach to the Roma has been taken under the (non-binding) decisions of the European Committee on Social Rights (ECSR) under the European Social Charter 1961.[340]

A small number of cases has been brought before the ECtHR by indigenous communities or individuals. Most of these have been declared inadmissible, including those concerning Sami reindeer grazing rights on private land in Sweden;[341] forced relocation from and loss of hunting rights on traditional lands due to the building of a United States military base in Greenland;[342] and the mass expulsion of Chagos islanders to build a British military base in the Indian Ocean.[343] Prior to the establishment of the Court in 1998, the European Commission on Human Rights also usually declared inadmissible cases involving indigenous communities. These mainly involved Sami in Scandinavia, including legislative interference in the customary hunting and fishing rights on traditional lands of 39 Sami villages;[344] disputes between different Sami groups over land and reindeer herding and grazing rights;[345] exclusion from membership of a Sami village, and denial to individuals of immemorial hunting and

338 See, eg, *Chapman v United* Kingdom, Application No 27238/95, ECtHR Judgment (18 January 2001); see also *DH and others v Czech Republic*, Application No 57325/00, ECtHR Judgment (13 November 2007), [182].

339 *Chapman v United Kingdom* (n 338).

340 Many such cases have also arisen under the European Social Charter 1961 and the individual decisions of the European Committee on Social Rights made under it: see, eg, *European Roma Rights Centre v Portugal*, ECSR Complaint No 61/2010 (30 June 2011), [49]–[53]; see also *European Roma Rights Center v Greece*, ECSR Complaint No 15/2003 (8 December 2004), [25]; *European Roma Rights Centre v France*, ECSR Complaint No 51/2008 (19 October 2009), [80]; *European Roma and Travellers Forum v France*, ECSR Complaint No 64/2011 (24 January 2012), [109]; *International Federation of Human Rights v Belgium*, ECSR Complaint No 62/2010 (21 March 2012), [73].

341 *Handölsdalen Sami Village v Sweden*, Application No 39013/04, ECtHR Admissibility Decision (17 February 2009).

342 *HINGITAQ 53 v Denmark*, Application No 18584/04, ECtHR Admissibility Decision (12 January 2006).

343 *Chagos Islanders v United Kingdom*, Application No 35622/04, ECtHR Admissibility Decision (11 December 2012).

344 *Könkämä and 38 Other Saami Villages v Sweden*, Application No 27033/95, ECommHR Admissibility Decision (25 November 1996).

345 *OB and Others v Norway*, Application No 15997/90, ECommHR Admissibility Decision (8 January 1993).

fishing rights on traditional lands;[346] and a private landowner's challenge to Sami elk hunting rights on his land.[347]

Council of Europe Framework Convention on the Protection of National Minorities

As might be expected, the focus has been on the legal concept of 'minorities', not indigenous peoples, under the Council of Europe Framework Convention on the Protection of National Minorities 1995.[348] The Framework Convention requires states to ensure full equality of minorities in all all areas of economic, social, political, public and cultural life; enable them to express, preserve and develop their culture, religion, language and traditions; guarantee their freedoms of assembly, association, expression, thought, conscience, religion and media; and protect linguistic freedom and educational rights.

The Framework Convention's procedures have, however, addressed indigenous issues over time. In its thematic commentary on minority language rights, the Advisory Committee which monitors state implementation of the Convention has emphasised the link between language and the preservation of indigenous traditions and cultures, and urged states to pay special attention to indigenous languages as being particularly threatened.[349]

Further, in its commentary on participation in economic and social life, the Advisory Committee called on states to give special protection to land traditionally used by indigenous peoples, and to closely involve indigenous representatives in decision-making on traditional land use and rights.[350] It also observed that indigenous peoples (and Roma) are more at risk of obstacles to, and exclusion from, their participation in socio-economic life than other minorities, and thus may require special protection.[351] The Committee likewise identified more significant difficulties for indigenous people (particularly women) in accessing the labour market, education and training, housing, healthcare and social protection.[352] It also noted the underemployment of indigenous people in public administration, which it felt required special attention by states.[353]

346 *Östergren and Others v Sweden*, Application No 13572/88, ECommHR Admissibility Decision (1 March 1991).

347 *FROM v Sweden*, Application No 34776/97, ECommHR Admissibility Decision (4 March 1998).

348 Council of Europe Framework Convention on the Protection of National Minorities (adopted 1 February 1995, entered into force 1 February 1998, ETS No 157).

349 Council of Europe, Advisory Committee on the Framework Convention on the Protection of National Minorities, *Thematic Commentary No 3: The Language Rights of Persons Belonging to National Minorities under the Framework Convention*, ACFC/44DOC(2012)001 rev (24 May 2012), 22–23.

350 Council of Europe, Advisory Committee on the Framework Convention on the Protection of National Minorities, *Commentary on the Effective Participation of Persons Belonging to National Minorities in Cultural, Social and Economic Life and in Public Affairs*, ACFC/31DOC(2008)001 (27 February 2008), 5, 19.

351 Ibid 14.

352 Ibid 18.

353 Ibid 31.

The Advisory Committee has further highlighted indigenous issues when periodically reviewing state implementation of the Framework Convention. Indigenous movements have sometimes fed information into this process. To take one illustrative example, the peak Russian indigenous movement, the Association of Small Peoples of the Soviet North (RAIPON), has submitted information to the Committee since 2006.[354] In 2013, for instance, the Committee recommended that Russia implement its plan for the sustainable development of indigenous communities; consult indigenous representatives; and refrain from legislating to undermine preferential indigenous access to land, wildlife and other natural resources.[355]

In reviewing Russia's performance in 2011, the Committee highlighted a wide range of concerns about indigenous people. As regards indigenous attachment to land, the Committee noted that a law to establish federally protected indigenous territories had not been put into practice and potentially allowed commercial exploitation by others.[356] Existing territories had also been decreased in size and status. Other federal amendments to land, forest and water laws undermined indigenous rights to preferential, free and non-competitive access to land and natural resources, thus impairing indigenous rights to maintain their culture and traditional and evolving economic activities.[357] The Committee was further concerned about the granting of licences to private oil and other companies to extract natural resources from indigenous lands, and the resultant environmental harm.[358] The Committee was also concerned that formal guarantees of consultation in decision-making (particularly on land and resources) were often not accessible or adequate in practice, or did not lead to meaningful results.[359] There was also an absence of an effective federal-level consultative structure.

As regards socio-economic rights, the Committee was concerned about indigenous health, including lower life expectancy, alcoholism, poor or inaccessible health services, and the health consequences of environmental degradation.[360] It was further concerned about inadequate indigenous education in schools,[361] as well as reductions in higher education quotas for indigenous people and the restriction of quotas to certain fields of study.[362] In relation to labour rights, the Committee was concerned about unlawful wages and working conditions for indigenous people engaged in traditional activities (such as fishing), including payment in food

354 Johannes Rohr, *Indigenous Peoples in the Russian Federation*, Report 18 (International Working Group for Indigenous Affairs, Copenhagen, 2014), 58.

355 Council of Europe, Advisory Committee on the Framework Convention on the Protection of National Minorities, *Resolution CM/ResCMN(2013)1 on the Implementation of the Framework Convention for the Protection of National Minorities by the Russian Federation*, adopted by the Committee of Ministers (30 April 2013).

356 Advisory Committee on the Framework Convention on the Protection of National Minorities, *Third Opinion on the Russian Federation Adopted on 24 November 2011*, GVT/COM/III(2012)004 (25 July 2012), 21–23.

357 Ibid 8, 21–23.

358 Ibid.

359 Ibid 9, 48–49.

360 Ibid 49–50.

361 Ibid 42, 45, 47.

362 Ibid.

or alcohol.[363] It called for measures to promote indigenous access to the labour market and commercial opportunities, since current state initiatives were confined to preserving traditional economic activities.[364] The Committee noted that subsidies for the economic development of indigenous peoples were insufficient, sometimes misappropriated, not based on adequate consultation, and subject to inaccessible procedures that favoured corporations.[365] In other areas, the Committee expressed concern about threats to indigenous languages and difficulties in registering indigenous religious associations.[366]

CONCLUSION

Indigenous cultural rights have been protected expressly under the African Charter and implicitly under the American Convention. Indigenous association with ancestral lands has been recognised as critical to indigenous cultural survival and is therefore protected as part of the right to take part in the cultural life of the community in Article 17 of the African Charter. Interference with cultural rights has been found to require a high threshold of justification, which would not be met, for instance, by creating a game reserve which excludes indigenous people from the ritual sites on which their culture depends, or the resources on which their livelihood depends.[367] Additionally, indigenous spiritual beliefs and ceremonial practices have been recognised as protected 'religion' under the African Charter.[368]

The American Convention does not explicitly recognise a right to culture. However, as mentioned in the previous chapter, the Inter-American system has implied a right of cultural identity into the right to property under Article 21 of the American Convention.[369] In other cases, culture has been taken into account in interpreting other American Convention rights. Thus, the right to life requires respect for indigenous burial practices, while freedom of conscience and religion encompasses respect for indigenous farewell rites. Protection against the risks of cultural extinction stemming from forced displacement was found to come within the ambit of freedom of movement and residence. The rights of the child have been interpreted to ensure indigenous children can live according to their own culture, religion and language, and not be forced to live amongst non-indigenous families.

In addition, cultural rights are recognised in Article 13 of the American Declaration and Article 14 of the San Salvador Protocol (albeit being non-justiciable). The Inter-American system has drawn on these sources, and international standards (such as Article 27 of the ICCPR and ILO Convention No 169) to protect indigenous

363 Ibid 7, 16–17.
364 Ibid 49–50.
365 Ibid 21–23.
366 Ibid 35, 38.
367 *Endorois Welfare Council v Kenya* (n 1) [249]–[250].
368 Ibid [165]–[168].
369 *Yakye Axa v Paraguay* (n 41), [131]–[137]. See also *Moiwana Community v Suriname* (n 41), [130]–[134]; *Sawhoyamaxa Indigenous Community v Paraguay* (n 41), [118]; *Saramaka v Suriname* (n 41); *Kichwa Indigenous People of Sarayaku v Ecuador* (n 41), [212]–[220].

cultural interests. In the case of the Miskitos, the Commission implicitly recognised a right to culture when holding that Nicaragua could not assimilate indigenous peoples and must protect their language, religion and cultural identity.[370] In another case, the Commission extended the protection of Article 13 of the American Declaration to cross-border trade in indigenous cultural goods, and culturally distinctive practices associated with cross-border trading.

While few economic and social rights are expressly protected under the constituent instruments of the African and Inter-American systems, both regimes have implied them when interpreting other rights. In Africa, the right to life has been found to protect against grave pollution and environmental degradation affecting survival resources such as land, food and water. A right to food has been implied into the rights to life, health and development. Rights to food and water have been further recognised where their deficiency impacts on the right to a decent existence and the conditions necessary to exercise other rights, such as education and cultural identity. In the Inter-American system, the right to life was found to be violated by a denial of the right to communal property that negatively affected a community's right to a decent life, by depriving them of access to their traditional means of subsistence and natural resources, clean water and traditional medicines. The poor living conditions of forcibly displaced indigenous people have also been held to engage the right to life.

A right to housing has also been implied in both regional systems. In Africa, forced evictions and the destruction of shelter have been found to adversely affect express rights to health; property; the protection of the family; freedom from cruel, inhuman or degrading treatment (including where committed by non-state actors); liberty and security of person; freedom of movement and residence; and collective economic, social and cultural development (by denying people the opportunity to engage in economic, social and cultural activities, and to educate their children). The African system has accordingly provided protection against forced evictions and for security of tenure.

In the Inter-American system, forced displacement has been held to violate the rights to life; personal integrity; freedom of movement and residence; and freedom of conscience and religion. Displaced indigenous peoples have been recognised as particularly vulnerable to cultural or physical extinction, destruction of social structure, disintegration of families, and loss of cultural and traditional practices and language, because of their cultural and material dependence for survival on their ancestral lands. Precarious resettlement conditions have also engaged the right to life and freedom of movement and residence, where services (such as clean water, toilets, health, education and electricity) are inadequate; people are unable to resume traditional economic activities or earn a stable income; and the effects of displacement have not been mitigated. A right against forced displacement has been implied into freedom of movement and residence.

[370] IACHR, *Report on the Situation of Human Rights of a Segment of the Nicaraguan Population of Miskito Origin*, OEA/Ser.L./V.II.62, Doc 10 rev 3 (29 November 1983), Part II, [B(15)].

A right to health is expressly protected under the African Charter. It has been found to be infringed by the destruction of homes, livestock and farms; the poisoning of water sources; and oil pollution by private companies. Oil pollution has additionally been found to infringe the express African right to a satisfactory environment favourable to development, upon which the fulfilment of economic and social rights depends, including because of the state's failure to evaluate and monitor environmental impacts, and inform and consult communities. The Inter-American system has sporadically addressed health rights in relation to indigenous people, such as where the right to life has been impaired by the denial of traditional lands and resources (including traditional medicines), and poor alternative living conditions (including inadequate healthcare).

Various kinds of violence against indigenous peoples have been dealt with in Africa and the Americas as violations of numerous rights, including the rights to life, liberty, personal integrity, humane treatment and freedom from torture. Usually such rights are applied in the ordinary way and not in ways specific to indigenous peoples. In the Americas, however, the cultural particularities of indigenous family life have been taken into account in identifying the successors of victims for the purposes of reparations and compensation. In most other cases, the victims were nonetheless targeted for being indigenous or indigenous leaders, or because they were defending their lands from developers, or they were human rights defenders (including non-indigenous peoples) working with indigenous communities. In such cases, impunity for the perpetrators and lack of remedies for victims is commonplace.

Finally, in Europe there is comparatively less jurisprudence specifically on indigenous peoples, with minority rights being the predominant normative framework (including the Council of Europe Framework Convention on the Protection of National Minorities 1995). Attention has, however, been given to indigenous language and cultural rights; economic and social protection (including in employment, healthcare, housing, education and social protection); and special protection for traditional lands and environment, including through indigenous participation in decision-making.

Conclusion

Future Normative and Implementation Challenges

INDIGENOUS PEOPLES HAVE long struggled for visibility and the recognition of their unique collective concerns in international law. It is true that international law has long contemplated the position of indigenous peoples, ever since first contact with European colonial powers in the Americas in fifteenth and sixteenth centuries.[1] Despite occasional (and usually paternalistic) acknowledgement of their interests, international law often affirmed the sovereign right of expansionist states to absorb or suppress them, and was generally created without their participation (with 'treaties', albeit unequal, being the rare exception).

As chapter 1 showed, however, the legal nomenclature of 'indigenous peoples' only gained currency in the twentieth century, beginning with ILO treaties and regional attention by American states. This universal labelling and conceptualisation of indigenous peoples helped to facilitate transnational indigenous activism directed towards articulating and securing indigenous rights. Particularly from the 1960s onwards, national and transnational indigenous movements gradually increased the legal visibility of indigenous peoples, including through their use of international and regional human rights mechanisms to advance their interests. Lingering ambiguities at the margins of who is regarded as 'indigenous' have not seriously hindered the progressive recognition of a framework of indigenous rights, even if some recalcitrant states, particularly in Africa and Asia, continue to politically resist the concept.

As chapters 4 and 5 demonstrate, the Inter-American human rights system pioneered the earliest contemporary jurisprudence in the 1970s, when confronting the varied abuses against indigenous peoples in numerous American states. The contribution of the UN human rights treaty bodies is comparatively more recent, and has only really taken off since the 1990s. The African regional protection of indigenous rights is even more recent, in concert with the late establishment of a regional human rights protection system on that continent. Despite the fairly recent provenance of most of the international and regional jurisprudence, a remarkably thick and extensive case law has emerged addressing most issues vital to indigenous peoples.

As chapters 2 and 3 show, the UN treaty bodies (particularly the Human Rights Committee (HRC) and Committee on Economic, Social and Cultural Rights (CESCR)) have interpreted the right of self-determination in ways specific to indigenous peoples, and with special attention to control over traditional lands

[1] See James Anaya, *Indigenous Peoples in International Law* (2nd edn, Oxford University Press, 2004), 15–34.

and natural resources. The HRC has otherwise focused on how the right to take part in cultural life manifests for indigenous peoples, again with special reference to land and resources. The HRC has also been attentive to the socio-economic dimensions of civil and political rights. As might be expected, the CESCR has focused on economic, social and cultural rights, which are often the most vital to the livelihoods, survival and cultural integrity of indigenous groups. Other committees have also been concerned about socio-economic and cultural conditions, and land and resource issues, including the Committee on the Elimination of Racial Discrimination (CERD), Committee on the Elimination of Discrimination Against Women (CEDAW Committee), and the Committee on the Rights of the Child (CRC). All of the committees have been concerned about the many guises of discrimination against indigenous peoples (including inter-sectional and indirect). All committees have also been alarmed by violence against indigenous peoples, excessive or negligent law enforcement, and the barriers to access to justice and remedies. Some committees have highlighted issues of political participation (CERD and CEDAW Committee), while the CRC has focused on family and child rights.

Jurisprudence on indigenous rights has been most extensively developed at the regional level, particularly in the Inter-American system and more recently in the African system. As chapter 4 demonstrates, the right to property has been expansively interpreted in both systems to encompass the collective rights of indigenous peoples to their traditional lands and natural resources, in accordance with their culture and customs. This includes rights to have their communal lands recognised, titled, delimited and demarcated; to be protected against state or third party intrusion (including resource exploitation, environmental degradation and forced eviction); to restitution of lands from which they have been dispossessed, or to receive lands of equivalent extent and quality; and to be consulted in decision-making affecting their lands and resources, and to give consent to major projects. In the African system, indigenous lands and resources have been accorded further protection through the application of the rights of peoples to development, and to control their wealth and resources.

Chapter 5 explored how the regional systems have protected indigenous rights to life, physical integrity and culture. In both systems, cultural rights have been expressly or impliedly recognised as protecting indigenous land and resource rights, as well as other cultural interests. Various civil and political rights have also been interpreted to protect socio-economic rights, given that the latter are not as extensively protected in regional treaties. For example, rights to food, water and housing have been implied into rights such as the right to life (in the Americas and Africa) or health and development (in Africa). In addition, in the Americas protection against forced displacement has been implied into the rights to life, personal integrity, freedom of movement and residence, and freedom of conscience and religion. Indigenous health rights have also been protected in both systems. Different kinds of violence against indigenous peoples, from massacres to threats to leaders and human rights defenders, have been found to violate rights such as life, liberty, personal integrity, humane treatment and freedom from torture.

The international and regional bodies have incrementally constructed an impressive and particularised array of human rights standards covering many issues of concern to indigenous peoples. While the Inter-American system has produced the most voluminous and detailed jurisprudence, the UN and regional systems have often synergistically informed, cross-pollinated and mutually reinforced one another. In turn the case law and standard setting of the UN and regional bodies have influenced political efforts to develop international law, most notably in the adoption of the UN Declaration on the Rights of Indigenous Peoples (UNDRIP) in 2007, but also in the many 'soft' law instruments adopted by international organisations, particularly those involved in development, finance and investment, and the environment.

The UNDRIP itself is gradually being referenced in the work of the UN and regional bodies, and this interaction will stimulate ongoing normative consolidation and evolution in the future. While much of the UNDRIP may reflect customary human rights law, reflecting back the practice of states through the UN and regional bodies, not all of it is settled law, at least as far as some states are concerned. This normative contestation will continue to play out in the future UN and regional bodies' jurisprudence, either to sharpen or resolve disagreements over matters such as the scope of indigenous self-determination and 'sovereignty'; entitlements in respect of historically dispossessed lands; the extent, modalities and interlocutors of consultation and consent in development; and the resolution of rights conflicts between indigenous groups and others (including other vulnerable social groups, such as landless peasants or those displaced by war), between individuals and their indigenous communities, or between indigenous individuals within communities. In this respect, an increasingly important issue arising in some states, such as Australia and Canada, is whether indigenous lands held on a collective basis can be alienated so as to permit individual members of a community to privately 'own' portions of indigenous land or even to sell or lease it to non-indigenous persons or entities. While such initiatives may generate wealth or stimulate economic development for present generations of indigenous peoples, such commodification may have stark implications for inter-generational equity, if future generations of indigenous peoples are dispossessed of their entitlement to formerly communal lands and resources.

As in any area of law, and particularly in international law and human rights law, problems of implementation of indigenous human rights[2] are more pressing than any residual normative gaps. The fairly rapid generation of indigenous rights has not been matched by implementation on the ground. Too often states fail to comply with even binding international decisions,[3] such as the merits judgments of the Inter-American Court. The dialogic, 'soft' monitoring of states by UN treaty bodies, and the African and Inter-American commissions on human rights, including through individual complaints processes, is often insufficient to change behaviour, including because diplomats are often far removed from their states' line ministries on the ground at home. The Permanent Forum on Indigenous Issues has highlighted, for instance, the limited effects of naming and shaming on norm internalisation by states,[4] as well as the problem of 'rights ritualism', whereby states proceduralise rights without substantively securing them.[5] It has further noted the lack of resources

[2] PFII, *Expert Group Meeting on the Theme 'Dialogue on an Optional Protocol to the United Nations Declaration on the Rights of Indigenous Peoples'*, Note by the Secretariat, E/C.19/2015/8 (17 February 2015), [39]; *Report of the Special Rapporteur on the Situation of Human Rights and Fundamental Freedoms of Indigenous People*, UN Doc E/CN.4/2006/78 (16 February 2006), [5].

[3] PFII, *Expert Group Meeting* (n 2) [39].

[4] Ibid [34]–[36].

[5] Ibid [41]–[43].

available to indigenous peoples even to access international (or regional) human rights mechanisms.[6] For these reasons, the creation of more or stronger international monitoring mechanisms, such as an Optional Protocol for individual complaints, or state reporting under the UNDRIP,[7] while welcome, may only have fairly marginal effects on state practice on the ground.

Questions of political economy also militate against effective domestic implementation of indigenous rights. In quite a few countries, indigenous peoples live upon traditional lands which harbour vast natural resources, from minerals to timber to agricultural land. The logic of state-led economic development, which dominated development discourse in the developing world from the 1960s onwards, has often viewed indigenous peoples as obstacles to national economic self-determination and the exploitation of sovereign natural resources. On this view, natural resources are seen as the birthright of the whole territory and its population, not a sub-group, and particularly where traditional land and resource use by indigenous peoples are not regarded as economically 'productive' in a 'modern' sense. The effective recognition of indigenous land rights presupposes a re-orientation of development discourse and the thinking of powerful constituencies, state and private, which drive it. Structural discrimination and racist stereotyping, and the low levels of political power wielded by non-dominant indigenous populations, also impede norm internalisation.

In the end, indigenous rights must be fought and won at the national level. International and regional standards can provide normative ammunition in those struggles, whether in domestic litigation, legislative reform or NGO and public campaigns. UN and regional bodies can increase the visibility of local causes, pressure governments, and sometimes provide political cover to indigenous peoples. Much work remains to be done to raise awareness about indigenous rights amongst governments; to counter-act ignorance, racism and hostility; and to build state capacity[8] to incorporate indigenous rights into the business of everyday governing.

[6] Ibid [28]–[30].
[7] Ibid [49]; see also PFII, *Study on an Optional Protocol to the United Nations Declaration on the Rights of Indigenous Peoples Focusing on a Voluntary Mechanism*, E/C.19/2014/7 (4 March 2014).
[8] PFII, *Expert Group Meeting* (n 2) [37].

Index